NAIPAUL'S TRUTH

NAIPAUL'S TRUTH

The Making of a Writer

LILLIAN FEDER

ROWMAN & LITTLEFIELD PUBLISHERS, INC.
Lanham • Boulder • New York • Oxford

ROWMAN & LITTLEFIELD PUBLISHERS, INC.

Published in the United States of America
by Rowman & Littlefield Publishers, Inc.
4720 Boston Way, Lanham, Maryland 20706
http://www.rowmanlittlefield.com

12 Hid's Copse Road
Cumnor Hill, Oxford OX2 9JJ, England

Copyright © 2001 by Lillian Feder

A slightly different version of the section on *Guerrillas* first appeared in *Trauma and Self,* edited by Charles B. Strozier and Michael Flynn (Rowman & Littlefield, 1996).

British Library Cataloging in Publication Information Available

Library of Congress Cataloging-in-Publication Data
Feder, Lillian.
    Naipaul's truth : the making of a writer / Lillian Feder.
        p. cm.
    Includes bibliographical references and index.
    ISBN 0-7425-0808-0 (alk. paper)
        1. Naipaul, V. S. (Vidiadhar Surajprasad), 1932—Criticism and interpretation. 2. West Indies—In literature. I. Title.

PR9272.9.N32 Z68 2000
823'.914—dc21

                                                                                00-029082

Printed in the United States of America

∞™ The paper used in this publication meets the minimum requirements of American National Standard for Information Sciences—Permanence of Paper for Printed Library Materials, ANSI/NISO Z39.48-1992.

In loving remembrance of my brother,
Milton Feder, my first friend

The choice between possessing the truth and giving up all claim on it does not exhaust all the possibilities that lie before us.

—Tzvetan Todorov, *Literature and Its Theorists*

Truth begets hatred.

—Terence, *Andria*

I am afraid of those who look for a tendency between the lines and who want to see in me either a liberal or a conservative. I am not a liberal, nor a conservative, nor a meliorist, nor a monk, nor an indifferentist. I should like to be a free artist and nothing more.

—Anton Chekhov, letter to A. N. Pleshcheyev

CONTENTS

Acknowledgments   ix

1   Introduction   1

2   Autobiography   25
    Becoming a Writer   25
    "The Traveler's I"   42

3   Travel Narratives, History, and Journalism   79
    The Bonds of the Past   80
    Fantasies, Lies, and "Political Myths"   107
    Continuity and Change: An Idea of Nationhood   123
    Islam—1979; 1995   134

4   Fiction   161
    Comic and Tragic Realism   162
    Outsiders Everywhere   184
    Violence, Selfhood, and the Ambiguities of Truth   205
    The Author in History   235

5   Afterword   249

Chronology of Works by V. S. Naipaul   253

Index   254

About the Author   271

ACKNOWLEDGMENTS

I am grateful to V. S. Naipaul and to Sidney Huttner, former Curator of Special Collections at the McFarlin Library, the University of Tulsa, for permitting me to read some of the notebooks and other material in the V. S. Naipaul Archive.

I also wish to thank my editors, Stephen Wrinn, whose interest and encouragement were invaluable during the years I worked on this book, and Mary Carpenter, on whose knowledge and support I relied in good times and trying ones. Other people who helped with advice and practical matters or by just listening sympathetically are Milton Feder, Paul Metz, Robert Shapiro, Felicia Bonaparte, Bernard Dick, Sylvia Brody, Leo Steinberg, Prema Subramaniam, Richard Gottlieb, Sanjay Malik, and Mitu Hirshman.

1

INTRODUCTION

V. S. Naipaul has described the genesis of his long commitment "to deliver the truth"[1] as an early struggle to rid himself of the model of the writer derived from late nineteenth-century aestheticism, "the ideas of Bloomsbury, ideas bred out of empire, wealth and imperial security," which he had absorbed as a boy in Trinidad. Acknowledging his "colonial-Hindu self" was his initial step in uniting the "man and writer" who, releasing "the worlds I contained within myself,"[2] inadvertently was to become one of the most controversial of contemporary literary figures. He has been acclaimed for his penetration into the lasting impairment of postcolonial societies, especially the deprivations of individuals who inherited a history of exploitation, and he has been excoriated as a reactionary loyal to imperialist values. He has been praised for his creative use of autobiography in his travel narratives and for converting autobiographical material into poignant fiction, and he has been accused of projecting his own neuroses onto his narrators and characters. Even the clarity and elegance of his prose, universally admired, have been treated by his detractors as mere sophistic devices for promulgating his views.

Among the criteria applied to Naipaul's work has been the objectivity he claims. Some critics have lauded his commitment to the truth of what he perceives, however disturbing; others have discredited his vision as blurred by self-serving prejudice. Naipaul's admirers and defenders represent various cultural and political positions; among the best known are John Bayley, Conor Cruise O'Brien, Alfred Kazin, Nadine Gordimer, Brent Staples, Ian Buruma, and Irving Howe who, though an "uneasy admirer," reiterates qualities that other supporters have noticed: Naipaul "writes with a strict refusal of romantic moonshine about the

moral charms of primitives or the virtues of bloodstained dictators. . . .
He is the scourge of our disenchanted age, as free of colonialist bias as of
infatuation with Third World delusions."[3] Conor Cruise O'Brien finds
"no trace of a racialist bias in Naipaul."[4] Defending Naipaul, Brent Staples alludes to prevailing preconceptions of his detractors:

> Few writers of V. S. Naipaul's stature have been so consistently and ag-
> gressively misread on account of ethnic and racial literary politics.
> Much of the criticism stems not from what Mr. Naipaul writes but
> from expectations about what he *ought* to write, given that he is a
> brown man (of Indian descent) born into the brown and black soci-
> ety that is Trinidad. Alas, after a 40-year voyage as a writer, Mr.
> Naipaul has arrived at a time when his work is too often viewed
> through the filter of race. This would seem an impoverished way of
> seeing in any case. In V. S. Naipaul's case, a strictly racial reading
> amounts to no reading at all.[5]

Racialist, imperialist, colonialist—these are descriptions of Naipaul's
work repeated by recent detractors, who consistently refer to their predecessors' views, deviating chiefly in their emphases. Selwyn Cudjoe, who
subjects Naipaul's writings to "A Materialist Reading" (as his subtitle indicates), refers to the "imperialist intent"[6] of Naipaul's work and to him
as an apologist for neocolonialism. In *London Calling: V. S. Naipaul, Postcolonial Mandarin*, Rob Nixon analyzes the rhetorical strategies of
Naipaul's travel narratives for evidence of his commitment to "the idealized imperial England of his imaginings,"[7] particularly the Victorian
era, which results in "a tone of outrageous superiority that blends easily
into racism."[8]

Both Nixon and Cudjoe attribute Naipaul's fundamental social and
cultural values to his psychological reactions to his immediate and extended family. Although Cudjoe claims in his introduction that his "book
will be an examination of Naipaul's work rather than an attempt to understand him as a person," his references to Naipaul's "ego," his "repressed
fears," his "neuroses," his "almost narcissistic concern for his prose style,"
and "the author's own perception of his sexuality [which] relates to the
question of his identity" contradict his stated aim. To be sure, Cudjoe
does not know the man whose psyche he so confidently analyzes. It is on
the basis of quotations (sometimes only a phrase or two) from the works
of Freud, Lacan, and LaPlanche, supported by his reliance on Marx, Louis
Althusser, and Terry Eagleton, among others, that Cudjoe constructs from
Naipaul's writings a psychopolitical biography of the man. One of his

comments on *Guerrillas* conveys assumptions that determine the quality of his judgments: "Much of *Guerrillas* . . . ought to be read as a script of Naipaul's unconscious, a neurotic response to his country."[9]

Although Rob Nixon mentions Cudjoe only once in *London Calling*, he seems to follow Cudjoe's lead as he begins with a psychological explanation for the colonialist bias that he considers the defining quality of Naipaul's nonfiction. Less judgmental than Cudjoe in this approach and mercifully sparing in his use of jargon, Nixon nonetheless reduces Naipaul's complex, often ambivalent, reactions to his early family life and social setting to the "idées fixes" which he finds "expressed for the first time in an explicit and concentrated manner" in *The Middle Passage*. Using selective brief references to Naipaul's autobiographical revelations, Nixon attributes his "tenacious disdain for collective values of any ilk, community feeling, political institutions, and women" to his "negative construal of his woman-dominated family." Even Naipaul's struggle for autonomy seems to Nixon to lead only to "arrogance and bigotry." He quotes a passage in which Naipaul describes his ambivalent feelings about the clan, which Nixon regards as "central to any psychological explanation of his hostility toward mobilization for political change":

> The clan that gave protection and identity, and saved people from the void, was itself a little state, and it could be a hard place, full of politics, full of hatreds and changing alliances and moral denunciations. It was the kind of family life I had known for much of my childhood: an early introduction to the ways of the world, and to the nature of cruelty. It had given me, as I suspected it had given Kala, a taste for the other kind of life, the solitary or less crowded life, where one had space around oneself.[10]

Nixon's premise that Naipaul is consistently hostile "toward mobilization for political change" is belied by the evidence of the very book he quotes from, in which Naipaul applauds the various political movements now demanding change in India. Furthermore, why should one assume that a writer or anyone else who has grown up in a turbulent atmosphere and now seeks peace and privacy is necessarily hostile to the political aspirations of those who seek change? This is "psychological explanation" at its most superficial. Nixon does concede: "Manifestly, community contains equivocal possibilities—it can be stifling or sustaining." Yet, denying the very evidence of his quotation and other similar passages in Naipaul's works, he remarks, "But Naipaul almost never acknowledges the latter as a possibility."[11]

In the latest extended censure of Naipaul's work, Fawzia Mustafa is troubled by the persistence of what he considers Naipaul's "misperceptions and inappropriate inquiries" regarding "Third-World issues" and "the exemplary space his writings have helped create in the understanding and making of late twentieth-century literary history."[12] Like Homi Bhabha, Nixon, and others, Mustafa exaggerates the importance of Conrad's influence, especially that of *Heart of Darkness*. His chief source is the brief essay "Conrad's Darkness," in which Naipaul discusses his varied responses to Conrad's work from his boyhood, when his father read him "The Lagoon," to 1974, the time of writing.

The key passage on which Mustafa stakes his claim is the one in which Naipaul describes his first reaction to Marlow's discovery of Towson's *Inquiry into Some Points of Seamanship*, a scene, Naipaul says, that "now makes less of an impression" than in his early first reading. But Mustafa ignores this last comment, choosing to magnify as permanent what is clearly the young aspiring writer's "fantasy" of "coming to England as to some purely literary region, where, untrammeled by the accidents of history or background, I could make a romantic career for myself as a writer." Naipaul soon abandoned this fantasy, discovering the "new politics, the curious reliance of men on institutions they were yet willing to undermine, the simplicity of beliefs and the hideous simplicity of actions, the corruption of causes, half-made societies that seemed doomed to remain half-made: these were the things that began to preoccupy me." If "to understand Conrad . . . it was necessary to begin to match his experience,"[13] it was *not,* as Mustafa says, because "Naipaul's map is Conrad's writing rather than colonial history and his quest canonical rather than historical." "Conrad's Darkness" is chiefly a reminiscence of Naipaul's responses to Conrad, whom he has reconsidered and essentially outgrown. Nonetheless, he values Conrad as "someone who sixty to seventy years ago meditated on my world, a world I recognize today," and he twice quotes Conrad's avowal that he endeavored to convey "a scrupulous fidelity to the truth of my own sensations." Elsewhere his quotations from or allusions to Conrad convey the injustice common to disparate places; for example, he compares the Argentine plunderers of the lands belonging to the Indians to the Belgian imperial conquerors, whose talk, Conrad says in *Heart of Darkness*, was that "of sordid buccaneers."[14]

Like many of Naipaul's analyses of fiction, which often assess their fidelity to actual social and cultural conditions he has studied or observed, his responses to Conrad are ambivalent. He describes a "multiplicity of Conrads, and they all seemed to [him] to be flawed" in their "explicitness," their lack of "imagination and fantasy and invention." In the story "Karain," "Reality hasn't fused with the writer's fantasy." Sometimes it is their very "explicitness" that leads to "mystification." Thus, *Lord Jim*, which is generally "held to be about honor," in Naipaul's view, is "about the theme of the racial straggler." He regards *Lord Jim* as "an imperialist book," and dismisses much of Conrad's fiction—*The Secret Agent* and *Under Western Eyes* (novels that we would expect to elicit more subtle responses) and, most surprising, *Nostromo*, which Naipaul never finished reading—perhaps because its brilliant depiction of imperialist corruption treads too closely on his own conception. So much for maps and canons.

Mustafa is unremitting in his attacks on "Naipaul's obsessive privileging of the Word and Book and the 'coherence' and 'order' leading to 'knowledge' they represent." Simple logic might assume that a writer is deeply involved with words and books, (with the upper case hardly necessary to make so obvious a point), but, alas, even logic is suspect where ideology lurks. To Mustafa, Naipaul's concern with language and the knowledge to which it leads "is partially responsible for his implication within colonialist discursive practice." Thus, combined with what Mustafa has judged to be Naipaul's "manufacture of 'lived experience' in his travels and sojourns," his "bookishness can with justification be read as Orientalist." Mustafa's next sentence reads like a summons from a Star Chamber or Orwell's Thought Police rather than a literary critique: "His writings, therefore, lend themselves to an indictment, the charge of which is political and, by extension, one which not only explores the issue of a writer's 'authority,' but also of the *ethics* (italics his) of writing and reading about non-western worlds."[15]

I cite the above examples only to note the predominant ideological emphases that are diametrically opposed to my own method. These emphases seem to me at times inappropriate and at others simply wrong. At worst, such approaches dehumanize Naipaul: they strip him of his ambivalence, his spontaneity, his "eye," the immediacy of his experience, and his ever-changing reactions, and they recreate him as the offspring of their own formulas. I have no intention of responding to them point by point—to do so would produce yet another commentary that replaces judgment of "the text as a coherent whole"[16] with polemics.

What is lost between critical lines drawn on ideological grounds is Naipaul's own declared strategy, his methods of searching for truth, a term he uses frequently in his autobiographical writings, interviews, fiction, and nonfiction. I will refer to various commentators in later sections, but only when my agreement with or objections to them elucidate the method and content of particular works, or in Umberto Eco's phrase, "the intention of the text." The reader, having joined me in exploring Naipaul's harsh avenues to truth, will, I hope, be equipped to evaluate these critics' claims to the truth of their positions as well as my own.

Naipaul's comment "A man must write to report his whole response to the world"[17] evokes the voice and the method that characterize the body of his work. It includes his effort "to reconcile" the colonial Trinidad of his youth and England, where he studied at Oxford and has lived as a writer. His travels throughout the West Indies, South America, India, Pakistan, Malaysia, Indonesia, Zaire, Iran, and the American South extend the terrain. In fiction and nonfiction he has explored the intricate connections between human history and the forces that determine its directions. Inherent in even his most despairing vein is a classical concept of justice, tragic in the consistency with which it is violated.

His claims as a seeker of truth are always contingent on his individual role in history and the possibilities of discovery within a particular time and place. In a lecture delivered in 1975, he said, "I begin with myself: this man, this language, this island, this background, this school, this time. I begin from all that and I try to investigate it, I try to understand it. I try to arrive at some degree of self-knowledge, and it is the kind of knowledge that cannot deny any aspect of the truth."[18] Throughout his work, brief and extended accounts recall his childhood—the strains and rewards of his relations with his extended family and the formative role of his father—and his later years in London and Wiltshire. Studying seventeenth-century documents of Trinidad's early history, he tries to "understand how my corner of the New World . . . had become the place it was."[19] He experiences the origins and evolution of his homeland as part of his personal history. No less revealing are his reactions to the lands and the people he comes to know in his travels, and his conversions of autobiography into fiction. Together these comprise the story of a writer whose pervading theme is a search for truth, an inner narrative of self-creation disclosed in the first or third person.

His means include observation, empathy, evaluation, self-criticism, and revision—an ever-expanding method in an ever-changing terrain. It is an ongoing process, an uncharted exploration of history, traditions, and values, of individual needs and desires, of the inner narratives of others, revised as they are enacted. Observing the intricate connections between the self and the observed world and its peoples stirs ambiguous memories and subliminal feelings that alter his responses. He has spoken of "two kinds of truth ... the real life [he] saw in Wiltshire" and the writer's "construct."[20] In his work the two kinds are never entirely separable; even words recorded in an interview are replies to the writer's particular approach to each speaker. Sometimes the tension between the author's immediate reaction and his awareness of the limits of his perception produces ambiguities that he later explores. Always subject to emendation, Naipaul's truth is the sum of continuous investigation in which his "eye" becomes keener and his knowledge of the seeker himself deepens. Throughout his career he has transformed self-creation into a cultural lens and a literary method that constitute his approach to truth, however contingent on the changing prospect of contemporary history and his own evolving skill as its interpreter.

His engagement with the "disordered and fast-changing"[21] world he observes, his empathy with the diverse people he describes in his travel narratives and creates in his fiction, his desire to "serve" his readers by disclosing the truth of their experience through the truth of his own, are rarely if ever discussed. Nor is his depiction of those whom no hospitable future beckons but who nevertheless enact a contemporary version of an ancient and continuous struggle to "exhaust the limits of the possible," unheralded but still representative of the history of their time. These issues at the core of Naipaul's work led me to write this book.

Naipaul's pursuit of truth, he has said, has released his own voice, his own views in opposition to received opinion and the seductions of language itself. Asked on one occasion whether he believed in "an objective truth," his answer was: "Yes. Provided that one takes everything into consideration, when one reacts to it. .... You have to become adept in looking for the truth of your own responses."[22] This was a daring position in 1971 and has become increasingly so ever since as the very notion of an author's individual voice and the possibility of objectivity are everywhere challenged. But Naipaul never meant and does not now mean to suggest that truth is some immutable essence, divine or historical. It is neither the "eternal objective truth" pervasive throughout both the Western religious and rational traditions, nor the "*rerum natura*" of natural law, nor the Romantic "personal truth,"[23] although it is necessarily the goal of an individual quest. When Naipaul speaks of the truth of one's responses, he refers to an individual mind contending with barriers to its authentic interpretation of experience. The outcome of this process depends on the capacity of human beings to create, out of their intellectual and emotional endowment, their background and education, a sound inner narrative in which the self reflects and confronts its world.

The issues implicit in this stance are not only literary ones. Naipaul's nonfiction and fiction portray the language of selfhood—words, gestures, acts—as a vehicle of truth. Still, questions arise: By what means can the individual self, as narrator or character, penetrate intractable personal and social barriers to regions of truth? How do fantasy, denial, and self-deception expose their ambiguous intentions? To what extent does the particular social and cultural background of the writer limit or enhance his comprehension of his own and other cultures? Do Naipaul's contradictions, reversals, detours, and regressions jeopardize the integrity of his quest? These are some of the issues I address.

In dividing the main body of this book into sections named for the genres Naipaul has used, I do not mean to suggest that these are discrete entities. On the contrary, I have found that this method discloses intricate connections among the various forms he redesigns for his own purposes. Long before "genre blur" became a trend, Naipaul was creating what I think is best described as genre fusion. In each section associations with works discussed under other headings will, I believe, elucidate Naipaul's assertion that he is "really writing one big book,"[24] fiction and nonfiction that confront the disjunction between his early background and later experience. His journalism, travel writings, and fiction expand this experience into a more general narrative of individuals' accommodation to their particular world—ambivalent even when seemingly firm, threatening the self, at once the product and the adversary of any reconciliation.

In Naipaul's work the development of selfhood, actual or fictive, is continuous exploration, inner narratives with referential affiliations among autobiography, journalism, and fiction. Such narratives are expressed in action, dialogue, and often in writing, all of which reveal individuals' drive to create themselves within the context, and often against the constraints, of their society and history. He portrays contemporary history in histories of the self devising its lot and enacting it privately and publicly. His fiction and nonfiction are complementary explorations of processes of selfhood stimulated and impaired by the nexus of familial, political, social, and cultural forces to which they are subject. In both forms a definitive expression of the self is the act of writing, which conveys the narrator or character reacting to public institutions and events, and divulges the equivocal connections between psychic and fictive narratives. Often, when his characters write, their words obliquely reveal desires and motives they have not previously acknowledged, even to themselves.

Diverse as the narrators of Naipaul's fiction are, none seem to fit the usual categories. Even when his narrator seems omniscient, the ways in which characters reveal themselves in relation to social history suggest that his knowledge is not given but gradually earned; when he is "unreliable," his motivation remains credible, his skewed perspective enlightening. In some novels, such as *Guerrillas,* related in the third person, and *The Enigma of Arrival,* told in the first person, the "implied author" seems to be discovering rather than establishing "the norms of the work"[25] in the act of narration. For Naipaul's writings, one needs a new term—perhaps investigative narrators, searching out the meanings of the events they recount and limited by a reality they cannot avoid.

Among the subjects I treat is the nature of these narrators: the kinship and divergencies among the I's of his autobiographical revelations, his travel narratives, and journalism and the first and third persons of his fiction. I track Naipaul creating himself as a writer and imbuing his characters, even the most poorly endowed, with the impulse toward selfhood. Author and characters as well as the people the traveler comes to know, however distant from each other in locale, personality, and class, are joined in a struggle to apprehend their roles within historical processes that often seem geared to defeat them, to render them dispossessed and homeless. These processes are their *moira,* their portion or fate, a tragic view which includes "the vision of the abyss" that pervades Naipaul's writings, even the comic ones. But the tragic apprehension of reality is not pessimistic. Paradoxically, the price of acknowledging the abyss is also the reward, the self-knowledge that stretches the limits it dares to reveal.

Naipaul has described his study of ancient Roman history as "the most awakening part of my formal education."[26] At school in classes based on a British model, he no doubt absorbed the heroic Rome of the European family romance, and it would have been easy for him to associate its history with his rather hazy image of "the India of the great civilization and the great classical past."[27] This kinship proved illusory on his first visit to India, but Rome was to become a multifaceted allusion, expanding the cultural affiliations of his narrators and characters. His many references to Rome and to Latin literature—brief but telling—convey his increasingly complex views of both the remoteness and the presence of the past in contemporary personal and cultural history, which are inevitably linked. Half a line from the *Aeneid* evokes an intense emotional experience of his own past. Elsewhere an epigraph from Tacitus elucidates some of the most insidious effects of colonialism. He reveals his affinity with Tacitus not only in this reference and another to Tacitus's digression on an ancient cult of Venus at Paphos, but also in his depictions of historical events through analyses of the character and acts of those involved in them. An epigraph from Polybius anticipates his approach to Islam. In Africa, the "colonial ruins of Stanleyville, now Kisangani," remind him of the ravages of Roman imperialism: "Rome and Belgium."[28] But Rome also provides an example of "pietas" comparable to the spirit inherent in Hindu ritual.

In 1975 Naipaul recommended that East Indians adopt toward their own past an "attitude . . . something like the attitude in Renaissance Europe toward the classical past." Like Fustel de Coulange, whose book *The Ancient City* he read with delight, Naipaul insists on a "recognition of the past as past," yet he acknowledges the necessity of "some understanding of all the strands in our upbringing."[29] In the strands of his own past, the classical and the Hindu meet as historical and emotional referents. In *An Area of Darkness*, recalling the death in London of a young Indian from Trinidad, and wanting to "offer him recognition," to have "his body . . . handled according to the old rites," he compares his own reaction to that of an ancient Roman: "So perhaps the Roman felt in Cappodocia." For the exile and unbeliever, history and tradition offer a sense of belonging without ideological ties or constraints on his imagination and judgments. On a visit to the Cave of Amaranth, he compares the "mystery" of the lingam of Shiva to that of the "Delphi of the older world."[30]

At a rest house in Luxor, furious at the treatment of young beggars by a waiter who whips them as they reach for food offered by a tourist, "an Egyptian game with Egyptian rules," Naipaul intervenes, shouting and grabbing the whip. Reflecting on his rage and the ultimate futility of his interference, observing a party of Chinese Communist circus performers tipping the "ragged waiters," he thinks of past imperial conquests of the land, of "the colossus on whose shin the Emperor Hadrian had caused to be carved verses in praise of himself, to commemorate his visit," and another "Roman inscription marking the southern limits of the Empire, defining an area of retreat." Rome here is but one of a series of imperial conquerors, whose pride is mocked by its very remains, which now bear witness to the transience of its rule. Naipaul sees the Chinese with their useless gifts as "another, more remote empire . . . announcing itself. A medal, a postcard; and all that was asked in return was anger and a sense of injustice." As the only tourist who reacted to the cruel game, he alone experienced the anger and the sense of injustice, the pain of the writer who could imagine an earlier time "at the beginning, when the ancient artist, knowing no other land, had learned to look at his own and had seen it as complete." Yet he finds it "hard to believe that there had been such innocence."[31]

In Luxor his Roman associations confront him with repeated violations of human dignity. In Iran he views Islam as a "divergence from the main belief . . . almost from the start . . . an imperialism as well as a religion." Its early history, he says, is "remarkably like a speeded-up version of the history of Rome, developing from city state to peninsular overlord to empire, with corresponding stresses at every stage."[32] When an old woman in Charleston, South Carolina, speaks of Sherman's burning of Columbia in 1865 as if it were a more recent event, Naipaul thinks, "perhaps Hannibal had been remembered in Italy and Rome in a similar way a hundred years after he had passed."[33] Rome is an opening into the historical life of places and people new to him, rendering them more familiar and more accessible.

Like their creator, several of Naipaul's characters regard Rome as a source of historical perspective and personal insight. Throughout *The Mimic Men,* the Latin language and Roman history and literature provide political enlightenment and personal "therapy" for the first-person narrator. A line in the *Aeneid* altered to signify the opposite of its original meaning, and inscribed on the remains of a monument in *A Bend in the River*[34] is critical to the protagonist's awareness of his own role in contemporary history. Planning *The Enigma of Arrival*, the narrator, clearly a version of Naipaul himself, means to draw on Vergil, Apuleius, Horace, Martial, and Petronius. "The ideal of living in my imagination in that classical Roman world was attractive to me. A beautiful, clear, dangerous world, far removed from the setting in which I had found myself." Although he obviously rejected this plan in writing *The Enigma of Arrival*, the ancient world remains in the novel as a vital part of the autobiographical narrative.

Naipaul's reminiscences of his early life in Trinidad and his efforts as a youth in London to make himself a writer recur throughout his work. Although many of the details remain the same, this is not mere repetition. His relations with people he meets in his travels affect the very nature of his memories and enlarge his perspective on his heritage: the religion and customs of immigrants from colonial India who settled in colonial Trinidad. In his travel books, his "Prologue to an Autobiography," and several of his novels, his returns to his roots are part of a continuous narrative of commitment to his "vocation" as writer, a means of assuring himself that his readers are acquainted with "this man," the author, where he comes from and where he is going.

His use of this technique is reason enough to devote a separate section of this book to a portrait of the artist as he emerges in the body of his work. But it is not only his own writings that disclose his origins and development. A central influence of his youth, the stories of his father, Seepersad Naipaul, amplify this background. Paul Theroux's view that Naipaul "may be the only writer in whom there are no echoes of influence"[35] is valid if he refers only to echoes of specific writers in his work. But Naipaul's originality is complex. In forging his way of looking at the world, he has assimilated centuries of Western culture to his own purposes. Even the Latin language, to which he returns when reading the historians, or Martial via the Loeb editions seems to have informed the precision and clarity of his prose. But far deeper than the early influence of Conrad or other writers he admired was that of his father, a gifted journalist and storyteller, his son's first example of a writer, who engaged the boy in the composition of his fiction and later became the model for Mr. Biswas, V. S. Naipaul's most moving fictional character. Reading his stories in the light of Naipaul's recollections of the years they shared, one can understand how Seepersad Naipaul's life and work led his son to confront the truth of his own experience, his memories, and emotions.

To define the narrators of his travel books, Naipaul uses his memories of the past and more recent times, both unbidden and deliberate, even an occasional dream. He reveals his immoderate personal reactions, his remorse at his own conduct, and the relief that friendship affords. Self-revelation is one of his means of relating to people he meets on his journeys, and it informs the composite creation of the characters of his fiction. His vivid portraits of people from a variety of economic and social classes are increasingly the product of a dialogue in which the reporter's disclosures of his own past, his values, and his reactions elicit candid responses from his subjects. As he compares his experience with theirs, both narrator and subject seem to discover as well as to reveal aspects of themselves. Naipaul's continual revaluations of his techniques as observer and listener demonstrate how closely his desire to apprehend the aspirations of the people he interviews and the obstacles they face is related to his development as a reporter recording the truth of his findings. The accretion of information—the relevant past and present history of the nations he visits, economic, social, and domestic details, literary references and interpretation—is often conveyed by a narrator whose pain and admitted rage sometimes blur his vision, yet also enhance it. The reader is engaged in exploring the lives of West and East Indians, Africans, Iranians, Pakistani, Malaysians, Indonesians, and American Southerners, led by a guide who is himself finding his "way in the world."

In every country he visited, Naipaul was concerned with the relation of the historical past—even in its seeming absence—to the present. The most intense personal reaction he records is empathy with the heirs of a history of slavery and colonialism: the economic, cultural, and psychological oppression, and especially the assaults on individual identity, a legacy with which they still contend.

Among his travel books, the three on India penetrate most deeply into his development as a man and a writer in intense, ambivalent, evolving relations with the society he explores. *An Area of Darkness* (1964), *India: A Wounded Civilization* (1976), and *India: A Million Mutinies Now* (1990) trace the changes in Naipaul's contradictory ties to his ancestral heritage rooted in the Indian community in Trinidad, trapped in the poverty, the limited opportunities for amelioration, from which its forebears had migrated, yet sustained by a "community identity" forged out of the "independence movement, the India of the great names," and its past grandeur. From his first visit in 1962, when he found no communal identity in the vastness of India and was shocked by the "poverty" and "abjectness" [56] that assaulted his sense of self, through many subsequent journeys over a period of twenty-seven years, he gradually came to terms with the actual India changing under his very gaze and in his internalized image.

Naipaul's journeys to India have been descents into himself as much as explorations of the land. On his first visit, the Himalayas were an inner landscape of the fantasized magnificence of his boyhood imagination; they were also the mountains where he observed pilgrims worshipping a melted lingam of Shiva with a detachment that seems a defense against his fear of self-abnegation. The millions with whom he identifies himself in his most recent book on India seem far removed from these pilgrims, yet their demands for social and economic reform do not preclude the profound religious devotion that many profess. The breadth of knowledge gained over years of travel, study, and self-examination have sharpened the "eye" Naipaul refers to so often, enlarged his receptivity, and refined his skills as a reporter. More secure in his "Indian identity," he welcomes the new assertiveness of Indians of diverse political and religious affiliations.

Not only in India and the West Indies, to which he has the closest personal ties, but also in Muslim countries and the American South, Naipaul associates his own background, his memories, and the feelings they evoke with the hardships and aspirations of the people he meets. Such affinities are one of his means of approaching the "politics" of a nation, which "can only be an extension of its idea of human relationships."[37]

It was during his travels in the Muslim countries, Naipaul says, that he arrived at his view of the "universal civilization," which he discussed in a lecture delivered to the Manhattan Institute in 1991. Visiting the holy city of Qum in Iran, he saw remnants of the "great medieval Muslim world, the great universal civilization of the time."[38] In Pakistan, in the poetry of a young medical student, who identified himself as a "rationalist," he sensed a fusion of the "worldly" aspects of the Shia Muslim religion in which he was raised and his attraction to the West which, Naipaul believes, now "leads" in the values and accomplishments that this concept encapsulates. In the young man's "fumbling response to the universal civilization," he says, "I thought I could see how Islamic fervor could become more than a matter of prayers and postures, could become creative, revolutionary, and take men on to a humanism beyond religious doctrine: a true renaissance, open to the new and enriched by it, as the Muslims in their early days of glory had been." This contrast between the humanism he perceives as inherent in Islam's past and its present fundamentalism, allied with an essential worldliness, no doubt enters into Naipaul's formulation of the universal civilization as neither a unitary system of values nor a single concept of truth. Even more cogent were his encounters with "the colonizations that had come with the Arab faith," [39] the loss of cultural traditions, of history prior to Islam, identities determined by an imposed religiosity.

In his lecture, "Our Universal Civilization," Naipaul responded to a series of questions posed by one of his hosts, in which he perceived a "pessimism" he did not share. These questions had to do with the efficacy of "beliefs or ethical views" in the life of a community, the most relevant to Naipaul's work being the last, which asks if such beliefs or values are "arbitrary" or if "they represent something essential in the cultures where they flourish." His lecture offers "no unifying theory of things," but reviews the disparate elements—personal, historical, cultural—that the concept of his title comprises. As always, beginning with his own experience, he believes that the universal civilization provides the conditions that create the "literary vocation" and make its fulfillment possible. The cultural development and continuous "needs" of such a civilization encourage intellectual growth through "the ideas of inquiry and the tools of scholarship" as well as a knowledge of history, which challenges nationalistic or religious claims to "the only truth." What is universal is "the idea of the pursuit of happiness," which embraces cultural differences even as it comprises particular values: "So much is contained in it: the idea of the individual, responsibility, choice, the life of the intellect, the idea of vocation and perfectibility and achievement."

Obviously, the idea of a universal civilization can be used to justify colonialism, as Samuel Huntington argues, in "the white man's burden" during the nineteenth century and, at present, in "Western cultural dominance of other societies and the need of those societies to ape Western practices and institutions." Huntington refers to Naipaul's article only to conclude that as one of the "intellectual migrants to the West," he finds in the idea of a universal civilization "a highly satisfying answer to the central question: 'Who am I?'" To indicate that Naipaul's need to establish his identity as a writer is one of the deleterious products of the belief in a universal civilization, Huntington answers his own question by quoting from Brent Staples's quotation from Edward Said, "White man's nigger," without a hint that Staples objects strongly to this description.[40]

Huntington interprets universalism as Western interference in the concerns of other civilizations and as the assumption that "non-Westerners will become 'Westernized' by acquiring Western goods." Even more contemptuous of the contemporary West is his rhetorical question: "What, indeed, does it tell the world about the West when Westerners identify their civilization with fizzy liquids, faded pants, and fatty foods?"[41] Sadly, he is equally cavalier regarding the issue of human rights and other democratic values that Naipaul emphasizes and that prevail in Western and some non-Western societies. In a review of Huntington's book, Patrick Glynn points out that Japan, for example, is "'Western' in the only sense that matters for purposes of geopolitics: it is a liberal democracy . . . Taiwan, too, has advanced significantly along the road from authoritarianism to genuine democracy. . . . The point of Western values in this sense is precisely that they are not so much 'Western' as universal."[42]

Admitting that the "West is now everywhere, within the West and outside; in structures and in minds," Ashis Nandy acknowledges its challenge to contemporary postcolonial commitments to autonomy. But, as Nandy points out, "the West is not merely a part of an imperial world order; its great classical traditions and its critical self are sometimes a protest against the modern West. This influence, as Nandy reminds us (and as Fawzia Mustafa should note), has been seminal in the very lan-

guage in which some of the West's harshest critics formulate their con-
demnations: "Let us not forget that the most violent denunciation of the
West produced by Frantz Fanon is written in the elegant style of a Jean-
Paul Sartre.[43] Nandy's concern is with "the Indian mind" as it has survived by adapting the influences of colonialism to its own ends, the ways
in which it has "tried to capture the differentia of the West within its own
cultural domain, not merely on the basis of a view of the West as politically intrusive or as culturally inferior, but as a subculture meaningful in
itself and important, but not all-important in the Indian context."[44]

Nandy's view of this "alternative universality" applies beyond his
immediate subject. The idea of the universal civilization of the West is
an amalgam of ancient Greek and Roman concepts of democracy, law,
and oratory; their styles of architecture; their languages; their history, art,
and literature; adapted to the changing economic and political developments and social values of individual nations. The reciprocal nature of alternative universality can be observed in the complex ways in which
Western European countries and the United States influence one another. Scientific discovery, technology, literature, and the fine arts are
often cosmopolitan products. Particularly in the United States, a large
immigrant and refugee population from the West and the East has expanded the concept of a universal civilization in science, industry, and
the arts.

Naipaul's conception of a universal civilization is based on his belief in individual potentiality and individual responsibility. It is not unlike the position of Isaiah Berlin, whose advocacy of cultural pluralism is
well known. In an interview,[45] replying in the negative to the question:
"Don't you think that there is a contrast between the principle of universality and cultural relativism?" Berlin explained his position on the
basis of common values: "No culture that we know lacks the notions of
good and bad; true and false." One of the most prominent authorities on
the "great differences" among cultures, he nonetheless argues that there
are universal values that make it possible to empathize with those whose
beliefs and assumptions differ from one's own. These values are similar
to Naipaul's:

> Understanding oneself and others, rational methods, verification, the
> basis of our knowledge and of all science, as well as the attempt to
> check intuitive certainties, are of cardinal importance. The idea of
> human rights rests on the true belief that there are certain goods—free-
> dom, justice, pursuit of happiness, honesty, love—that are in the inter-

est of all human beings, as such, not as members of this or that nationality, religion, profession, character; and that it is right to meet these
claims and to protect people against those who ignore or deny them.

Naipaul and Berlin, like George Orwell, to whom both refer with
admiration, defy ideological classification. Scorning utopias, they seek no
single truth, but rather, in Berlin's words, "roads to the truth," the continuous endeavor to translate into various eras and terms the truths that
seemed "self-evident" to those who framed the concept of the pursuit of
happiness. This "immense human idea," says Naipaul, "cannot be reduced
to a fixed system. It cannot generate fanaticism. But it is known to exist;
and because of that, other more rigid systems in the end blow away."

Naipaul has often said that the society that fosters intellectual
growth and imaginative creation did not exist in the Trinidad of his
youth. But, encouraged by his father and determined to be a writer, he
assumed that he was "part of a larger civilization," which he joined when
he left for Oxford. The values delineated in "Our Universal Civilization" are adumbrated in his travel books and in articles written prior to
his visit to the Muslim countries. His concern with the opportunities inherent in the idea of the pursuit of happiness is evident in his methods
of observation and engagement, his selection of data, his revisions of earlier judgments, and his reactions to people and their history. These
largely determine his "whole response to the world," which I examine
for its credibility as a source of information and sound interpretation.
Among his means of being "true to one's experience . . . and true to
what one's learned about it"[46] "are complex skills" that he acquired as a
reporter: openness to the unexpected—"encounters," "adventures," and
pondering on "what questions to ask, how to get on with people, how
to let people talk . . . what would prejudice my grasp of any given country or situation."[47] It is chiefly his interaction with a great variety of people—intellectuals and illiterates, guides, business executives, servants,
teachers and students, atheists and orthodox Hindus, Muslims, Sikhs, and
Jains—that demonstrate the advantages and limitations of his method of
seeking truth.

In evaluating the credibility of Naipaul's reporting, I consider issues
such as: How valid are his interpretations of the links between the historical past of a country and its present economic, political, and social
development, especially a history of invasions and colonialism? How
convincing are his views of the inbred "self-contempt" of subject populations and of the nature of their struggle for a measure of self-realiza-

tion, of personal dignity, within the bounds of what is often a spurious emancipation? How is his conviction that societies "have continually to create themselves"[48] related to and possibly limited by his own mode of self-creation? Does recent or current history support his representations of the societies he has explored?

Naipaul's journalism and fiction are linked by the author's presence as observer and participant in the action. In his travel books, the reporter analyzes fiction by the Iranian writer, Nahid Rachlin; the Indians R. K. Narayan and U. R. Amantha Murthy; and others, for their validity as interpreters of their societies. Describing Gandhi's persistent influence on India, Naipaul uses a telling simile: "Like a novelist who splits himself into his characters, unconsciously setting up consonances that give his theme a closed intensity, the many-sided Gandhi permeates modern India."[49]

In *A House for Mr. Biswas*, which appeared in 1961 when Naipaul was twenty-nine, the boy Anand's reactions to his father—longing, attachment, fear, rage, and reconciliation—are a foil for Mr. Biswas who, like Naipaul himself, wrests comedy from frustration and pain. Father and son, constructed from Naipaul's youthful "way of experiencing,"[50] evoke both an individual and a historical past. Naipaul's most recent novels, *The Enigma of Arrival* (1987) and *A Way in the World* (1994), are even more overtly autobiographical. But even these, and certainly the novels that appeared in the intervening years, are not to be taken as literal versions of their author's life. Naipaul splits various facets of his personality among his narrators and characters, including some seemingly very different from their creator. Many of his protagonists are writers. As he depicts them composing their narratives, he discloses the manifold ways he uses and distorts his own personality to create his fictitious progeny.

Naipaul has said, "An autobiography can distort; facts can be realigned. But fiction never lies: it reveals the writer totally."[51] But it is not only the author that fiction discloses: in *Among the Believers*, introducing his discussion of Nahid Rachlin's novel, *Foreigner*, he says: "People can hide behind direct statements; fiction, by its seeming indirections, can make hidden impulses clear." Recalling the years when he worked on *A House for Mr. Biswas*, he says that in the process of writing, the "novel called up its own truth." For him, the "wonder" of fiction lies in "the unsuspected truths turned up by the imagination."[52] These and other comments on the kinds of truth fiction reveals, as well as his protagonists' painful acceptance of such truths, must be considered in assessing his recent addition to the periodic death knells for the novel in the *Observer* (January 25, 1996), where he declared that it had not been a viable form since the end of the nineteenth century. It is not enough to say as Salman Rushdie does in a brilliant defense of the novel in the *New Yorker* (June 24 and July 1,1996) that if Naipaul "no longer wishes or is no longer able to write novels, it is our loss." Naipaul's contradictory statements actually convey both the continuous themes and the alterations in form that characterize his fiction throughout his career.

His disparagement of "invented stories" is not as new as it may seem. In 1979 he found novels about "London life" and "suburban misery" uninteresting, lacking a quality of "instability," which he valued in fiction.[53] He has long regarded the novel as "a form of social inquiry,"[54] and has converted places and events he covered as a reporter into the settings and plots of his fiction. In various and complex ways his characters internalize their heritage of slavery and colonialism and respond to each new "tide of history." This last phrase is from *A Bend in the River*, which is based on events in Zaire that he covered in his essay, "A New King for the Congo: Mobutu and the Nihilism of Africa." James Ahmed, a major character in *Guerrillas*, is a fictional version of Michael X, a.k.a. Michael Abdul Malik, a Black Power leader in London and Trinidad, whose career Naipaul had recounted in his essay, "Michael X and the Black Power Killings in Trinidad." Other novels also revolve around historical events, for example *The Mystic Masseur, The Mimic Men, In a Free State, The Enigma of Arrival,* and *A Way in the World*.

Rushdie's remark that Naipaul "is currently to be found at the leading edge of history, creating this new postfictional literature" (meaning "factual writing") is only partly true. His most recent novels, *The Enigma of Arrival* and *A Way in the World*, like many of his earlier ones, blend historical fact, autobiography, and fiction. However, his technique in integrating these components is at the cutting edge of his own craft. His emphasis is on autobiography, no longer oblique, now the chief vehicle of truth. But it is autobiography rooted in history, ancient and modern, political and cultural, from which the individual writer emerged.

Speaking of *The Enigma of Arrival*, following its publication in 1987, he clarified this new approach: "The writer, the observer, that is scrupulously myself. The minute other people are in the picture, that's where the fictive element comes in. . . . In the other work, someone like myself is doing the writing or observing. In this book I do it in my own person. It's closer to the truth; and I blend it in with my fiction."[55] It is "truth to a particular experience, containing a definition of the writing self."[56] The subject of *The Enigma of Arrival* is the creation of the writer's self and of his work; its plot is the act of writing. The truth he seeks, the integration of the psychic narrative of the man with the written narrative of the author, involves the convergence of many elements: his childhood in Trinidad, which "had fed my panic and my ambition," the other places he has lived in, his travels, the books he has written and the one he is writing, his dreams, his absorption in history, past and present, all are linked with his life in Wiltshire and with the characters he invents as catalysts in this chronicle of self-definition. The union of autobiography and fiction is most moving in his identification with one of his characters, Jack, a farm worker, whose life and death generate the writer's acknowledgment of his mortality, the central reality of his life and of this work.

In *A Way in the World*, Naipaul's most recent novel, he again employs fact and fiction, history and autobiography to explore the genesis of the "writing self." Here he converts the archival material he used in *The Loss of El Dorado* to an exploration of how closely the history of Trinidad from centuries before his birth to the time of his youth is interwoven with his personal history. As in *The Enigma of Arrival*, historical persons and fictional characters are involved in his intellectual and artistic autobiography. I discuss *The Enigma of Arrival* and other fiction that depicts a narrator or a character becoming a writer in chapter 2, autobiography, and *A Way in the World* in chapter 3 as history. Still, I return to these works in the last chapter, where I approach the body of Naipaul's fiction as part of a composite opus, the central theme of which the lifelong process of self-creation, an individual narrative of a search for truth that incorporates the historical and social framework in which it is enacted.

NOTES

1. Aamer Hussein, "Delivering the Truth, An Interview with V. S. Naipaul," *Times Literary Supplement* (September 2, 1994): 3.

2. V. S. Naipaul, *The Enigma of Arrival* (New York: Knopf, 1987), 146–47.

3. Irving Howe, "Epilogue: Politics and the Novel after *Politics and the Novel,*" *Politics and the Novel* (1957; reprint, New York: Meridian, 1987), 265–66.

4. Conor Cruise O'Brien, "The Intellectual in the Post-Colonial World," *Salmagundi* 70–71 (Spring/Summer 1986): 79.

5. Brent Staples, "'Con Men and Conquerors,' a Review of *A Way in the World,*" *New York Times Book Review* (May 22, 1994): 1.

6. Selwyn Cudjoe, *V. S. Naipaul: A Materialist Reading* (Amherst: University of Massachusetts Press, 1988), 191.

7. Rob Nixon, *London Calling: V. S. Naipaul, Postcolonial Mandarin* (New York: Oxford University Press, 1992), 37.

8. Nixon, 50.

9. Nixon, 172–255.

10. V. S. Naipaul, *India: A Million Mutinies Now* (1990; reprint, New York: Viking, 1991), 178.

11. Nixon, 172.

12. Fawzia Mustafa, *V. S. Naipaul* (New York: Cambridge University Press, 1995), 1–2.

13. V. S. Naipaul, "Conrad's Darkness" (1974), *The Return of Eva Perón* (1980; reprint, New York: Vintage, 1981), 232-33. Writing this essay, Naipaul could hardly have imagined that he was to match something of Conrad's posthumous experience as well. Reactions to Conrad's fiction—especially *Heart of Darkness*—have ranged from admiration at his foresight in exposing the atrocities of colonialism in the Congo Free State to condemnation of what are considered his racialism and his colonialist sympathies. There are, of course, more moderate reactions that view Conrad as a writer who both reflects and exceeds his time. Thus, Edward Said believes that the "imperial attitude" of "Western centrality" is "beautifully captured in the complicated and rich narrative form of Conrad's great novella *Heart of Darkness*." But he goes on to show that Conrad is also "ahead" of his time in his and his characters' understanding that the very "'darkness' has an autonomy of its own, and can reinvade and reclaim what imperialism has taken for *its* own." Still, "as a creature of his time, Conrad could not grant the natives their freedom, despite his severe critique of the imperialism that enslaved them." See *Culture and Imperialism* (1993; reprint, New York: Vintage, 1994), 22-30. Actually, Conrad had no such choice. As Adam Hochshild demonstrates in his recent book, *King Leopold's Ghost: A Story of Greed, Terror, and Heroism in Colonical Africa* (Boston: Houghton Mifflin, 1998), in *Heart of Darkness* Conrad was depicting the horror of real events in the Belgian Congo, and Kurtz is a composite of actual persons.

14. See chapter 3, p.140.

15. Mustafa, 27.

16. Umberto Eco, *Interpretation and Overinterpretation*, ed. Stefan Collini (New York: Cambridge University Press, 1992), 65.

17. "V. S. Naipaul, An Interview with Adrian Rowe-Evans," *Transition* 40 (1971): 58.

18. V. S. Naipaul, "Introduction," *East Indians in the Caribbean: Colonialism and the Struggle for Identity* (New York: Krause International Publishers, 1982), 7.

19. "Prologue to an Autobiography," *Finding the Center: Two Narratives* (New York: Knopf, 1984), 36.

20. "Delivering the Truth," 3–4.

21. "An Interview with Adrian Rowe-Evans," 62.

22. "An Interview with Adrian Rowe-Evans," 56.

23. These quotations are from Isaiah Berlin, *The Sense of Reality: Studies in Ideas and Their History*, ed. Henry Hardy (1996; reprint, New York: Farrar, Straus, Giroux, 1997), 172–183.

24. "The Novelist V. S. Naipaul Talks about His Work to Ronald Bryden," *The Listener* (March 22, 1973): 367.

25. These terms, introduced by Wayne Booth in *The Rhetoric of Fiction* (Chicago: University of Chicago Press, 1961), can be helpful. Even when inapplicable, they raise important questions, particularly about the unpredictability of fictional narrative. See 140–43, 158–59.

26. "Prologue to an Autobiography," *Finding the Center*, 46.

27. *India: A Million Mutinies Now*, 8.

28. V. S. Naipaul, *A Congo Diary* (Los Angeles: Sylvester and Orphanos, 1980), 23–24.

29. "Introduction," *East Indians in the Caribbean*, 6.

30. V. S. Naipaul, *An Area of Darkness* (1964; reprint, New York: Vintage, 1981), 93, 163.

31. V. S. Naipaul, *In a Free State* (1971; reprint, New York: Penguin, 1973), 243–46.

32. V. S. Naipaul, *Among the Believers: An Islamic Journey* (1981; reprint, New York: Vintage, 1982), 7.

33. V. S. Naipaul, *A Turn in the South* (New York: Knopf, 1989), 99.

34. V. S. Naipaul, *A Bend in the River* (1979; reprint, New York: Vintage, 1980).

35. Paul Theroux, *V. S. Naipaul: An Introduction to His Work* (New York: Africana, A Division of Holmes and Meier, 1972), 7.

36. *India: A Million Mutinies Now*, 8.

37. V. S. Naipaul, "The Return of Eva Perón" (1972) in *The Return of Eva Perón with the Killings in Trinidad* (1980; reprint, New York: Vintage, 1981), 166. First published in *The New York Review of Books* as "The Corpse at the Iron Gate" (August 10, 1972) and as "Argentine Terror: A Memoir," (October 11, 1979).

38. *Among the Believers*, 53.

39. V. S. Naipaul, "Our Universal Civilization," *The New York Review of Books* (January 31, 1991): 22-25.

40. Samuel Huntington, *The Clash of Civilizations and the Remaking of World Order* (New York: Simon and Schuster, 1996), 66.

41. Huntington, 58.

42. Patrick Glynn, "The Swelling Democratic Tide," *Times Literary Supplement* (April 11, 1997): 10–11.

43. Ashis Nandy, *The Intimate Enemy: Loss and Recovery of Self under Colonialism* (Delhi: Oxford University Press, 1983), xi–xvi.

44. Nandy, 75–78.

45. "Philosophy and Life: An Interview," with Ramin Jahanbegloo, *The New York Review of Books* (May 28, 1992): 46–54.

46. "V. S. Naipaul: 'It Is Out of This Violence I've Always Written,'" interview by Mel Gussow, *New York Times Book Review* (September 16, 1984): 45.

47. Bharati Mukherjee and Robert Boyers, "A Conversation with V. S. Naipaul" (May 1979), *Salmagundi* 54 (Fall 1981): 11.

48. "Introduction," *East Indians in the Caribbean*, 8.

49. V. S. Naipaul, *India: A Wounded Civilization* (1977; reprint, New York: Vintage, 1978), 189.

50. V. S. Naipaul, "Writing *A House for Mr. Biswas*," *The New York Review of Books* (November 24, 1983): 22.

51. V. S. Naipaul, "Michael X and the Black Power Killings in Trinidad," *The Return of Eva Perón*, 67. First published in London as "The Killings in Trinidad" in *The Sunday Times Magazine*, on May 12, 1974, and May 19, 1974.

52. "Writing *A House for Mr. Biswas*," 22–23.

53. Mukherjee and Boyers, 11.

54. *India: A Wounded Civilization*, 10.

55. Mel Gussow, "The Enigma of V. S. Naipaul's Search for Himself in Writing," *New York Times* (April 25, 1987): 16.

56. V. S. Naipaul, "On Being a Writer," *The New York Review of Books* (April 23, 1987): 7.

2

AUTOBIOGRAPHY

BECOMING A WRITER

By the time Naipaul was eleven, he and his father assumed that he was to be a writer. Fulfilling this ambition, he believed, entailed winning a Trinidad government scholarship to Oxford, his sole means of escape from the strictures of his background. He achieved these goals by the age of eighteen, only to face a greater challenge—the unforeseen demands of his vocation.

His conception of the writer as "a person possessed of sensibility," instilled by his education and early reading, resulted in what the mature Naipaul describes as a "separation of man from writer," the denial of the "colonial-Hindu self below the writing personality."[1] But this division was never intact. In *The Enigma of Arrival*, looking back after more than thirty years to the beginning of his journey to England, Naipaul describes his younger self as half-consciously recognizing but unwilling to accept his anxiety and loneliness, "a dwindling of the sense of the self." Yet if the diary he wrote in the Hotel Wellington during a stopover in New York was "suppressed, half true," it was also "half intensely true." Paradoxically, the diary's entry, however oblique, "of truth not fully faced," itself records a truth. It adumbrates a fundamental motif of Naipaul's life and work: the difficulty and necessity of releasing subliminal feelings into consciousness, one of the manifold ways of knowing. The unity of the self and the work was to become his lifelong commitment, ongoing processes of creation in which the truth of personal and social history are intertwined.

Naipaul says that "the two personal narratives" that comprise *Finding the Center* "are about the process of writing. Both pieces seek in different ways to admit the reader to that process."[2] This statement defines most of the autobiographical revelations that appear throughout his work. In brief or extended comments, in first or third person, directly or obliquely, the writer discloses himself practicing his art. Variations in moods and judgments, rage expressed and rued, altered responses to past events: all convey the persistent demand he makes of himself—that the work be true to his experience.

In his Foreword to *Finding the Center,* he tells of needing a story for the first narrative, "Prologue to An Autobiography," that would relate the middle-aged author's "particular truth" of his "literary beginnings." "The Crocodiles of Yamoussoukro," the second narrative, discloses the traveler and writer of 1982-83 "in his latest development . . . adding to his knowledge of the world, exposing himself to new people and relationships." Both explicate the book's title, which, as he explained to an interviewer, "has many meanings—finding the center of the narrative, the center of the truth of every experience, the philosophical center for one's belief." It is the link between the author's inner and literary narratives. Having lived through the chaos of this century, who can withhold assent to Yeats's pronouncement that "the centre cannot hold"? Yet Naipaul's response to his interviewer's allusion to this line must be reckoned with: "Yes, it was meant to be an inverted reference to that too. For many people, they find the center and it does hold." [3] The truth may be provisional and ambiguous, but for the writer this center beset by opposing forces was his first and remains his continuous pursuit.

Without Naipaul's later explications in *Finding the Center* and *The Enigma of Arrival* it would be virtually impossible to realize that his first transformations of his early life into fiction constitute the resolution of almost five years of conflict, denial of the self and its insistent demands to be heard. The voice that emerges in *Miguel Street* is confident; the writer has turned to his most authentic resource, his memories of the people and "the life of the street" of his boyhood.[4] Explaining that the young narrator is not himself, Naipaul points out that for the sake of simplicity the boy is given no father and no extended family, only a mother. He is indeed an independent creation, but he, the contents, and the tone of the stories he tells have a literary ancestor in the author's father, Seepersad Naipaul. Only in the last sentence of *Miguel Street* does the narrator become the author: "I left them all and walked briskly towards the aeroplane, not looking back, looking only at my shadow before me, a dancing dwarf on the tarmac."[5] This sentence, Naipaul says, "held memories of the twelve years, no more, I had spent with my father. . . . And it was with that sudden churlishness, a sudden access of my own hysteria, that I had left my father, not looking back. I wish I had. I might have taken away, and might still possess, some picture of him on that day."[6] The absence of the narrator's father in *Miguel Street,* along with his reenactment of the author's refusal to look back, suggests that what Naipaul calls "churlishness" and "hysteria" is actually a more specific reaction, combining psychological and aesthetic need. His father was indeed absent for long periods of his childhood. Yet their relationship was fundamental to Naipaul's early development and his later career. But to the young man, becoming a writer meant breaking away from the limits of his past and the mutual dependence of father and son in this very endeavor. Naipaul's explanation of the formal value of omitting the father in *Miguel Street* is no doubt valid, but creation is always overdetermined. A father is absent until the writer has completed his first return to the past, having avoided the complications of love and pain associated with his own father who had nourished his gift. Only at the end could he risk awakening more ambivalent feelings about the heritage he was to explore in making himself a writer.

Writing *Miguel Street* was the genesis of self-knowledge, a recognition that the "worlds I contained within myself, the worlds I lived in" were his "subject."[7] As he continued to write, these worlds were to unfold as the history of Trinidad, of his parents and his extended family, which were incorporated into his own past as well as his present life in an alien setting. Within this heritage, the context of his inner narrative, the central figure was his father.

Seepersad Naipaul is a remarkable figure as he is rendered in his son's portraits in *Finding the Center* and in his Foreword to his father's stories, *The Adventures of Gurudeva and Other Stories.* Although his stories do not deal with his personal life, his narrators, perhaps inadvertently, reveal something of his nature and certainly his early familial and village background. In fiction his character is most poignantly recreated in the protagonist of V. S. Naipaul's *A House for Mr. Biswas.* Versions of Seepersad Naipaul's struggle for autonomy in an inhospitable setting are also woven into the plots of several of his son's later novels. The facts that emerge chiefly from these sources describe a man who was paradoxical in many respects, yet consistent in defying the barriers of his personal and social history in order to make himself a writer and finally to live in his own home.

Although Seepersad Naipaul's father, a pundit, died when he was an infant, his mother's tales of his cruelty oppressed him throughout his life. Left without resources after the father's death, his family was divided among relatives whose decisions regarding the children seem to have been determined by their age. Seepersad Naipaul, the youngest, was to be trained as a pundit, and thus was able to learn both English and Hindi. Rereading his father's stories and perceiving "the brahmin standpoint from which they are written," V. S. Naipaul speculates that it was the "Hindu reverence for learning and the word, awakened by the beginnings of an English education and a Hindu religious training" that instilled "the desire to be a writer"[8] in Seepersad Naipaul. Surely his social and economic circumstances would seem to have precluded such an ambition. He never became a pundit and had no training for any other work. Married into a wealthy family of landowners, he resented his dependence on them for housing and at times for menial employment.

The drive of Seepersad Naipaul's talent exploiting whatever meager opportunities were open to him within the disparities of his background accounts, at least in part, for both his achievements and their psychic cost. If his brief formal education made him skeptical of pundits, it did provide an introduction to Hinduism, enhanced no doubt by the storytellers whose recitation of the Hindu epics were a tradition of village life.[9] His secular education, however limited, made him aware of writing journalism and fiction as a vocation, a prospect of self-fulfillment or at least a form of self-expression.

In 1929 he started writing for the *Trinidad Guardian*. Encouraged by its new editor, Gault MacGowan, Seepersad Naipaul wrote articles that drew on his knowledge of Indian life in Trinidad and reflected the influence of "the reforming movement known as the Arya Samaj, which sought to make of Hinduism a pure philosophical faith."[10] But such views offended orthodox members of his wife's family. A crucial episode that was to affect the future course of his life as well as his son's occurred in 1933, when he wrote an article critical of the Hindu remedy for an outbreak of paralytic rabies among cattle—the sacrifice of a goat to the goddess Kali. In return he received an anonymous letter probably, says V. S. Naipaul, from a member of his wife's family, threatening him with death unless he performed "the very ceremony he had criticized." Although his accounts of this threat in the *Guardian* had declared that he would not perform the sacrifice, in fear of death he complied. One can only imagine the conflict of a man who had begun to establish his identity as a writer, to find his own voice, forced into the role of orthodox priest performing a rite of self-renunciation.

Soon afterward the editor who had taught and believed in him left the *Guardian*. To make matters worse, he was removed from the staff and demoted to the position of "stringer." His confidence, largely dependent on the success he had begun to achieve as a writer, was shattered. As V. S. Naipaul was to learn from his mother many years later, "He looked in the mirror one day and couldn't see himself. And he began to scream." No more graphic example of the loss of identity can be imagined. Fleeing the scene where he had been compelled to deny his own truth, the heart of his vocation, he roamed about doing odd jobs and depending on various relatives.

During this absence from home he sent his son a little book of poetry in which he inscribed the child's exact age: "3 years, 10 months and fifteen days" and his counsel: "Live up to the estate of man, follow truth, be kind and gentle and trust God." This gift, which V. S. Naipaul describes as "really a decorated keepsake," reminded the son of his father's devotion even in his absence, but it was also, Naipaul says, "something noble, something connected with the word." The counsel to a child not yet four, perhaps premature in a more conventional family, expresses ideals that even in his despair Seepersad Naipaul had not abandoned and wished to bestow on his son. Certainly this is true of the father whom V. S. Naipaul was to know after his return to the family. Seepersad Naipaul managed to regain his job at the *Guardian*, and the family moved from the maternal grandmother's household in Chaguanas to a house she owned in Port of Spain.

The position Seepersad Naipaul now held was that of reporter, which offered little satisfaction, but his earlier writing for the newspaper, in which he was free to express his own point of view and to forge his own style, remained for him the genesis of a vocation, which he transmitted to his son. The boy read his father's early articles as "memorials of a heroic time I had missed."[11] His father read to him: "Charles Kingsley's story of Perseus," chapters from Dickens's novels, stories by O'Henry and, when he was only ten, Joseph Conrad's "The Lagoon." In an essay on Conrad written in 1974, Naipaul tells of his lasting response to the atmosphere "of night and solitude and doom" and his later feeling for the Conradian "passion, the abyss, solitude and futility and the world of illusions" that this brief story creates.[12]

Despite Naipaul's reservations regarding Conrad's fiction, to which I referred in chapter 1, he continued to value his commitment to the truth that narrative can produce, but this lifelong challenge has its origins, I believe, in earlier and more personal impressions. Surrounded by domestic turmoil—a reluctant move from Port of Spain back to a communal household, animosity within the extended family, lack of a modicum of privacy, and then a return to Port of Spain to a house increasingly occupied by relatives—Naipaul began to read stories his father had written for *The Guardian* in the past. Also during these turbulent years, when Seepersad Naipaul found relief from his anger and depression by once again writing fiction, he engaged his son in the process. The boy listened to the stories as they were created in version after version, and was asked for and gave advice. He observed his father's efforts to depict the Hindu village life of his childhood. In his "Prologue to an Autobiography," he tells of his participation in the creation of a long story, "Gurudeva," "its slow making . . . from the beginning to the end. . . . It was the greatest imaginative experience of my childhood. . . . It was my private epic." He was eleven years old when this story and a few others were published in a booklet in 1943. Having empathized with his father in the act of writing, he now "shared his hysteria" at the errors of the linotypists.[13]

This shared interest in writing continued even after V. S. Naipaul left home for Oxford. Until Seepersad Naipaul's death in 1953, father and son corresponded about their work,[14] about finding an English publisher for "Gurudeva" and other stories (which was not accomplished until 1976), and about V. S. Naipaul's short stories and his first novel, which was finally rejected. They praised, advised, and encouraged each other. Seepersad Naipaul assured his son that if he could not find a job, he would provide the opportunity that he himself had missed—time to be devoted entirely to writing. In another letter he suggested that his son use him as a subject, and that, of course, was exactly what his son was to do.

The word "hysteria" appears often in V.S. Naipaul's autobiographical revelations, not only as an overreaction to a specific concern, but more fundamentally as the "fear of extinction," the annihilation of the self that his father continued to endure and "transmitted" to his son. This, Naipaul says, was the "subsidiary gift" of his father. Only "linked with the idea of the vocation," his father's primary gift, could the fear "be combated."[15]

As an avenue to the truth of one's memories and observations, as the product of "seeing," writing could allay that fear. But Seepersad Naipaul could go only part of the way back to his early life. He wrote eloquently about the setting and customs of his childhood and about members of his extended family, but only one of his plots is based on an incident involving his parents. Although he said that he wished to write an autobiographical novel, he never produced one. It seems likely that recreating the deprivations of his youth, the cruelty he was told of and witnessed, his later humiliations by his wife's family, and his continuous frustrations at home and at work constituted too great a threat to the emotional stability he struggled to maintain. Years later his son would write that novel, fulfilling Seepersad Naipaul's aspiration in *A House for Mr. Biswas*, which he describes as "very much my father's book . . . written out of his journalism and stories, out of his knowledge. . . . It was written out of his writing."[16]

Seepersad Naipaul's stories are a vital portion of his heritage to his son, who considers them "a unique record of the life of the Indian or Hindu community in Trinidad in the first fifty years of the century." He refers to the "knowledge" and "sympathy" that made it possible for Seepersad Naipaul to comprehend the changing course of this community rooted in "old India" as it gradually blended into its setting in colonial Trinidad.[17] It seems likely that one of the offshoots of the evocation in the stories of ancestral beliefs and rituals was V. S. Naipaul's early and lasting attraction to the ancient world. In his Foreword, he says that when reading Fustel de Coulange's *The Ancient City* it "was entrancing to me . . . to discover that many of the customs, which with us in Trinidad, even in my childhood, were still like instincts, had survived from the pre-classical world." *The Ancient City* deals primarily with the religion of ancient Greece and Rome, but Fustel de Coulange finds many parallels with the beliefs and rituals of the ancient brahmins. Early in *The Ancient City* he suggests that we study ancient Greek and Roman civilizations "without thinking of ourselves, as if they were entirely foreign to us, as if we were studying ancient India or Arabia." But he is also aware that, without distorting early societies into semblances of ourselves, we are nonetheless ultimately their "product." "Fortunately, the past never dies for man. Man may forget it, but he always preserves it within him."[18] Seepersad Naipaul's stories create this strangeness, this distant past of an unknown world, which, however different the context, suggests the remoteness of his readers' own past and evokes its presence in their inner narratives.

His characters, Hindus who are either descendants of indentured workers or have themselves discharged their indentureship, range from landowners to the very poor, living in mud huts under the most primitive conditions. In a passage characteristically precise and imaginative, he conveys the atmosphere of one area, flooded for half the year. Engaging the reader through the phrase "made you think," he says: "From a quarter of a mile these huts made you think of some gargantuan, prehistoric monsters that had rambled in the slime and slush of the lagoon and then, no longer able to carry themselves, had died, greyed, become fossilized, and remained rooted and inert for ever." Yet its inhabitants rejoice in the rain and the mud as "a godsend for the paddy crops" ("My Uncle Dalloo").

In his "Foreword," V. S. Naipaul remarks on the variation between the romantic and satirical approach of these stories. He believes that for the writer romance was "a way of concealing personal pain." While it is true that "there is nothing of protest . . . the barbs are all turned inwards," Seepersad Naipaul's "way of looking" does not exclude the suffering inherent in customs that the romance of ceremony cannot redeem. In the story "Dookhani and Mungal," a loving wife serves rice to her husband "as though performing a ritual" when he returns from his work in the sugar fields. But this wife, though loved in return by her husband, has just endured the hatred of her mother-in-law who finds many occasions to insult and beat her, especially for her failure to bear offspring. Her husband, bound by tradition not to defend his wife against his mother lest the villagers say that "Kali-yuga—the Black Age [has] come upon the world," can express his concern only by telling her to return to her own mother. While the story ends in the couple's joy in the knowledge that she is pregnant, they remain victims of the very traditions that give their lives meaning. The husband of this story is uncommon in his tenderness toward his wife. Usually it is the husband's cruelty that generates the need for appeasement in the romance of "the old way."

Seepersad Naipaul wrote to his son: "I have hardly written a story in which the principal characters have not been members of my family" ("Foreword"). In two of these family stories, "Panchayat" and "They Named Him Mohun," tradition serves to rationalize a husband's right to mistreat his wife. In "Panchayat," even under rapidly changing social conditions, as the narrator says, "in these amazingly modern times," a mother chooses to bring her daughter's charge that her husband has repeatedly deserted her during her pregnancies before a village tribunal rather than before a court of law. The husband, bold in his sophistic arguments, wins the case. His mother-in-law remains unconvinced: "Just talk," she says, "Talk and nothing more." But the wife, ever submissive, agrees to return to him. The story ends not in the liberation of romance but in conformity to the demands of custom.

The wife in "Panchayat," V. S. Naipaul reveals, was based on his father's sister, whose unhappiness in her marriage pained him. "They Named Him Mohun" was inspired by the writer's parents and his own birth. Once again a pregnant woman has sought her mother's protection from the abuses of her husband, in this case, his stinginess and his anger, expressed in words and blows. The child Mohun's birth is inauspicious.

While he was still in his mother's womb, his grandmother had encapsulated her feelings about him and his father in the word "Shame." Born under "a bad planet," "in the wrong way," and "with six fingers on each hand," he is declared by the midwife a child "bound to eat its mother and father." Nevertheless, his grandmother, on the advice of a pundit, performs a ritual to mitigate these bodings and holds a celebration of Mohun's birth. At the first of these the father's presence is required; he insists on attending the second, and at the end, even the grandmother agrees that he may remain with his wife.

V. S. Naipaul describes this story as "a tale of pure romance, in which again old ritual, lovingly described, can only lead to reconciliation." Yet the story contains many realistic details—the husband's meanness, the pregnant wife's seven-mile journey on foot to her mother's house, and especially her mother's open contempt for the husband's lack of "shame," a traditional epic insult. If Hindu "law" uttered by the pundit compels her to capitulate, she certainly is not reconciled to her son-in-law, whose cruelty tradition has condoned. Seepersad Naipaul could not endure the pain of further self-revelation, but his son, having "cannibalized" "They Named him Mohun" for the opening section of *A House for Mr. Biswas*, compensated for his father's resistance to expressing the full measure of his hatred for his own father by making his protagonist, Mohun Biswas, fulfill the prophecies that attended his birth when inadvertently but effectively he is instrumental in his father's death.

In the first part of the title story, "The Adventures of Gurudeva," Seepersad Naipaul adapts conventions common to both Indian and Western epic—the security and constrictions of the clan, the desire for glory, the example of the gods and the heroes of the past—only to expose the degeneration of such norms in the career of the protagonist, a cowardly village hoodlum. Like "They Named Him Mohun," though less directly, this story expresses both its author's veneration of tradition and his reformist deprecation of its observance in unreflecting routine or, more culpably, in arrogance and cruelty. Gurudeva's ambition to be a fighter, "a bad-John," his inability to distinguish "notoriety from fame," lands him in jail, where he turns to his meager knowledge of religion for comfort, and from which he emerges determined to become a pundit. The second part of the story portrays him in this unlikely role.

V. S. Naipaul explains disparities between the first and second parts of the story in his "Foreword." "The story was written in two stages"; the first, which takes place during the 1930s, was written in 1941–42, and the second ten years later, by which time the writer's and his protagonist's "society had been undermined; its values had to compete with other values; the world outside the village could no longer be denied." Naipaul sees Gurudeva in the second part as "an easy target" of satire and feels that "the satire defeats itself." The absence of the heroic tone of the early episodes against which the ignorance and distortions of tradition are measured does reduce the power of the later section of Gurudeva's story. Still he remains a striking comic figure as he masks his shyness, his smattering of Hindi and Hinduism, with bravado.

The first part of "Gurudeva" reveals Seepersad Naipaul's reverence for traditional beliefs and customs in details of rural life, the second part his ambivalence regarding changing religious and cultural attitudes through various characters. The reformist is here represented by Pundit Biswas whose name he was to inherit in his son's autobiographical novel. Gurudeva's semi-literate challenge to Biswas in a lecture ends in disorder but makes him a "celebrity." One can also sense the author's presence in Schoolmaster Sohun, who resembles him in only one respect: he is learned in Hindu thought and its various interpretations of worship. Even Gurudeva, "turning satirist himself," says V. S. Naipaul, "begins to approximate to his creator; at the end, abandoned by wife and girl friend and left alone, he is a kind of brahmin, an upholder of what remains of old values, but powerless. He has traveled the way of his baffled creator" ("Foreword"). This convergence continues in still another fictive transformation in V. S. Naipaul's *The Mimic Men*, in which the narrator's father takes the name Gurudeva when he leaves his family and his job to lead a protest movement of the poor.

Listening to these stories as they were written, offering encouragement and suggestions, V. S. Naipaul was learning a great deal about the writer's craft. His father's stories, he says, gave him "a way of looking, an example of labor, a knowledge of the literary process, a sense of the order and special reality (at once simpler and sharper than life) that written words could be seen to create." Before he could apprehend the context of the message, he had received his counsel to "follow truth." Much later, in a letter to his son written in 1951, Seepersad Naipaul had recalled his editor's advice, "Write sympathetically," and had added his own, "and this, I suppose, in no way prevents us from writing truthfully, even brightly" ("Foreword").

In so far as he could, he adhered to this principle. The very disparities that characterize his style render his fidelity to the truth of his observations: the contraposition of an epic tone with wit and satire; the remnants of a ceremonial heritage and the pleasures of quotidian existence juxtaposed against the details of its poverty, ignorance, deceit, and cruelty. His repression of his own pain and anger at the deprivations of his past and the continuous humiliations of dependence does not diminish these stories. But in his daily life his frustrations were expressed in bizarre and sometimes violent behavior.

Although V. S. Naipaul did not learn about the circumstances of his father's breakdown until 1970, from his sixth to his eighteenth year he was exposed to the lasting psychological effects of Seepersad Naipaul's surrender to the will of the clan. The boy participated in the act of writing that remained his father's refuge, his means of restoring his fragile sense of selfhood. Inevitably, the self-confidence such trust could bestow on a child was tempered by his assimilation of his father's anxieties, the conflict produced in suppressing his own truth, his writer's identity, and his simultaneous need to articulate it. It is not surprising that the son incorporated his father's fear of psychic dissolution along with his vocation. Yet, if Seepersad Naipaul's trauma exemplified the psychic cost of commitment to the truth of his convictions, it also served as a warning against the repression of memory and the denial of perception. Furthermore, his belief in his son's gifts, his determination that he escape the bonds of the clan and the limits of his society, fostered V. S. Naipaul's commitment to the truth of his own past, to his emotional and intellectual vantages in the stages of his development as a writer.

Naipaul drew on material from his childhood in *Miguel Street* and set other early fiction—*The Mystic Masseur* and *The Suffrage of Elvira*—in Trinidad, but he has said that it was the writing of *A House for Mr. Biswas*, his "most personal" book, that "changed" him. After completing that novel, he returned to Trinidad for a visit in 1960 with "a sense of security that was entirely new, the security of a man who had at last made himself what he wanted to be."[19] In reconstructing his father's life he was also tracing the inception of his own process of self-creation.

The son of Mr. Biswas, Anand, endures domestic strife and poverty, his father's illness and absences, frequent moves from Hanuman House, the home of his grandmother in Arwacas (the fictional Chaguanas), to Green Vale, to Port of Spain, from there to Shorthills, and then back to the city, all of which are fictional versions of experiences Naipaul has recalled in later autobiographical surveys. But the "truth" that Naipaul has said this novel evoked concerned not only events and feelings Seepersad Naipaul could not bear to face, but the son's ambivalent relationships with his father, his mother, and her extended family, in whose houses he lived for much of his youth.

In various contexts Naipaul has disparaged the clan with its emphasis on caste, a system he denounces. Yet, looking back in his "Prologue to an Autobiography," he acknowledges, it could have been a psychological advantage: "For all its physical wretchedness and internal tensions, the life of the clan had given us all a start. It had given us a class certainty, a high sense of the self." Undernourished and mistreated in the household of his grandmother—often for his father's transgressions—Anand is depicted as gradually conceiving a private sense of self within the contradictions of his extended family: their pride as prominent Hindus who observe the religious rituals but do not practice the values they profess, their petty tyrannies, their stinginess, their outright cruelties. In the novel, as no doubt in reality, his father's alternating submission to and rebellion against that family, his skepticism, his rage and wit, his idiosyncrasies and fastidiousness, however unsettling, provoked the boy to develop his own multifaceted way of perceiving the world around him.

A House for Mr. Biswas portrays the tentative approaches and withdrawals of the early relationship between father and son. Having been absent during much of his son's early childhood, Mr. Biswas gradually reaches out to the boy who had "belonged completely to the Tulsis,"[20] among whom Mr. Biswas includes his wife Shama as antagonist. Her acceptance of the life assigned her by the clan, even its "established emotions," elicits Mr. Biswas's irony and often his rage. The boy lives in a household of constant tension.

Naipaul has said that *A House for Mr. Biswas* was "created out of what I saw and felt as a child."[21] Those perceptions and feelings emerge in Anand's gestures, in his silences and laconic responses, in his sudden exclamations of anger and oblique expressions of affection and loyalty. Episodes involving the boy that are not necessarily autobiographical in external detail elucidate his inner life, especially what seemed so "astonishing" to Naipaul as an adult, his internalization of his father's "fear of extinction" along with his vocation. His fictional portrayal of Anand's unconscious identification with his father reveals psychological affinities that he does not probe in his autobiographical writings.

Both Seepersad and V. S. Naipaul were deprived of a father's presence in early childhood, and both were dependent on the arbitrary benevolence of their extended families. In the novel this similarity initiates an empathy that slowly develops between Mr. Biswas and Anand. During Mr. Biswas's visits to Arwacas, when he is living apart from his family at Green Vale, a sugarcane estate owed by the Tulsis, Anand is generally shy with him, avoiding any physical contact. Yet on one occasion, when he has defended the boy who has been unjustly punished, Anand seems "unwilling to let him leave. He said nothing, he simply hung around the bicycle, occasionally rubbing up against it." Only the gesture discloses his need and gratitude for his father's protection. He is silent when his father asks: "You want to come with me?" He "only smiled and looked down and spun the bicycle pedal with his big toe," displacing his longing on the surrogate object. Each feels the other's vulnerability: Mr. Biswas "touched by the boy's fragility," the shabbiness of his clothing, his subjection to the harsh rule of the Tulsis. Anand is aware of their disapproval of his father, of the loneliness of his exile. Yet neither can express his feelings openly.

A more critical episode takes place during the period when Shama and the children come to spend the Christmas holidays with Mr. Biswas at Green Vale, where he is working as a "driver" or "suboverseer." Trapped in a position for which he is utterly unfit, threatened by laborers evicted from the land they had rented, alone for much of the time in one room of barracks that houses twelve families, he has grown increasingly fearful and despondent. Tormented by nightmares, by feelings of depersonalization, he begins to hallucinate. Still he struggles to remain lucid. When Shama and the children arrive, he tries to disguise his terrors and his hostility toward Shama, pretending that his strange behavior is due to physical illness, perhaps malaria. Yet, needing help so badly, he responds to her innocuous question, "Something on your mind, man?" with a hint that it is indeed his "mind" that is the problem, obliquely disclosing the contents of a hallucination: "Clouds. Lots of little black clouds," and then is outraged when she cannot grasp the "truth" in his play on words.

Soon he is desperate and, when Shama tries to help him, fearing even her touch, he kicks her. Concluding that she has no choice but to take the children and return to Hanuman House, she is unprepared for Anand's decision to remain with his father. Neither the narrator nor Anand is explicit in rendering the boy's feelings, but they emerge empathically in silence and finally in a few words that seem forced out of him. Urged by his mother, by neighbor women, and his sister to leave, at first he says nothing, then simply, "I staying with Pa." Only after the others have left, when Mr. Biswas asks why he remained, does Anand reply: "'Because—' The word came out thin, explosive, charged with anger, at himself and his father. 'Because they was going to leave you alone.'" It is not that he sides with his father; he has taken on the burden of their shared weakness.

Still, during their days together, the roles of father and son are ambiguous. For a brief time Mr. Biswas finds relief from his distress in his rare paternal capacity: he makes toys for Anand and teaches him bits of religion and science. In a scene characteristically Naipaulian in its blend of humor and pathos, he tells Anand about "people called Coppernickus and Galilyo." Even in his disoriented state he urges his son to "Remember Galilyo. Always stick up for yourself." He has taught Anand a lesson in self-assertion, a challenge he himself will not relinquish despite all obstacles. In contrast, when he cannot control signs of his terror, he makes the boy "recite Hindi hymns after him." Anand, "affected by his father's fear[,] repeated . . . the hymns like charms."

But nothing can avert Mr. Biswas's breakdown or his son's identification with his father's fear of disintegration. Mr. Biswas's last effort, his "positive action," a move from the barracks into the one finished room of his first ill-fated house, proves disastrous. Pieces of asphalt that melt and leak from the roof are metamorphosed into snakes that inhabit his dreams. When their dog is killed by vengeful laborers, Anand grows hysterical and demands to go home. But before Mr. Biswas can take him to Arwacas, there is a storm, the house is flooded, and winged ants appear, increasing their terror. When lightning strikes the house and the lamplight is extinguished, their room becomes "part of the black void" that Mr. Biswas had feared all along. Father and son are overwhelmed by hysteria.

Although Seepersad Naipaul's breakdown had occurred during different circumstances, when his son was an infant, this episode, however fictional in chronology and setting, depicts the psychological conditions that determined V. S. Naipaul's assimilation of his father's fear of the abyss, the "subsidiary gift" of his dual legacy. Anand's need to identify with the father he had never before had the opportunity to know is revealed in brief but important incidents. He responds avidly to the attention Mr. Biswas pays him, to his efforts to teach him. When his uncle, a formidable presence at Hanuman House, appears and urges him to return home, he repeats a theological saw his father has just taught him and, obeying his admonition, "Remember Galilyo," he decides to stay. Even as he takes on Mr. Biswas's fear, he finds "compensations" in an experiment they perform together and in making an "electric buzzer." Mr. Biswas's hunger for knowledge, his singularity and playfulness, shocking to the Tulsis, are attractive qualities to the child who has for so long been deprived of a father's example. Angry and frightened as Mr. Biswas abandons him for his delusions, Anand has no psychological refuge from the "void" his father's terror evokes.

The differences between the chronology of Mr. Biswas's breakdown as well as of subsequent episodes in the novel from those of Naipaul's autobiography intensify the intricate connections between the "fear of extinction" and the vocation of writing that the father transmitted to his son. Seepersad Naipaul's most rewarding years on the *Trinidad Guardian* were those before his breakdown. The job to which he returned entailed mere reporting, which he found unsatisfying. In the fictional version, as soon as Mr. Biswas has recovered sufficiently, he leaves his family and finds a job as a reporter on the *Trinidad Sentinel* in Port of Spain. This is V. S. Naipaul's reconstruction of his father's first experience on the *Guardian* when, guided by a sympathetic editor, he was able to channel his bizarre fantasies in journalistic drama. Mr. Biswas's pleasure in his job and his pride in seeing his name and articles in print give him a new confidence, and he is able to return to his family with a sense of his own worth.

When he appears at Hanuman House, Anand observes his father, who had been rescued by the Tulsis when he was sick and disoriented, now a successful writer, recognized by the other children as the *Sentinel's* adventurous "Scarlet Pimpernel" who rewards those who identify him. Anand is still shy and laconic but, in a subtle contrast with an earlier scene, he no longer expresses his need for his father through a surrogate object: "Mr. Biswas held Anand to his leg and Anand rubbed against it." Mr. Biswas's achievements impress even Mrs. Tulsi, who suggests that he and his family share a house with her and one of her sons in Port of Spain. It is here that Mr. Biswas, like Seepersad Naipaul begins to supervise his son's education, to temper Anand's impatience—so like his own—by saying that the boy is helping him. Here too he begins to write stories.

Even during this brief period when Mr. Biswas's discovery of his vocation seems to be a redemption from his fear of extinction, its persistence is suggested in an episode involving father and son. On a Sunday at the beach with Anand and his two brothers-in-law, Mr. Biswas overreacts when the other men playfully duck him in the sea; he is irate, frightened, even tearful. Anand's danger of drowning is more decisive. When he is rescued by his uncle, father and son displace their terror on each other. But the next day Mr. Biswas writes "an angry article about the lack of warning notices at Dockside." For Anand the threat of drowning becomes the subject of his first original composition. In "A Day by the Seaside," he avoids the stock phrases prescribed by his teacher—"pounding surf," "laden hampers," and "delirious joy"—and instead describes the water filling his mouth, stifling his effort "to cry for help," his fear of dying. It is not his father that he censures but the sea.

The threat of annihilation has demanded a truth to his actual experience that his education would deny.

Despite fierce quarrels, father and son reach an understanding grounded on the assumption, suggested in Naipaul's autobiographical writings and explicit in *A House for Mr. Biswas*, that the father is training the son to leave him, to attain the fulfillment he was deprived of. Like Seepersad Naipaul, Mr. Biswas encourages his son to compete for a government scholarship, he shares his reading with him, he asks for his advice about his writing. All this is preparation for the boy's escape. When he makes Anand "write out and learn the meanings of difficult words" in Dickens, he explains, "I don't want you to be like me." Ironically, this concern only draws them closer in their aspirations and their fears: "Anand understood. Father and son, each saw the other as weak and vulnerable, and each felt a responsibility for the other, a responsibility which, in times of particular pain, was disguised as exaggerated authority on the one side, exaggerated respect on the other."

But the inverse of their bond is inevitable anger at the circumstances that have forged it. Their temperaments are similar—high-strung, sensitive, quick to cover hurt with barbed words they later regret or, in Mr. Biswas's case, as his job and living conditions deteriorate, with violent acts. Anand, who uses expressions he has learned from his father to retort to an insulting classmate, also turns Mr. Biswas's words against him. Unaware that Anand wants to see a certain film in order to meet another student's challenge, Mr. Biswas says: "When you get to my age you wouldn't care for Westerns." Anand retaliates by joining his father's opening clause to words he had used earlier to express the wish that his son surpass him: "When I get to your age I don't want to be like you." He has turned obedience into cruelty. Both are contrite, but Mr. Biswas's efforts to make amends only lead to further conflict, which he lovingly resolves.

There is a significant difference in V. S. Naipaul's depiction of a painful incident in "Prologue to an Autobiography" and in *A House for Mr. Biswas*. In the autobiographical account, he describes an especially difficult period when his father, overwrought by lack of privacy and insufficient food for the extended family, quarrels among and with them, "one Sunday evening, in a great rage . . . threw a glass of hot milk. It cut me above my right eye; my eyebrow still shows the scar." In the novel, Mr. Biswas, after flinging about and breaking objects in his room, "threw a glass of milk at Anand and cut him above the eye. He slapped Shama downstairs." The extent of his violence, particularly when aimed at the boy and his mother, intensifies the ambivalence of the relationship between father and son. It hardly matters whether such details are fictional or Naipaul omitted them from his autobiography out of respect for his father, out of a sense of decorum. They heighten a recurring motif in *A House for Mr. Biswas*: anger as a desperate means of self-assertion. It is a response to mistreatment and, in a broader sense, to injustice. It is an impetus to writing and can be a solace. Near the end of his life, when he is fired by *The Sentinel*, Mr. Biswas misses his son, who is now in England. He "needed his son's interest and anger."

In 1981, on hearing a section of *A House for Mr. Biswas* read on the BBC World Service, Naipaul could only weep. His tears, he says, were "*lacrimae rerum*, 'the tears of things,' the tears in things: to the feelings for the things written about—the passions and nerves of my early life—there was added a feeling for the time of the writing—the ambition, the tenacity, the innocence. My literary ambition had grown out of my early life; the two were intertwined; the tears were for a double innocence." It may seem surprising that Naipaul uses *lacrimae rerum*, that most resounding of tragic phrases, to signify his response not only to remembrances of his childhood in Trinidad but to those arduous years in London when the joy of writing *A House for Mr. Biswas* was his "Eden." But the victory of creation emerged from "the fear of destitution," from "a vision of the abyss . . . that lies below the comedy of this book."[22] Vergil's line, "Sunt lacrimae rerum et mentem mortalia tangunt," includes the mind's awareness of destruction and death; Naipaul's quotation links the fear of extinction with the drive to creation in the minds of the author and his protagonist. Beginning with *A House for Mr. Biswas*, he transmits this legacy of his father to many of his fictive characters.

The structure of *A House for Mr. Biswas* also reveals the genesis of the man as writer. Originating in his memories of early childhood, the "pattern in the narrative [is] of widening vision and a widening world."[23] This pattern includes the gradual disintegration of the traditional Hindu community of Trinidad and the resulting instability along with new opportunities for its youngest members. It is the background of Naipaul's own preference for instability as a subject. Like Seepersad Naipaul and himself, the most moving figures of his journalism as well as his fiction struggle against historical constraints to create an opposing personal history that incorporates and defies its setting.

Naipaul often refers to the disadvantages of growing up in the colonial society of Trinidad shadowed by a mythicized ancestral past in India. But in the composite portrait of the writer that emerges from the body of his work this point of departure at times seems a blessing. No doubt, his feelings of rootlessness, the role of exile, resulted in personal insecurity as well as cultural instability, but it also produced an independence of spirit and a need to "extract the truth about all my varied life, culturally varied, geographically varied."[24] Explaining to an interviewer his effort to "make a whole, an integrity," by reporting or recreating an authentic version of his experience, he says, in his early writings, "my first four or five books (including books which perhaps people think of as my big books) I was merely recording my reactions to the world."[25] But these reactions express the psychic and intellectual risks he had begun to take in making himself a writer.

"THE TRAVELER'S I"

In one of these early books, *The Middle Passage*, it seems clear that Naipaul is not "simply recording." He is beginning to develop a technique that is to characterize his travel narratives: the examination of the reporter as part of the territory he covers. His serendipitous method—minimum advance planning, openness to new situations, people, friendships, recordings of his instant reactions, along with later revisions—almost always leads to self-discovery.

In *The Middle Passage*, his personality emerges in a multitude of comic and painful episodes, from his care for a distressed fellow passenger, whom he supplies with the "pills, "tablets," and "cornplasters"[26] that he carried with him on his journey, to his dread of returning to Trinidad. During his years in England, Naipaul had had recurrent nightmares that he was again in Trinidad, but he "had never examined this fear; it is only now, at the moment of writing, that I am able to attempt to examine it." The immediacy of this effort ("only now") and its difficulty ("attempt to explain") suggest how vulnerable he remains to the influence of the past. He has returned to Trinidad in 1960 in a celebratory mood, confident that he has "made [himself] a writer."[27] But at this time Trinidad remained for him a place that could countenance only failure, where it was said that "brilliant men—scholarship winners . . . had died young, gone mad, or taken to drink." This atmosphere, which haunted his past, hangs over him, the scholarship winner, the successful novelist, like a hex, threatening his sense of self. His rage at Trinidad's denial of heroism, its resentment of talent, is a kind of amulet, protecting his own gifts, but it is also an oblique hope that the land for which he is later to express nostalgia and a bitter love will come to value the creativity of its people. The extremity of his reactions reveals how deeply allied to his inner narrative of self-creation is his conviction that societies must come to terms with their weaknesses and failures as well as their inherent strengths.

Looking back in *The Enigma of Arrival*, he describes the conflicting personae of his younger self who undertook the journey that was to produce *The Middle Passage*. His "model" might be the "metropolitan traveler," whose "education and culture" he had acquired, but the writer could not deny his consciousness of himself as "a colonial among colonials who were very close to me." Not only had he shared their way of life during his formative years, but it was, after all, in Trinidad that he had developed a desire to know the world outside, "the idea of civilization, and the idea of antiquity—the island had given me the world as a writer, . . . the themes that in the second half of the twentieth century had become important." The uneasy resolution of these disparities is intrinsic to the reporter's truth to his experience, his exasperation at and empathy with those who could not escape the effects of colonialism: its economic, cultural, and psychological oppression, and particularly its assault on individual identity. Long before the term was debased by over- and misuse, he insisted, "everyone has cause for self-esteem," and the reporter's own personality emerges in his efforts to reach beyond the political and social conditions he deplores to what people "esteem in themselves."[28]

Throughout his travels for *The Middle Passage* he observes and records the ways in which colonialism "distorts the identity of the subject people." In Trinidad, in Surinam, in Martinique, in Jamaica, the damage resulting from identification with the aggressor elicits compassion and despair. Still striving to define his role as a writer, he is especially sensitive to the difficulties of those who struggle for a measure of self-realization, of personal dignity, deprived as they are of an authentic cultural history in their spurious emancipation. The range of responses in *The Middle Passage* conveys the ambiguities of the truths Naipaul is in the process of discovering. Empathy, alienation, bitterness, admiration, hope, rage—all reflect contradictory elements in the conditions he encounters as they express his own ambivalence to the West Indies.

His anger at the Trinidadians' passivity in accepting the "borrowed culture" that exploits them is countered by his praise of their "natural sophistication and tolerance." Identifying with their lack of "sanctimoniousness" as he draws on his own experience in the larger world, he says they "can never achieve the society-approved nastiness of the London landlord . . . who turns a dwelling-house into a boarding-house, charges exorbitant rents, and is concerned lest his tenants live in sin." Trinidadi-ans, on the other hand, have a "tolerance for every human activity and af-fection for every demonstration of wit and style." His pleasure in these qualities is tempered by changes he perceives as Trinidadians become "more reliable and efficient. . . . Class divisions are hardening," the ac-ceptance of the idiosyncratic replaced by middle-class ambitions and val-ues. The "fluidity of the society has diminished," destroying "the com-munity spirit," isolating "people in their separate prisons of similar ambitions and tastes and selfishness: the class struggle, the political strug-gle, the race struggle."

This passage is a striking example of the contradictions in Naipaul's attitude toward Trinidad. Earlier in this chapter he had said that in Trinidad "there was no community." What then is the "community spirit" he now views as being eliminated? It seems that even while lamenting the absence of an established community with its unique cul-tural history, he also values the "cosmopolitan" spirit that characterized the Trinidad of his youth, which, no doubt, helped to form his own character and to nourish his own gifts, the spirit that is so lovingly com-municated in *Miguel Street*.

In an evaluation of his chapter on British Guiana written many years after *The Middle Passage*, he attributes his earlier failure to foresee the goals of the two Marxist leaders, Cheddi Jagan and Forbes Burnham, to the fact that he "shared to some extent the background of both."[29] But his lack of insight in this respect was also due to his distrust of ide-ological positions on either front of the Cold War and his effort to bridge the gap between observer and observed. The rift he describes here between perception and acknowledgment continues to preoccupy Naipaul throughout his fiction and nonfiction. As he explores the mo-tivations for avoidance or denial of one's own perceptions, his narrators and characters define themselves.

After completing *The Middle Passage*, determined "to acknowledge more of myself,"[30] he set out on a year's journey to India. It was to pro-duce the first of three books that, he has said, were about him "as much as India."[31] Nothing Naipaul has written exposes the man and the writer more unsparingly than does *An Area of Darkness*. Here he infringes on an inbred decorum to ransack his soul for every trace of peevishness, rage, shame, and guilt, dwelling on feelings that many travelers experi-ence but few admit. For the writer who, in *The Middle Passage*, had reit-erated his bitterness at the "self-contempt"—the direst individual rem-nant of colonialism—that he encountered in the West Indies, the extreme forms of self-abnegation he witnessed during the sea voyage from Athens to Bombay were a personal assault. The sight of men who "had been diminished and deformed," who "begged and whined," produced "hysteria" and what he calls "a brutality" in response to what seemed to threaten his "new awareness of myself as a whole human being and a determination, touched with fear, to remain what I was." These are defenses against his old fear of merging with the helpless in a psychic abyss, and he immediately rejects his "Superficial impressions, intemperate reactions." Yet these extreme responses anticipate his involvement in the lives of people he is to observe and come to know in his year's journey. Approaching Bombay, he cautions himself against overreacting: "Now I tried to remember that in Bombay as in Alexandria, there could be no pride in power, and that to give way to anger and contempt was to know a later self-disgust."[32]

Continual revisions of his impressions and reactions are fundamental to Naipaul's method in *An Area of Darkness* and much of his later travel writings. Deliberate exposure of intense feelings, which include nostalgia, pleasure, and friendship, as well as pain, contempt, and rage, followed by regret and self-deprecation, are intrinsic to the articulation of his own truth, in his view an author's responsibility. In personal engagement with a variety of people he stresses physical and cultural deprivations—he is enraged by corrupt bureaucracy, shoddy solutions, and hypocrisy; he deplores recurrent injustice. The objectivity he strives for is often a tense union of his own "experience and emotions," which he considers "the only way of understanding another man's conditions,"[33] and his effort, not always successful, to temper his feelings through a sense of historical perspective. This approach limits his assessment of the India of 1962, but it discloses connections between individual human history and the forces that determine its direction and, for the author, the profound effect of an unfamiliar territory on an inner landscape, "an area of darkness," the ancestral past.

Like the village life of Seepersad Naipaul's stories, the hardly imaginable past that V. S. Naipaul recalls extends beyond his particular experience. It is shared, however different their origins, by other offspring of diaspora. In many immigrant families settled in America during the early years of this century, for example, the customs of the homeland gradually mingled with those of the new country. New ideas and aspirations were brought home from school by the children or were assimilated by their elders in the business of daily life. Their parents' references to the old country created in the consciousness of first generation Americans

an inaccessible region. Yet they retained ancient prohibitions and phobias as well as values such as respect for study and learning, the security
of communal bonds. To readers of this background Naipaul's disappointment on arriving in "the mythical land of my childhood" only to
confront the reality of buildings and people that "seemed ordinary and
inappropriate," appears inevitable, a common response under the circumstances. But the extent of his rage and his psychic vulnerability signify the idiosyncratic character of the narrator. From the onset he converts emotional turmoil, as well as the satisfactions of exploration and
discovery, into his individual mode of travel narrative.

In *An Area of Darkness* he says he feels like a "stranger" in India although his memories of Hindu myth, rituals, customs, and attitudes remain from his formative years. The ancient past of India is merged with
his own past. Yet, an unbeliever from birth[34] and, at least consciously,
having rejected Hindu ritual, he is unprepared on his first visit for the
emotional impact of these memories, which complicate his reactions to
the actual life of the society he had envisioned. He refers to the "newer
and now perhaps truer side of my nature," which is appalled at what he
regards as India's ossification in its past. But there is also the older side,
which "had an answer": remembrances that evoke the aesthetic quality
of ritual, ingrained assumptions and values, surprising him with their
poignancy as they enlarge his vision. "I understood," he says, "better than
I admitted." Making explicit the subliminal feelings his observations
elicit is another means of characterizing himself as narrator, acknowledging a truth beyond his immediate reaction.

Proceeding on his journey, he learns more about himself as he tries
to understand why his resolve to moderate his feelings so often fails him.
When he returns to Bombay ten months after his first visit, he revises his
earlier impression, realizing that "it was my eye that had changed," a
statement he repeats near the end of his year's sojourn. The technique of
"seeing," in which he had trained himself from childhood, cannot always
save him from reacting to the "obvious." Reviewing the extremes of
neglect and poverty he had seen in the villages, the "starved child," the
"wasted" bodies, he reacted with "fear," which seems to be a form of
self-protection, as is his struggle against "contempt." "To give way to
that," he says, "is to abandon the self I had known." He could counter
such immoderate and inappropriate feelings only by learning "to separate myself from what I saw," to "separate things from men," the beauty
and accomplishments of India from the degradation to which so many
of its people were subject. At times he manages neither to deny nor to

indulge his immediate responses but to incorporate them into a broader view of the great contrasts that India comprises.

But these are only temporary resolutions. Uncovering links between India's cultural history and his own past is both enlightening and disturbing. The fantasy of "India as a country still whole," uninvaded by an "alien presence," he now realizes, was a form of "self-deception," peculiarly Indian, "part of a greater philosophy of despair, leading to passivity, detachment, acceptance." Only through the "processes of writing and self inquiry" does he now acknowledge "how much this philosophy had been mine." If it had limited his loyalties to personal ones, it had produced the independence and integrity of his life and his work. Still, his conviction of autonomy could not shield him from a recognition of the "England of India" and with it "an encounter with a humiliation I had never before experienced . . . the colonial humiliation I did not feel in Trinidad."

Naipaul's most fruitful explorations of himself in relation to his earlier image and present cognizance of India occur in his interactions with a great variety of people. Reaching out to even casual acquaintances through his own "experience and emotions," he sometimes creates composite figures whose psychic core belies their outward appearance, a technique that is to characterize the body of his travel writings. One example is Bunty, a fairly typical business executive, whose nickname, clothing, and social activities with his colleagues in Bombay or Calcutta are colonial "mimicry" in post-colonial India. But Bunty's "inner world," says Naipaul, "continues whole and untouched." His Indian heritage is central to his selfhood. "Bunty's caste is European; but Bunty carries within himself a strong sense of Aryan race and ancientness as exclusive possessions." It is this pride in an ancient heritage with which the narrator empathizes, Bunty's and Naipaul's own defense against a history of exploitation, the effects of which are everywhere still apparent.

Other figures are highly individualized. Two of the many who become part of Naipaul's inner narrative are Aziz, a Sunni Muslim who is a servant at the Hotel Liward in Kashmir, and an unnamed Sikh, whom he later meets on a train. The vast differences in his relations with these two men disclose how he uses the particularities of his own personality as means of investigating the intricate connections between individuals and the society they inhabit.

At his first meeting with Aziz, Naipaul is struck by the man's "quaintness, something of the Shakespearean mechanic was given him by his sagging woollen nightcap." He is soon to learn how "misleading can first impressions be." Aziz is to take various roles in his life starting with personal servant "magically improvising, providing everything." But that is only the beginning. Magic is soon replaced by the realities of daily life in the small hotel on the lake where he cannot avoid involvement with the staff, especially Aziz. He now faces what he had known only from books and conversation: that having a personal servant "creates dependence . . . and can reduce one to infantalism."

Aziz is moody, demanding, and quarrelsome; he can be a bully. His dignity violated, he is furious. But he is also intelligent, imaginative, and responsive to the demands of an exacting guest. Perhaps unintentionally, Naipaul's detailed analysis of Aziz's behavior suggests that, however opposing their roles, the personalities of servant and guest are similar. They are sensitive to each other's moods; they exact one another's loyalty, and they suffer immoderately when disappointed, becoming sullen and in Naipaul's case, angry, then, as usual, appalled at his own irrationality. Although their vulnerability reveals concern and affection, Naipaul continues to fret over Aziz's motives.

The Liward Hotel has become a haven, his privacy guarded by Aziz, his needs attended, when his idyll is disrupted by twenty Hindu pilgrims and a "holy man" they revere. Furious at their appropriation of the premises for their religious requirements, Naipaul confronts Aziz, threatening to leave if they remain. Once again Aziz finds a solution, suggesting that this is a good time for Naipaul to visit his friends in Gulmarg and pleading to be taken along. It is to him that Naipaul's account of this visit is almost entirely devoted. About his friends he remarks only on Aziz's way of "binding them to himself." Wondering why Aziz was so eager to go to Gulmarg, a small vacation spot surrounded by mountains, he speculates that it is the ponies that drew him. Riding, Aziz relinquishes the demeanor of servant; he is a horseman delighting in his skill. But Naipaul also realizes that in his role as servant he too exercises a particular skill: his method of appraising the people he works for. Increasingly for Naipaul, as for Aziz, "people [are] his material."

As the months in Kashmir go by, Naipaul and Aziz become more protective of each other's feelings even when differences in their stations create conflict. Despite Aziz's sometimes unreasonable demands when he accompanies Naipaul on a pilgrimage to the Cave of Amarnath, Naipaul's description of his conduct is filled with admiration for his intelligence, his ingenuity, his consideration, his delight in the adventure. The pilgrimage takes place annually in August when a large ice lingam, a symbol of Shiva, generally forms in a cave high in the Himalayas. Although it has no religious meaning for Naipaul, he is drawn to the myth of Shiva's continuous presence and power, and particularly to the setting of the rite. It is the Himalayas that are his "special joy." He is "linked" to them by the fantasy India of his childhood, stimulated by memories of pictures in his grandmother's home. Their grandeur had no connection with the actuality of his early life, "but in that corner of the mind which continues child-like their truth remained a possibility." Now the truth of the mountains for him has become loss, recovery, and acceptance of their "unattainability." Inevitably, he must relinquish their promise to memory again, as perhaps the pilgrims must do, their reality unclaimable, their recovery "only in pilgrimages, legends and pictures." The Himalayas have linked him not only to the boy he was but to the pilgrims, even as they remain remote in their religious devotion.

Faced with the huge crowds climbing the long approach to the cave where the inner sanctum of the god is located, Naipaul gives up the effort to see the god, but Aziz, though a Muslim, cannot resist this opportunity. Naipaul's description of him struggling against the press of the crowd is affectionate and admiring. He returns triumphant, only to report that "there was no lingam." Whether it simply had not appeared that August or had melted, its absence mattered little to the pilgrims; it was the "spirit" that counted. To Naipaul it had become "the symbol of a symbol. In this spiralling, deliquescing logic I felt I might drown." Yet, if he cannot participate in veneration of the deliquesced lingam, the mountains remain his myth. He imagines a later time, when he will return to the mountains and the streams, unspoiled by crowds, still the magical sphere of his childhood fantasy.

Near the end of his sojourn in Kashmir, Naipaul discovers another aspect of Aziz's complex character when he is invited to dinner at his home on a houseboat in the lake. Here as host, "behaving with an ancient courtesy," Aziz is "grave, independent, a man of substance, a man of views." Underlying the mercurial servant is the "responsible family man," the reserve of confidence and dignity that his private self maintains distinct from his prescribed social role.

Yet when Naipaul leaves the hotel to continue on his journey and Aziz, weeping, bids him farewell, he cannot "be sure that he had ever been mine." The basis of this uncertainty is implicit throughout his characterization of Aziz. Contending with the harsh conditions of his historical destiny, Aziz cannot afford the luxury of absolute loyalty to an outsider, however eagerly he responds to his knowledge and influence. Since Naipaul has portrayed the inevitability of such reservations, his disappointment is all the more touching. Having grown accustomed to Aziz's empathy, he has withheld neither his wounded feelings when his demands were unmet nor their source in his craving for unqualified affection in unlikely circumstances. His deepest insights and his most painful reactions result from his involvement in the lives of people he encounters and his tendency to expose himself to emotional intimacy despite the consequences.

Even when he resists acquaintance, he is sometimes unable to curb a curiosity that eventually invites it. On a train traveling south he cannot refrain from looking at a Sikh although initially the man's arrogant bearing repels him. The Sikhs, he says, "puzzled and attracted" him because in some respects they reminded him of the Indians of Trinidad. So eager is he to associate his own background with his discovery of India, to locate himself within the actual land, that he is "misled by [his] Trinidad training." He soon realizes, however, that what he took for Trinidadian irony in the Sikh's declaration that he is "color-prejudiced" was not intended as such. Disturbed by the man's racialism, his contempt for his countrymen—even other Sikhs—and his intrinsic violence, he cannot escape him on the long train journey. But it soon becomes clear that there are more basic reasons for his willingness to allow the relationship, which "had begun in mutual misunderstanding" to continue. The very violence of the Sikh's reaction to the impoverished countryside and the towns they passed "steadied" him: "He became my irrational self." The rage and contempt he himself had felt witnessing unheeded deprivation have shamed him throughout his visit to India. Now he has displaced these feelings in the Sikh's bitterness and rage. He can attribute reactions he abhors in himself to a man he dislikes and distrusts.

The process does not end with the train journey. In fact, when they meet again, as arranged, in an unnamed town in the Punjab, the identification intensifies to the point where Naipaul fears that he cannot avoid being infected by the irrationality of his companion. Only when the Sikh strikes a man in a restaurant and later threatens to kill Naipaul, does he break free.

The violence he has encountered in this strange pseudo-friendship evokes "photographs of the Punjab massacres of 1947 and of the Great Calcutta Killing," and the trains "ferrying dead bodies across the border." Although he had known of these terrible events, India had never before seemed to him a violent country; only now his personal anguish at his involvement with the frenzied Sikh has confirmed the reality.

Naipaul continues to analyze his immoderate reactions, trying to replace rage and contempt, even "compassion," with acceptance. But such efforts at understanding cannot protect him from the emotional devastation of his visit at the end of his year in India to his maternal grandfather's village in eastern Utter Pradesh. On his arrival he admits that he has "not learned acceptance." As one follows him through the psychic demands of this last phase of his journey, one wonders whether at this time acceptance is possible or even salutary. At first he is moved as shrines and religious images, old photographs taken in Trinidad, and a song he had heard in his childhood merge past and present. But the expectations of his hosts that he partake of the life of the village—eat, drink, accept the subservient postures—and finally the repeated demands for money by Ramachandra, "the present head of [his] grandfather's branch of the Dubes," break down his defenses. He can only flee. As he describes his peevish refusal to give a boy a lift to town in his jeep, he seems for a moment to be identifying himself with the child who had bathed and dressed for the occasion. Certainly he elicits sympathy for the boy, the innocent victim of what Naipaul calls his "gratuitous act of cruelty" immediately followed by "self-reproach and flight."

In Madrid for a few days on his way back to London, he thinks of his year in India as "a journey that ought not to have been made; it had broken my life in two." Yet he remains ambivalent. Once again, when with himself "contented least," it is friendship that offers consolation and self-knowledge. He thinks of an architect he had met in India, the "affection and loyalty" they had professed. "This was part of the sweetness of India; it went with everything else." Later he dreams about a gift his friend had given him, Indian cloth for a jacket. In the dream he knows that if he cut "a specific section of this cloth," not only the cloth but finally "all matter" would "unravel . . . *until the whole trick was undone*." The cloth, he says, contained "clues" that he "desired above everything else to find, but which [he] never would."

The subsequent paragraph, which concludes the book, contains those very clues: "I saw how close in the past year I had been to the total Indian negation, how much it had become the basis of thought and feeling. . . . I felt it as something true which I could never adequately express and never seize again." His friend's affection, like the protective cloth he provided, released fears often cloaked in rage, his vulnerability to the negation, the "abyss," the ethnic and paternal heritage with which his own talent contended and flourished.

He was to deal with this subject again, more objectively in *India: A Wounded Civilization*, in which he continued to explore his distance from and affiliation with the land he had imagined, visited, and revisited. His focus in this book is the extent to which "Indian attitudes" based on Hindu philosophy and religion have determined the country's political and cultural history. Having striven for more than a decade to understand his initial reactions to India, he has come to recognize "how far the 'Indian attitudes' of someone like myself, a member of a small and remote community in the New World, have diverged from the attitudes of people to whom India is still whole." This divergence centers on the issue of identity, especially on the ways in which individuals and the mores of their societies continually react on one another. No doubt because of his own efforts to unite the self with the writer, his analyses of novels by R. K. Narayan and U. R. Anantha Murthy illuminate the intimacy of his changing approach to India: that of the "stranger" whose "starting point. . .has been myself," the self which retains "phantasmal memories of old India which for me outline a whole vanished world."[35]

Before Naipaul had been to India, the land of Narayan's fiction had seemed similar to the Trinidad of his childhood, becalmed in colonial subjection. After his first visit, he found himself still drawn to Narayan's "older India," his certainty of India's continuity, no matter the circumstances. But he also deplored the very qualities he admired: the limits of this "Indian truth," which Narayan has captured, its "negative attitude," its absence of "self-assessment."[36] Thirteen years later in *India: A Wounded Civilization*, he regrets that Narayan's fiction has not conveyed the actuality of the India that in his travels he has found "cruel and overwhelming." Narayan's world was no longer one he could "enter into." To do so was "to ignore too much of what had been seen, to shed too much of myself: my sense of history, and even the simplest ideas of human possibility."[37]

Applying these persistent themes of his own work—the self, past and present history, and human possibility—to Narayan's novels, he finds that they distort, or even more telling, deny these essential determinants of individual fulfillment. Having come to know something of the variety and complexity of India, he now regards these novels as "less the purely social comedies I had once taken them to be than religious books, at times, religious fables, and intensely Hindu."[38] Yet the differences he points out in the two works he discusses, *Mr. Sampath* and *The Vendor of Sweets*, are not only assessments of Narayan's themes but of changes in India and in himself.

Even when Srinivas, the hero of *Mr. Sampath*, reluctantly takes on the responsibilities of work and marriage, these are secondary to his preoccupation with "the perfection of nondoing," Hindu negation, to which he eventually returns. Naipaul regards the attitude of this feckless man as an all too common misinterpretation of "Gandhian nonviolence," which was actually intended as a "form of action, a quickener of social conscience." Linked with other distortions—"self-realization, truth to one's identity"—that "disguise an acceptance of karma, the Hindu killer," nonviolence has come to mean "something very like the opposite of what Gandhi intended," a denial of individual responsibility. Whereas karma is a passive assent to the consequences of a past life, identity entails assessing one's actions, development, and change, all of which enter into the making of the self that contributes its aspirations and skills to society.

By 1967, when *The Vendor of Sweets* appeared, history had intruded on Narayan's idealized "fictional world," which, Naipaul says, has been "cracked open, its fragility finally revealed, and the Hindu equilibrium—so confidently maintained in *Mr. Sampath*—collapses into something like despair."[39] The protagonist of *The Vendor of Sweets*, Jagan, is no more impressive than Srinivas. Although he is a successful businessman who sells candy, his fundamental belief, uttered in the first sentence of the book and repeated on the second page, is "Conquer taste, and you will have conquered the self."[40] In his effort to achieve purity, he has given up sugar and salt. When his cousin remarks that he has become "self-dependent," that he has "perfected the art of living on nothing," he misses the irony and proudly announces that he has also "given up rice." Yet he avidly collects each day's proceeds, setting aside a portion on which he withholds payment of taxes. Naipaul considers this novel "a key to the moral bewilderment" of postindependence India."[L]ike *Mr. Sampath*, it is a fable"[41] which, he believes, misinterprets Gandhian ideas to rationalize personal withdrawal from a changing society. Both Srinivas and Jagan are depicted as ordinary men, comical in their petty self-involvement and their ineffectiveness in dealing with the world outside their personal realm. Yet they embody Narayan's belief that renunciation is the ultimate self-knowledge, open to all.

Jagan's antagonist, his son Mali, who rejects his father's Hinduism, is presented as a ridiculous caricature of the rebel. Influenced by Western ideas of "human possibility," he violates food and drink prohibitions and drives a car. But to Jagan, more unsettling is his announcement that he wishes to be a writer. Narayan's most severe condemnation of the changes Independence has wrought is his treatment of what seems at first the touching if far-fetched ambition of this naive young man. Jagan assumes that a writer is merely a "clerk," but when his son tries to enlighten him, it is clear that Mali has no more understanding of this vocation than does his father. He returns from a brief stay in the United States with a Korean-American woman whom he introduces as his wife and with "a story-writing machine," which he intends to use for his own writing as well as a model for those he plans to manufacture and sell in India. With one of them, he explains to his father, "anyone can write a story." Narayan's rather obvious metaphor—a machine that supplies subject, characters, and so-called techniques—conveys his contempt for stories without a spiritual core. His own fruitless efforts to write after his wife's death led him to a medium who used automatic writing to summon her salutary presence. He was then able to achieve "psychic contacts" on his own and to return to writing. He imagines an ideal state that exceeds the limits of mere physical existence and combines psychological with spiritual enlightenment: "If one could have a total view of oneself and others, one would see all in their full stature, through all the stages of evolution and growth, ranging from childhood to old age, in this life, the next one, and the previous ones."[42]

Of course, Mali's commercial venture fails, as does his feigned marriage. Jagan, having left his business and his home, "polluted" by the unmarried couple, goes off to a retreat "to watch a goddess come out of a stone." To be sure, he has taken his bankbook with him. Mali, jailed for hiding half a bottle of liquor in his car, is deserted by Jagan, who merely writes a check for his bail and promises to pay any further legal expenses.

Naipaul's analyses of Narayan's fiction reflect changes in his own approach to "Indian attitudes." The two novels he has chosen to discuss exemplify the "passivity," the "negation," that he regards as having been so detrimental to progress in India, feelings he himself endured on his first visit. In the intervening years, he has been able to integrate his early environment in the Indian community of Trinidad, his education there and in England, his travels, and his career as a writer into his self-image, and thus to achieve a greater objectivity toward India. Without relinquishing his respect, even his nostalgia, for Hindu ritual and custom, he has become an uncompromising modernist in his views on India's future. Thus, he does not seem to be aware of the ambivalence in the totality of Narayan's work regarding the inevitable changes in the lives of people trapped in oppressive traditions or bending to inevitable change. Narayan's *The Dark Room,* which appeared in 1936, is the story of a woman whose only means of protest against her traditional role as the subservient Indian wife is a passivity that destroys her. Commenting on this novel in his *Memoir*, Narayan says: "I was somehow obsessed with a philosophy of Woman against Man, her constant oppressor. This must have been an early testament of the 'Women's Lib' movement. Man assigned her a secondary place and kept her there with such subtlety and cunning that she herself began to lose all notion of her independence, her individuality, stature, and strength. A wife in an orthodox milieu of Indian society was an ideal victim of such circumstances."[43] This is hardly the position of an unregenerate traditionalist. In later novels, for example, *The Painter of Signs* (1976) and *The World of Nagaraj* (1990), the inhabitants of the provincial town of Malgudi cannot escape the outside world of constant change and some even begin to gain a new understanding of themselves and others. Still, as Narayan gently satirizes their resistance to technology, to children who leave home to study abroad or to work in factories, to women who refuse their traditional role, he depicts their inability to integrate change into their daily lives and their place in their society. Naipaul's own diverse experience, his touchstone in reacting to India and other nations, has made him especially sensitive to the necessity and difficulty of achieving such integration, contingent as it is on inherited tradition, the opportunities and limits of particular societies, unpredictable personal responses, and the changing direction of all human life. Thus, he is unsympathetic to Narayan's mild humor in exposing the follies of those who are drawn to the new, too often mere novelty, and those who resist any alteration in age-old customs and routines.

Naipaul's determination to hone his method of observation, of "seeing," is reflected in his chapter "A Defect of Vision," in *India: A Wounded Civilization*, where he deplores "an absence of the external world" in Gandhi's *The Story of My Experiments with Truth*. Although Gandhi's "self-absorption was part of his strength," in excluding other people, even the landscape of South Africa, where he lived for many years, it was also "a kind of blindness." According to Dr. Sudhir Kakar, a psychotherapist, whom Naipaul cites, "the Indian ego is 'underdeveloped.'" Quoting from a letter from Kakar, Naipaul appears to concur with his view that "[g]enerally among Indians . . . there seems to be a different relationship to outside reality compared to one met with in the West." Kakar characterizes this difference "as closer to a certain stage in childhood when outer objects did not have a separate, independent existence but were intimately related to the self and its affective states."[44] Such early stages of development are hardly restricted to Indians; they are reflected in common fantasies in individual and national histories. Still Naipaul finds this analysis useful in his continuing effort to understand the particular ways in which Indians conceive of the self.

Once again, to explore the subject further, he turns to fiction, to a "remarkable novel, which "takes us closer to the Indian idea of the self without too much mystification." The novel, U. R. Anantha Murthy's *Samskara*, depicts the psychic struggle of Praneshacharya, an Acharya, a "spiritual guide" and leader of the "agrahara, an exclusive settlement of Brahmins."[45] The novel begins with a dilemma occasioned by the death of Naranappa, an unprincipled member of the community: how can brahmins perform the "death rites" for a man who has violated every prohibition of food and drink, befriended Muslims, killed the sacred fish in the temple tank, and left his wife for a low-caste woman? Since he has never been excommunicated, does he remain a brahmin despite his depravity? If so, will he pollute the sect? Can members of the community allow a rival sect to perform the rites? They turn to the Acharya to settle these issues. Since the brahmins must fast until the body has been cremated, the matter is pressing. Even worse, Naranappa died of a fever, and his rotting corpse causes a plague while the Acharya seeks a solution. Ironically, during this crisis the Acharya faces a personal crisis, to him even more compelling, which profoundly alters his life.

The Acharyra is famous for his purity and learning. At sixteen he married a twelve-year-old invalid, with whom he lives as an ascetic, devoting himself to feeding and tending her, sacred duties that will lead to his salvation. In the current quandary he follows the prescribed path, seeking his answer in the holy palm-leaf texts. When he finds none as several people die and the community is infested with vultures and rats, he goes to the Maruti temple, seeking the god's help, but the god does not respond to his plea. On the way back, he encounters Chandri, the beautiful mistress of the dead Naranappa. Discouraged and hungry, he responds to her compassion, her beauty, and her desire for him. He eats the plantains she offers him and then engages with her in the first sexual act of his life. So concludes Part I of the novel.

In Part II the Acharya returns to the agrahara to care for his wife, but he is now repelled by her body. His pleasure in making love with Chandri, which he does not deny, has challenged his inner narrative created during a lifetime in which he followed the texts prescribed for the man destined to become "the Crest-Jewel of the Vedanta Philosophy." Yet, "like a baby monkey losing hold of his grip on the mother's body as she leaps from branch to branch, he felt he had lost hold and fallen from the rites and actions he had clutched till now." When his wife dies, still another victim of the plague, he has her cremated and leaves the agrahara, unaware that Chandri, with the help of Muslim friends, has had Naranappa's body cremated.

The third and last part of the novel depicts the Achayra wandering about the countryside, seeking self-knowledge: in order to shed the "self-deception" of his past, to accept the responsibility for making love with Chandri, his lasting desire for her, his new "awareness" of pleasures he had never before known. "This is me," says his inner voice, "this, this is the new truth I create, the new person I make."

As he walks through the forest he meets Putta, a young man who insists on accompanying him and leads him to a fair, a cockfight, and a prostitute whom he desires. During a "time of mourning and pollution," he partakes of a feast in a Brahmin temple, and invites Putta, who is of lower caste, to join him. He considers returning to the agrahara to report his adultery and the prohibitions he violated when he wandered about with Putta, not as "repentance for sins committed. Just plain truth. My truth. The truth of my inner life." At the end of the novel he sits in a covered wagon, being driven home, still uncertain what his future holds.

Naipaul, though deeply impressed by this novel, and finding "the narrative hypnotic," views the Acharya's defection not as a transformation but merely as a new phase of his previous way of life. He assumes that the Acharya will continue to be "self-absorbed and that his self-absorption will be as sterile as it had been when he was a man of goodness." He predicts that "No idea will come to him, as it did to Gandhi, of the imperfections of the world, and of a world that might in some way be put right." Yet *Samskara*, as A. K. Ramanujan, the distinguished translator and poet, points out in his Afterword, though "a religious novel," is much more than that. The characters are "frankly allegorical," he says, "but the setting is realistic." It is outside the confines of the agrahara, in the world of ordinary people, that the Acharya begins to define himself as "the new person I make." Even his return to inform the community of his transgressions is left open to question. "The novel," says Ramanujan, "ends but does not conclude." There is no "climax or closure. Such inconclusive, anticlimactic use of tradition is very much a part of this modern tale."

It is this blend of the archetypal and the realistic that appeals to the secular reader, especially the portrayal of a noble figure, surrounded by pettiness and corruption, compelled to acknowledge his own transgressions. Even more affecting is the dreamlike atmosphere in which the

Acharya's turmoil begins: unconscious fears and desires released in the forest at night and faced in the daylight of ordinary circumstances—a fair featuring a cockfight, shops, and acrobats. Secular as well as religious issues inhere in the Acharya's resolve to overcome a lifetime of denial, to come to terms with his sexual desires, with the knowledge that even as he "lost control," he was responsible. The novel's open ending leaves the Acharya's future, like all our futures, uncertain.

Still, one can understand Naipaul's position. In *India: A Wounded Civilization,* he defines the novel as "a form of social inquiry, and as such outside the Indian tradition." It "had come to India with the British." Now, after independence, in a time of "instability," he would seek in fiction evidence of change, "an anxiety about man as an individual."[46] These have long been his concerns as a writer whose own identity was formed within an Indian community that "had begun to disintegrate."[47] Like Naipaul, the Acharya seeks truth, but it is the truth of his "inner life," the resolution of conflict between his desires and his inhibitions, seemingly to be achieved in contemplation. Naipaul's search is centered on the "world": the societies of his early life and of his later voyages of exploration and discovery; the history of injustices that human beings have visited on their fellows; the political, social, and cultural institutions organized to justify conquest; and the concept of the self, including his own, that this history engendered—from all of which he continually creates and recreates the world within himself. The Acharya's truth is not Naipaul's truth.

Naipaul opposes Jagan's argument in *The Vendor of Sweets,* "Why do you blame the country for everything? It has been good enough for four hundred millions," with evidence that the present "seven hundred millions" are by no means satisfied. Like Jagan, the Archarya is remote from the "millions on the move" from the villages to the cities, escaping the bondage of karma and caste as they seek a new way of life. Naipaul's hopes for India lie in these millions to whom he refers many times. Among them are those who have become part of "the Indian industrial revolution, which offers more than just a job. Men handling new machines, exercising technical skills that to them are new, can also discover themselves as men, as individuals." It is in this opportunity, as yet offered to only a few, that Naipaul sees a true transformation. In the making of the self through constructive work, in the "urgent new claim on the land" by the "millions on the move" Indians are employed in putting themselves and their world right.

India: A Million Mutinies Now, which appeared in 1990, deals with the vast changes in India brought about gradually by these millions forging new identities over many years. These are manifested in a variety of mutinies—psychic, political, social, economic—which Naipaul tracks with a new optimism in interviews with a great many people of diverse backgrounds. More secure in his relations with India, he can empathize with those reconstructing the nation and themselves. But this path is less direct than it may seem. It is best to follow him on voyages he made to other lands in the intervening years before returning to his third book on India. Though charged with less personal signification, these journeys enlarged his vision and deepened his insight into the extent to which people's aims and frustrations are determined by their societies.

The very title of *Among the Believers* indicates Naipaul's approach; he makes no claim to a comprehensive study of Islam in the four nations he visited or the many others where it prevails. His emphasis is on the reporter finding his way among people committed to a monolithic truth he tries to understand by seeking the multiple historical, social, and personal roots of their faith. His remark at the very beginning of *Among the Believers* that, although he grew up among Muslims of Indian descent in Trinidad, his knowledge of Islam consisted of little more than that they "had a Prophet and a Book; they believed in one God, and disliked images" introduces limits he must face as he investigates new parts of the world, and tries to overcome cultural and personal distances. He first thought of a journey to Muslim countries while watching an American television news program on the Iranian revolution, finding that "as interesting to me as the events in Iran were the Iranians in the United States who were interviewed on some of the programmes." What primarily engaged him was their simultaneous attraction to and rejection of the educational opportunities and social freedom America offered them. This "expectation of the alien, necessary civilization going on," which is "implicit in the act of renunciation" is a major subject of his book.

The method he employed combined studying the past history of Islam and the current observance of its various adherents: the Shiites of Iran; the Sunnis, the Shiites, and the dissident Ahmadis of Pakistan; and the new fundamentalists of Malaysia and Indonesia. Characteristically, he tries to apprehend subtle religious and political manifestations of Islam through the eyes of people he has either arranged to meet or has encountered by chance. Sometimes, especially starting out in Iran, he is frustrated, lacking the language and the temperament to gain access to a society in which religious devotion penetrates every feature of life.

Early on he realizes that the "dream of the society ruled purely by faith . . . that dream of the society of believers excluded me." Visiting the offices of the *Times*, an English-language newspaper, which displayed the motto, "May Truth Prevail," he is aware that he must deal with a conception of truth for which "nothing of the intellectual life that I valued was of account." When he tries to comprehend the faith, or the dissent from it, through his contacts with individuals—his guide, journalists, students, their teacher, the Ayatollah Shirazi, and Ayatollah Khalkhalli, "Khomeini's hanging judge"—he is constantly thwarted by their reticence or misunderstanding and his inability to empathize with a fixed concept of truth so alien to his ambiguous findings. Both believers and their opposition, exemplified by his guide and translator, Behzad, a communist, "depended on revealed truth," impervious to introspection or argument.

Still, Naipaul persists, trying to elicit individual responses despite the barriers of religious dogma. When, in the holy city of Qom, Behzad tells him that students are arranging a meeting for him with Shirazi, he reacts "with the child's part of my mind . . . amazed . . . nervous" at the opportunity to talk with a counterpart of medieval schoolmen like "Peter Abelard or John of Salisbury." Alas, his overvaluation of this occasion, his insecurity and dependence on Behzad for translation and counsel, prevent any authentic communication. Reluctantly, he takes Behzad's advice that he conceal the fact that he is an unbeliever of Hindu ancestry and agrees to let Behzad say he is a Christian. But he immediately regrets the falsehood:

> Shirazi hadn't been taken in by my equivocations; he knew that something was wrong. And I decided that I would never again, on my Islamic journey, out of nervousness or a wish to simplify, complicate matters for myself like this, and consequently falsify people's response to me. Strain apart, it would have been more interesting now—it would have served my purpose better—to get Shirazi's responses to me as a man without religion, and as a man of an idolatrous-mystical-animistic background.

This resolution makes Naipaul less diffident when he interviews the hanging judge. Determined to be direct, he still cannot achieve what he desires—"to enter his mind, to see the world as he saw it." Before a large crowd of admirers, Khalkhalli's responses to Naipaul's written questions about his decision "to take up religious studies," his father, his "happiest day," aim at humor, even mockery. Naipaul can only conclude that "he had forced me, in that room full of laughter, to be his straight man." He seems neither bitter nor hurt at what could be felt as inhospitable, even humiliating, treatment. Refused admission to the inner life of the judge and his circle, denied any intellectual or emotional connection with them, he objectifies the scene as a bit of comedy which exposes more about the judge than he might have wished to reveal.

The only mind in Iran that Naipaul succeeds to some extent in entering is Behzad's. It is Behzad who, recounting his own past, tells him how it was possible even in Iran, "to do without religion." His explanation is both personal and historical. On the one hand, it was simply that he "hadn't been instructed in the faith by his parents; he hadn't been sent to the mosque." Behind that simple fact lie centuries of political and religious history: "Islam was a complicated religion. It was a revealed religion with a Prophet and a complete set of rules. To believe, it was necessary to know a lot about the Arabian origins of the religion, and to take this knowledge to heart." Furthermore, Shia Islam, the religion of Iran, was particularly complicated with "divergences" and hostilities that at times had led, as Behzad says, to poisoning or murder. Behzad had supported the revolution but not the "religious revolution," which fulfilled none of his hopes for Iran. Influenced by his father, an unbeliever and a communist imprisoned under the Shah, Behzad had inherited the ideal of revolution as a substitute for religion that exalts the downtrodden and would imprison or kill their oppressors—justice as reward and punishment.

Trying to comprehend their different conceptions of poverty and deprivation, Naipaul realizes that his model—his early life in Trinidad—is inapplicable to Behzad's situation. Half Naipaul's age, Behzad had lived "nearly all his life under the Shah" at a time when "the world had opened up in ways unknown to his grandparents." For him "national wealth" and the "expansion of his society" were givens. When Behzad speaks of his poverty, Naipaul can only regard the young man as "privileged."

Near the end of their time together, Naipaul, understanding Behzad's wrath and his pride, becomes his guide. When a soldier orders Behzad and his girlfriend to stop playing cards on a train to Tehran, Naipaul calms him, advising him to "forget" the soldier. "You don't have to fight every battle," he says. "Fight only the important ones." Their divergent cultural backgrounds and their opposing views on democracy and communism hardly seem to matter at this moment; the older man offers the young one advice garnered from his own excessive reactions of rage and pride. Six months later, when they meet again in Tehran, Naipaul resumes this role, listening sympathetically to Behzad's sad account of his estrangement from his girlfriend, advising him not to abandon his studies despite his pessimism about finding a job, the hopelessness of his life in Tehran.

In Pakistan, Naipaul finds people more approachable than in Iran. He is himself more open, his responses to their devotion to Islam at once keener and more ambivalent. Replying to the question of an official in the government information office in Karachi, Naipaul is frank about his lack of religious belief. To his surprise, the man is "delighted." Interpreting the remark as evidence that the visitor is not "prejudiced," he predicts that his "investigations" will lead to his conversion to Islam. However imperceptive he is in regard to Naipaul's character, he is motivated to escort him that evening during Ramadan to various mosques where he is able to observe not only "Islam in action" but the intensity of his guide's devotion to his faith.

Naipaul's relations with people in Pakistan reflect the conflict he perceives throughout the Muslim countries he visits: rejection of the "West, or the universal civilization it leads," and simultaneous reliance on Western technology and medical advances. The outcome, he concludes is "parasitism," dependence on the creativity of the very civilization it eschews. Yet he also perceives the "attractions" of Islam to university students, even as their faith dominates and limits their learning, for "fundamentalism . . . equalizes, comforts, shelters, and preserves." Years later in *A Turn in the South*, he is moved by the communal spirit, the "consoling union," of a Baptist service in Bowen, North Carolina: "as in Muslim countries, I understood the power a preacher might have."

Several of the people he meets in Pakistan confide in him, admitting their doubts even as they cling to their faith. A doctor tells him of a dream that restores his belief in the afterlife. His son, Syed, a medical student and a poet, is both a "rationalist" and a believer. In the young man's interest in the world outside, in "English books" and "Western music," in what he calls "basics,"—personal and political relationships—Naipaul finds hope for a revival of an earlier Islamic cosmopolitism. Of his poetry Naipaul says, "in his fumbling response to the universal civilization, his concern with 'basics,' I thought I could see how Islamic fervor could become more than a matter of prayers and postures, could become creative, revolutionary, and take men on to a humanism beyond religious doctrine: a true renaissance, open to the new and enriched by it, as the Muslims in their early days of glory had been."[48] Naipaul's hopes for Syed and for Islam itself express his own humanistic values: the preservation of what is valuable in art, history, and tradition revitalized by new challenges which science and technology inevitably produce.

In Malaysia, Naipaul finds that the "universal civilization" of the West has penetrated society on all levels, from town to village. Malaysia's wealth of natural resources ("tin, rubber, palm oil"), has generated education and technological development along with discontent and conflict. It is in Malaysia that Naipaul establishes the closest of his relations with the many people he interviews throughout this journey. Although he had increasingly overcome barriers of religion and tradition in his contacts with several Pakastanis, in Malaysia he and his guide become friends as each expresses his own convictions and questions the other's.

Shafi, who works for a Muslim youth movement, exemplifies the personal conflict of an intelligent, sensitive young man dedicated to the new Islam. Nostalgic for the village life of his boyhood, he nonetheless feels impelled to reform the "pre-Islamic . . . old ways of the village," a commitment Naipaul regards as a "contrary missionary wish . . . to cleanse his Malay people of an important part of themselves." Although Shafi rejects the materialism that recent wealth has produced in the cities, he admits that he traveled to the United States, where he expected to observe only the "technical developments, the material developments." Still, he was disappointed in not finding people concerned with "the universal creation."

Naipaul's interest in Shafi, the provocative questions he asks, his frankness about his own beliefs, encourage him to open himself to an outsider: "Shafi, you think you have found the answer?" "I think so," Shafi replies. When Shafi defines civilization as closeness to "the creator," Naipaul asks, "So you don't think too much of me?" As Naipaul increasingly personalizes Shafi's answers, Shafi is prompted to question him in turn and the interview becomes a dialogue. When Naipaul, responding to Shafi's comment that in the United States "life revolves around money and sex," asks him, "Do you think my life revolves around money and sex?" Shafi's reply is a question: "What is the purpose of your writing? Is it to tell people what it's all about?" When Naipaul says, "Yes. I would say comprehension," Shafi asks, "Is it not for money?" When Naipaul answers, "Yes. But the nature of the work is also important," he has introduced the "idea of a vocation" to Shafi, whose reply, for all that it is qualified by his religious beliefs, reveals a new understanding of his interlocutor from the civilization he rejects: "You are not doing justice to yourself. You have been searching for truth and yet you haven't got the truth." If Naipaul's vocation is irreconcilable with his own dedication to an unchanging truth established by dogma, he has learned that truth can be sought through observation and writing.

Despite their disagreements, the two men have felt an affinity that the disparities in their backgrounds and aspirations would seem to preclude.

During their last meeting, when Naipaul asks, "Is it really true? You've never thought or talked about your life as you've done with me?" Shafi replies, "It's true." Responding to Naipaul's affection, he has reminisced about his past, "those good old times," which he now feels he must "uproot" in embracing the truth of the new Islam, but he has also become acquainted with an alternate approach to truth. Even as he disparages Naipaul's search, he has participated in it by revealing his own conflicts.

Naipaul leaves Malaysia saddened by Shafi's suppression of his feelings for the past of his village and his people, his emotions displaced in religious abstraction and ritual. Yet Shafi's ambivalence helps him to understand the complex reactions to the new Islam of people he encounters in Indonesia. In Jakarta Naipaul feels he is "in a country with a sense of its past." Not only in other Muslim countries but in the West Indies, India, and Zaire, he had related the general ignorance or distortions of history to the loss of a national culture. Now he observes how the survival of the pre-Islamic past in the cultural and religious life of the Javanese is fundamental to "the feeling of their uniqueness." Here Islam is "part of the composite religion," which includes Hindu-Buddhist elements. In his view, the most important remains of the Hindu legacy are its epics, the *Mahabharata* and the *Ramayana* performed "in the puppet plays, the wayang," for inherent in these stories are "ambiguities" of ethics and conduct as each of the figures "is engaged in his own search," an interpretation that might apply not only to the characters and audience but to the writer and his readers as well.

But this blending of religious and cultural traditions is not generally reached as harmoniously as in the puppet plays and even their techniques can be adapted to propagandistic ends. Ever alert to infringements on individual development, Naipaul finds that the increasing acceptance of Islam in Java is a reaction to anxiety, resentment of recent technological and economic advances, a retreat to the rigid demands of fundamentalism. In a section entitled "The Loss of Personality," Darmasastro, "a high civil servant in one of the new departments concerned with technology," tells him of people who have lost their "identity." Having left their villages and acquired wealth, they still "are not individuals in the Western sense. They cannot stand on their own and as individuals interact on an equal basis with others." Another acquaintance, Prasojo, who guides him in the villages, says that the poor have also lost the security of village life and with it have "lost their personalities."

In Bandung Naipaul observes a class in "mental training," where "children of the middle class, people faced with this special Indonesian threat of the loss of personality," engage in exercises in "communication," from which, they conclude, they have learned "important things: the value of inquiry, rational analysis." Their teacher Imaduddin, as Naipaul describes him, embodies the contradictory and sometimes conflicting influences of tradition and modernity, religion and politics, in his varied commitments. Born in Sumatra, he was trained as an electrical engineer in Jakarta and the United States and had traveled to Europe and to Mecca. His involvement with the Muslim youth movement in Malaysia made him "suspect to the Indonesians," who "were especially nervous of radical developments in the Bandung Institute." Released from prison only five months before Naipaul's meeting with him, he is still, as he says, "fighting for my freedom."

Now he conducts "a three-day Islamic 'mental training' course at the mosque of the Institute of Technology," where he is an instructor. Naipaul describes a section on "communication," in which students are asked to retell a story that has been read to them and, accustomed as they are to the techniques of puppet shows, react with "hilarity" to the disparate versions. Recalling Naipaul's earlier description of the "good puppet-master [who], whatever his interpretation of the story, political, mystical, leaves the issues open" so that members of the audience can respond in their own ways, the reader expects that this is to be Imaduddin's method throughout the class. But Naipaul's further depiction of the session only highlights the differences in the intentions of the "good puppet-master" and Imaduddin, the trainer of minds who leads his class from the hilarity of puppet-show ambiguity to the solemnity of Islamic conformity. No longer taking the role of "the actor or the puppet-master," he assumes that of "the mullah, the man in a mosque, reciting the Koran on some day of Muslim passion."

The puppet master, through his art, elicits individual responses to traditional myths, appealing to "the common imagination" mingled with contemporary associations, both personal and social. The stories themselves raise questions concerning motivation, morality, cause and effect, stimulating each member of the audience to seek his or her own way to truth. The mullah closes all paths that do not lead to the Koran. In the opposition between these two figures, one in the theater and the other in the mosque, Naipaul creates a modern myth, which, like many traditional ones, discloses the necessary yet ambivalent, and often hostile, links between individual and communal life, psychic and social truths that quotidian reality often denies. It is also an assertion of his lifelong objection to the tyranny of ideology, its repression of the changing perceptions of the "eye," and the imagination's transforming operations. What Naipaul finds most surprising about Imaduddin is that he is "indifferent to the wonder of his life." He had known Sutan Sjahrir, "the secretary-general of the Indonesian Socialist Party" and the "prime minister of Indonesia in the first year of independence," and other famous Indonesians. He had himself fought in the war for independence and had witnessed and profited from a period of turbulence and change in Indonesia. Yet he cannot identify himself with the history through which he has lived; he remains rooted in his beginnings as a Muslim who "could separate his country from its history, traditions, art: its particularity."

"I travel to discover other states of mind," Naipaul says in "The Crocodiles of Yamoussoukro,"[49] which, along with "Prologue to an Autobiography," reveals how the mind functions in the process of writing. The states of mind he investigates include his own as well as those of the people he is drawn to and comes to know. One of the most vivid episodes he describes exposes him to magic beliefs and rituals that he may fear, even abhor, but which become means of entering the hidden life of the country, the fragility beneath its stable surface.

After observing a gruesome sacrifice of chickens to feed the president's crocodiles and hearing about sacrifices of children whose heads are needed for the burial of some important person, Naipaul has a dream in which he is "on a roof or bridge" that "had begun to perish," and was told it would not "be mended." Still, he is assured he can cross the bridge. "And in the dream that was the most important thing, because I wasn't going to pass that way again." Having unconsciously internalized the cruel rituals as a personal threat, in his dream he assures himself that he is safe; the bridge "seemingly melted at the edges" is his means of apprehending the insecurity of people through whom he perceives the land. In the morning the dream continues to inform him: "The buildings of Abidjan, seen in the morning mist of the lagoon, seemed sinister: proof of a ruler's power, a creation of magic, for all the solidity of the concrete and the steel: dangerous and perishable like the bridge in my dream." Observing a ritual sacrifice to the point where he must turn away, enriching his understanding through dream symbols, interpreting them in the light of day and of history—all this is transmitted to the reader as part of the writing process.

Naipaul refers to a more technical aspect of writing in *A Turn in the South*, where he discusses his need "to establish some lines of inquiry, to define a theme," which "has to develop with the travel." And so it does. Traversing the American Southeast from North Carolina to

Mississippi, he finds a close alliance between religious observance and the internalized history of the region. As the past of many of the Southerners he meets—both blacks and whites—is a kind of religion, so religious belief incorporates the history of slavery, segregation, and the long struggle to overcome its ravages. Here, as in many of his travel narratives, his pervading theme is the indelible, often painful links between individual identity and the historical past persisting "as a wound" which inhibits, reduces, but can also challenge individuals and communities. It is this wound that is the source of his empathy with people seemingly so different from himself who have shared with him a cruel and violent history in the New World.

At a party at an estate in northwestern Georgia, informed that American Indians "might have lived" there, listening to talk of the connections between "religious faith and identity," Naipaul is moved by the history of the land itself, "resting layer upon layer." It seems to him that the turbulent past of slavery, civil war, racism, and segregation is deeply involved with "the need everyone felt . . . in his own way, to save his soul." A shared absorption in history, however different the lens from which it is viewed, unites him, if only temporarily, with people whose background, beliefs, way of life, and even vocabulary are distant from his own.

In Tallahassee, when Naipaul asks the Reverend Bernyce Clausell how she explained "the strong religious instinct black people had," she says, "it comes from slavery. And even from before slavery. From Africa." Although she admits that for some, religion "might be a form of escapism, she views Christianity as "a way of life" with continuous historical affiliations, from the prayer meetings of slaves—which, as Eugene Genovese has demonstrated, instilled "pride," "self-respect, . . strength derived from direct communion with God and each other"[50]—to the present, when religion, she believes, "has had a great part in helping to break down segregation."

Naipaul responded so strongly to Bernyce Clausell's account of the Quaker prayer meetings where she was trained not to react to abuse when she worked to desegregate Washington D.C., that he began to cry. Clausell seems to offer comfort as she assures him, "People have changed. And now some of those people wouldn't believe that they were that cruel back there." That she did not "offer a personal forgiveness" but instead "spoke of a larger change of heart" he finds "immensely moving." Regarding her own history within the larger framework of the links between past and present, she has not "dug into" her family history before 1900. For her, as for many black Southerners, history, religion, covert resistance to slavery in the past, and public opposition to racism in the present are one.

As often in his travels, it is memories of Trinidad that ally Naipaul most keenly with the land and its inhabitants. In Atlanta, interviewing a woman who had worked with poor white people in the Appalachians, he asks how "identity was important" to them. Though at first unable to understand their difficulties, relying as he has so frequently done, on memories and associations, a "half-buried part of myself," he recalls the "stress" of those living in a multiracial society. From childhood he had known "how important it was not to fall into nonentity." He then remembers his intense emotional reaction, his "feeling of taint and spiritual annihilation," the threat to his autonomy, when, traveling in the Caribbean, he encountered Indians in Martinique who had lost all cultural affiliations with their past, and years later "a similar feeling of the void" in response to the "small, lost, half-Indian community" of Belize.

There are other memories of Trinidad and of earlier voyages, nostalgia blended with the pain of past and contemporary history. In North Carolina, when James Applewhite, a poet and teacher at Duke University, comments that there is "no landscape like the first that one knew," Naipaul's feeling is "he couldn't have known how directly he was speaking to me (the scarcely bearable idea of the beginning of things now existing only in my heart, no longer existing physically in the ravaged, repopulated Trinidad of today)." Applewhite's recollections of the "old days" when the "marks of the sweeping" of yards would be left as a sign of pride in their cleanliness remind Naipaul of "the African huts and their clean yellow-brown yards" he had seen on the banks of the Congo or Zaire River. Later he is moved by an older memory of marks made by a "cocoye broom" in the sand of Trinidad, signs of "order and cleanliness, almost the piety of a house." A poem of Applewhite's elicits one of Naipaul's most empathic associations with the Southern landscape: a reference to a tobacco harvest celebration, "originally the slave crop," evokes a memory of "the sugarcane fields, acres upon acres, scene of bitter labor" in Trinidad.[51] Like so many other places he has visited, the American South conjures up a history of exploitation—slaves, indentured laborers, and their descendants, coming to terms with their past.

Muslim acquaintances who sometimes became friends, people in the Ivory Coast who, "not unlike myself . . . were trying to find order in their world, looking for the center,"[52] American Southerners bearing a heritage of violence and humiliation—all enlarged Naipaul's understanding of the different personal and social means individuals use to salvage their self-respect, to maintain the integrity of their religious observance, to evaluate their past, to conceive a future. In *India: A Million Mutinies Now*, the product of his sojourn in India in 1988–89, his relations with his informants are distinguished by an affinity born of such knowledge. Exploring their ancestral heritage, their homes, their beliefs, the rituals they enact or reject, the streets they walk on, their workplaces, the narrator continually reflects on his own psychic and cultural links to India. In greater detail and with deeper empathy than in *India: A Wounded Civilization*, he writes of the common need of the Indian people, in all their diversity, for both a secure material existence and an identity released from the humiliations of poverty and the bonds of karma. Having assimilated his Indian heritage, he identifies himself with many of the people he encounters.

Before he begins this person-to-person narrative, he describes the two images he had formed of India in his youth. The first was of "a most fearful place," which produced "an anxiety" a kind of "neurosis," when he observed Indians still trapped in Trinidad by the poverty they had tried to escape by migrating. The second, in contrast, was a supportive image: the India of the struggle for independence, of "the great civilization and the great classical past," the basis of his "identity" on his initial visit in 1962. As is apparent in *An Area of Darkness*, this identity could not withstand the distress of the actual country he encountered. It was not merely disillusionment that produced his extreme rage and pain, nor even the poverty of India "scratching at [his] old neurosis." Meeting degradation where he had sought the roots of his communal identity, he felt his hard-won awareness of himself "as a whole human being" threatened. In the vastness of India, without his own "region, clan, caste, family,"[53] the union of the man and the writer, his protection against the abyss of dissolution, was impaired. Still, his illusions shattered, he was forced to recognize how profoundly his Indian roots had formed his character, even aspects of a way of life seemingly removed from their influence.

Thirteen years later, on the visit that is the subject of *India: A Wounded Civilization*, he no longer needed defenses based on an idealized past; instead he saw "the possibility of a true new beginning." Yet, writing about the "ambiguities of India's history" in *India: A Million Mutinies Now*, his "old nerves" still respond to "the many accidents" that saved the country from "cultural destitution," and introduced conceptions of "law and freedom and wide human association—which gave men self-awareness and strength." He considers the irony that among its British conquerors were those who "gave to Indians the first ideas they had of the antiquity and value of their civilization." An apprehension of their common heritage and its function in promoting "self-awareness" is Naipaul's deepest connection with the Indians he meets during this visit.

As he travels from Bombay to Goa, Bangalore, Madras, Calcutta, Lucknow, Chandigahr, Amritsar, and finally to Kashmir, his own memories and associations are guides to the intricate connections between tradition and change in India. Renewing his friendships with people he had met in previous visits and making new acquaintances among Hindus, Jains, Dalits, Muslims, and Sikhs, he investigates the manifold ways in which Indians resist and adapt to the demands of continual upheavals. Although he encourages his informants to tell their own stories, he focuses on "the new sense of self" emerging in individuals of every political or religious affiliation. However alien or opposed he may be to such positions, he empathizes with those who seek their identities within them.

In earlier years, as Naipaul acquired the skills of travel narrative, occasional recollections of his past mitigated feelings of alienation. But on his first trip to India, these memories came unbidden, antithetical reactions to his conscious judgments. Now, the product of many years of reckoning with his past, they are means he uses deliberately to understand the ways in which people adapt to or exceed their limits, as he recognizes his bond with them.

One remembers his congenial relations with several of the Muslims he interviewed for *Among the Believers*, especially his friendship with Shafi, his guide in Malaysia. Now, visiting a Muslim father and son in India, he reacts even more intimately to the circumstances that govern their lives, their poverty, the "traffic fumes," the "mill smoke," the thefts and quarrels in their neighborhood. He admires "the humanity that remained to them, the old man's calm acknowledgement of the better health and strength of others, the better conditions of life of others." Beginning to feel an affection for them both," Naipaul imagines himself living as they do: "I felt that if I had been in their position, confined to Bombay, to that area, to that row, I too would have been a passionate Muslim. I had grown up in Trinidad a member of a minority and I know that if you felt your community was small, you could never walk away from it; the grimmer things became, the more you insisted on being what you were." The poverty he had known in Trinidad, to which he had once attributed an "old neurosis," is now a source of empathy.

In a later interview, the issue of financial means, which occurs repeatedly in Naipaul's investigations of family life, reveals more subtle changes in his feelings about his background. Responding to Naipaul's question about whether he felt "poor" when growing up, Subramaniam, a brahmin scientist living in Bangalore, says, "There was never money to spare" in his family, but his "background was poor only in an economical sense. Not at all in a cultural sense." In this instance Naipaul shares his own experience to indicate how he understood. "It was what I felt—in a lesser or different way—about my own Indian family background in far off Trinidad. I felt that the physical conditions of our life, often poor conditions, told only half the story: that the remnants of the old civilization we possessed gave the in-between colonial generations a second scheme of references and ambitions, and that this equipped us for the outside world better than might have seemed likely." This is a far cry from his position in *The Middle Passage,* where he observes that for Trinidadians the only source of identity was "our belonging to the British Empire." Both this judgment and his summation of his background in 1973 as "fairly simple, barbarous, and limited"[54] refer more specifically to their context, his exposure of one of the dire effects of colonialism—the erasure of people's own history and culture—than to his familial environment. Still, Naipaul, like most of us, has long been ambivalent about his childhood. In interviews, in *The Enigma of Arrival,* in *A Turn in the South,* and elsewhere, he has expressed nostalgia, even love for his homeland and has acknowledged that his early environment, with all its hardships, nurtured his imagination, his curiosity about the great world beyond it, and his vocation as a writer. Yet he has never romanticized it. His first impressions of Kinshasa are of "a leafy Trinidad-like suburb." The people remind him of "Trinidad negro crowds."[55] Trying to get his bearings in an unfamiliar city, he associates a restaurant with "a Trinidad caff." For better or worse—"the magnificence of the women," the "climate . . . more humid and more sapping than Trinidad," a slum "vaster than the shanty town of Port of Spain"—Trinidad is a continuous point of reference.

Now speaking with Subramaniam, he remembers "the shoddiness of the Indian books we bought. . . . The idea of India was part of our strength, and it received part of our piety; yet there was this other idea of the Indian reality, of poor goods, of poor machines poorly used." His insistence on this reality elicits his informant's reaction to the same "shoddiness," actually to a more complex view of its effect. The poor quality of Indian products compared with English or European ones, says Subramaniam, did not diminish people's "innate feelings of old cul-

tural strength." He never doubted that India would one day become in-
dustrialized. Yet, like Naipaul, he admits to a "feeling . . . compounded
of shame, ignorance, and hope."

As the conversation continues, each man's remembrances enrich the
other's understanding of the different personal effects of their common
cultural heritage. When Naipaul recalls his early concerns as to "whether
the culture . . . which in one way supported and enriched some of us,
and gave us solidity, wasn't perhaps the very thing that had exposed us
to defeat," Subramaniam says he has similar feelings. But then he emphasizes the essential difference in their circumstances: "The foreigner
was here." Naipaul's reminiscences have drawn Subramaniam into a discussion of India's past, its reliance on the continuity of its culture and its
"social organization" as autonomous even as it accommodated itself to
centuries of foreign invasion. It was the British conquest that brought
about change, unwillingness to accept defeat, a new awareness that attracted people to English schools run by orthodox Hindus," who taught
"English, science, technology." Subramaniam's "pattern of Indian history" provides further clues to the relation between national assumptions, historical events, and the course of individual lives, Naipaul's recurrent theme.

From Pravas, an engineer who also lives in Bangalore, Naipaul learns
how the "expanding economy" offered him opportunities for education
and employment, how "cultural change" led him to adapt the "brahminic
value system," the tradition of learning, to his pursuit of science. Although
he does not perform the prescribed rituals, he retains "a nostalgia" for and
an understanding of their meaning. When Naipaul compares the changes
Pravas has described to those that occurred in the Indian community of
his childhood—the loss of "language" and "the reverence for rituals,"
even as the forms survived—Pravas, like Subramaniam, emphasizes the
different consequences: "For you the change was not subversive," by
which he means that "the change was not from within. It was external."
Naipaul seems to accept Pravas's distinction, but his additional comments
refute this rather facile judgment. Naipaul attributes "a further, and fundamental, difference between the new generation in India and our own
immigrant community far away" to the declining knowledge of and
commitment to Hindu theology in Trinidad, "part of a more general cultural loss, which has left many with no strong idea of who they were."
This is certainly an "internal" change. In India, he believes, the loss of ritual and other external changes will not have such consequences. The
new "identities" of the "millions" who have rejected the strictures of

caste and ritual will preserve remnants of the ancestral past, "the customs . . . which were still like instinct" that Naipaul found so moving in Fustel de Coulange and in his father's stories, and recurrent in memories as he defined his ambivalent link with his Indian heritage.

Discussion of caste, ritual, and especially of the nature of the clan becomes an occasion for sharing this ambivalence. When Kala, a young independent woman who works in publicity in Bangalore, reveals the suffering her mother endured submitting to the traditional role of a young wife in her husband's family, Naipaul relates her story to his own childhood within his extended family. He has often referred to the security that the clan provided and the tyranny it imposed, the most flagrant example of which was the threat of death leveled at his father for opposing the orthodoxy of his wife's family. Unlike Kala, he views the cruelty of the clan as less a matter of "double standards" than an aspect of a "ritualized" way of life, "no more than the cruelty of life itself." Yet he understands and shares her need for independence as a reaction against the authority of the clan. Once again, a common heritage, however distant its recipients both socially and geographically, creates a psychological bond.

Naipaul's reminiscences help to create a congenial atmosphere as he reaches out to people of divergent political and religious positions. Both similarities and differences in his background from that of his Indian informants clarify their roles in a changing society and deepen his knowledge of his Indian community in Trinidad. With Vishwa Nath, the editor of *Women's Era*, a committed anti-brahmin, whom he met in New Delhi, Naipaul shares a lifelong "love of print." "I felt he was speaking for me," says Naipaul, as Vishwa Nath's memory of being introduced to printing by his father evokes a similar episode of his own youth. Talk of printing leads to further revelations and to Naipaul's discovery of the ambiguities of this complicated man: "iconoclasm" allied with a regard for tradition, "a concern for the family," which in India "was like a wish to preserve the old social order." These "contradictions," which grow out of India's and Vishwa Nath's own history, are a truer guide to his character than the term "conservative," with which younger people have labeled him.

As always in his travels, Naipaul examines his methods of acquiring knowledge of people, social developments, and change. "Knowledge can sometimes come slowly," he says; listening can be "selective," the traveler taking "too much for granted." This is his introduction to his visit to Kakusthan, "who was trying to live as a full brahmin" in an agrahara in

Madras. His receptiveness to this brahmin is in sharp contrast to his disparagement of the Acharya in the novel *Samskara*: "I didn't understand how unusual and even heroic this resolve of [Kakusthan's] was." He is to discover what Ramanujan called the realism in *Samskara*, the signs, even in the agrahara, of the inevitable changes taking place in contemporary India. Kakusthan, who as a youth had rebelled against his father's brahminism, now a middle-aged employee of a business firm, had returned to the "little urban slum" of the agrahara in order to adhere to religion and ritual. As Naipaul comes to know him, he admires the integrity of the man who "belonged now, by his profession, to the modern world" and yet, under the most difficult conditions, observed the brahmin prohibitions not only at home but at work where, garbed as "a brahmin priest," he could not partake of unconsecrated food or even water throughout the day, no matter how hot it was. But Naipaul's sympathetic reaction to Kakusthan and the colony as a whole is also based on their willingness to make the "compromises" that belonging to the modern world exacts.

In the colony in Madras compromise does not signify corruption, as it does in *Samskara*. It acknowledges the need to work at jobs "not dreamt of by traditional brahmins," in industry, in offices, as a cook. Even within the agrahara caste strictures are sometimes blurred by the necessities of daily life. In the course of his acquaintance with Kakusthan, Naipaul realizes that "accommodations with the world outside," far from undermining the agrahara, as he had first assumed they would, could only save it. "The community was learning to adapt; that was its strength." In his several visits to the brahmin colony Naipaul observes and at times is moved by the presence of traditional objects—the "style" of a lamp "that took me back to the ancient world"—and customs however compromised, such as eating of banana leaves now "bought in the market," but still a reminder of the days when fresh banana leaves evoked "one's remote origins."

As in the agrahara, throughout this visit to India, Naipaul is impressed by the preservation of cultural history adapted to social and economic change. Even in Karnataka, a new state created after Independence, with its "new sense of self," the persistence of "[r]eligious myths . . . gave antiquity and wonder to the earth people lived on." Individuals like Subramaniam and Pravas who no longer partake in Hindu rituals retain a faith in or at least a nostalgia for an ancient ritual, a family god, a prohibition no longer observed but still respected. Naipaul's sympathy for such attitudes reflects and confirms his reconciliation of many disparate elements of his own life: the Hindu heritage of his youth in Trinidad; the fantasy India of his childhood, now "lost and irrecoverable," replaced by the actual country of the present; his attraction to the ancient worlds of India and the West; and his conviction that change is essential despite its disruptions and sometimes questionable consequences.

In the last phase of this journey, Naipaul returns to Kashmir where, on his first trip to India, he had found a measure of tranquility at the Hotel Liward, now enlarged and modernized, its name corrected to Lee-ward. Visiting the place that twenty-seven years before had been his haven for more than four months, he finds Aziz unchanged. He has grown stout and prosperous, becoming, as his son Nazir says, "com-mander-in-chief" of the hotel, but he retains the "energy, the lightness of step, . . . the assessing intelligence" of his younger self. When Aziz shows him photographs of his pilgrimage to Mecca, Naipaul's reaction sums up his admiration for the man: "What a taste he had for life!" evok-ing for this reader Aziz's pleasure in riding a pony, his elation during the pilgrimage to the Cave of Amarnath so many years before.

Naipaul finds many changes in Kashmir—new hotels and shops, government buildings, the streets and lake crowded with inhabitants and tourists. Yet, surrounded by tall new buildings, "the centre of the old city" remained as it had been on his first trip. His reactions to India have become more temperate, more pleasurable, with his deeper comprehen-sion of its history and of his own links to its past and present. If "old Kashmiri irritations" and others have occasionally returned, "telescoping the years," they have not exacted the psychic toll of his earlier visits. When he says farewell to Nazir, uncertainty similar to but not quite the same as he had felt with Aziz recurs. How to repay the young man who had accompanied him on "excursions?" Aziz, whose advice he seeks, will only say that a tip (baksheesh), not "payment," might be acceptable. But when Naipaul does offer the young man money, his response trou-bles him. Realizing that his relationship with Nazir, "with his new ideas of elegance and self" was "more complicated" than that with Aziz, he tries "to save the moment" by explaining that it was "a gesture . . . made out of friendship," and to some extent he succeeds. His extreme sensi-tivity to people's reactions are now more rewarding than disturbing as he seeks their aid and friendship in his travels.

Naipaul's three books on India record changes both in the country and in himself that are sometimes analagous. He attributes India's achievement of "a central will, a central intellect, a national idea" to its revaluation of its past, along with its openness to new ideas and discoveries, a growing "self-awareness," its very "movements of excess" aiming at "law and civility and reasonableness." For him the million mutinies are expressions of individuality, the adaptation of multiple cultural traditions to the demands of a nation remaking itself. On a larger scale, these movements reflect his own struggle to assimilate his Indian past, his own complex social and personal history, his continual self-evaluation and self-criticism, his sometimes excessive reactions, and the core of creative intelligence, which for him manifested itself in writing, his way of "ordering events and emotions," as he records his expanding view of his ancestral heritage and envisions the manifold possibilities of the millions whose views may coincide with or differ from his own.

Defining the "writing self," Naipaul quotes from Proust's *Against Sainte-Beuve*, which he greatly admires: "a book is the product of a different self from the self we manifest in our habits, in our social life, in our vices. . . . What one bestows on private life—in conversation, however refined it may be . . .—is the product of a quite superficial self, not of the innermost self which one can only recover by putting aside the world and the self that frequents the world."[56] It is true that the self that speaks to the reader in Naipaul's work does not divulge details of his domestic or social affairs, but it is clear that his "innermost self" has, to some extent, been formed by his interaction with the worlds he has explored. In the next chapter, my emphasis is on the products of this fusion: How do his twin aims, personal discovery and objective reporting, function in interpreting the problems and achievements of the nations he visits and revisits, as both the reporter and the terrain change over time?

NOTES

1. *The Enigma of Arrival*, 146–48.
2. "Prologue to an Autobiography," *Finding the Center*, vii.
3. Gussow, 45–46.
4. "Prologue to an Autobiography," *Finding the Center*, 9.
5. V. S. Naipaul, *Miguel Street* (1959; reprint, New York, 1979), 172.
6. "Prologue to an Autobiography," *Finding the Center*, 33–34.
7. *The Enigma of Arrival*, 147.
8. V. S. Naipaul, "Foreword," *The Adventures of Gurudeva and Other Stories by Seepersad Naipaul* (London: Andre Deutsch, 1976), 8–13. Subsequent references to Foreword are to this volume.
9. R. K. Narayan, *Gods, Demons, and Others* (1964; reprint, New York: Bantam, 1986), ix–x.

10. My source for the events summarized on 31–33 is "Prologue to an Autobiography," *Finding the Center*, 66–72.

11. "Prologue to an Autobiography," *Finding the Center*, 25.

12. "Conrad's Darkness," *The Return of Eva Perón*, 224.

13. V. S. Naipaul, "Foreword," *The Adventures of Gurudeva and Other Stories*, 19.

14. V. S. Naipaul, *Letters Between a Father and Son* (London: Little, Brown 1999).

15. "Prologue to an Autobiography," *Finding the Center*, 72.

16. "Prologue to an Autobiography," *Finding the Center*, 60.

17. V. S. Naipaul, "Foreword," *The Adventures of Gurudeva and Other Stories*, 19.

18. Numa Denis Fustel de Coulange, *The Ancient City* (1864; translated into English by Willard Small;1873; reprint, New York: Doubleday Anchor, 1956), 11–14.

19. The quoted passages are taken from "Writing *A House for Mr. Biswas*"; "Prologue to an Autobiography," *Finding the Center*, 60; and *The Enigma of Arrival*, 151. In "Writing *A House for Mr. Biswas*," Naipaul says: "Colonial Trinidad had sent me to Oxford in 1950, and I had made myself a writer."

20. V. S. Naipaul, *A House for Mr. Biswas* (1961; reprint, New York: Penguin, 1969), 216.

21. "Writing *A House for Mr. Biswas*," 22.

22. "Writing *A House for Mr. Biswas*," 22.

23. "Writing *A House for Mr. Biswas*," 22.

24. Gussow, "It Is out of This Violence I've Always Written," 46.

25. "An Interview with Rowe-Evans," 56.

26. V. S. Naipaul, *The Middle Passage* (1962; reprint, New York: Vintage, 1981), 21.

27. *The Enigma of Arrival*, 153.

28. Mukherjee and Boyers, 21.

29. V. S. Naipaul, "A Handful of Dust: Return to Guiana," *The New York Review of Books* (April 11, 1961): 16.

30. *The Enigma of Arrival*, 153.

31. "Travel Plus Writing Plus Reflection Equals V. S. Naipaul," an interview with Mel Gussow, *New York Times* (January 30, 1990): 9.

32. *An Area of Darkness*, 15–18.

33. *The Enigma of Arrival*, 244.

34. *An Area of Darkness*, 34, 38; *Among the Believers*, 11, 50.

35. *India: A Wounded Civilization*, ix–x.

36. *An Area of Darkness*, 227–28.

37. *India: A Wounded Civilization*, 13.

38. *India: A Wounded Civilization*, 13.

39. *India: A Wounded Civilization*, 32.

40. R. K. Narayan, *The Vendor of Sweets* (1967; reprint, New York: Penguin, 1983).

41. *India: A Wounded Civilization*, 33.

42. R. K. Narayan, *My Days: A Memoir* (1975; reprint, New York: Penguin, 1989), 138–45.

43. *My Days*, 115–16.

44. *India: A Wounded Civilization*, 107.

45. U. R. Anantha Murthy, *Samskara: A Rite for a Dead Man*, translated by A. K. Ramanujan (1965; reprint, New York: Oxford University Press, 1978), 149.

46. Mukherjee and Boyers, 5.

47. *India: A Million Mutinies Now*, 169.

48. *Among the Believers*, 173–78.

49. "The Crocodiles of Yamoussoukro," *Finding the Center*, 90.

50. Eugene Genovese, *Roll Jordan Roll: The World the Slaves Made* (London: Andre Deutsch, 1975), 237–38.

51. *A Turn in the South*, 268–71.

52. *Finding the Center*, ix.

53. *India: A Million Mutinies Now*, 7–8, and *An Area of Darkness*, 16.

54. "The Novelist V. S. Naipaul Talks about His Work to Ronald Bryden," 367.

55. *A Congo Diary*, 1.

56. "On Being a Writer," 7.

3

TRAVEL NARRATIVES, HISTORY, AND JOURNALISM

The autobiographical motif that pervades Naipaul's writings attests to William James's conviction "that there is no truth without some interest, and that non–intellectual interests play a part as well as the intellectual ones."[1] I hope to show in this chapter how Naipaul's standpoint shifts, his "eye" changes as his "interest" merges with that of the postcolonial societies he explores. His chief concerns are the lasting political, economic, and social effects of past foreign domination: lack of education and training in the development of natural resources, long exploited by colonizers; the absence of preparation for independence and consequent wide-spread poverty; retreat to fantasy when there are no established institutions to provide social cohesion and solutions to economic problems and social conflict; the rise of despots who amass great wealth by robbing populaces denied participation in government, opportunities for financial security, cultural enrichment, a sense of their own dignity, the freedom to develop their own abilities and talents, to pursue their "vocation," and thus their particular version of "happiness." Linked with these issues is that of cultural identity as are questions similar to those Wole Soyinka raises in his recent *The Open Sore of a Continent*: "does the superimposed idea 'nation' harmonize or conflict with our given a priori, humanity? If not, what are the causes? What are their histories, and what futures do such histories further threaten?"[2] Another question frequently asked, which is related to Naipaul's approach, is whether nationalism entails unification and creation or pernicious exclusion of individuality and dissent. "Nationalism," says Isaiah Berlin, "springs, as often as not, from a wounded or outraged sense of human dignity, the desire for recognition. This desire is one of the greatest

79

forces that move human history. It may take hideous forms, but is not in itself either unnatural or repulsive as a feeling."[3]

THE BONDS OF THE PAST

Naipaul often evokes ancient civilizations—Rome, India, medieval Islam, and others, sometimes as proleptic paradigms in epigraphs, there and elsewhere for the meager consolations of historical perspective. References to the ancient world also heighten his personal reactions, backing them with historical associations. Two epigraphs to the chapter on Trinidad in *The Middle Passage* anticipate the ambivalence of the reactions he records on this visit: his pain and anger at the deprivations of its people combined with a recognition of the historical inevitability of their situation. The first, from Thomas Mann's novella *Tables of the Law*, describes the dilemma of the ancient Israelites:

> Because several of their generation had lived in a transitional land, pitching their tents between the houses of their fathers and the real Egypt, they were now unanchored souls, wavering in spirit and without a secure doctrine. They had forgotten much; they had half assimilated some new thoughts; and because they lacked real orientation, they did not trust their own feelings. They did not trust even the bitterness that they felt toward their own bondage.

The second epigraph, from Tacitus's *Agricola*, on the Roman conquest of Britain, even more telling in the context of this section, reiterates the cultural and psychological effects of domination by a foreign power:

> In place of distaste for the Latin language came a passion to command it. In the same way, our national dress came into favour and the toga was everywhere to be seen. And so the Britons were gradually led on to the amenities that make vice agreeable—arcades, baths, and sumptuous banquets. They spoke of such novelties as "civilization" when really they were only a feature of enslavement.

The similarity of the consequences of the imperial conquest of Trinidad to those suffered by two ancient civilizations negates an assumption generally held by Trinidadians: "Though we knew something was wrong with our society, we made no attempt to assess it. Trinidad was too unimportant and we could never be convinced of the value of reading the history of a place which was, as everyone said, only a dot on the map of the world."

Naipaul's epigraphs recounting the effects of ancient conquest on the lives of its victims, imaginatively reconstructed from biblical narrative and described by a contemporary Roman historian, revise this impression. They suggest that the psychological and cultural ravages of Trinidad's history are vital for understanding himself and the society that from boyhood, fearing its "threat of failure," he wished to flee. Within these historical contexts his view that Trinidadians had little regard for themselves is far more than a personal indictment.

In his youth, he says, values, such as "dignity," "generosity," and pride in one's accomplishments were absent or disparaged. He could encounter them only in books and, no doubt, in his father's aspirations for him. The lack of communal spirit, of a national identity, he attributes to a heritage of colonialism, a past of slavery, indentured labor, and continual immigration. Ironically, whatever frail sense of communal values existed was an offshoot of the eradication of Trinidadians' diverse history: "It was only our Britishness, our belonging to the British Empire, which gave us any identity."

Tacitus's description of the British who, when conquered by the Romans, had no more inherent capacity to resist a "borrowed culture" than those they later conquered reduces the imposed model to a prototypical case history. Introducing Naipaul's chapter on Trinidad, it locates the island within the long history of conquered lands left unprepared for the autonomy they sought.

This is only the beginning of Naipaul's effort to restore to Trinidad the history of which it had been robbed. He was to pursue it in two later books: in *The Loss of El Dorado*, "the creation of a colony in the New World—the bringing of a part of the New World into 'history'—by men from Europe,"[4] and most recently, in *A Way in the World*, the inevitable transformations that are history manifested in the writer and in his ties to Trinidad, now changed by political, economic, and social upheavals from the world of his childhood, but still bearing evidence of its colonial past.

In *The Middle Passage* Naipaul is concerned with the conditions that produced an exploited population of different races, denied their own history, "unanchored" in Trinidad as members of a "materialist immigrant society," where, as throughout the West Indies, "nothing was created, . . . no civilization as in Spanish America, no great revolution, as in Haiti or the American colonies. There were only plantations, prosperity,

decline, neglect." It is a society without common goals or values, enduring the intellectual and psychological effects of ignorance, which is actually denial, of its own history and the inevitable identification with the
aggressor. Because of their heritage of slavery, the black population is
most vulnerable in this respect. Slavery, he says, taught blacks "self-contempt," among the greatest evils human beings can inflict on one another. Having internalized their masters' values—"the ideals of white
civilization"—even when emancipated, blacks continued to reject the
self they scarcely knew and had few opportunities to develop, having
only the model of their white oppressors.

The East Indians, who arrived in Trinidad as indentured laborers,
Naipaul says, were better able to establish a community where religious
rituals and taboos, cultural ties within their extended families, and their
commitment to India's independence were bases of their identity. But as
religion declined into mere forms and strictures and India achieved Independence, the Indian community of Trinidad adapted to the "easy, un-
demanding society" of the island. Those who visited India were repelled
by its poverty and "returned . . . convinced of their own superiority."

Naipaul objects to the view that "Indian Independence in 1947 encouraged Indian racialism in Trinidad" as "too simple." It was rather the
"first elections . . . under universal adult suffrage" in 1946 that intensified
long-held biases: Indian belief in their own racial preeminence combined
with the adoption of "white prejudice against the Negro." Black racialism,
he believes, is "more complex," combining "an overdue assertion of dignity" with "bitterness" and "something of the urban mob requiring to be
satisfied with bread and circuses. It has profound intellectual promptings as
well, in the realization that the Negro problem lies not simply in the attitude of others to the Negro, but in the Negro's attitude to himself." The
contrast between Naipaul's perception of the onset of black pride and self-
knowledge and his comparison of black demands with those of a Roman
mob implies that reasonable needs unmet can lead to desperate compromises by those unfamiliar with popular organization for reform.

The rivalry between blacks and Indians for political power, their
mutual distrust and contempt, aroused Naipaul's fears that "Trinidad in
fact teeters on the brink of racial war." Although racial antagonism has
not led to war in Trinidad, there was ample cause for such concern. His
essay, " Michael X and the Black Power Killings in Trinidad," and his
novel *Guerrillas*, refer to the Black Power rebellion of March 1970:
"There were daily anti-government marches in Port of Spain; revolutionary pamphlets appeared everywhere, even in schools; sections of the

regiment declared for the marchers. Even the Asian countryside began to be infected. A spontaneous, anarchic outburst: a humane society divided in its wish for order and its various visions of redemption."[5] The situation was sufficiently dangerous for a state of emergency to be declared, but within a few months the uprising was ended and its leaders were arrested.

Twenty years later a seeming repetition of this rebellion occurred but, larger in scope and more violent, it seemed a greater threat to any hope of permanent stability in Trinidad. In July 1990 an armed group of Black Muslims led by Abu Bakr occupied the Parliament and held Prime Minister Arthur N. R. Robinson, and his cabinet hostage, threatening to kill them if their demands were not met. In the armed combat that followed, the looting and burning, many people on both sides were wounded and killed. After a state of emergency was declared, Robinson, who had been shot, was released on August 1, but forty hostages remained. The next day Abu Bakr surrendered, and was arrested and imprisoned. Naipaul refers to this episode in *A Way in the World,* regarding it as part of a "chain of events" beginning with blacks and Indians he had encountered in the past, manifesting their particular desperation, and moving forward to "the nihilism of the moment."

No doubt the loss of income from falling oil prices in the early 1980s and widespread unemployment were at least partly responsible for the discontent that sparked this rebellion. Some Trinidadians discounted racial antagonism, but a black truck driver quoted in the *New York Times* (September 24, 1990) seemed to echo Naipaul's observation of 1960 as he described racial division and the violence it continued to threaten in Trinidad: "Them Indians—them already get all the business. . If they take over the government, we're going to have a war." Furthermore, the return of Abu Bakr and his followers, who were freed in July 1992 by order of the British Privy Council, and even awarded damages, caused concern among many Trinidadians. The number of Bakr's adherents had increased, and he remained an intimidating figure, ever ready for confrontation with the government. According to Lloyd Best, an editor of the *Trinidad and Tobago Review,* as quoted by the *New York Times* (November 11, 1992), "Abu Bakr has transformed the politics of this country in the sense that most people never thought there could be a coup. The question is whether he will be able to profit from it. Now that he is being watched by everybody, including the man in the street, he is no longer a novelty and he has lost the element of surprise." A new transformation in the politics of Trinidad was the election in December 1995 of Basdeo Panday, its first prime minister of Indian descent, a victory that seemed a further threat to blacks who have feared the increasing Indian presence in government and business. More recently, however, a booming economy resulting from the development of Trinidad's natural gas resources has encouraged cooperation between the two groups.

In 1961 Naipaul observed a racial division in British Guiana. In an article he wrote on his return to now-independent Guyana in 1991,[6] he describes his younger self—the writer of *The Middle Passage*, as "an artless traveler. . . . As a political observer I was uncertain and diffident. I thought that in this kind of writing I had to take people on trust," particularly in British Guiana, the leaders, Cheddi and Janet Jagan and Forbes Burnham. Thus, he suppressed his doubts about the Jagans' Marxism, viewing it as "a British Labour party kind of socialism," and did not acknowledge his "feeling that Burnham was a sensualist and dangerous, someone at once wounded and spoilt, full of vengefulness." Still, his portrayals of these people in *The Middle Passage* suggest that he was not as naive or as easily swayed by appearances as he claims in retrospect.

He introduces his account of his first meeting with Janet Jagan, who was then "Minister of Labour, Health and Housing," with an admission that he "was prejudiced in her favour," a skeptical response to the "many malicious accounts [he] had read and heard" about her. He describes her as a strong woman, intelligent, hardworking, well-informed about and devoted to the country, who regarded herself as a "pessimist." An American who had come to British Guiana as the young wife of Cheddi Jagan, she had shared her husband's political victories and defeats, including imprisonment after the British occupation of 1953. Although the Jagans' party was returned to power in 1957, she was troubled by the rupture of the alliance between Indians and blacks, which had "become a major issue in British Guiana."

In his travels throughout the country, Naipaul observed this division and heard objections to Cheddi Jagan as a communist, but in his meeting with the couple in Georgetown, and during his trips with them to other parts of British Guiana, he was convinced of their integrity as individuals, though he is noncommittal about their ideological position. In regard to the split that occurred between the Jagans and Forbes Burnham, their former ally, Naipaul clearly favors the Jagans. Yet he remarks on Burnham's charm, his extraordinary gifts as a speaker and, in a moving passage, speculates that "there remains a mutual sympathy and respect stronger than either [Jagan or Burnham] suspects, each perhaps regretting the other for what he was."

Ultimately, Naipaul's accord with the Jagans rested on their struggle against the persistent depredations of colonialism, which, he believed, could be countered only by "nationalism" as a "revitalizing force." Although he does not elaborate on this concept, here and in his later writings it seems to be an extension on a national level of his belief that individual and cultural identity are essential components of dignity, of self-respect. A "positive nationalism," which "existed in British Guiana in 1953 . . . the achievement of the Jagans and Mr. Burnham and their colleagues . . . was destroyed by the suspension of the constitution in that year and—gratuitous humiliation—by the dispatch of troops." Once again the nation was divided. As a result, says Naipaul, "the energy which, already gathered, ought to have gone towards an ordered and overdue social revolution was dissipated in racial rivalry, factional strife and simple fear, creating the confusion which is today more dangerous to Guiana than the alleged plot of 1953."

If Naipaul underestimated the Jagans' adherence to Marxist principles, he also discerned the integrity of their commitment to social justice throughout the years when they were deposed and treated as "pariahs." In his reports on speeches delivered by Cheddi Jagan and Forbes Burnham, the differences in the characters of the two men are clear. Jagan is well-informed, specific in details of the government's achievements and in answering questions from the audience. Burnham holds his audience with his brilliant technique and his wit. But, says Naipaul, "Unfortunately Mr. Burnham had little to say." He spoke of his "general disapproval of what was going on," and made disparaging remarks about Mrs. Jagan. Most revealing is a quotation from a speech in which Burnham turns Jagan's effort to control the economy into a racial challenge, "I warn the Indians. . . . Jagan has said he wants to gain control of the commanding heights of the economy. The commanding heights. Let me translate for you: your businesses, your land, your shops." As Naipaul's comment suggests, the intent of these remarks is self-evident: "To the Negroes in the audience the message was clear." These speeches recall earlier ones that Jagan and Burnham delivered at Oxford in 1953. The comparison confirms Naipaul's view that "Dr. Jagan remains what he then was. The same cannot be said of Mr. Burnham. In 1953 he spoke, however uncertainly, like a man with a case. In 1961 I felt he had none."

In his recent article Naipaul reviews Guyana's history since 1961, the decline of its economy and its currency, its "communist-style tyranny of the state [which] was also a racial tyranny." Burnham, who led the so-called conversion to socialism from 1971 on, was soon discredited by members of his own African party. Naipaul quotes a former follower of his who accused him of having "introduced slave labor." After his death in 1985 his estate was "declared to be a million Guyana dollars." An article in the *New York Times* (November 3, 1992) describes the fraudulence of his "cooperative socialism," which his opponents considered "a thin cover for a thuggish system of personality cult, graft and cronyism." Under his government and that of his successor, Guyana's resources of "bauxite, gold, diamonds and timber as well as its agricultural potential . . . went untapped" while the nation was reduced to poverty.

All the while, says Naipaul, "Cheddi Jagan has sat at his post, the leader of his party, always there, the possessor of a purer Marxist way, waiting to be called." His view of the man remained unchanged, despite his later awareness of Jagan's political naïveté and consequent failures. Yet Naipaul sensed that, even in his defeat, "Cheddi Jagan, in an essential personal way, had been a success," an insight that Jagan confirmed: "Even my enemies recognize our integrity in politics." In 1991 Naipaul speculated that with the end of European communism and with it the Cold War mentality, free elections might be held in Guyana, and Cheddi Jagan "may at last win." Both predictions came true in October of 1992 when Jagan, then seventy-four, was elected president of Guyana, an office he held until his death in March 1997. Unfortunately, this reconciliation did not extend to his widow. When Janet Jagan won a majority of votes for president in December 1997, a large number of demonstrators, claiming she had been elected by fraud, were quelled only by police using tear gas. Racial politics persist.

Assessing Naipaul's endeavor to understand the problems of Caribbean nations caught between a history of subjugation and the prospects of independence, one must consider his own admissions of oversight and distortion, in British Guiana, for example, his inability to foresee that Burnham and Jagan, "these two Marxists between them would actually overturn the society. I saw what I thought I should see, what I was more comfortable seeing. In this way I was like the people of Guyana."[7] His empathy with this colonial people may have produced a bias, but it was essentially a salutary one. Certainly, he did not "go in with preconceived notions,"[8] political or ideological.

Reviewing *The Middle Passage* in *The Nation* (October 26, 1963), Norman Thomas di Giovanni begins with a warning that newspaper accounts of the Caribbean are not to be trusted: "We are not committed to truth and understanding in that part of the world, but have instead chosen Cold War sides." He juxtaposes Naipaul's approach to British

Guiana, which he accepts as "not political," with that of American re-
porters intent on the "U.S.–USSR power struggle" and praises Naipaul's
"incisive summaries of social problems and situations" throughout the
West Indies. Naipaul's mistrust of ideological positions on either front of
the Cold War and his ease in bridging the gap between observer and observed were early indications of his later stance as a mature reporter. He
may have been unable to predict the havoc that Jagan and Burnham
were to create, but he did apprehend the characters of the two leaders;
he did perceive the threat of increasing racial strife, the deep-seated
detriments of colonialism, which could be remedied only by a national
commitment to social and economic reform.

   The Middle Passage, like all of Naipaul's travel narratives, elicited
strong and contradictory reactions. Whereas di Giovanni refers approv-
ingly to Naipaul's representations of the Jagans "at home and out poli-
ticking (they appeared human beings, not monsters)," Bertram B. Johansson, who reviewed the book for the *Christian Science Monitor*
(October 30, 1963), finds Naipaul "quite partial to Marxist-Leninist Premier Cheddi Jagan." Although Johansson remarks on Naipaul's "love for
his native Trinidad," he takes exception to the "extremes" he describes
in his discussion of Jamaica.

   Naipaul's portrayal of Jamaica is indeed harsh, a land that is hardly a
nation at all, where humanity is partitioned into three impermeable sections: tourists, the middle class, and slum dwellers. He emphasizes the divisions between middle-class Jamaicans, who had adopted American materialist values, and the unemployed workers of the sugar estates; between
the races—"black against brown, yellow and white, in that order." He describes "young intellectuals," educated "to enrich a developing stable society," finding no outlet but talk, "frenzied in their frustration," powerless
before the "pressures . . . not simply of race or those of poverty" but of
the island's heritage of slavery and colonial domination, "the under-de-
veloped, over-populated agricultural country." This social and economic
predicament, he says, "required not a leader but a society that understood
itself and had purpose and direction." Acknowledging the dire consequences of past subjection, he suggests that they could be alleviated by accepting responsibility for the making of present history. There can be little doubt that he here extends his conception of self-creation to a society
where racial division, extreme poverty, and inequality of opportunity have
led to a "psychology of survival" that is only self-defeating, to a movement such as the Ras Tafarians, which he describes as "like a mass neurosis." Naipaul's observations are confirmed by Noni Jabavu (*New York*

Times Book Review, October 22, 1963), who describes herself as a "black South African" who lived for a time in Jamaica. She begins with questions for the reader: "Have you visited the West Indies? Do you hope to holiday there sometime?" Seemingly a come-on in a travel brochure, evoking the popular image of the island merely as a tourist attraction, these questions actually introduce her own experience of the "desolation" Naipaul encountered in Jamaica.

Expecting to "feel a sense of community" with its people, "whose political and social freedoms [she] long had envied," she "was disturbed, dismayed to find myself haunted by an inability to enjoy living in this reputedly most beautiful of enchanting islands." Reading *The Middle Passage*, she says, helped her to understand this reaction. Among the Jamaicans she came to know she found "Rootlessness, a historical sense of dereliction, absence of tradition, search for identity." Ironically, coming from a much more oppressive social and political environment, Jabavu was able to perceive the deprivations of West Indians in the light of her own cultural "heritage imbedded in my language, tribal loyalties, stored treasures of legends, events." Her view, like Naipaul's, is at once informed and limited by her personal background, but it seems undeniable that her assent to Naipaul's judgments is rooted in the truth of her own experience.

Over the years much has been made of Naipaul's quotations from nineteenth-century writers in *The Middle Passage*, especially two epigraphs from James Anthony Froude's *The English in the West Indies* (1887) as evidence of Naipaul's so-called racist and imperialist allegiances, somehow related to his psychological problems. Gordon Rohlehr "wonders at Naipaul's hypersensitivity and asks [himself] whether the neurosis is completely controlled by the irony." In his next sentence, which seems to have little relation to the one just quoted, Rohlehr asks, "Is not this complete acquiescence with Froude that there are 'no people there in the true sense of the word,' a formula for evading the complex sympathy which the West Indian experience seems to demand?" [9] To make his dubious point, Rohlehr omits part of the sentence from Froude that concludes Naipaul's epigraph to *The Middle Passage*. Froude's sentence actually says: "There are no people there in the true sense of the word, with a character and purpose of their own." This is not to say that Naipaul agrees with Froude even when he clearly means not that West Indians are without humanity, but without a stable identity and chosen purpose. In fact, a comparison of the complete and truncated sentences reveals more about Rohlehr's method than about Naipaul's views. This would have little significance were it not an instance of repeated evasions of the ambiguity of Naipaul's "complex" reactions, sometimes immoderate but certainly not mere "sympathy" for the condition to which a history of conquest has reduced the West Indies. Among Selwyn Cudjoe's chief objections to *The Middle Passage* is what he sees as the influence of Froude, Anthony Trollope and, more generally, "many English attitudes," which, he believes, determine Naipaul's admiration for "the values of the dominant colonialist-capitalist society."[10] Rob Nixon, convinced of what he calls "Naipaul's Victorian obsession," attempts to demonstrate its role in promoting racist and colonialist prejudices. Like Rohlehr, he cites as evidence the epigraphs from Froude's *The English in the West Indies* that appear in *The Middle Passage*. Since such importance has been placed on these passages, it seems necessary to give them a closer scrutiny than they would seem to deserve.

The first epigraph, which introduces the book as a whole, is unquestionably superficial and obtuse in its assessment of the colonies:

> They were valued only for the wealth which they yielded, and society there has never assumed any particularly noble aspect. There has been splendour and luxurious living, and there have been crimes and horrors, and revolts and massacres. There has been romance, but it has been the romance of pirates and outlaws. The natural graces of life do not show themselves under such conditions. There has been no saint in the West Indies since Las Casas, no hero unless philonegro enthusiasm can make one out of Toussaint. There are no people there in the true sense of the word, with a character and purpose of their own.

The second epigraph, which heads the first chapter of *The Middle Passage*, describes representative imperial types on their way to the West Indies for various purposes, "officers . . . planters, young sportsmen. . . . The elders talked of sugar and of bounties, and of the financial ruin of the islands." Quotation of such imperialist assumptions, according to Nixon, along with others from Anthony Trollope's *The West Indies and the Spanish Main* (1859) and Charles Kingsley's *At Last: A Christmas in the West Indies* (1871), expresses Naipaul's concurrence with their views. "Indeed," he says, "Naipaul is so set on 'confirming' his observations by quoting from this trio that his travelogue becomes shrouded in an atmosphere of colonial atavism."[11] Nixon should know better. He is a trained scholar, surely aware that quotation serves a variety of purposes. Is it not at least possible that Naipaul introduces a book on the rapaciousness and arrogance of the colonizers with the evidence of their own words?

An earlier critic, Peggy Nightingale, whose book on Naipaul Nixon does not mention, perceiving that such quoted passages "may be misunderstood by some readers," points out both their obvious and more subtle implications: "Naipaul's ironic intention in quoting Trollope's lyricism regarding Demerara [in Chapter III] is hard to miss, but in quoting Froude's unflattering statements, Naipaul is not necessarily invoking him as a corroborating witness." She considers this reference in relation to others Naipaul makes, particularly his illustration in *An Area of Darkness* of differences in the use of the word "British" by Jane Austen and E. M. Forster, "showing how a geographical designation has come by degrees, in the writings of a series of intervening authors, to describe an entire way of life." She might have added Naipaul's comment: "Between the two uses of the word lie a hundred years of industrial and imperial power." It is a sense of unearned superiority and arrogance based on such power that the quotations from Froude connote. Can one not speculate that Naipaul was conscious, as was Nightingale, that "Froude's indictment of the West Indies is an indictment of English colonialism whether he was aware of it or not?"[12]

Ignoring the fundamental differences in their attitudes toward British colonialism, Nixon is bent on fitting Naipaul to Froude's procrustean bed. Another example is his reference to two sentences that Naipaul quotes in his chapter on Trinidad on the conflicts between Indians and blacks: "'The two races,' Froude observed in 1887, 'are more absolutely apart than the white and the black. The Asiatic insists the more on his superiority in the fear perhaps that if he did not the white might forget it.'" Nixon omits Naipaul's introductory remarks to this passage, in which he deplores the lasting social effects of colonialism, the identification of both Indians and blacks with the aggressor, whose "values of white imperialism at its most bigoted" they incorporated and used against each other. Instead Nixon quotes only one sentence from Naipaul's extended commentary preceding and following the passage from Froude: "Like monkeys pleading for evolution, each claiming to be whiter than the other, Indians and Negroes appeal to the unacknowledged white audience to see how much they despise one another." Seizing on what he calls the "self-consciously Victorian trope of the evolving monkey," Nixon concludes that "Naipaul blends his voice with Froude's as if the seventy-four years of Caribbean history that lie between *The English in the West Indies* and *The Middle Passage* were irrelevant." He then informs the reader of what anyone who has even skimmed Naipaul's work must surely know: that he is himself a Trinidadian Indian, that in the 1880s, the period when Froude "was penning his anti-Indian poison," Naipaul's grandfather was on his way from Uttar Pradesh to indentured labor in Trinidad. Following what he seems to regard as this revelation, Nixon comments: "Naipaul's remark thus throws into relief a dangerous rift in his attitude toward his own West Indian origin, as Naipaul alias Froude peers down at Naipaul alias evolving monkey."[13]

Naipaul's simile is unquestionably derogatory, bearing connotations that extend far beyond the Victorians, to whom Darwin's influence is hardly restricted. But it must be understood both in its present context and in others where he either uses or quotes references to monkeys as incongruous comparisons, not identifications: *Omne simile est dissimile*. In fact, it is the inherent dissimilarity in the comparison, the very points at which it is inadequate, that contain its greatest emotional force. In this passage it expresses Naipaul's rage at the abominations inflicted on subject people by their imperial conquerors. His tone is immoderate but understandable to readers who empathize with his frustration at perceiving how injustice has turned victim against victim, arresting political development that could lead to unified action to repair the economic and psychological damage done to both blacks and Indians. He is not saying, as Nixon implies, that blacks and Indians (himself included) are "monkeys." His simile dramatizes a particular internalization of the prejudices of the classes that enslaved blacks, exploited Indians, and usurped the resources of their lands, depriving them of their own history and culture.

On another occasion Naipaul's response to the trope—monkeys—further elucidates his assumption that this image is not to be taken as mere identification. In *An Area of Darkness* he describes his reaction to a Sikh's reference to Indians he disapproves of as monkeys. Misled by his own background, Naipaul had taken the remark as Trinidadian "irony," only to realize to his dismay that the man meant it literally. Elsewhere, that irony emerges in Naipaul's use of the monkey simile to depict himself, by no means as an inferior species, as Nixon has suggested, but enjoying an early triumph, the recognition of himself as a writer who has found his true subject, his early life in Trinidad, and now is composing *Miguel Street* in the freelancers' room of the BBC Caribbean Service, sitting in "something like a monkey crouch."[14]

At the risk of belaboring what has begun to seem obvious, I mention one more example of the monkey simile from a passage I have quoted earlier:[15] U. R. Anantha Murthy's description of the Acharya in *Samskara* who, in a state of devastating inner conflict, is compared with "a baby monkey losing hold of his grip on the mother's body as she leaps from branch to branch." Not Darwinian or racist or colonialist, the simile evokes emotional associations broader and more fundamental than any particular context or ideology.

Nixon is so intent on exposing Naipaul's colonialist bias via his improper trope that he seems unaware that the similes in the epigraph he has chosen for his own book from Derek Walcott's "The Unfortunate Traveller" undermine his argument:

> Like lice, like lice, the hungry of this earth
> swarm to the tree of life. If those who starve
> like these rain-flies who shed glazed wings in lights
> grew from sharp shoulder blades their battle vans
> and soared toward that tree, how it would seethe
> —ah, Justice! But fires
> drench them like vermin. . . .

If one wishes to view them through a Darwinian lens, Walcott's lice, vermin, and rain-flies belong to a lower species than Naipaul's monkeys. Needless to say, to do so would reveal only the interpreter's insensitivity to the poet's subject and his language. Regarding Walcott as an ally, Nixon seeks no evidence of impropriety in the tone and diction of outrage. Turning to Naipaul, even when making an innocuous observation, he cannot resist denunciation. He ascribes Naipaul's reluctance to return to Trinidad to fear of "the place where writers, like his father, disappeared into the quicksands of oblivion," a reasonable inference which he then goes on to overinterpret: "This helps account for the fierceness of *The Middle Passage*, which . . . set the tone—wounded, supercilious, and choleric—for much of the nonfiction that would follow."[16]

Naipaul has himself acknowledged his testiness, the pain and anger vented in his nonfiction, but the three adjectives Nixon has chosen, even if occasionally accurate, are clearly inadequate to characterize the various tones or voices that can be heard in the large body of his work. The "tone" Nixon finds so consistent, despite his mild reservation in the word "much," indicates his method of fulfilling his "ambition," as he calls it: "to account for and contest Naipaul's distinctive authority" as a commentator on the Third World "by exploring the rhetorical character and political circumstances of his nonfiction,"[17] a method that evades contradictory evidence in the text.

A fair examination of the tones of *The Middle Passage* entails listening to the humor in Naipaul's description of himself on his arrival in British Guiana: "It was perfectly ridiculous . . . to feel on that first day that I was in a frontier town of the Wild West." Yet even as he associates "the wooden buildings" and "the empty wide streets" with Western films from his childhood, the self-mockery in "I felt I had come to rescue Georgetown" wryly discloses his compassion for the Guianese exploited by the Bookers, "merchants and planters" whose name appeared on "hardware stores, foodshops, machine-tool shops, drugstores, taxis."

Another example of Naipaul's various tones is one of lamentation expressing his despair in Surinam as he recognizes how "many things in these West Indian territories . . . speak of slavery":

> There is slavery in the vegetation. In the sugarcane brought by Columbus on that second voyage when, to Queen Isabella's fury, he proposed the enslavement of the Amerindians. In the breadfruit, cheap slave food, three hundred trees of which were taken to St. Vincent by Captain Bligh in 1793 and sold for a thousand pounds, four years after a similar venture had been frustrated by the Bounty mutiny. . . . There is slavery in the food, in the saltfish still beloved by the islanders. Slavery in the absence of family life, in the laughter in the cinema at films of German concentration camps, in the fondness for terms of racial abuse, in the physical brutality of strong to weak: nowhere in the world are children beaten as savagely as in the West Indies.

As Naipaul analyzes it, the relationship between past history and the striving toward nationhood, which he treats throughout *The Middle Passage*, is most paradoxical in Surinam: "Nationalism in Surinam, feeding on no racial or economic resentments, is the profoundest anti-colonial movement in the West Indies." But even there nationalism, which generally grows out of a shared history, is threatened by Surinam's assimilation of the Dutch language and Dutch culture, which has also served as a source of unity. The vestiges of slavery, the history of slave revolts and escapes of the seventeenth and eighteenth centuries, the mixture of races and customs, the widespread use of the Dutch language and admiration for Dutch culture despite independence since 1955, the counter movement to establish a form of "Negro English"— all these comprise what Wole Soyinka calls the "histories" that determine the struggle for national identity.

The lasting consequences of such histories are emphasized throughout Naipaul's writings. In an article published in 1969 he locates the history of St. Kitts on a "narrow coast road [which] encircles the island," where "Sir Thomas Warner landed in 1623, to found the first British colony in the West Indies." Plantation workers continue to "live beside this road, squeezed between sugar-cane and sea." There also are "two rocks crudely carved by the aboriginal Caribs, whom the English and the French united to exterminate." Also remaining is the square where slaves were auctioned. This is the setting for the conflict between the Premier Robert Bradshaw and the opposition, who "are not allowed to broadcast" and are said to have difficulty getting jobs. Whether or not this is true, Bradshaw's career does sound like "the politics of kingship." When young people reject work on the sugarcane plantations, they place their hopes in tourism, which thus far remain unfulfilled. It is all too clear that "the past crowds the tiny island like the sugar-cane itself."[18]

Mauritius, in 1972 independent for only three years, after a history of colonization successively by the Dutch, the French, and the British, retains the "economy, and the social structure . . . of an agricultural colony" with sugar "the main crop and virtually the sole export." The island, "overpopulated," with few opportunities for employment, is a "lost paradise" to tourists, who leave with "a feeling of peace." "To the Mauritian who cannot leave it is a prison." Naipaul depicts these powerless descendants of slaves and indentured laborers as trapped between the opposing platforms of the government and "the holders of economic power." Inhabitants of "the overcrowded barracoon," surrounded by "the slave crop," they have no means of the escape they long for.[19]

In *The Loss of El Dorado*, Naipaul was particularly concerned with "the subjects of slavery and revolution. More than I knew or felt when I was growing up in Trinidad, slavery had helped to make my world." The book comprises two stories: the first is "the end of the search for El Dorado" and the second, which "occurs two hundred years later," is "the story of the British-sponsored attempt from the newly captured island of Trinidad to set going a revolution of high principles in the Spanish Empire." Both stories tell of plunder of the New World and the enslavement, torture, and murder of its people, the conquistadores for legendary gold, the English for trade. Both involve Port of Spain, where as a boy Naipaul first observed the ways of the city, a place which having "no independent life . . . alters with the people who come to it." *The Loss of El Dorado*, based on archives of the late sixteenth, seventeenth, and eighteenth centuries, is nonetheless the product of Naipaul's personal effort to recover the generally unknown history of the island, and within it something of his own roots as well. What interests Naipaul is "the human story," material appropriate to the method of the "novelist," which he has chosen.

History is recreated largely through the individuals whose roles Naipaul reconstructs from letters and documents they produced or appeared in. The theme that emerges from this material is the disparity between the heroic images history has imposed on the protagonists, or they themselves conceived, and the greed, the lust for fame and power, especially the illusions, the evasions and deceits their ambitions entailed. In 1967, two years before the publication of *The Loss of El Dorado*, reviewing Bjorn Landstrom's *Columbus*, Naipaul, without claiming the title of new historicist or revisionist, without fanfare, wrote a scathing revaluation of the legendary discoverer: "He was looking less for America or Asia than for gold." In fact, "the Indies, the source of his gold, where he thought he had discovered the Terrestrial Paradise, had become, largely through his example, the *anus mundi*." From Columbus's own words, Naipaul educes his egotism, his banality, and always, his greed. This brief commentary serves as an antidote to the "heroic gloss" on Columbus's reputation and the "traditional gloss" of Landstrom's book.[20] It can also be regarded as a prelude to the first story of *The Loss of El Dorado*.

Actually, Naipaul quotes from his review in depicting the search for El Dorado by the Spaniards, Antonio de Berrio, who occupied Trinidad, and Domingo de Vera, who "took formal possession" of the island and of the Indians who were native to it in 1592. Their claims were religion and riches, God and El Dorado. Fearful of competition with the British, Berrio "sent Vera . . . to take possession of the lands on the Orinoco and to look around." When Vera, returning with "seventeen golden eagles and jackals," declared that he had discovered El Dorado, the legend grew. But, in its wake shipwreck and starvation ensued. "The quest for El Dorado," says Naipaul in his review, "became like a recapitulation of the whole New World adventure, a wish to have it all over again." In *The Loss of El Dorado* he demonstrates how Berrio "links the two fantasies." He compares "an aspect of what the El Dorado quest had become," as he had earlier compared Columbus's ventures, to legendary voyages, particularly Robinson Crusoe's. His story "in its essential middle part is a monologue; it is all in the mind." In language differing slightly from that of his review he describes the common fantasy of these adventurers: "to be the first man on the earth, to see the first shoots of the first crop, to let off 'the first gun that had been fired there since the creation of the world.'" Naipaul's repetition of this passage describing a primitive fantasy of survival and conquest indicates the importance he places on it as a continuous psychological offshoot of political and economic exploitation: the grandiose aims that drove the would-be conquerors of the New

World who were ignorant of its geography, its actual resources and dangers, and the lives of its inhabitants. As El Dorado proved to be no more than an illusion, the Indians used it as a defense against their conquerors, and Berrio adopted it as his own when he was himself defeated by Sir Walter Raleigh.

Naipaul's portrait of Raleigh includes the usual headings of courtier, soldier, adventurer, and writer. But the most striking feature of his portrait links Raleigh's contempt for his followers and his victims, and his brutality, with his tendency to escape from the consequences of his actions in fantasies of his own glory. Naipaul emphasizes the vacillations of the courtier and the soldier, the timidity of the adventurer, dreaming of liberating the Indians who never believed in the legendary gold he sought. He praised them not for their bravery and skills but as "the greatest carousers and drunkards of the world." Naipaul thinks of the Tower of London, where Raleigh was twice imprisoned, as "his perfect setting, perhaps subconsciously sought, where, liberated from his inadequacy in the role the age imposed on him, he reached that stillness where the fact of life and action was reconciled with the act of death." These musings are part of "the human story" of Naipaul's narrative, the method of the novelist combined with that of the historian, a measure of dignity afforded to even the most deluded of men in the contemplation of his mortality. But the historian is never absent for long: Raleigh's notes reveal that he was enough a man of his world to turn with hatred against his old friend and comrade in his expeditions, Laurence Keymis. Even as Raleigh awaited execution, he blamed Keymis for his own failures.

The second story Naipaul reconstructs deals with many figures, chief among them Thomas Picton, Francisco Miranda, William Fullarton, and Luisa Calderon, people from divergent backgrounds whose lives were involved in the history of the British effort at the end of the eighteenth century to create a revolution in Venezuela from their base in Trinidad. Picton and Miranda, both active supporters, had very different motives. Picton, a Welshman, "a professional soldier who had fought no battle" when he was appointed governor of Trinidad, was a harsh ruler, supporting torture and execution. He regarded the revolution as his opportunity for military glory. No one could have been more different in character and personality than his ally, Miranda, a Venezuelan, the son of an immigrant from the Canary Islands, a dedicated revolutionary who had traveled and lived in Europe and the United States for many years. Yet in one respect they were alike: each cherished an idealized image of himself which brought him more grief than glory: Picton as a military hero, Miranda as a glamorous revolutionary who embodied the graces of the old world along with the ideals of liberty and equality of the American Revolution.

A typical example of the way in which the two men worked against each other occurred early in the plans for the revolution. Miranda, stationed in London, unable to obtain a passport, sent his agent Caro, a Cuban exile, to Trinidad, where Picton accused him of being a Spanish spy and, lacking a ship in which to expel him, kept him in virtual isolation. It is Caro's complaining letters to Miranda, Naipaul says, that reveal how ineffective were the Venezuelan revolutionaries in Trinidad in their commitment to independence. The following passage, which Naipaul quotes from one of Caro's letters, deals with the distance between their goal and their will to effect its fulfillment:

> The Venezuelans have no concentrated plan. . . . They do not work with foresight. They are better prepared to change their masters than to become free. They believe that it is the same to acclaim independence as to be independent, and that independence will be accomplished simply by rejecting the yoke of Spain and placing themselves under the protection of some other nation.

Although these shortcomings do not fully explain the failure of the revolution, they do account for a basic weakness in its organization and in the future prospects of movements for independence in the region. Self-delusion was by no means restricted to the Venezuelans. Picton, who read Caro's letters, forwarded them to the "Under-Secretary of War in London as proof of Miranda's untrustworthiness." Caro was himself both victim of and contributor to the failure of the revolution. Finally, like several others, he played both sides.

Naipaul's summaries of and quotations from his sources are surely evidence that the careers of Miranda and Picton exemplify the self-destructive illusions of those serving British aims in plotting the revolution. Along the way their Venezuelan allies were tortured, imprisoned, and poisoned by the Spanish, as were the slaves, free Negroes, and mulattos suspected by the British of treachery and theft. One of these was Luisa Calderon, a free mulatto, falsely accused of theft, imprisoned and tortured until she confessed to a crime she had not committed. The injustice to the young woman was disregarded until after the failure of the first revolution. When Picton's view of Trinidad as a slave colony (he had himself become a slave owner) conflicted with British intentions to establish Trinidad as "a colony of free settlers, . . . the centre of British trade with South America," complaints regarding his brutality were taken seriously, and the British ordered that his powers be limited.

Picton was demoted to Second Commissioner and in 1803 Colonel William Fullarton was dispatched from London to assume the position of First Commissioner. Once again Naipaul portrays a man whose conduct often belied his stated aims to provide "justice and protection." Fullarton was easily swayed. When his objections to unlawful imprisonment and physical punishment were protested, he modified his position, allowing prisoners to be "chained and whipped" but, what seems an incredible contradiction, "not to be punished too severely."

Increasingly Fullarton and Picton were at odds. Their animosity reached such proportions that Fullarton, determined to be rid of Picton, sent thirty-seven charges against him to the Privy Council in London, chief among them the torture of Luisa Calderon. Despite efforts at reconciliation, Fullarton persisted, and Picton was arrested, tried, and convicted. Luisa Calderon, the chief witness, was brought to England, the torture scars on her wrists exhibited not as evidence of the injustices she had endured but as means of discrediting Picton. After she had served this function for five years of trial and retrial, after Picton was finally acquitted, she returned to Trinidad, her future unrecorded. Naipaul regards Picton's trial as actually having little to do with Luisa Calderon. Picton, he says, "was being tried for being governor of a slave colony. . . . He was the victim of people's conscience, or ideas of humanity and reason that were ahead of the reality." Picton's heroic ideal, centered entirely on himself, was finally realized when he fought and died at Waterloo.

In the end Miranda did not have even this satisfaction. A second failed invasion in Venezuela, which he had led, ended in his humiliation and betrayal. Imprisoned in Puerto Rico, when he learned that he was to be transferred to a prison in Cadiz, he responded, "Thank God." He remained there for two and a half years until his death in 1816. "Prison," says Naipaul, "was perhaps the setting that Miranda, like Raleigh, subconsciously required. It dramatized inaction, failure and the condition of exile." The similarity of the language he uses in imagining the end of the lives of Columbus and Miranda—the prison "setting," the word "perhaps," and "subconsciously sought" in the first passage, "subconsciously required" in the second—points up one characteristic shared by two very different men: forced into solitude and "inaction," they turned from the grandiose fantasy on which their careers were based to what Yeats called "the desolation of reality."

The slaves also suffered the consequences of their grandiose fantasies. Naipaul writes of the "underground life of fantasy linking creole Negroes and new Negroes, French Negroes and English Negroes" who, after days of subjection and hard labor, at night would secretly take on the roles of kings and courtiers. Dressed in discarded finery, they gathered to mimic the power of those at the summit of the chain of being. But latent in their mimicry was mockery of their oppressors: "The moment would occur when secrecy became its own assurance, when fantasy submerged and ridiculed the world of labour and property." Small episodes of "impudence" and songs of protest were noticed. It was not long before the nightly gatherings with their threat of defiance and plans for an uprising were uncovered, and many of the participants were tortured and murdered.

Naipaul refers to the anonymity of the slaves whose personal roles in their history are accessible only to the imagination. One exception, Jacquet, the "head-man" of a sugar estate who turned poisoner, has an individual story that can be interpreted as the violent outbreak of long-repressed resentment. Yet his motivations can only be imagined, as can those of the slaves who participated in the secret nightly pomp, their only access to a measure of dignity. Though the archives that Naipaul studied and quoted tell us much more about Picton, Fullarton, and their associates, the inner lives of these men who participated in revolution as pawns of empire remain hidden. Nor can we fathom what Luisa Calderon endured and learned in prison and in her five years in England. Only Miranda emerges as a man whose ambition and ideals, even his frustrations, reflect his vision of himself as a humanist and revolutionary. Disillusioned, imprisoned, no longer believing in the support of the British or any other power, he seems to have clung to this self-image, which even failure could not invalidate. But this is an unfinished portrait, to be altered in Naipaul's reevaluation of Miranda twenty-four years later in *A Way in the World*.

His research for *The Loss of El Dorado* evoked late eighteenth-century Trinidad. In the street of Port of Spain where he had spent much of his childhood and that later became the setting of *Miguel Street*, he could now feel the presence of the homes, "the street life," the languages of the people, no longer obliterated in its "long nineteenth-century colonial torpor."[21] But this was by no means the end of his concern with the history of Trinidad and his need to locate himself further in the consequences of its occupation by conquistadores, revolutionaries, and colonizers. The title of his most recent work on Trinidad, *A Way in the World*, places the writer within that framework, uniting history, autobiography, and fiction, each genre commenting on the others.

In the chapter on autobiography I discussed Naipaul's growing knowledge and embrace of the history of his two nationalities, Trinidadian and Indian, as fundamental to his development as a writer. His observations in *A Way in the World* of continuous transformations in Trinidad integrate past and present history, such as changes in its populations and place names. Yet, he points out, the skills of the extinct aboriginal Indians were "passed to their successors," among them Asian Indians, his own people. "I had arrived," he says, "at a way of looking that contained both the fabulous past and the smaller scale of what I had grown up with." *A Way in the World* is also a return to the lives of men who were products of and participants in historical events that reached beyond any one individual life. As in *The Loss of El Dorado*, along with the central historical figures—Raleigh, Keynis, Miranda, Hislop, and Picton—are references to slaves, tortured, mutilated, and hanged, and as many "new Negroes" as possible imported from Africa when traders learned that slave trading was soon to be outlawed. Once again, the contrast between the toil of daytime and the fantasy nightlife of the slaves is described, here from the point of view of General Hislop, the governor of Trinidad, who "hates the island and the people."

Following the publication of *A Way in the World*, Naipaul remarked in an interview that history is "an interplay of various peoples, and it's gone on forever. I can think of no culture that's been left to itself."[22] In *The Loss of El Dorado* he had quoted extensively from archives in depicting the interactions of historical figures from various cultures. *A Way in the World*, like an epic inspired by Mnemosyne, records the remembrances of its author and his protagonists, some from tales told before by him and by his predecessors, the invaders and the vanquished. Using dramatic narrative and imagined dialogues, he recreates history as internalized by those who enacted it and those who inherited its ongoing effects.

In *A Way in the World,* Raleigh is depicted as a sick old man on his last fruitless voyage to the New World in 1617 aboard a ship, the *Destiny*, during long interviews by his surgeon about his continuous obsession with El Dorado. The "land, which in his mind and writings existed as a kind of Arcadia," is now hostile territory, where he is not even permitted to disembark. He has staked his survival on his claim to knowledge of the location of the gold of Guiana and his promise to mine it, counterfeit pledges that ignore his earlier history of failure. Raleigh's version of that history, quoted and challenged by his surgeon, is, of course, Naipaul's own way of reading and appraising the historical records. But these dialogues are also a commentary on the relationship between two men with opposing motives: the one to weave his memories into epic tales, the other to question their intent. When the surgeon arrives to give him his dose of medicine, Raleigh speaks of the pleasures of his voyage in 1595, of balsam and oysters and cassava, remembrances that would deny his present unwelcome return. The surgeon insists on his own view of both the past and the present: Raleigh's grandiose claim that he "could be king of the Indies," which lured men to sickness and death. But it is in the surgeon's detailed critique of Raleigh's book, *The Discovery of the Large, Rich, and Beautiful Empire of Guiana,* that the writer's evasions and distortions are most convincingly exposed, revealing what he intended to hide. No doubt one hears Naipaul's voice in the surgeon's analyses of Raleigh's distortions, as one does in the speech of several of the other historical figures, but this seems less the stylistic awkwardness detected by Stephen Schiff[23] than Naipaul's deliberate attempt to participate in the history that made his world, joining his voice with those who discover the truth beneath the legends, some, like the surgeon, exposing Raleigh's deceptions, and others finally revealing their own.

The surgeon finds Raleigh's book "slippery," alternating between clarity and an obscurity that causes the reader to feel he has "not been paying attention." He soon realizes, however, that it is not the reader's carelessness but the writer's intention that creates these inconsistencies. In fact, the reader must focus on the very passages in which "the writing has changed," for these are "where the writer decides to add or to hide things." What Raleigh hid was his awareness that El Dorado did not exist, a truth that emerges in the disparity between the two parts of the book: his descriptions of "the eastern side, the Trinidad side," are specific and accurate, but those of "the main Orinoco," the way to El Dorado, are pure fantasy. The surgeon's emphasis is on the contrast between Raleigh's actual role in the continuity "of blood and revenge" in the Gulf and his depiction of the region as "an untouched paradise on the rivers."

He wants to understand how Raleigh "arrived at that book, at that version of your adventures." The answer he comes up with is Raleigh's need to counteract the mockery he met when he returned to England not with gold but with sand, to show that he was not "a fool," that he had discovered "a new empire for England." This explanation is credible, but Naipaul in the surgeon's persona has suggested a more complex one as well. The two styles of the book disclose Raleigh's ambition to take his place among the Renaissance explorers and adventurers, Sir John Hawkins and his kinsman, Sir Francis Drake, but he could not match their accomplishments. Thus he fantasized his own discovery, a land to be conquered and exploited without risk of failure, a denial of all those sacrificed to his ambition: his own followers ravaged by disease and starvation; two English boys left in the forest in exchange for the son of an Indian chief to serve as evidence, on Raleigh's return, that his voyage was authentic; the Spaniards killed in Port of Spain, whose deaths were avenged fourteen years later when their compatriots retaliated by cutting the throats of thirty-six English traders.

A year after Raleigh's interview with the surgeon, in New Granada, the Indian Don José, who had been the servant of the Spanish governor, Don Palomeque, gave his version of Raleigh's voyage of 1617 to the priest Fray Simón for his history of the Spanish New World. Naipaul had referred briefly to both these men in *The Loss of El Dorado*, and had quoted a bitter comment on the death of Raleigh's son from Simón's history. In Don José's narrative and the priest's responses in *A Way in the World* we hear the voices of the two historians, but there is also a third, that of the author who sets the scene and creates a portrait of Don José, whose resilience and integrity helped him to survive the cruelty and humiliations of conquest. His account, from the point of view of the vanquished, tells of his relationships with men from different cultures and classes who could never overcome such barriers. Only the victims could at times reach out to one another, and even to their conquerors in defeat, grief, and impending death.

Recounting his memories of the expedition led by Keymis against the Spanish town of San Thomé, Don José tells of having claimed half-Spanish lineage to English soldiers only to be saved from hanging by the interference of Negroes who insisted he was entirely Indian. He laments the cruelty of the English, grieves even for the dead Spanish governor, whom he hated, but also for the English commander, who was ill-equipped for leadership, whose men were hungry and sick. He tells of desertions and deaths, the weeping of women, bodies left unattended, "like a weight on the earth, a weight on the soul."

Sent by Keymis to deliver the "parcel of papers, a roll of tobacco, and a tortoise," for which the chapter is named, Don José was also the bearer of a letter informing Raleigh of the death of his son in the expedition led by Keymis against San Thomé the year before. Almost immediately Don José's fear of Raleigh was replaced by trust. He remained on the *Destiny* with Raleigh and returned with him to England where he stayed until after witnessing his execution. Raleigh was drawn to Don José perhaps, as Fray Simón speculates, because the young man bore "some resemblance" to the son he mourned, or was "among the last people to see" him. As Don José turns from Raleigh to his own fate ("I was full of my own grief," he says), it seems that it is grief as much as anything else that drew them together, a sense that they were doomed to extinction. He tells Fray Simón that from the time he left his home in New Granada and accompanied the Berrios to Guiana he felt he had lost his bearings, that he was doomed. Having nothing else "to hold on to," he accepted "doom" itself, which he imagined as merging with the sea and the sky beyond the various trials he encountered among human beings. Paradoxically, this was a means of enduring the historical conditions he faced without retreating into heroic fantasy or extricating himself at the expense of others.

When Fray Simón questions him about Raleigh's initial response to him, Don José can only respond, " I just felt the old man's eyes falling on my face, and I felt at ease with him." Fray Simón becomes impatient: "I was hoping to get something else from you, I must confess. My feeling now is that as an historian I should deal as simply as possible with the moment of news. I should present only the facts." Naipaul's rejoinder to this limited view of history lies in Don José's return to his narration of the suffering and compassion on all sides, which illuminate the moments of news Fray Simón seeks.

Don José reveals contradictions inherent in his relationships with the invaders of his homeland through what would seem to be unimportant details, for example, the relief he felt in removing the clothes of the Spanish governor which he had worn, oversized and bloodstained though they were, and donning the new clothes Raleigh gave him when he took up his role as "the general's personal servant." In this role he pitied Raleigh who was sick, unable to eat, grieving for his son, yet still the "general," issuing orders, acting out the fantasy that he might succeed, while everyone else aboard the *Destiny* humored him even as they knew he was doomed to execution.

When Don José accompanied Raleigh to England, the servant's ambiguous identification with the man he continued to honor as the "general" was manifested in his feeling that "the world had become like that picture in my head." Once again, he experienced the sense of doom he had felt at leaving familiar surroundings; he was "now in a world changed forever, for me and for everybody else." His own identity was submerged in the compassion he felt for Raleigh, one of the invaders responsible for the loss of his own land, its sky and sea, its familial and social history. In England, in Raleigh's home, he was so unhappy, he says, "I wanted to die." Repeatedly he refers to Raleigh's "doom." When, at Raleigh's request, he witnessed his execution, he was so upset, he says, "I turned my face to the wall and looked at the sky in it," the picture of doom he had created. He could have remained in England, in the home of a nobleman, but his "grief was too great," grief, paradoxically, for the invaders of his land whom he had known, Spanish and English: the Berrios and Don Palmita, Keymis, and Raleigh, "moving on in a chain of death from one man to his enemy." His own salvation, he felt, lay in returning to "the first world I knew," a way of reclaiming his identity long submerged in the service of those who had neither his courage nor his integrity.

Naipaul's version of Don José's narration is a realistic portrait of a survivor of colonial oppression, and particularly of the psychic cost to the subjugated generally unrecorded in history. In his return to Francisco Miranda, whose career as delineated in *The Loss of El Dorado* was based entirely on archives, his method is very different. The section on Miranda, "In the Gulf of Desolation," is the product of "imaginative truth." "For twenty-five years," Naipaul says, "I've wanted to portray the slave society . . . the parent of the one I grew up in. I did it here indirectly." Returning to Trinidad after thirty-five years, Miranda at first does not "see Negroes." He hears their language, and looks out the window at "Africans working," but later he "again doesn't see."[24] His assumption that African slaves were necessary to the plantations along with his inability to "see" them as individual human beings was among the moral and political limitations that led to his downfall. Looking without seeing, a form of moral blindness, is a continuous theme of Naipaul's work. Here it is part of his creation of a "historical myth" for Miranda who, he believes, warrants but lacks a place in the history of the West Indies and South America equal to that of Columbus and Raleigh. As Naipaul tells this historical myth he examines its nature—its protagonist's ambition, his striving for power and lasting fame, his compromises, and the tragic consequences of his tarnished idealism. It is an archetypal story of pride and ruin: Miranda's myth is linked to those of Columbus and Raleigh by "madness and self-deception—followed by surrender."

Miranda, says Naipaul, is not a known figure because "he achieved little and because the South American revolution doesn't have the universal appeal of the three great revolutions—the American, the French, and the Haitian—that came earlier." Also, when Miranda was betrayed by those who had chosen him to head the Venezuelan revolution, the papers he had kept so carefully out of "a sense of history and personal destiny" were lost and not recovered for more than a century. On first reading these papers and in them the lost history of the Caribbean, the background of his childhood and youthful memories, Naipaul felt that Miranda was not only the "precursor, the man before Bolívar," for Venezuelans, but a precursor of himself "as a very early colonial." Now he realizes that, "carried away by a private idea of ancestry," he "overlooked too much that was obvious." If Miranda's "political cause cannot be denied," he himself was "something of a confidence man."

This is the theme of Naipaul's long account of Miranda's career from the time he left Venezuela to take up the commission of captain in the Spanish army that his father had bought him. Even at this early age—he was then twenty-one—Miranda displayed the arrogance, the susceptibility to affront, that were to characterize him throughout his life. He was cruel to subordinates; he engaged in dubious schemes. He "begins to steal the regiment's funds, a practice . . . not unusual among officers who have bought their commissions," but only the prelude to more serious crimes. He conspired with the governor of Cuba to deliver two ships loaded with contraband—slaves and British china and linen—for which he was arrested. Before the king of Spain's sentence was announced, Miranda had fled to the United States where, armed with a letter from the governor of Cuba, he met "distinguished people" and became known as a supporter of the South American revolution. By now he had established a pattern that he was to follow for the rest of his life: he had become a prototype of the tainted idealist, self-serving in the name of a worthy cause.

Traveling throughout Europe, he ingratiated himself with the powerful; he amassed titles and valuable possessions. Catherine the Great "makes him a colonel in the Russian service." In France he was a general in the Revolutionary forces, only to be arrested and tried after a military defeat. Although his first invasion of Venezuela failed, he returned to Trinidad in 1806 in a second disastrous attempt. Naipaul's portrait of Miranda during his last years in Trinidad and Venezuela is of a man determined to claim his place in history as a revolutionary leader at any cost to himself and others.

Don José and Miranda were both self-made men, Don José by necessity, Miranda by choice. No doubt that is their attraction to Naipaul. Don José returned to New Granada no longer a provincial, in Fray Simón's words, "a well-travelled man," who had been to England and

had "seen some of its great cities and buildings," to Spain—Toledo, Sala-
manca, and Seville—and had "met important men." He had earned his
identity as "Don José in name and deed." But his experience had en-
compassed far more than travel and sightseeing. He had witnessed and
participated in historical events that were to become legendary. He deplored the harshness and arrogance of those he served, yet he could not
deny them compassion in their downfall.

Miranda's self-creation was more deliberate. In a dialogue with General Hislop in Trinidad, he says that at twenty-one, embarking to claim
the coat of arms his father had bought for him, he "knew precisely who
I was, and was proud of my father, and very proud of our money," but
also "that I was another kind of person, and that I was travelling to Spain
to claim my rightful inheritance, of which the coat of arms was a part."

He was never to resolve the contradictions of these two views of
himself. Born in Caracas, the son of a wealthy linen merchant, he was
"neither a proper Spaniard from Spain nor someone accepted by the creole Spanish aristocracy." All the titles and honors he managed to acquire,
the culture he sought in his travels and readings, could not assure him of
the authenticity of rank and leadership he gained through machinations
and fraud. Naipaul's portrait reveals the unbridled egotism inherent in
Miranda's heroic self-image, in his constant striving to renew himself, to
compensate for each failure with new adventures, new risks.

Having joined Bolivar's revolution in 1810 and enjoyed an early triumph, he was soon deserted by former colleagues and followers. Imprisoned in Puerto Rico, he was visited by the Venezuelan Level de
Goda whose memories, written many years later, were to record Miranda's final insights into his ambitions and failures. Level's sympathy
elicited Miranda's confession that his grandiose fantasies, his literary
models of revolution and democracy, were the basis for all his action:
"Most of my ideas about liberty," he says, "came to me from conversation and reading when I was abroad." His models—Plato's republic,
Thomas Paine, Rousseau—were personal ideals, which he hoped to im-
pose on Venezuela, the "country I created in my mind"; "my revolution
was a personal enterprise," which, as Level reminds him, "left out two of
the colors. You left out the black and you left out the mulatto." Miranda's
excuse that "[t]here were no Negroes in Tom Paine or Rousseau," that
these people were "accidental to the truth I was getting at," suggests that
at best he is being disingenuous.

Deserted by his former allies, as "Everybody focussed his resentment or fear or hate on me—republican, royalist, all the four colors," Mi-

randa could expect only imprisonment for the remainder of his life. Yet the recognition that self-aggrandizement was the root of his revolutionary zeal was "a kind of release," he says. Had he admitted earlier that he was ignorant of the people he aimed to free, that the revolution he imagined could not be won, he could never have faced the harsh reality of his own motives, his own character. At this point it is hard to resist identifying Miranda, as he no doubt identified himself, with a tragic protagonist in his final *anagnorisis*, gaining a measure of "release" through this insight. But weighed against the cruelty, destruction, and death wrought by his misguided exploits, this self-discovery—Miranda's sole achievement—seems to be his final effort to assure himself a role in history through the only channel still open to him.

Naipaul's account of Miranda's career as material for a historical myth comparable to those of Columbus and Raleigh is also an exposure of the process of mythmaking. Interpreting the records of the "fabulous and original" pursuits of these three men, he demonstrates how they adapted to their individual purposes the imperial values and goals of their eras, in order to create exalted images of themselves based on earlier explorers and literary heroes. Faced with failure or, in Miranda's case, confessing moral blindness and arrogance, they still did not renounce this mythical role, which became part of the history Naipaul investigated in order to apprehend the background of the self that he too, as explorer and adventurer in a different world and with very different aims, was continually creating.

FANTASIES, LIES, AND "POLITICAL MYTHS"

Fantasy, in Naipaul's view, was also a dominant modus operandi of despots, political leaders, and their followers from the Spanish conquest until the eradication of Peronism in the early 1990s. In four articles covering the years from 1972 to 1991, he traces the role of myths and lies in sustaining the heritage of that conquest—"greed and . . . cruelty, the ideas of blood and revenge, money and the enemy"[25]—in Argentina's recent history. Fortifying this hold was the destruction of the pampas Indians in the late 1870s and the seizure of their land. "Vast estancias on the stolen, bloody land: a sudden and jealous colonial aristocracy."[26] Along with this genocide the Argentines eradicated the authentic traditions of the land, and neither they nor the "immigrants, mainly from northern Spain and southern Italy" who came to work on the *estancias*, could create a genuine society of their own.

Culturally and economically undeveloped, when the British Empire withdrew and efforts "to industrialize, to become balanced and autonomous" failed, Argentina had nothing to rely on, not even "its most precious myth, the myth of wealth." This history of unlawful seizure of the land and the murder of those to whom it belonged, of immigrant workers with no attachment to the past of the country or to its land, of the failure of leaders to meet the challenge of independence and industrialization—this is the background Naipaul sketches for the rise of the Peronist cult. His essay "The Return of Eva Perón" reviews the conditions—historical, economic, cultural, and psychological—that can impel a populace to accept, even, to their sorrow, to welcome, dictatorship.

In 1972, seventeen years after Perón was ousted from his first presidency, after his imprisonment and exile, Peronismo remained a potent force in Argentine politics, and Perón himself was to be elected once more by a large majority in September of the next year. Inflation, poverty in a vast country rich in natural resources, riots, guerrilla attacks, and the murder of an industrialist and an army general, himself known as a "torturer"—these would seem reason enough for people to replace the military rulers. But why choose a dictator who in the past "had filled the jails and emptied the treasury"?

One explanation Naipaul offers is that, lacking ties to a common history and traditions, having no attachment to the land or to their fellow countrymen, Argentines sought mystical experience to fill their need for commitment, "the new enthusiastic cult of espiritismo, a purely native affair of mediums and mass trances and miraculous cures, which claims the patronage of Jesus Christ and Mahatma Gandhi." Closer to home were two major figures who reinforced such mystical solutions: José López Rega, Perón's "companion and private secretary through all the years of exile," who was "known to be interested in astrology and espiritismo" and Eva Perón who, dead since 1952, had become a "saint."

Rega's aim was to induce a feeling for the land through a mystical alliance with ancestral "blood," that of the Indians whose actual history had been obliterated and whose presence was now resurrected in the "Argentine racial mixture . . . enriched by Indian blood." Naipaul sees "unconscious irony" in this claim, but it seems more likely that it was a deliberate, cynical transformation of murder and greed into a retroactive ritual sacrifice to enrich what Naipaul calls "the blighted land."

The role Eva Perón had cast herself in during Perón's first presidency enacted other fantasies: as the dispenser of "power, justice, and revenge," at least in her pronouncements, she was the foe of the rich, the protector of the poor. Her early death, her embalmed body, only en-hanced her self-created legend, which had already been resurrected by the time Perón returned. In 1972 Naipaul could find little factual infor-mation about Eva Perón either in her ghosted autobiography or in re-ports of people who had known her: "Memories have been edited; peo-ple deal in panegyric or hate, and the people who hate refuse to talk about her." She is perhaps the best-known example of how "the truth begins to disappear; it is not relevant to the legend." It is difficult to ex-plain how a great number of people could place their faith in so tawdry a symbol, but Naipaul's suggestion that Eva Perón is part of the *espiritismo* that substitutes for authentic Argentine history does offer a clue. It seems that, lacking the continuity of a communal past, the security of "reliable institutions" or "secular assurances," her followers, in identifying with her, could deny the fragmentation of their own lives and could believe, during each mass they attended in her honor or in each visit to the vault where her sarcophagus is placed, that they too could achieve the in-tegrity they projected on this most compelling of Peronist fabrications.

Naipaul often seeks the effects of a country's past and contempo-rary history on individual lives in the works of its writers. In *The Return of Eva Perón*, his interpretation of Borges's poetry and his conversations with him and with his translator, Norman Thomas di Giovanni, suggest that Borges's image of Argentina, with its particular ambiguities, is both a denial and an oblique protest against the rule of torture and terror. "Like many Argentines," says Naipaul, Borges "has an idea of Argentina; anything that doesn't fit into this is to be rejected." This idea seems to be based on his status as a "criollo, someone who came to Argentina be-fore the great immigrant rush, before the country became what it is; and for the contemplation of his country's history Borges substitutes ances-tor worship." In conversations with Naipaul he seems to divide his con-ception of history into a heroic past and a debased present: Perón, for ex-ample, "represented the scum of the earth," yet Borges feels obliged "to admit he is an Argentine—an Argentine of today." The history Borges acknowledges in his poetry consists of "his military ancestors, their deaths in battle, . . . and old Buenos Aires." Even in his detective fiction, "gangsters are given epic stature."

All the themes he has developed throughout his life, Borges con-fided to Naipaul, are "contained in his very first book of poems, pub-lished in 1923." A passage Naipaul quotes indicates that in this book, *Fer-vour of Buenos Aires*, Borges intended to celebrate the new city by identifying it with an idealized antiquity: "Akin to the Romans, who would murmur the words '*numen inest*' on passing through a wood, 'Here dwells a god,' my verses declare, stating the wonder of the streets. . . . Everyday places become, little by little, holy." Not only places but events are transfigured in his poems. Starting with what Naipaul calls the "petty battles and wasteful deaths" of his military ancestors, he has created an epic world based on the ancient heroic code by which a man achieves immortality through death in battle and passes on this glory to his descendants. Claiming this heroic past for himself is Borges's version of patriotism.

It would seem that Borges, at the opposite social and cultural pole from those who worship Eva Perón has, like them, fallen prey to fantasy and mythmaking. But there is a difference: Borges was all too aware of the dangers of Peronismo. "Now the country is in a bad way," he said in 1972. "We are being threatened by the return of the horrible man." Naipaul points out that "This is how Borges speaks of Perón: he prefers not to use the name." What's more, both Borges and his ninety-five-year-old mother had been personally threatened. Yet he cannot acknowledge that, if Argentina was then "in a bad way," it was never a land of godly presences and gallant warriors seeking deathless fame, that this anachronistic ideal has no basis in actual truth. It is a means of retreating from reality—"horrible" leaders, their pusillanimous followers, the absence of common values, the terrors of everyday life. Somewhere, if only in a literary tradition existing from ancient times into his own present, the poet insists, there was a conception of heroes committed to a cause for which they were willing to sacrifice their lives. This credo is Borges's personal and aesthetic defense against what he regards as his country's loss of the honor it once possessed. But this defense could not protect even Borges. A "recurring theme of his later stories," says Naipaul, "is of cultural degeneracy," and this disillusionment is conveyed in his poetry as well.

Naipaul, of course, would disagree with Borges's claim that Argentina was once "an honorable country," as indeed would anyone familiar with its actual history of civil war, military coups, dictatorship, conquest, and cruelty. "The land is full of military names," Naipaul says, "the names of generals who took the land away from the Indians and, with a rapacity that still outrages the imagination, awarded themselves great portions of the earth's surface, estates, estancias, as large as counties." Regarding this plunder as part of the "great imperialist push" of the time, he compares President Roca "systematically exterminating the Indians" with the Belgian conquest of the Congo, and evokes Conrad's voice from *Heart of Darkness* to further express his own rage at these crimes of his-

tory. "Their talk was the talk of sordid buccaneers: it was reckless without hardihood, greedy without audacity, and cruel without courage;
there was not an atom of foresight or of serious intention in the whole
batch of them, and they did not seem aware these things are wanted for
the work of the world." Naipaul sees this "frenzy" of the Belgian impe-
rialists as similar to the "frenzy" of the Argentines; Conrad's words "contain the mood and the moral nullity of that Argentine enterprise which
have worked down through the generations to the failure of today." He
turns to *Heart of Darkness* again in "The End of Peronism?" quoting a bit
more of the same passage, suggesting that Conrad's description of the
Belgians' greed, their obliviousness to the suffering around them, conveys
the iniquity of the Argentine theft of the Indians' land.

The section entitled "The Terror," dated March 1977, delineates the
extreme cruelty that a history of denial and falsification has bred: the
"killer cars," torture, an "Argentine institution," and the constant seizure
of those who came to be known as "the disappeared." The war that
began "between the guerrillas on one side and the army and the police
on the other," Naipaul says, is now "a war [that] touches everybody." It
seems inevitable, from his account, that the ruthlessness of the military
junta, which assumed power in 1976, would emerge from the lawless-
ness that had long pervaded Argentina, and was tolerated by various political factions, on the left and the right, and by the rich who believed
themselves safe from its threat. Now no one was safe. The "shocked and
damaged people" of Buenos Aires, "can see no cause in Argentina and
can acknowledge at last the barbarism by which they have for long been
surrounded, the barbarism they had previously been content to balance
against the knowledge of their own security," their material wealth and
dependence on "the goods and fashions of Europe." They had no concept of nationhood, no tradition of law, no knowledge of history to
awaken them to the horrors of Peronism and its offshoots. Only when
they themselves were threatened did they admit that anarchy and sadism
had infected their land.

In the first of two articles Naipaul wrote fourteen years after the
visit that produced "Argentine Terror: A Memoir" ("The Terror" in *The
Return of Eva Perón*), he returns to the "'dirty war' against the guerrillas"[27] of 1977. Beginning with his first-hand experience of that war, he
tries to fathom the nature of the guerrillas, their various motives, and
their relation to the "old Argentine idea of revolution." Suspected of
being a guerrilla, he was removed by two policemen from a bus headed
for the town of Jujay and taken to a shed where a third policeman stood

near a table on which Naipaul could see "close to his hand, the black-and-gray metal of a machine gun lying flat." As if this was not menacing enough, he was then taken to a "police post or sub post." After fruitless questioning and many efforts by the police to phone sources unknown to Naipaul, he was finally saved by his pipe, "a small black Tanganyika meerschaum," which convinced the police that he was truly a foreigner. In two short sentences Naipaul recreates his sense of impending violence and the psychic defenses he summoned: "My idea of time changed. I learned to wait."

Naipaul wrote "Argentine Terror: A Memoir" soon after he left the country but, dissatisfied with the article, he put it aside only to find it "fair enough" two years later. This "confusion," it seems, had to do with his feelings of "how close" he had come "to the dirtiness of the dirty war," with the episode itself as an example of the terror, and at the same time with his "writer's instinct [which] had wanted me to keep the emotion of that day to myself, and not to expose it indirectly in an article." He was to use it, he says, in "a long imaginative work set in Central Africa," obviously *A Bend in the River*. Only after he had completed this novel did actual memories of Jujay return.

Attempting to broaden his comprehension of the terror of the 1970s in "Argentina: Living with Cruelty," Naipaul recalls other experiences and conversations of his earlier sojourns, probing the social forces and personal impulses that led people of divergent backgrounds and beliefs to become guerrillas. They included "people of the left," old-time Peronists, those who "wanted Peronism—a mixture of nationalism and socialism and anti-Americanism—without Perón, . . . simple gangsters," and "educated, secure, middle-class people." Naipaul's informants spoke of various motives for joining the guerrillas: "mimicry" of the American and French students of the 1960s, "the old Argentine idea of revolution" as renewal, "high political principles" that ended in "the blood feud." Naipaul himself neither rejects nor unreservedly accepts such explanations.

In extended interviews in 1991 he continues to seek the origins of the guerrilla movement and the motivations of its members. He finds few answers that are entirely satisfactory, although most confirm his view that denial of Argentina's cruel and violent past, the fantasies substituted by its political leaders and absorbed by its populace, the sentimental slogans that disguise suspicion and hatred created a society based on enmity, internal and external. "Argentina made people dream too much," says Ricardo, one of Naipaul's informants. "When the dreams fell apart the response was anger and looking for the guilty." Ricardo's explanation of his own role as a guerrilla suggests the complexity of the movement itself. Obviously an intelligent, articulate man, he reveals the doubts he had even as he remained loyal to the movement; for example, his support of the Montonero guerrillas' opposition to the army and his objection to their resolve to restore Perón to power. Having responded to Naipaul's question, "What did the guerrillas want?" with a twenty-year-old formula: "To destroy the army," he soon goes on to explain the ambiguity of this opposition. Many of the guerrillas and members of the army, he says, "were grandchildren of immigrants. There were many family links between the two sides, because it was basically a fight within a social segment of society." Neither "big landowners," nor "working class," these immigrants, not unlike many in the United States and other Western countries, one cannot help thinking, "expected a certain social development based on education," but "they were beginning to feel that for various reasons the doors were closing." Products of a despotic government and a failing economy, each blamed the other for the failure of their dreams.

Other informants had different explanations for their allegiance to the guerrillas. One man spoke of the convergence of Catholicism and the leftist "idea of the New Man, the idea of the revolutionary as an identity, the revolutionary confronting injustices" and the "self-esteem" that resulted "from doing the right thing." Yet this high-sounding account ends with an apparent retraction: "What resulted was sometimes a perversion." Both his bravado and his last sad commentary on his own words confirm Ricardo's belief that he "was presenting himself to [Naipaul] as a defeated man, part of a defeated generation." In the reminiscences of former revolutionaries that Naipaul records this is the dominant tone.

In 1991, eight years after democracy has been restored to Argentina, even as the economy is being stabilized and revolution no longer threatens, Naipaul still sees evidence of "the enduring cruelty of the Spanish conquest," especially the absence of the "high idea of human possibility," which he describes as "the opposite of the idea behind" that conquest. He sees this heritage of cruelty and deprivation in the details of life in Argentina, for example, in the short stature and "bow legs" of a young Indian nun singing in a church during Easter, "who had made peace with the world in her own way." More broadly it exists in "government jobs" created by politicians, which demand no work, only the presence of bored, restless "pensioners," granted "this largesse [that] comes with a touch of Spanish-Argentine cruelty."[28]

Despite lasting remnants of the past, Naipaul is encouraged by changes in the perception of Argentina's future by people he meets and by the government led by President Carlos Menem. In "The End of Peronism?" he refers to a businessman's conviction that "Argentina no longer believed in the foreign enemy; no longer believed it was a European country; and had lost the idea of the limitless wealth of the land," all of which amount "to an intellectual revolution." Furthermore, Menem, elected as a Peronist, gradually "began to shed old and fundamental elements of Peronist doctrine. . . . Perhaps only a Peronist," Naipaul says, "could have declared Peronism over and put an end to that particular idea of revolution and justice." The word "perhaps" and the question mark in the title of his article are signs that Naipaul's optimism is tempered by his awareness that Argentina still lacks a "moral idea," an ethical stance that fosters national cohesion and individual potential.

At this writing in 1998, Naipaul's reservations seem justified. Privatization (which, Naipaul warned, Menem was instituting "not always wisely"), as part of globalization has caused volatility in the stock market and in the economy in general. Foreign investors in land and business are transforming the terrain. "There are more fences going up in Patagonia, as the internationally wealthy install themselves on newly acquired estates," reports Roger Cohen in the *New York Times* (February 6, 1998). He goes on to quote an Argentine observing these changes: "I used to go and camp or fish, but now I hear that Ted Turner is here, Rambo there, the Terminator somewhere else. And I say, no, this is not my Argentina." Any incipient sense of nationhood that followed the restoration of democracy is imperiled by greed and expediency.

Still, farming and cattle raising have been modernized and expanded. As a result Argentina's exports of beef and agricultural products have greatly increased, providing jobs and a measure of security to people who for a long time had had none. There are heartening signs that Argentines are coming to terms with the truth of their past. Amnesty for admission of torture and murder has begun to seem insufficient as a means of dealing with the horrors of the dirty war. After twenty years of marching by the Mothers of the Plaza de Mayo and protests by defenders of human rights, the Congress has faced the reality that the amnesty laws cannot allay the anguish of the past, that the perpetrators must bear responsibility for their crimes. This determination, and the recent decisions to extradite Nazi war criminals, after so many had found safe haven under past governments, suggests that Argentines are struggling to establish the "moral idea" of which colonial conquest with its legacy of tyranny had robbed them.

The cult of the leader, which persisted for so long and with such dire consequences in Argentina, was also the chief means of political repression and economic exploitation in Zaire when Naipaul visited it in 1975, as it was throughout much of Africa. "Mobutu in Zaire; Bokassa in the Central African Republic. Bongo in Gabon, Kenyatta in Kenya. Amin in Uganda. Banda in Malawi. Nyerere in Tanzania. How odd this situation, in which the most revealing thing is that every country produces only one man who is known. The leader, the leader. Nobody else exists."[29] In *A Congo Diary* and "A New King for the Congo," Naipaul examines this most flagrant symptom of national corruption in Zaire— the dictator who perpetuated the worst crimes of imperialism, exploited a populace made vulnerable by the loss of its history and traditions, and used propaganda, fantasies, and lies to consolidate his power.

Having seized command in a military coup, Mobutu appointed himself president in November 1965. Until he was ousted in May 1997 he held absolute power, controlling a large portion of the national revenue, which he used as his personal means. Supported by the United States and other Western nations as a bulwark against Soviet inroads into Central Africa, Mobutu instituted African "authenticity" as a national policy that ruled out all foreign influences such as place and personal names, clothing, and even farm machinery. He confiscated the property of foreigners and then nationalized all businesses. His economic policies, aimed chiefly at enriching himself and his associates, finally bankrupted the nation. Roads deteriorated, new ones were not built, workers' and soldiers' salaries were not paid or were paid in worthless zaires, unemployment and poverty were widespread in a country rich in natural resources such as diamonds, copper, and cobalt, which either provided the president with enormous wealth or lay untapped. At the end of the Cold War, when Western countries recommended democratic measures in Zaire, Mobutu ordered that student rebels be killed and made bogus promises to reform. But neither increasing demands from the West, nor the withdrawal of its support, nor uprisings within Zaire in the early 1990s, followed by violence and looting by Mobutu's soldiers, ousted him. It took the united forces of Rwanda, Angola, and Uganda, and a citizen army led by Laurent Desire Kabila to finally drive him out. Why did it take so long? How did a self-serving tyrant manage for almost thirty-two years to usurp his country's wealth and deny its citizens the necessities for a productive and dignified way of life?

As in many newly independent countries, Zaire's history left its people colonized in their outlook, unprepared to organize for effective democratic reforms. But Naipaul's observations make it clear that it also took the particular character of Mobutu to take full advantage of the vulnerability of the people and the potential but undeveloped mineral wealth of the land. In "A New King for the Congo" he describes him asserting his African identity as Mobutu Sese Seko in his "leopard-skin cap," carrying his "elaborately carved stick," his "official handbook" declaring "a profound respect for the liberties of others." "He is citizen, king, revolutionary; he is an African freedom fighter; he is supported by the spirits of his ancestors; like Mao, he has published a book of thoughts." These claims did not preclude his reliance on the "despotic legislation" of Leopold II, which had "passed down through the Belgian colonial administration to the present regime, and is now presented as a kind of ancestral African socialism—like Leopold II, Mobutu owns Zaire."[30]

In his many roles, professing to blend African traditions with progressive change, both of which were his own specious inventions, "unpredictable" in his alternating disapproval and "magnanimity," appearing to trust his commissioners one day, on the next dismissing a number of them, Mobutu relied on confusion and fear as psychological bases for obedience. No social contract existed in Zaire, not even the concept of a loyal opposition, let alone its presence. Mobutism, like Peronism, turned out to be whatever the "chief" or his commissioners, following his orders, demanded at the moment. And always there was a disparity between the promise of progress and prosperity and the reality of stagnation and decay.

In Zaire, as in other postcolonial societies that Naipaul explored, he is troubled by the absence of a sense of the past. Many of the victims of their country's history were ignorant of the tyranny of colonialism that was their heritage. He returns again and again to this theme in *A Congo Diary:* "History has disappeared. Even the Belgian colonial past." This is by no means a plea for nostalgia. Quite the opposite; clearly he feels that knowledge of the past can instigate resistance to despotism and support self-determination in society. He regrets that even a teacher at the university, "the first of his village and his family to be educated," speaking of Belgian rule, can only say: "The Belgians gave us a state. Before they came we had no state." Naipaul's sadness, an emotion that pervades *A Congo Diary*, regarding what seems to be lack of curiosity about past history, but is more likely denial, is to some extent mitigated in his oblique hope that remembrance will eventually function in creating a viable future: "Passion comes later, where memory takes over."

A trip to the university begins with "despair" at the "run-down city" through which he is driven, the "non-creation of the Belgian intervention in the Congo," but his spirits are lifted as he responds to the "intelligence of the students." The questions he raises convey empathy and concern for their future opportunities. When they tell him that they would be given positions in the government, he worries about "power-fights." "Would an Amin come and turn everything upside down?" Their "dignity," he feels, "deserved a better country, a country better equipped." This thought is extended in his "feeling about Africa"—that "the individual, awakening to history, discovering injustice and the past, discovering ideas, was not supported by his society." Considering this dilemma as particularly relevant to these students in "A New King for the Congo," Naipaul fears that, exposed to ideas, discovering their history and "a sense of their own dignity," these young people "can only awaken to pain." Then, an afterthought seems forced upon him: "But no. For most there would be jobs in the government; and already they are Mobutists to a man." What choice had they, with no opposing social and cultural support, but to become functionaries in the government of a state in which "inquiry is restricted," in which "Mobutu himself has warned that the most alienated people in Zaire are the intellectuals"? Later events in Zaire only confirm Naipaul's apprehensions. Mobutu proved to be as corrupt as Amin and more tenacious. Zaire became the site of "power-fights," increased suppression, social unrest, and economic crises.

If some intellectuals are "alienated" from "the dream of an ancestral past restored . . . allied to a dream of a future of magical power," others are both drawn to and repelled by "authenticity" and *la negrité*. Naipaul quotes the "French African writer," Seydou Lamine, who raises the question of whether the designation "Africanness" is merely a myth used by the rulers of Africa "to strengthen their own position." For many people, he says, "authenticity and Negroness . . . are only words that stand for the despair and powerlessness" of the African "faced with the discouraging immensity of his underdevelopment."

Visiting the presidential domain at Nsele, where conferences are held and foreign dignitaries and scholars are entertained, Naipaul is caught up in the contradictions with which the intellectuals of Zaire are obliged to live. On the one hand, he sees the extravagance of the domain as an effort to heal the "wound" of Africa, which also "explains the harassment of foreign settlers, the nationalizations." On the other hand, the domain is "shoddy," pretentious; the nationalizations "bogus, . . . self wounding."

The visitor, he says, "swings from mood to mood, and one reaction cancels out another." Such contradictions and the relations between the domain as a "hoax" and as a place where intellectual growth may be possible are explored in "The New Domain," a large segment of *A Bend in the River*, Naipaul's novel that grew out of his experience in Zaire.

Naipaul senses a profound wrath in educated Zairians who seemingly have gained from nationalization, have become managers, and have developed a "new sense of the self." Their commitment to authenticity has made them all the more suspicious of foreign influences, of "foreign attitudes to African art." He depicts Simon, one of these managers whom he comes to know, as typical of those "adrift and nervous in this unreal world of imitation . . . finding that they have been fooled and affronted," and most likely to rebel. Evoking Conrad once again, he refers to the violent rebellion of 1964 led by Pierre Mulele who "camped" at Stanleyville, Kurtz's "heart of darkness." Only this time it was not a white man "maddened" by "wilderness, solitude and power," but a black man "maddened" by "the civilization established by those pioneers who now lie on Mont Ngaliema, above the Kinshasa rapids."

Rob Nixon objects to what he considers Naipaul's equation of Kurtz with Mulele "in a fashion that sets up a causal relation between their locale and their morality"; thus "Kurtz's behavior and Mulele's become most intelligible as emanations of place." To this reader their "emanations," their source, are the horrors of the "civilization" created by their imperial conquerors, to whom Naipaul refers in the passage quoted above and elsewhere in the essay. It is not "civilization" per se, as Nixon's truncated quotation suggests, but the colonial civilization left by the so-called—mostly Belgian—"pioneers." Although Nixon admits that "the Mulelists' actions were violent," he finds that they did exercise "'restraint': they made a policy of respecting traditional chiefs, while attacking officials whom they considered to be colonial appointees."[31] Since he provides no evidence of the chiefs' innocence and the officials' guilt, his defense of Mulele on this basis seems a flimsy excuse for elitism.

The revolution of 1997 in Zaire grew out of the conditions that Naipaul described and was fought, at least in part, by acts of violent rage, but this time of Africans against Africans. Early reports of its history maintained that Laurent Kabila, a longtime dissident who had led an unsuccessful rebellion against Mobutu in the 1960s, was able in the fall of 1996 to gather allies aiming to reanimate a spirit of nationalism that independence had promised and to overthrow Mobutu. Soon an army of rebels, untrained, with inadequate equipment, but determined and resilient, joined up. Their victory seemed inevitable as Zairian civilians and the Zairian army supported them.

Facts soon emerged, however, which clouded this picture of the rebel's victory. It became known that Rwandan officers had helped to plot the revolution from its beginnings. A great number of Tutsis from Rwanda and Congo fought in Kabila's army, seeking vengeance against the Hutus, driving thousands of them out of the refugee camps on the Congo/Zaire border into the bush, where they were slaughtered. Kabila's efforts, abetted by Rwanda and Uganda, to cover up these atrocities, his exclusion of former opponents of Mobutu from his government, his intolerance of dissent, evidence of corruption by newly appointed officials, all signified still another cult of the leader in the land he renamed The Democratic Republic of the Congo. At the beginning of August 1998 a new rebellion aimed at ousting Kabila was led by the Congo's Tutsi minority, backed by its former allies, Rwanda and Uganda. Although Angola and Zimbabwe have supported Kabila, he has lost the confidence of the Congolese who face continuous war, inflation, and unemployment. One of Naipaul's "half-made societies," Congo seems unlikely in the near future, or ever, to achieve the stability of nationhood.

The Ivory Coast, which Naipaul visited in 1981, had "its own cult of the leader."[32] To be sure, President Felix Houphouët-Boigny appeared to be a benevolent autocrat in contrast with the rapacious tyrants who ruled Argentina, Zaire, and other African nations of the time. Still, as head of the one political party, he had been president since independence in 1960. His ancestral home, Yamoussoukro, the site of his palace, seemed at once a sign of the wealth and progress of the country and an execution of the myth of his superhuman authority, most dramatically illustrated in the "man-eating crocodiles" installed in "an artificial lake" near his palace. Naipaul describes these as "totemic, emblematic creatures" that attest to the "chief's magically granted knowledge of his power as something more than human, something emanating from the earth itself."

The president's actual powers were exerted in trying to unite the traditional "idea of African completeness" with a modern conception of Africa's future. Like other commentators, Naipaul attributes the peace and wealth of the country, surrounded as it is by nations in various states of poverty and chaos, at least in part to the president's willingness to employ French "technicians, advisors, administrators." Nonetheless, Naipaul's expectation that he would find "France in Africa" turned out to be his own "fantasy." His recognition that French technology and

African "officially approved 'culture'" were still "like separate ideas" makes him wonder about the signs of success in the capital, Abidjan, and "the continuing order of the state" as a whole.

Typically, he seeks understanding through people he comes to like who, in the Ivory Coast, turn out to be chiefly "expatriates, white and black." "I saw the country through them," he says, "and through their varied experience." Their views also exemplify a variety of attitudes toward the country and disclose the advantages and limits of judgments based on standards formed in other civilizations. Each person Naipaul gets to know has a different conception of the Ivory Coast and of what is intrinsically Africa: its gods and sorcerers, its mysticism, its traditional culture, its "idea of completeness." Sometimes, inadvertently, people reveal their prejudices and allegiances, their ambivalence despite their alleged commitment.

One such person is Philip, an English expatriate married to a beautiful black Guyanese woman who had grown up in England. Philip "had spent most of his working life in Africa, and it was one of his sayings that in their mixed marriage Janet was the English partner; he was the African." Naipaul makes no comment on this claim, but in an earlier conversation, when Naipaul questions Philip about his feelings regarding "personality cults" in African countries, Philip's response seems to this reader that of a condescending Englishman rather than that of an African: "You must understand that Africans like the cult of personality better. It is what they understand. A multiplicity of parties and personalities confuses them. I've seen this happen."

Clearly Africans were not entirely satisfied with a cult leader. At an embassy lunch the day after this conversation, Naipaul learns that the president "had become aware of the growing discontent in the Ivory Coast" and had offered a way to "democratize." At the last election voters, instead of being presented with a list of the one-party candidates for whom they could vote "for or against, . . . anyone in the party could contest any seat." As a result, for "the 140 or so seats in the assembly there had been more than 600 candidates." The problem, as Naipaul sees it, was not a matter of Africans preferring a cult leader, or being confused by choice, but rather the African tradition whereby an elder (in this case, the large number of defeated deputies) could not return "to being an ordinary villager; he had been personally degraded." The reaction to this situation, which "had damaged the cohesiveness of village life," was a call for "reconciliation," an "African idea" rather than the "imported one" of democracy. It is at once a more traditional and more sophisticated response to a multiplicity of choices than Philip seemed to apprehend. Yet Naipaul's portrait of Philip as a good man, who had "become more thoughtful than he might have done if he had stayed in England, . . . more knowledgeable and more tolerant," is convincing. His identification with the Africans seems an expression of his caring, his "special conscientiousness to his job" in the "interstate African organization for which he worked."

From "the public affairs officer of the American Embassy," Naipaul learns of the persistence of African religious and "magical practices," even in their modern incarnations in "the masks in souvenir shops, even in the dances beside the swimming pool of the Forum Golf Hotel." Arlette, a black woman who "worked in an arts department of the university in Abidjan," tells him of the divisions between the French, the French West Indians, and the Africans of the Ivory Coast. Arlette came from Martinique; although she "loves the culture of France," she is drawn to "the Africa that followed its own ways." Hers is one of Naipaul's most compelling portraits. As she explains African customs and beliefs to him, illustrating them with anecdotes, she validates her belief that "To live in Africa was to have all one's ideas and values questioned." She seems incapable of stock responses; her loyalties are all her own. She helps not only Naipaul but the reader to "understand many things about the country," one of which is "the two worlds, the world of the day," quotidian reality, and "the world of the night," imagination, creation, music, and drama.

Arlette's friend, Andrée, also an expatriate from the West Indies, identifies herself with the French. She feels "trapped" in the Ivory Coast, and when she speaks of "home," she means France, not Guadeloupe, her birthplace. Yet Andrée is the secretary of Georges Niangoran-Bouah, an anthropologist, whose specialty is "Drummologie . . . communication of tribal drums," a term and controversial subject he invented. Andrée's help is acknowledged in his book, and despite her alienation from Africa, she is proud of her "patron." Furthermore, as Naipaul points out, in her work for Niangoran-Bouah, whose "cause is the 'talking drum' as a record of tribal history and tradition," she is also serving this cause. Later on, when Naipaul meets Niangoran-Bouah and listens to his recordings of "first the tribal song or ballad, then the drum that mimicked the beat of the word," he begins to apprehend "the richness of the material he had made his subject and his passion to present this material adequately to Africans and the world."

Even as Naipaul sees the country through these and other people he meets and empathizes with their commitment to African rather than to an imposed foreign culture, or understands a need, such as Andrée's, to adopt an alien culture as one's own, he is conscious of the disparity between the modern Ivory Coast—Abidjan with its "urban highways," its "skyscrapers," its "university campus"—and the continuity of myth and magic as bases for morality in private life and qualifications for success in governance. His prime example is the president's creation of Yamoussoukro, which, vast as it may be, is still "far from completed" and "would not be completed in the president's lifetime." Even before he sees it, hearing of this "monumental city meant to make an African ruler immortal," he thinks of "the monuments of ancient Egypt where the cartouches of one pharaoh could be defaced by his successors," where monuments "could be broken up and used unceremoniously as building stones." Moreover, Yamoussoukro was being built not by Africans but by "French and Israelis and others." Learning of the president's role, Naipaul's "first impression of modern African success began to be qualified." Success depended on this representative of "an established ruling family" which "rested on an African ideal of authority. And at the bottom of it all was magic."

From newspaper reports Naipaul learns that "mysterious fires" in the home of a schoolteacher were caused by an "Evil Spirit" identified and expelled by the Celestial Christians and that in this way "the Ivory Coast had itself been cleansed." He hears of sorcerers and *feticheurs*. But he finds the most dramatic evidence of the reliance on magic as a form of religion in his visit to Yamoussoukro. The room in The Hotel President, where he stays, is "opulent"; the "parkland created out of the African bush" is now a "famous golf course" with impressive views. There is a town, a market, a wide main street, and workers' settlements. All these are evidence of the president's power. But it is the rituals connected with the feeding of live chickens to the crocodiles in the lake beside his palace, the "public ceremony of kingship," that symbolize his role as a descendant of an ancient priest-king.

In the Ivory Coast, as in Argentina and Zaire, loyalty to a cult leader became a substitute for national cohesion and thus a deterrent to the realization of nationhood. Naipaul shows how Perón, Mobutu, and Houphouët-Boigny, each in his way, could rule by symbol, propaganda, and suppression. Even educated, intelligent people could be duped by a leader's rites and concealments. When Naipaul asks his friend Arlette about the meaning of the crocodiles, she replies, "Nobody knows. Only the president knows," seemingly content to accept the mystery. But this is not an innocuous puzzle. Since it was said that the crocodiles, "by a particular movement of their heads, warned the president of danger to the state," no one could be safe from this political threat in the guise of magic.

After the president's death in 1993 it became known that the erection of his magnificent city with the largest church in the world left the Ivory Coast with huge debts. Félix Houphouët-Boigny has gone down in history as a man who neglected the health and education of his people in order to spend lavishly for his own ephemeral glory. Today his decisions would be questioned by opposition parties and by a free press. It seems doubtful that any subsequent president will attempt to unite the authority of his tribal heritage with the aspirations of a modern technocracy as confidently as he did.

CONTINUITY AND CHANGE: AN IDEA OF NATIONHOOD

"Five hundred years after the Arab conquest of Sind, Moslem rule was established in Delhi as the rule of foreigners, people apart; and foreign rule—Moslem for the first five hundred years, British for the last 150—ended in Delhi only in 1947."[33] This chronology is the historical background of Naipaul's views—largely based on his own observations and thus changing, contradictory—on post-Independence India's capacity to forge a national identity. His travels in India during the 1960s and 1970s convinced him that "India is without an ideology—and that was the failure of Gandhi and India together." Lacking an "idea of the state" and the accompanying "attitudes" toward their history, Indians, he says, have "no identity beyond the tenuous ecumenism of Hindu beliefs." During "centuries of conquest," Indian civilization adopted as "an apparatus for survival ... magical practices and imprisoning social forms." Under such conditions the "key Hindu concept of dharma" cannot be followed on its highest level.[34]

A. K. Ramanujan construes dharma as "a central word in Hinduism, therefore multi-vocal, untranslatable; usually glossed 'law, righteousness, duty, code, etc.,'"[35] a term that seems analogous to the ancient Greek concept of *themis*. To "established order" R. K. Narayan adds "virtue," "moral merit," and "justice."[36] Naipaul, regarding dharma as "an elastic concept," defines it as "the right way, the sanctioned way, which all men must follow, according to their natures." He interprets it not only as a philosophical ideal but as a personal creed that "[a]t its noblest ... combines self-fulfillment and truth to the self with the ideas of action as duty, action as its own spiritual reward, man as a holy vessel." Because dharma binds human beings to their societies, "this ideal of truth to oneself . . . can also be used to reconcile men to servitude and make them find in paralyzing obedience the highest spiritual good."[37] This is the way, Naipaul suggests, in which dharma was interpreted in the India he visited in 1975 and 1976. Inevitably, dharma signifies the quality of individual life within the limits and possibilities of a particular society, and he observes "dharma, as expressed in the Indian social system . . . shot through with injustice and cruelty."

Conditions Naipaul despairs of in *India: A Wounded Civilization*—the continuing poverty, the tendency of Indians to cling to their idea of their country's "established past," the persistence of caste restrictions and humiliations, the "dismantled institutions" of the Emergency—would seem to be limits impossible to overcome. He is especially hard on Hinduism which, he says, "has exposed us to a thousand years of defeat and stagnation. . . . It has given men . . . no idea of the state. It has enslaved one quarter of the population and always left the whole fragmented and vulnerable," unable "to respond to challenge."

Reviewers have stressed the darkness of Naipaul's vision, his harsh judgments of Hinduism and of Gandhi's legacy—his opposition to industrialization, his failure to engage in political action that would lead India to a concept of nationhood, his withdrawal instead "from the difficult world." All these do comprise wounds of India's civilization. Yet there is also optimism in this book, hope that Naipaul places in movements of the oppressed, which are both protests against the status quo and positive action for their future and India's. He writes of "unknown India on the move," entering the cities, seeking and finding work, experiencing pride in achievement, a new sense of self. Among these is the Shiv Sena, a movement emerging from "squatters' colonies," in Bombay. Downplaying their anti-Muslim stance, their tyrannical methods, Naipaul stresses the salutary effects of their quest for the dignity of community and identity. "Within the past ten years," these squatters have used both the past and Hinduism—"bits and pieces" of both, to be sure—but inspiring nonetheless—to identify themselves with the "army of Shiva," not, Naipaul explains, "the god, but Shivaji the seventeenth-century Maratha guerrilla leader, who challenged the Mughal empire and made the Marathas, the people of the Bombay region, a power in India for a century."

In *India: A Wounded Civilization*, Naipaul's acceptance of the Shiv Sena reflects his compassion for the "dispossessed," even as it conveys his belief that the past, a nation's history, must not be dismissed or merely venerated but should be revitalized by its contribution to present needs. The Shiv Sena has roots not only in the seventeenth century but in "the early pre-Gandhi days of the Independence movement." It has adapted to modern independent India and to "industrial Bombay." If it is "a contracting out . . . from a Hindu system," it is also "in part a reworking of the Hindu system. Men do not accept chaos; they ceaselessly seek to remake their world; they reach out for such ideas as are accessible and fit their need." Although Naipaul is aware of the Sena's shortcomings—he refers to it as "xenophobic"—he emphasizes its determination to provide for its members. It has gotten even the government to agree that "eighty percent of all jobs shall be held by Maharashtrians." More disturbing was its "persecution in its early days of South Indian settlers in Bombay." Such extreme means as the exclusion of outsiders, seemingly a condition of its very existence, a necessity for the movement, with its limited means and goals, to avoid "chaos," is part of the group's identity, which Naipaul later calls its "destructive chauvinism" in *India: A Million Mutinies Now*. But in 1975–76, during the journey that was to produce *India: A Wounded Civilization*, he is impressed by the Sena's "municipal self-regulation," its engagement in politics. Its members are "industrial workers beginning to apply something of the discipline of the factory floor" to their settlement, "a low huddle of mud and tin and tile and old boards." They are men "rejecting rejection" who in discovering their own identities exemplify the potential "dynamic" quality of "Indian identity."

Fourteen years later, in *India: A Million Mutinies Now*, Naipaul is more ambivalent. By then the Sena had grown in size and power. It "had won control of the Bombay Municipal Corporation" and it had "units" throughout Bombay and its suburbs. From the leader of one of its many branches Naipaul learns of the Sena's continuous "resentment against" outsiders, especially Muslims, its drive "to keep Hinduism alive." This "area leader," Mr. Patil, identifying himself with the "Maratha warrior pride," expresses his contempt for Gandhi's pacifism: "I hate the idea of non-violence," he says. Despite the success of the Sena, Mr. Patil, still nursing his rage at past injustices and, fearing for the future of his people, cannot understand the anger of the Dalits who, by any rational standards, surely had more cause for resentment than any other Indian group, condemned as they were throughout their history to a barely human existence. Naipaul neither denounces nor lauds the Sena's narrow vision. In his view the Sena enacts its own varieties of "twenty kinds of group excess." Each group, he believes, is aware initially of only its own rage, its particular history, the grounds of its own mutiny.

Other leaders reveal more benign personal attitudes even as they demonstrate the political power of the Sena in Bombay. As a result of the "victory of the Sena in the municipal elections," Mr. Raote had become "a man of authority, chairman of the Standing Committee of the Bombay Corporation." Like Mr. Patil, he is religious, but in Naipaul's portrait, he is more at peace with his Hinduism, his "devotion to the Shiv Sena and its leader," his life of "belief and action." Naipaul visits another "high Sena official" in the chawl (slum) where he has chosen to live. The disparity between the physical conditions of the chawl block—the "garbage," the odors, the foul air—and Mr. Ghate's dignity and sense of responsibility would suggest that he was uncomfortable in such a setting. On the contrary, though he deplores what he calls the "absence of civic sense" of some of the tenants, he is committed to the communal life and does not even want privacy. What counts is people's knowledge of and concern for one another, "the special philosophy of the Sena."

Sunil Khilnani's view of the Shiv Sena is harsher than Naipaul's. He considers the movement "a deep potential within modern Indian politics" rather than a potential contributor to India's nationhood. The Sena, he says, has succeeded both in its "ability to develop a quotidian local politics with local goals" and in "the skills of high electoral politics." He concedes that it has established its "reputation" by providing "real cultural, medical and educational services to Bombay's poor and lower middle classes." But the underside of these achievements has been the distribution of its social services to only some of Bombay's residents and the exclusion of others. More disturbing has been its use of violence. During the 1980s the Sena incited riots aimed at Muslims and from December 1992 to January 1993, it was involved in riots "directly after, and related to, the destruction of the Babri Masjid in Ayodhya by Hindu militants aspiring to construct a Ram temple in its place." Khilnani regards the Sena's "idea of India" as "provincial, partial." It conceives of India "as a hierarchical grid that contains internally homogeneous communities, each insulated from the others."[38]

The difference in Naipaul's and Khilnani's concerns is due in part to the different times in which they were writing, as well as to their fundamental approach to the concept of nationhood. Although Naipaul objects to the Sena's xenophobia, his response to the movement is generally favorable. His comments on the Shiv Sena in *India: A Wounded Civilization* and *India: A Million Mutinies Now* were written before its participation in the riots connected with the destruction of the Babri Masjid, events that would surely have modified his appraisal of its role as an ameliorative agency. But he was writing of an earlier time when the Shiv Sena was essentially a colony of people living in intolerable conditions who had banded together for survival through social action. His description of them as "unaccommodated [a word that insists on associations with Lear on the heath] men making a claim on their land for the first time"[39] suggests the desperation of their struggle for a place in their society. Typically, Naipaul's emphasis is on individual human beings reacting to and taking part in the history of their time. If their vision, as Khilnani demonstrates, is merely local—even "provincial"—for Naipaul, their very demand for recognition, their refusal to accept the bonds of caste, the strictures of their village past, are signs that India itself is in transition. The millions on the move, whatever their present limits, are leading to a new definition of the nation.

One of the groups Naipaul writes about, the Dalit Panthers, and especially its founder and leader, Namdeo Dhasal, exemplify the diversity of the rebellions and of India itself. Dhasal became known for his first book of poems written in demotic Marathi and "specifically in the language of the Bombay brothel area." A poem of his that Naipaul quotes in *India: A Million Mutinies Now*, "The Road to the Shrine," is a moving condensation of the life of the poet as representative of the "scheduled castes," a euphemism for "untouchables." Even in translation the poem speaks not only for the dispossessed of India but for anyone who has reason to feel "like an orphan in the land of his birth" (the poet's explication). In another poem he writes about water, which has been "taught class prejudices." The subject is important to him, says Naipaul, the origin of painful memories of being forbidden, as a child, "to touch any source of water" or to bathe in water used by "upper castes." Once, when he dared to bathe "in a pond with some upper-caste boys, . . . he was chased and stoned," and later was beaten by his mother for "defiling the pond." He could not even enter a classroom, nor could he be touched by a teacher. These are some of the most obvious humiliations he has endured, and the pain and suppressed rage of those times emerged in his political work, his poetry, and also in his marriage, which was certainly anomalous. His wife, Mallika, the daughter of a mixed marriage—Muslim and Hindu—was reared as a high-caste Hindu. Equally offensive to "people's caste sensibilities" was her autobiography, *I Want to Destroy Myself*, "a best seller" that revealed intimate details of her married life: her love for Namdeo and her pain at his neglect, his visits to prostitutes, his venereal disease. It is an account of conflict between dedication to "the freedom of women" and her own loss of "some of her autonomy" in her love for her husband. What's more, Namdeo has read the book and "defended" it, regarding it in both a social and personal context. According to Mallika, his "argument" is that she "has seen" their life together "with her middle-class eyes," and "has every right to express what she feels about the marriage."

Mallika's and Namdeo's story is but one example of how rebellion and change in India can affect the personal lives of people in fundamental ways: the rage at past degradation channeled into efforts at social reform, the inevitable personal cost and the personal satisfactions of political involvement, the greater freedom to face resentment and anger as inseparable from love. They have rejected the security of ritual and custom and accepted the responsibility of relying on their own feelings, their own judgment, in their personal life and in their writings. At sixteen Mallika idealized Namdeo as her rebel hero. Now many years later she feels bound to him because she married him in defiance of her class—"against everybody," she says— but also because she loves him even as she knows that his political commitments are paramount, that the humiliations of his past are a blight on their marriage.

Although he considers himself as much "politician" as poet, Namdeo Dhasal has not achieved the power that the leaders of the Shiv Sena possess. A meeting he holds for prostitutes to protest against conditions in the brothel area is badly attended. When he wished to expand the Black Dalits to "take in all the oppressed, not just the scheduled castes," he was defeated by what he calls "the reactionaries among the Dalits." Naipaul considers this talented, intelligent man "a prisoner of India, with its multiplicity of movements and desperate needs." Yet he has produced a body of revolutionary poetry, and he has founded the Black Dalits who, though "beginning to fragment" at the time Naipaul was writing, was one of the first organizations of "lower castes" who were to form regional parties or to ally themselves with those who supported their interests.

Naipaul's long discussion of the DMK, the Dravidian Progressive Movement, in Tamil Nadu concentrates almost entirely on a variety of people, those who supported the movement, ignored it, or resisted it. In 1967, five years after his initial visit to Madras, he realized that the rebellion he now observed had begun much earlier: "the revolt of South against North, non-brahmin against brahmin, the racial revolt of dark against fair, Dravidian against Aryan." Sugar, the friend Naipaul visited, managed to ignore the movement then, and twenty years later, when Naipaul was again in Madras, to have withdrawn into his own temple as a self-made holy man.

But he was unusual. Naipaul writes of his surprise that Periyar, founder of the Self-Respect Movement, from which the DMK descended, who in his writings "came over as a humorist and satirist, should have been received by the people of Tamil Nadu as a prophet," and continued even after his death in 1973, to be honored as a sage. In fact there is no more striking example of the rebellion against religious belief and caste discrimination than the wide acceptance in Tamil Nadu of Periyar's platform, which can be summarized as opposition to everything that Hindus professed. His claims to "rationalism," Naipaul says, included not only "his rejection of God," but "his rejection of the brahmins, their language," and their "caste prejudices." Clearly it was caste prejudice that prepared the way for Periyar's first triumph: in 1924 opposition to the denial of non-brahmins "free entry to temples" in Karala, and even to a "temple lane" resulted in a protest, to which Periyar was summoned. It took him a year, but he won his case. According to Naipaul, Periyar's history is of "a local figure" who, unlike Gandhi, "never outgrew his cause. Without Gandhi and the Congress and the independence movement his cause wouldn't have had the power it had; he was riding on the back of something very big."[40]

The DMK, "the political offshoot" of the Self-Respect Movement, achieved power in 1967, and won again in the election of 1989. Naipaul's informant, Sadanand Menon, "a writer living in Madras," is critical of the party, which he finds no longer "creative." Tamil, he says, has become "a fossilized language . . . reflected in the quality of Tamil journalism." When Menon remarks that ironically "a cult of the primal mother," a regression to Dravidian religion has arisen, Naipaul sees "a deeper irony" in the fact that the antibrahmin movement consisted "mainly of the middle castes." More disturbing to him than the decline of the DMK, "their narrowness, their regionalism, their caste obsessions," was their neglect of those who needed them most. "There was, as ever in India, a further lower level, a further level of disadvantage. For these people at the very bottom the DMK offered no protection."

Although Naipaul is critical of the DMK's rigid adherence to its founder's platform, their obsession with negation rather than devotion to active reform, their exclusion of the most needy, he does not discount the positive effects of the movement on the lives of some of its followers: "Periyar had touched something in these people, something deeper than logic and a regard for historical correctness; that also had to be taken into account." What Periyar seems to have inspired in people Naipaul interviewed was a determination no longer to accept the contemptuous treatment from brahmins that they and other non-brahmins had endured since childhood. One of these people, Mr. Gopalakrishnan, tells of indignities he suffered from his teachers and a priest. It took only exposure to "one of Periyar's meetings" for him to comprehend the brahmin prejudices which he had earlier "taken for granted." He began to read the literature of the Periyar movement and soon became "a complete rationalist," who can simply ignore Hindu ritual and religion. The extent to which the movement has determined his way of life is also evident in his work: he is "the proprietor of Emerald Publishers, publishers of school text books and books about the rationalist movement." From his own account, Gopalakrishnan seems to have gained a sense of his own worth through his affiliation with the nationalist movement; he certainly seems to be at peace with the path he has chosen.

Another rebel against brahmin discrimination, Mr. Palani, comes across as a more complicated man, to whom devotion to the rationalist movement has not brought a tranquil life. Like Namdeo Dhasal, he dwells on memories of discrimination endured by his younger brother and himself fifty years ago. It was actually an affront to his brother who, like Dhasal, was the victim of water prejudice in the presence of his classmates, that led Palani to question customs he had earlier accepted. He was only eleven years old at the time. A series of subsequent events—a speech by Periyar in which he warned against a plan to substitute Hindi for English in the schools, making Tamil "secondary to Hindi"; picketing of schools on this issue; a protest march that was successful and ended any imposition of Hindi; another successful protest against segregation of nonbrahmins in the mess hall of his college hostel—all led to his conviction that once "we start asserting our rights, they wouldn't have the temerity to oppose that."

Polani regards his own protest against the brahmins within the context of Tamil history, beginning with the "casteless society" of the ancient Dravidians. Only with the invasion of the Aryans, "the foreign civilization . . . from the north," did class differentiation arise. "Every century since then," he says, "there has been a protest by some Tamil intellectuals against the caste system." Now he has taken his place within that history. As an engineer, he has done all he can to assign "funds for backward areas," to create "facilities in remote places." Given the past and recent history of Tamil Nadu, for both Gopalakrishnan and Palani, educated middle-class men, protest as an assertion of their own rights was almost inevitable. Polani seems to have gone beyond this limited aim, beyond the official membership of the DMK, in his concern for the most deprived. Still, for the most part he has not been able to see beyond the narrow focus of the DMK. When Naipaul introduces the subject of India's independence, it is plain that Palani follows the example of Periyar, who "hadn't bothered too much about the national movement and independence." He is, as he says, "obsessed" with the DMK, his "cause." He lives with contradictions: "his own need for religious faith" and the existence of "caste structures in his own family." He is aware of the disintegration of municipal services in Madras, the corruption of the DMK government, which he admits but evades by blaming the wily brahmins in Delhi. His devotion to the Dravidian movement erases all doubts. As Naipaul says, his "passion was very great; it had to be respected." His own integrity and accomplishments persuade us that, despite its many shortcomings, the DMK, in Sadanand Menon's words, "still has a place." Belonging to the same movement yet so different in their manner of protest, Gopalakrishnan and Palani, like other rebels Naipaul interviews, illustrate a point he makes in a later commentary: "every man is a mutiny on his own—and I find that entirely creative."[41]

Even resistance to the DMK, while hardly a mutiny, is a form of individual and social protest. Amid "the undoing of a culture"[42] in Madras there is also a continuity of that culture in the agrahara that Naipaul visits, where he learns from the brahmin priest Kakusthan that brahmin customs and observances need not exclude the demands and even the influence of the modern world. Kakustan and other members of the colony work at professions and jobs, yet they maintain their commitment to a brahmin way of life. Kakusthan has twice been an outsider in Madras. As a boy, he says, in the "mid-1950s, when there was widespread movement against brahmins and their practices," he was forced by his father to dress as a brahmin and endure the ridicule of his classmates. He tried to resist their insults and to persuade his father to let him "switch to the new ways of life—particularly removing the churki and wearing trousers," but succeeded in neither attempt. Yet, after a period of rebellion against his father, against brahminism itself, after living and working in New Delhi for sixteen years, he returned to Madras in 1981, "a Brahmin fully committed, fully realized." Naipaul admires Kakusthan for his willingness to accept the necessity of "worldliness" along with "the life of the spirit," but even more perhaps because his return to the traditional ways of a brahmin priest is an act of defiance in contemporary Madras.

Usually Naipaul is sympathetic to the "rage" pervading India: "There had been a general awakening. But everyone awakened first to his own group or community; every group thought itself unique in its awakening; and every group sought to separate its rage from the rage of other groups." The Sikhs are the one group whose rage he judges as regressive, wounding to themselves and to India. He traces their history from the time of their first guru to the present: the brutality of the Moguls, the contempt of the British for the very Sikhs who fought on their side, their anguish during the partition of 1947, and, despite the discrimination of the Hindu establishment, their economic success in independent India; "they were among the leaders in every field." Yet "in the late 1970s their politics . . . became confounded with a Sikh fundamentalism," and their religion, having "reached its final form with the 10th Guru," they were isolated by their commitment to a rigid sectarian code of conduct. There seemed to be "a lack of balance between their material achievement and their internal life," the one "so adventurous and forward-looking," the other "close to their tribal and country origins."

When the fundamentalist leader Bhindranwale occupied the Golden Temple of Amritsar, "the Sikhs' holiest shrine," and, having fortified it, "declared war on the state," the violence against Hindus began. With the assault of the army on the temple it continued. After Indira Gandhi was murdered "by her Sikh bodyguards," there were executions of Sikhs in New Delhi and riots throughout India. "Out of that great fire in 1984 [the] terrorist incidents in the Punjab, on the frontier with Pakistan," which Naipaul read about every day in the newspapers, "were the embers."

During his many visits since 1962 Naipaul has witnessed India's gradual accommodation to "the outside world," which has produced its "intellectual liveliness in the late 20th century: a free press, a constitution, a concern for law and institutions, ideas of morality, good behaviour, and intellectual responsibility quite separate from the requirements of religion." These principles and institutions, along with "the idea of freedom" which, from the mutiny against the British in 1857–58 to the present has pervaded India, are the bases of its democracy. But freedom in India, as everywhere else, has its own costs. In India, says Naipaul, "with its layer-below-layer of distress and cruelty, it had to come as disturbance. It had to come as rage and revolt."

His optimism regarding India's future lies in "the beginnings of self-awareness." Rebellions against poverty, against caste and class discrimination, and against political corruption expose these injustices even as they are declarations of the right to self-respect in work and in private life. However varied such movements, however separate in their struggle, they are part of "a central will, a central intellect, a central idea." They have

contributed to the concept of nationhood as "the source of law and civility and reasonableness." Naipaul proposes three measures essential to
the future of Indian democracy: growth of the economy, political leaders
emerging from the people and cognizant of their needs, and the extension of education. Like Naipaul, Khilnani sees "[r]egional and caste politics and Hindu nationalism" as "direct products of India's first four
decades of independence." Both he and Naipaul are well aware of the
limits of the increasing democratic movements: "The compulsion to win
power publicly and legitimately has provoked unpicturesque illegalities,
old and innovative—violence, corruption, and 'booth-capturing.'"[43]
However, they remain convinced that democracy will continue to function as it comes to terms with and embraces the great diversity of India.

There are, of course, dissenting voices. Discussing the question of
the Bharatiya Janata Party's "ability to tackle corruption, Pankaj Mishra
seems to have little faith in the present or hope for the future of Indian
democracy:

> Fifty years after independence, politics is now little more than an in-
> vestment opportunity, an idea uncynically accepted in public dis-
> course where a politician's career is assessed with respect to the
> wealth he has amassed. The new "men of the soil," the politicians
> from Dalit and other so-called backward castes, are only more recent
> examples of a political culture that was spawned by the Congress, a
> culture in which being a member of the ruling class is all too often
> a license for criminal activity. The new politicians' several years of
> power in some Indian states have created a creamy layer of rich land-
> lords and business-men; for the millions underneath them, the dis-
> used public parks and broken roads renamed after low-caste politi-
> cians are the sole benefits of self-rule.

He then speculates on India's future:

> Democracy in India—that much-celebrated accomplishment—seems
> to have degenerated into a vast colorful circus of almost continual
> elections. And now, as the economy stumbles, and tough times, after
> the current euphoria, loom ahead for the middle class, the poor may
> find that the small portions of bread that occasionally went with the
> circuses have become even smaller.[44]

Doubtless there are grounds, if not for such despair, then for skepticism regarding the motives and practices of Indian politicians. Many

others have voiced similar prognostications. Perhaps that is why Naipaul, acknowledging the hurdles but putting his faith in the millions on the march, has proposed "the Hindu idea" to serve as "almost a necessary early stage. It contains the beginnings of larger, new ideas: the idea of history, the idea of the human family of India."[45] He sees Hinduism as a temporary unifying ethical principle sorely needed at a time of inevitable chaos and continuing political skullduggery. His is not the Hinduism that Mishra attributes to the "BJP ideologues": "a dated solution, a mishmash of ancient Vedic wisdom, overblown ideas of India's past glory, and now-forgotten nineteenth-century theories of European nationalism." Anyone who has read even one of Naipaul's three books on India knows that he has not fallen into this trap. On the contrary, he has tried to eradicate fantasies that were defenses against the depredations of invasion and colonial rule. He has warned against the hazards of retreat into Hindu passivity, the reduction of the meaning of dharma to unquestioning obedience.

During his travels in India in 1988 and 1989, Naipaul had witnessed the persistence of Hinduism adapted to the modern world in science, in politics, in domestic life, even in an agrahara. Now, he hopes, it can help in coming to terms with the past: "We should make ourselves see how far these old invasions and wars had beaten India down and how far we have come."[46] Naipaul's individual self-creation has served as a useful paradigm for his idea of a nation. He insists that truth about the past is the means of relaxing its hold. His focus is on "human possibility . . . the idea of individual talent,"[47] as the core of a nation's strength. On the basis of his own experience and his growing knowledge of India, he has provided reason to believe that, despite persistent inequalities, contradictions, and political venality, through "self-awareness," freedom and democracy can thrive. India is finding its center.

ISLAM—1979; 1995

In the chapter on autobiography I discussed Naipaul's journey to four countries—Iran, Pakistan, Malaysia, and Indonesia—as one in which, despite barriers of language and cultural differences, he was able to reach out to people and to apprehend the central role of Islam in their lives. These dialogues also answered some of the questions with which he arrived. The people he met in Iran and Pakistan came from various economic and social backgrounds and expressed divergent attitudes toward Islam—pessimism, despair, or wary hope regarding the future, unwavering belief in the faith as the bearer of truth—but all, in Naipaul's eyes, were victims of Islam as an Arabian imperial conquest. In *Among the Believers,* in his chapter "Killing History" in the section on Pakistan, he summarizes the history of Arabia's invasion of Spain, Persia, and "the great-Hindu kingdom of Sind" during the seventh and eighth centuries, the last "a bloody story," which is omitted in textbooks where only "the fairy tales" appear. In fact, in Pakistan, as in other Moslem countries, history now begins with Islam. "The time before Islam is a time of blackness: that is part of Muslim theology." Naipaul refers to a letter in a newspaper regarding the excavation of the ancient city Mohenjo-Daro, "one of the archeological glories of Pakistan and the world," in which the writer suggests that "Verses from the Koran . . . should be engraved and set up" in that city "in appropriate places," warning onlookers that such ruin awaited "idolaters."[48]

The loss of history as damaging to the growth of a society and to the "individual talent" of its members is a familiar theme in Naipaul's writings, but in the non-Arabic Muslim world he perceives this loss as fatal. Because of its tyrannical laws, the substitution of theology for education, the suppression of all individuality, he finds that "no colonization had been so thorough as the colonization that had come with the Arab faith."[49] Even those who reject Western civilization are all too willing to rely on its technology to provide the necessities of modern life. This dependency results in a lack of self-confidence and sometimes for the young, like Behzad in Iran or Masood in Pakistan, an inability to plan for their future. Masood, whose parents had left India for Pakistan in 1947, seems to speak not only for himself but for others who might fear being so direct, perhaps because he senses Naipaul's compassion. Having been denied a scholarship at an American university and without enough money to accept a place he has been granted in England, he expresses his despair about life in Pakistan: "In some countries you can believe in the life of struggle. You can believe there will be results. Here there is only luck."[50]

Naipaul's darkest pictures are of Iran and Pakistan. He arrived in Tehran in August 1979, only six months after Ayatollah Khomeini returned from exile in Paris to assume leadership of the Iranian revolution, which had begun in 1978. Almost immediately Khomeini, known for his strong opposition to monarchy, assumed an even more authoritarian role than the deposed Shah. Executions continued, music was outlawed, Revolutionary Guards were on the lookout for communists, for so-called immoral acts, and segregation of the sexes was enforced. As

Khomeini had ordered, "mullahs and ayatollahs" were elected "to the constitution-framing Assembly of Experts." Rule by cleric was under way. What Naipaul calls "the souvenir books of the revolution" consisted of photographs of "death, blood, and revenge," which heightened the mixture of ecstatic profession and underlying fear that pervaded Tehran in August 1979.

His reaction to the results of the revolution was no doubt influenced by his sympathy for Behzad, despite his disagreement with his young guide's communist credo, but even more by the contrast between contemporary Iran and the Muslim civilization of past history. On a street in Tehran, hearing two men selling medicines "invoking as medical authorities . . . Avicenna, Galen, and 'Hippocrat,'" he is reminded of "the Arab glory of a thousand years before, when the Arab faith mingled with Persia, India, and the remnant of the classical world it had overrun, and Muslim civilization was the central civilization of the West." This cosmopolitan tradition, with its capacity to inspire a responsive creativity, has been totally rejected, replaced by a narrow fundamentalism that declares that religion, politics, law, and government are one.

In Pakistan Naipaul finds that not only the deep past but the recent one is ignored. Quoting from a newspaper article that links Iran and Pakistan as Islamic states and refers vaguely to Pakistan's history, he lists the conditions and events its author omits: "the uprootings and mass migrations" after the partition; "the absence of representative government; the land of the faith turning into a land of plunder"; military rule in 1958 and at present; "the bloody secession of far-off Bangladesh in 1971"; the arrest and hanging of Bhutto, "the country's only elected prime minister. . . . All this history, all this secular failure and pain, had been conjured away by the logic of the faith."

The many examples he cites of the deterioration of institutions, of law, and daily life disclose how spurious this logic is. Despite, or perhaps because of, a failing economy, a despotic government controlled by the army, with thousands emigrating to find work and political asylum, there are people who identify the nation of Pakistan with God. For them Islam "is a complete way of life" quite apart from the actual sorry conditions of national and individual existence. To Naipaul more troubling even than the bizarre fantasy of a declining state as Godhood is the use of Islam to justify the atrocities of political despotism, which belies not only its cultural traditions but its spiritual heritage. Yet he comes to understand the personal faith of some of the people he meets, for example, one man who occasionally wavers in his belief but turns back to Islam, hoping for his son's success at school, and for the afterlife for himself, another devoted to the "idea of sacrifice and service." The integrity of their commitment within a society that offers them so little leaves Naipaul with the desperate hope that "in Pakistan, by the very excesses of fundamentalism, Islam might be preparing its own transformation."

Considering Islam in Malaysia and Indonesia, Naipaul stresses its arrival in Southeast Asia "as another religion of India. There was no Arab invasion, as in Sind," and none of the "slaughter" and other depredations inflicted on Iran. "Islam spread as an idea" conveyed by "merchants and priests." The implications of its gradual acceptance as it "mingled with older ideas" govern his approach to these two countries. During this first visit, he perceives the "mixed religion," which had assimilated elements of Hinduism and Buddhism, so vital in preserving the history and traditions of Malaysia and Indonesia, threatened by "Islamic missionaries," chiefly from Pakistan, whose aim is to "purify" the faith, to establish the new Islam modeled on Iran and Pakistan. True, "the pre-Islamic past . . . in Malaysia seemed to be only a matter of village customs," but among the people Naipaul met there was nostalgia for the security of this traditional way of life, which was passing, even as they tried to embrace the new Islam.

In 1979 Malaysia was enjoying wealth produced by "tin, rubber, palm oil [and] oil," which had provided education for young people, "new men," who now feel at home neither in the villages in which they grew up nor in the world outside, where there is no place for them. For these young men, Naipaul says, Islam is "a weapon" which "serves their grief, their feeling of inadequacy, their social rage and racial hate." Money spent on the products of foreign technology only emphasizes their "dependent relationship with the developed world." Their own insecurity encourages the long-standing discrimination against the Chinese, whose very financial success is held against them and who have no political influence. Although the population is only fifty percent Malay, "the country is officially Muslim," with "Muslim personal laws, . . . a kind of prying religious police," and "legal discrimination against non-Muslims," which Naipaul calls "outrageous."

The fundamentalists in Pakistan and Malaysia "believed that to follow the right rules was to restore the purity of the early Islamic way: the reorganization of the world would follow automatically on the rediscovery of the true faith." Reducing this grandiose fantasy to a simpler, more authentic meaning, Naipaul thinks of the person in Malaysia he knows best, his guide who has become his friend, Shafi: "for him the wish to re-establish the rules was also a wish to re-create the security of his childhood, the Malay village he had lost." But even this modest wish could not be realized.

"In Indonesia—or Java," Naipaul says, the pre-Islamic past "showed as a great civilization." Islam was "the formal faith," but the "Hindu-Buddhist past . . . survived in many ways—half-erased, slightly mysterious, but still awesome." This heritage remains even as Indonesians come to terms with their more recent history. Characteristically, Naipaul compresses in a paragraph more than three hundred years of oppression, uprisings, wars, rebellions, and finally independence won at the cost of countless Chinese and Indonesian lives. It is said by some that "half a million people thought to be communists," others say "a million," were killed in uprisings throughout Indonesia. This is the background to rule by the army at the time of Naipaul's visit, and he feels its proximity when people "talk of 1965," as if they were "looking, from a distance, at a mysterious part of themselves." The depersonalization of their violent past seems to result in what Naipaul perceives as restlessness at a time of apparent peace, technological advancement, and productivity. So many years of struggle against the cruel and humiliating domination of the Dutch and the Japanese have surely conditioned Indonesians to be wary of authoritarian rule, albeit that of their own countrymen.

In their restlessness they have chosen two very different sources of identity: on the one hand, a return to Javanese traditional culture and, on the other, a commitment to Islam. In either case, says Naipaul, "they were now always entering somebody else's world, and getting further from themselves." Nonetheless, as I pointed out in chapter 2, Naipaul believes that the puppet plays serve an important function in the villages, where the "living epics" of Hinduism, "its most human and literary side," the *Ramayana* and the *Mahabharata*, were performed. Contrasting the unyielding dogma of Islam with the adaptability, the freedom of interpretation, offered by the puppet plays, he observes that the Javanese "had taken what was most human and liberating from the religions that had come their way, to make their own." However, the old "composite religion" was gradually giving way before the new Islam that had begun to infiltrate the villages, bringing faith with "political roots."

Like Malaysia, Indonesia in these years had grown rich, chiefly from oil, but the effects on the very people who had prospered were so unsettling as to cause what one of Naipaul's informants calls a loss of "personality" or "identity," an inability to adapt to their new status and to enjoy opportunities to learn about cultures other than their own. Even when people have had the advantages of travel and education abroad, they remain villagers in mind and spirit. One solution to this problem is the course in "mental training" offered in Bandung by Imaduddin in the mosque of the Institute of Technology, where he is an instructor. Imaduddin's beliefs and attitudes, which determine his method in the classes he teaches,[51] are unacceptable to Naipaul: his efforts to disseminate an imposed ideology, to politicize religion, to oversimplify faith. He has no historical perspective, no tolerance for cultural differences. Yet Naipaul is moved by the adventurous life Imaduddin has lived, his involvement, despite his indifference to this phase of his career, in the history of Indonesia. He respects Imaduddin's integrity and feels compassion for the fourteen months' imprisonment he endured and for his present uncertain status in Bandung. And it is with an account of what has happened to Imaduddin between "the last day of 1979"[52] and their meeting in 1995 that he begins his most recent book on his return to the four non-Arab Muslim countries he had earlier explored.

In *Beyond Belief* Naipaul traces changes in the lives of some of the people he had met in 1979, and learns from them and from others how imposed political and religious structures, often fused as one, have affected their view of themselves and their world. In this respect it is a sequel to *Among the Believers*, but in one way it is quite different. *Beyond Belief* is rarely autobiographical. As Naipaul says, "It is less of a travel book; the writer is less present, less of an inquirer." One might add "less of an inquirer" of himself as well as of his informants. Rather, he is "a finder-out of stories." His search is by no means haphazard, however. As "a manager of narrative," he has gathered his stories around the theme of "conversion," which appeared earlier in *Among the Believers*, but is central to *Beyond Belief.* He states his position in the prologue: "Islam is in its origins an Arab religion. Everyone not an Arab who is a Muslim is a convert. Islam is not simply a matter of conscience or private belief. It makes imperial demands. A convert's worldview alters. His holy places are in Arab lands; his sacred language is Arabic." Such conversions are disruptive to individuals and their societies. Their own history is lost, replaced by "the Arab story." As a result they "develop fantasies about who and what they are; and in the Islam of converted countries there is an element of neurosis and nihilism."

Fouad Ajami, in his review of *Beyond Belief,*[53] calls this statement "an odd, obtuse view of religion." Islam, he says, "like Christianity . . . is a world religion. Its worldly and otherworldly ideals are universal. Strictly speaking, everyone outside the Hijaz—like everyone outside Galilee and Calvary—is a convert to these faiths." He discusses the many alterations that "converted societies" have made on the faith they accepted, particularly in Iran. These comments, as well as his learned summary of how Islam "made its great world-historical way" to people "who had not known or met the Arabs," point out the complexity of conversion, the variety of forces that govern this process. He also demonstrates that Naipaul, as an outsider, in the five months of his travels, could not go much beyond "the exterior of things."

If Ajami discloses some limitations of Naipaul's approach, he does not always give him credit for what he actually sees. For example, Ajami reminds the reader that Islam "is not quite as total and unworldly as Naipaul fears." But Naipaul, far from viewing Islam as "unworldly," says in *Among the Believers*: "No religion is more worldly than Islam. In spite of its political incapacity, no religion keeps men's eyes more fixed on the way the world is run,"[54] evidence of which is apparent in many of the narratives in *Beyond Belief*.

Furthermore, Naipaul's conception of conversion is not based on individual Muslim belief or on the ideals Islam shares with other religions. It signifies a political, social, legal, and cultural adherence to Islam, in other words an Islamic state, of which Iran and Pakistan are prime examples and, in his view, Malaysia and Indonesia are on the verge of becoming. Naipaul acknowledges that there "is another way of considering the theme of conversion. It can be seen as a kind of crossover from old beliefs, earth religions, the cults of rulers and local deities, to the revealed religions—Christianity and Islam principally." The disruptions these changes wrought are now past history, and it is through this lens that Naipaul also views the ongoing conversions to Islam.

Beyond Belief was written and published before the uprisings in Jakarta started in May 1988, which resulted in the downfall of Suharto. The opening section on Indonesia, "The Man of the Moment," in which Naipaul writes of his visit with Imaduddin, was published in the June 11, 1988 issue of *The New York Review of Books*, followed by an epilogue by Margaret Scott dated May 14, 1988, in which she discusses her meeting with Imaduddin after the rebellion was under way. Her comments fill out Naipaul's portrait of Imaduddin, one of his chief informants in the past and now a leading political figure, whereas Ajami, in his review which appeared two months later, raises questions about their common impression of the man.

After sixteen years Naipaul finds Imaduddin unchanged in his total devotion to Islam but no longer having a "university lecturer's manner," instead appearing as a "man of affairs." Indeed, that is what he has become. In Naipaul's account of Imaduddin's version of his past—his years of study abroad, his imprisonment and years of exile, suspected of trying to convert Indonesia into an Islamic state—Imaduddin seems to feel that his time in prison had some lasting value. There he came under the influence of Dr. Subandrio, a physician, formerly Sukarno's deputy prime minister, sentenced for his involvement in "a communist plot to kill the generals and take over the country." In his thirteen years as a political prisoner, Subandrio had changed. He had become religious, wishing to learn more about the Koran from Imaduddin. In turn, Subandrio, with his Javanese "courtly manners and special ways of saying difficult things," taught the blunt North Sumatran Imaduddin how to control his aggression. From Subandrio, Imaduddin feels, he received advice that has been the key to his success: "in politics you must not expect honesty and morality right through. . . . In politics the question of winning is the end result. So if you put your idea into the mind of your enemy, and he practices it, you are the winner. Above all . . . you must never confront the Javanese."

Having adopted a kind of Javanese discretion and "learned that he shouldn't try to act on his own," Imaduddin "found" or, as Naipaul indicates a little later on, deliberately chose, "a patron, Habibie." Of course, Imaduddin could not have foreseen the day when Habibie would replace the ousted Suharto, but some political instinct, inseparable from his Islamic fervor, must have intimated that this affiliation was a means to advancement. As minister for research and technology when Imaduddin came to know him, Habibie was already a powerful figure, "closer than anyone else in government to President Suharto." Habibie's "grand idea" was to have Indonesians "build, or at any rate design" their own airplanes. His plan, to Naipaul, a dubious one, was that the resulting technological knowledge and training would bring about "an Indonesian industrial revolution." As chairman of a new organization, the Association of Indonesian Intellectuals, Habibie was a proponent of the union of science and religious devotion, thus the perfect model for Imaduddin, who was one of the "principal early movers behind" the Association.

Imaduddin headed another organization, the Foundation for the Development and Management of Human Resources, a circumlocution that Naipaul interprets to mean convincing people to become "devout Muslims" by "weaning them away from old loyalties, whatever these were, and getting them to follow the technological-political line of Imaduddin and Habibie." Imaduddin's assertion: "Science is something inherent in Islamic thinking," suggests to Naipaul that "this was where Imaduddin was taking the war to the enemy, and making an immense power play on behalf of the government." Along with the Association of Muslim Intellectuals, his aim was "to take the islands to their destiny as the leader of the Islamic revival in the twenty-first century."

The portrait that emerges from Imaduddin's own words, supplemented by Naipaul's explications, is of a man who reveals little of his inner life, and certainly no conflict. Firm in his commitment to the fundamentalist path, he never questions his own motives or values or conclusions. The rare self-criticism he allows himself in his discussions with Naipaul is of his early lack of political savoir-faire, and he is frank about his efforts, even in prison, to improve so as to fulfill his ambitions. He seems to be merely an opportunist when he tells of "reading about" Habibie, then asking a friend to arrange an introduction because of Habibie's connection with Suharto, and of giving up engineering for what he calls "human resources," actually training students "to become good Muslims." His belief that he can win by simply getting his "enemy" (apparently anyone who disagrees with him) to accept his "idea" suggests that he has a simplistic view of the human beings he has chosen to "develop." Yet he seems sincere in his conviction that his effort to promote his career is only an expression of his zeal to proselytize for Islam. In working for this goal he has been uncompromising, as much in the past when he faced opposition as now when the Muslim movement is supported by the government. It is this quality, a certain serenity in the consistency of his faith amid the "[e]xtraordinary events" he has lived through, that gives him, in Naipaul's view, "a strange innocence that appeared to have protected him."

Margaret Scott's visit to Imaddudin took place more than three years after Naipaul's. By then what Imaduddin calls "our economic troubles"[55] had caused bank and business failures and widespread unemployment. Student uprisings had become a serious threat to Suharto's regime, which in a matter of days would be deposed. Aware that Scott has "come to talk about what has happened to him and Indonesia since Naipaul's visit," Imaduddin appears optimistic despite his weakness from recent heart bypass surgery. Scott depicts his initial response to her as jovial: "His heart may be failing him, he says, but he is very, very happy that Habibie, his patron, has now become vice-president," thus, "the presumptive successor—at least constitutionally—of the seventy-seven-year-old Suharto." To Imaduddin this is the fulfillment of the "dream" he had when he organized The Association of Muslim Intellectuals.

He admits that he did not foresee the economic problems that now beset Indonesia; they are among the surprises he did not plan for, and he underestimates their importance. Despite the government's intimation that money might not be available to support Habibie's "grand scheme to build the N-2130 jet" and the IMF's denial of "public funds to finance the plane," Imaduddin "says his belief in Habibie and his technological vision remains unshaken."

Even this naïveté, or willful denial, on the part of a powerful political figure seems less threatening to the stability of the nation than his refusal to acknowledge the seriousness of Indonesia's economic catastrophe, which he dismisses as "temporary." He twice refers to Subandrio, from whom he learned "Javanese politics, whose influence even now tells him that 'Suharto will win.'" To Scott, "it is clear that in his account Naipaul describes [Imaduddin's] cast of mind with great acuity. Islam remains Imaduddin's guide." In a single page of *The New York Review of Books* she has demonstrated how the man whom Naipaul depicted as the archetypal Muslim fundamentalist reacted to recent economic and political events in Indonesia. One would expect that Imaduddin who has participated in so much of modern history, who fought against the Dutch for independence, and has known and worked with many Indonesian leaders, would approach the present crises with more awareness of the dangers that threaten the nation. Scott writes of the "sense of dread in Jakarta. . . . Will there be enough food? How long will the recession last? How much strain can the system bear?" But Imaduddin is not concerned with such matters: "Suharto has been good for Islam and so he still supports Suharto."

Ajami, writing after Suharto resigned and was succeeded by Habibie, warns that "Imaduddin offers a cautionary tale about the glib imputation of the actions of Muslims to Islam." In "both of Naipaul's journeys," Imaduddin "raises . . . the risk of being taken in, the risk of looking for belief where there is only need and ambition." As Ajami sees it, this risk entailed a failure to see that "faith can be a pose," that Imaduddin's faith was but a means of advancing his career. Referring to the section on Indonesia in *Among the Believers*, he claims that Naipaul misses "the eclecticism" of the "culture and the religions of the place," the "ambiguity of people's belief."[56] Although it is Naipaul's version of Imaduddin's character that inspires such statements, Imaduddin seems the least likely person to whom they would apply. In both Naipaul's and Scott's accounts

Imaduddin presents himself as without conflict, without ambivalence. If this is a pose, as Ajami suggests, is it not possible that, sustained by years of dogma and prayer, of training himself and others, it has become a self-image so inflexible as to be impervious to doubt, and even to his own serious illness and the political and economic crises of the state?

In an article dated July 15, 1998, Margaret Scott refers to Clifford Geertz's view that Indonesia is "a would-be nation of nations, a collection of hundreds of different peoples and islands rather than just landscapes. 'And what is needed to join them,' he writes, 'is a story that convinces them that they belong, by fate and nature, politically together.'" In the spring of 1988 she witnessed "this search for a new story," and was able "to hear those whose voices often conflict in trying to create it."[57] The stories Naipaul narrates in some respects constitute the prolegomena to these strivings, and Imaduddin's is but one of them.

Mr. Wahid's story is linked to his "family story," which "contained, layer by layer, the history of the country over the last century and a quarter." In some respects it is not unlike Imaduddin's, whose roots are also in the nation's history and his paternal heritage, but its denouement is quite different. Wahid is known for carrying on the tradition of his grandfather and father, both of whom had established their pesantren, religious boarding schools, to teach "the Islamic way of life." He had also inherited the leadership of the NU (Nahdlatul Ulama), a revisionist Muslim party related to the pesantren, which his father had established in 1952. In 1984 Wahid had divorced the NU from politics, and he has persisted in his belief that Islam must not be politicized, that it "is a moral force which works through ethics and morality."

Wahid strongly objects to Habibie's "route of Islamization," which, he says, "means that he sees politics as an integral part of Islam," and he is eloquent in condemning this policy. "I feel it personally," he says, "because my father participated in the writing of the constitution which gives equal status to all citizens. People should practice Islam out of conscience, not out of fear. Habibie and his friends create a fear among non-Muslims and non-practicing Muslims to show their identity. This is the first step to tyranny." Clearly, among these friends of Habibie is Imaduddin, although he is not named.

Naipaul seems somewhat frustrated by Wahid's repeated denunciations of Islamic politics, hoping instead to hear more about Habibie: "a picture, some conversation, a story." Yet Wahid has told a story, his own, which is perhaps more vital to the future of Indonesia than Imaduddin's. As a Muslim scholar, he is the antagonist of the technocrat politician

Habibie. Descended from a grandfather and a father who made the pilgrimage to Mecca, a man who values and teaches Islamic traditions, he would protect the diverse non-Islamic population of Indonesia—Hindu, Buddhist, and Christian—against fundamentalism. Implicit in his way of life and his beliefs is one possible version of Clifford Geertz's hypothetical story: the political union of people brought together "by fate and nature," some inspired by the moral core of Islam, others free to follow the religion of their heritage or to find their own path.

From Dewi Fortuna Anwar, a civil servant, whom he meets in Jakarta, Naipaul hears a story that confirms his belief that "[r]eligious or cultural purity is a fundamentalist fantasy." A conservative Muslim, Dewi has nonetheless remained loyal to "the many strands of her background"—an orthodox Muslim education as well as an academic one and, most interesting to Naipaul, a familiarity with and respect for the remnants of the pre-Islamic village ways of her ancestors. At her suggestion he visits West Sumatra, where she grew up. There "the antiquity these plains suggested" evoke "the idea of the ancient world . . . the 'eternal forms'" that Hazlitt had found "in the landscapes of Poussin." He responds even more intensely on the next day during a visit to Pariyangan, "a big dip in the volcanic land with a hot-water spring," which gives him the feeling that, even without knowing its history or myth, one can realize that it had always been "a sacred place; it would always have had a power over human imagination."

Like Dewi's, his own "different worlds converge," as he associates this site with an ancient Roman myth to which Tacitus alludes in his *Histories* (II, 2, 3). To Tacitus's account Naipaul adds the Latin recognition of divine presence, *"Numen inest*: the Roman words fitted: the god or spirit of the place was there, more than it was for me at Paphos in Cyprus, where Venus was said to have issued out of the sea." He then refers to Tacitus's explanation that Venus was worshipped at Paphos as she was nowhere else, in her most elemental representation as "a rock cone sliced off at the top," in contrast, Naipaul says, with the "alluring feminine shape" of her presence elsewhere.

For Naipaul the religious traditions of ancient Rome and of pre-Islamic Asia merge to illuminate the very nature of the sacred, "the wonder of the site and the wonder of the water bubbling up from the earth for centuries." For the unbeliever this evocation of the ancient past is a spiritual bond with those who from time immemorial have acknowledged the mystery of natural and human life. Still, he is aware that Muslim visitors to this place who greet each other with "worship the god" would know "with one part of their minds that the salutation was idol-atrous." The nearby mosque was intended "not to honor or claim the sa-credness of the place, but to triumph over it. . . . The sacred places of the Muslim faith . . . were in another country." Yet it was, after all, Dewi, the conservative Muslim, who had sent him to her childhood home where the taboos of her clan and their sacred places endure.

Few of the people whose stories Naipaul tells are as fortunate as Dewi in her background or as content as she in her achievements and her way of life. During Indonesia's boom some have prospered in "the worlds of business and computers," but not all have been able to inte-grate their professional success with their origins. When Naipaul meets Budi who, with a partner, owns a software company, he seems "to ex-emplify what Imaduddin taught and what Habibie had committed the country to: the congruence of Islam and technology." Yet soon Naipaul is to learn that Budi "had not mastered the new society; he was one of its orphans or half-orphans."

Budi has never recovered from his father's bankruptcy, which oc-curred seventeen years earlier, but remained as a warning. Failing twice to pass the entrance examination to the Bandung Institute of Technol-ogy, he studied computer technology, and soon was successful in the field. Still his failure to be accepted at the Bandung Institute, like his father's bankruptcy, seemed a portent of his future. Although he has made the pil-grimage to Mecca and has become a devout Muslim, he has not found peace. His financial success is often a source of guilt; when he spends money on himself, his family's poverty comes to his mind. Most touch-ing of all is his loneliness. Unlike his colleagues at work, he has not at-tended a university and has thus "been cut off from a whole generation of his peers." Because of his insecurities, his inability to define his role in his society, he has been unable to find a girlfriend or a wife. No doubt some of his problems are those of a sensitive man who has succeeded in his profession at great personal cost, but others reflect "a time of crossover between faiths," amid rapid technological development linked to politi-cal power. Budi could not know that Habibie's world and that of his en-vied colleagues, which seemed so substantial, was as unstable as his own.

Naipaul does see signs of fundamental instability. The rapidity with which "new wealth" was accumulating "felt like luck, this wealth that could bless even the uneducated, because the technologies and the fac-tories that produced it had been imported whole. For that reason, it felt like plunder, something that had to end." Jakarta seems to him somewhat like his image of prerevolutionary Iran, even in 1979 retaining something of its grandeur as a cosmopolitan nation. In that year, six months after the revolution, he had seen signs of decay, but there had also been "the excitement of the immense crowds at Friday prayers at Tehran University," a sign, like the "revolutionary posters and graffiti everywhere," of hope for the future.

Now, sixteen years later, much has changed. The dominant tone of the section on Iran in *Beyond Belief* is sadness. At the beginning of Naipaul's stay in Tehran, when he speaks of "middle-class looking people" in the lobby of what had been the old Hyatt hotel, he is corrected by an acquaintance who tells him that "the true middle class of Iran, the class that had taken a century, and incalculable wealth, to produce had been destroyed or scattered." The people Naipaul had referred to "were the sad beginnings of a new middle class," a reminder of what they could not replace. Sandra Mackey, who has observed progress in Iran since 1979—the expansion of education, "health care," "social services," and even the rights of women—lists among the negative results of the revolution, the loss of millions of people who left the country, fleeing "either the rage against the privileged or the repression imposed by the clerics. In economic terms, they took with them the capital and skills necessary to build a new Iran. In terms of Iranian society, the exodus physically broke the great extended families, the foundation blocks of society."[58]

Even more than this loss, more than any other injury to the nation, more than strict censorship and seemingly endless forms of suppression, the eight-year war with Iraq has wounded Iran. The war, says Naipaul, "was the inescapable theme." Mehrdad, a university student who is Naipaul's guide, transmits his own version of a general despair. In his story, as he gradually relates it to Naipaul, and in his interpretations of the experiences they share, one hears the effects of the revolution and the war on the mind and spirit of an intelligent young man who could represent many of the youth of Iran. Through his eyes we see how the nation's trauma has affected every area of life—personal, social, and economic. When in response to Mehrdad's comment, "It is a war that was lost," Naipaul asks "what it meant to him," and Mehrdad replies, "Nothing," Naipaul is aware that this is "his way of speaking of an almost inexpressible pain." Pain at the plight of his sister who, as an unmarried woman in her thirties, cannot find a husband because too many men have been lost to the war. Given the restrictions imposed by the revolution, she is denied even a social life. Confined to a routine of work and home, she expresses her frustration in rages and tears, and Mehrdad and their mother are unable to help her.

Beyond his family's suffering is unremitting pain at the sacrifice of thousands of young lives depicted in his and Naipaul's visit to the Martyrs' Cemetery. The best known of these is the thirteen-year-old martyr who had "strapped a bomb to himself and thrown himself below an enemy tank." Now he lies buried beside his brother, who was also killed in the war. Khomeini's tribute to the young martyr as the true "leader" whose "little heart" exceeded the worth of "more than a hundred pens" seems a distortion of the faith to justify the sacrifice of boys too immature to resist the lure of instant heroism. The many gravestones marked "UNKNOWN MARTYR," followed by Mehrdad's explanation, "Families who don't know where their son is come and say their prayers over one of these stones" accentuates the loss of each young life deprived of its identity in death, assigned by parents a fantasized burial site.

Mehrdad, pointing out the flags of the Islamic Republic, "green, white, and red," now faded, remarks, "Losing their color. Losing its meaning." By now Naipaul knows him well enough to realize that "[what] appeared to be irony in his words was a form of pain. The army," in which he had served, "and the flag mattered to him; and these flags, never moving, never meant to catch a breeze, put up by the families of martyrs, were coated with the dust of the desert."

Arash, one of the young men to whom Mehrdad introduces Naipaul, had volunteered for the army when he was sixteen. Now at twenty-seven he talks frankly about his disillusionment: "This war didn't have anything for me. Let's see whether my memories of it have something for others." Indeed they do. He tells of the hypnotic chanting to inspire those at the front with "thoughts of death and martyrdom and going to paradise and having freedom," of his engagement in battle, his wound and recovery. Sent back to fight despite the promise that, as a Basiji, he could return home when he wished to, he simply left. He soon went back to the army, but left again and returned twice more, obviously ambivalent about his commitment to possible martyrdom.

One source of his disillusionment was life in Tehran during and after the war. It was as if there were no emotional connection between the city and the battlefield. In "the same alley" where the funeral of two of Arash's martyred friends was taking place, "there was a wedding party." All that the people in Tehran seemed to care about, he says, was "fashions and music. . . . In Tehran nobody cared about the war. Everybody was looking for money." The Basijis "hounded people for violating Islamic rules and they extorted money from them."

Despite Arash's "openness," Naipaul feels he has omitted his actual experience of the war. It seemed from his account to have been "a war without death and with very little blood." When pressed, however, despite his unwillingness to recall the deaths he had witnessed, he says, "A regiment of fourteen hundred men went on an attack. And only four hundred came back." Asked what he thinks now, he replies, "I am indifferent," like Mehrdad, Naipaul comments, "really saying that he couldn't express his pain." Yet Naipaul's empathy with Arash, transmitted in the words, "I feel you are a lonely man," does break down some of his defenses as Arash admits, "I prefer to be alone," and soon after he discloses the core of his pain, the violation of his youthful ideal of Islamic justice: "Everyone was looking for Ali's justice. But after a while they saw it wasn't getting done." To Naipaul's question, "Do you think you can get such a thing as Ali's justice in the world again?" Arash responds, "Never." At the age of twenty he had come to the conclusion that not only was justice unobtainable in his time but even the great Ali, during the seventh century "in a short period of time . . . had many enemies, and he couldn't do it. It is always like that." The revolution he had risked his life to defend had failed him, leaving him without ideals, without a profession, his means of support a taxi that is not even licensed.

At the opposite end of the economic and social scale, a contemporary Ali tells an even more harrowing story of disillusionment. The son of "a rich and famous and admired father," Ali had many advantages, among them the opportunity to study at a theological school in Mashhad and later to take "technical courses" and one in the humanities in the United States, where he spent eight years. After the freedom he enjoyed in America, he found the atmosphere in Iran, still ruled by the Shah and his secret police, oppressive—even dangerous. Ali acquired great wealth in the 1970s yet, as a proponent of freedom, he supported the revolution "morally and financially." Like Arash, he committed himself to an ideal—in his case, "a revolution based on heavenly laws and laws of nature." He soon found, however, that his wealth, which made it possible for him to contribute generously to the cause, made him suspect. Regarded as a member of the "old regime," over a period of three years following the revolution he "had been kidnapped more than once; arrested and imprisoned many times; even tried. He had been bled of tens of millions of dollars."

It was not only his own victimization that turned Ali against the revolution. He describes the court that the Ayatollah Khalkhalli used "as the instrument of his executions"; he recounts the "anarchy and terror" induced by Khomeini himself. By the time Ali was tried and acquitted, he had "learned how to live with the revolution." As he had survived the harsh rule of the Shah, he manages to deal with the present theocracy. If the revolution turned out to be a far cry from "something done by God," at least he has had a calmer period since his trial. "The government had got rid of many of the wilder people," the types who had tormented him during the first years of the revolution.

Among those ousted from power is the hanging judge Khalkhalli, whom Naipaul tried to interview in 1979, only to be met with evasions in the guise of humor. On his return to Iran in 1995 he once again visits Qom to interview Khalkhalli and, "if possible, get from him some new angle on old times." The old times of Khalkhalli were gone: "He had been cast aside by the revolution long ago as one of the old brigade." As Naipaul waits for Khalkhalli he examines photographs of him with Khomeini displayed in a sitting room, "like proof of his power in the old days, his closeness to the Imam, the leader of the revolution." The Khalkhalli who appears is much altered from these images—aged, sick, "his eyes without mischief now and seemingly close to tears," appearing to elicit pity. But in one respect he is unchanged; he makes it impossible for Naipaul to reach him. Evading Naipaul's questions, he "turned everything to abstraction. As an ayatollah that was his talent. It pleased him to be baffling my purpose." Even after all his experience and achievements as a reporter, Naipaul, evaluating his own technique "many weeks later," wonders whether he should have asked about the photographs of the days when Khalkhalli was the hanging judge, Khomeini's "jester," whether this method might have led to other things. But it seems clear that, as in 1979, Khalkalli is determined to reveal nothing about himself.

One of the few subjects that interests Khalkhalli is a visit he wants Naipaul to pay to the Ayatollah Montazeri, which Naipaul later realizes was "possibly even an attempt by Khalkhalli to involve me in his cause." After he and Mehrdad have left, Mehrdad warns Naipaul that "such a visit is the way of death." Naipaul's assertion that "these men are back numbers. They are very old and can't be dangerous to anybody now," seems naive regarded from Mehrdad's viewpoint: "In this situation even the dead are dangerous."

Even with the old guard gone—replaced or dead—fear, like a persistent infection, seems to have spread throughout Iran. Mehrdad says, "Everyone is frightened. My father and mother are frightened." He speaks of their fear for the future of their younger son, still a child. Another person, a Mrs. Seghir, who left Iran and has returned to visit her parents, tells of how her husband, "frightened after the revolution," had become stressed and ill and had died of cancer. From a diplomat Naipaul hears of parents, frightened when they are called to their nine-year-old daughter's school, wondering what she could have said about them, only to learn that they had been invited to witness her receiving a prize for being "the best reciter of the Koran."

The most chilling story Naipaul hears, also from the diplomat, has "a quality of folk myth." As such it enacts the intensity of the fear and pain that individuals repress. The story is about "a middle-aged lady in a chador" who repeatedly takes a blind young man to see a specialist in a local hospital to have his eyes examined. The doctor considers the boy "just 'a piece of meat,' mutilated beyond rehabilitation, without hands, without feet." He cannot see any point in restoring his eyesight, since he can never "return to any sort of life." After a while the woman confesses to the doctor that the boy is the son of a neighbor. Because he betrayed her son who belonged to an antirevolutionary group and was thus the cause of his execution, she wants him to live. Alive, he is her "revenge." The tale ends with her statement: "I want his mother to grieve for him every day." This perversion of the archetypal episode, a mother grieving for her son, connotes many sources of the pain that afflicts Iran—the fear pervasive in quotidian life, the betrayal of the innocent, the consequences of martyrdom in warfare, the impossibility of finding consolation. As Naipaul writes in another context but is certainly fitting here: "All that could be said was that the country had been given an almost universal knowledge of pain."

Implicit in the sadness of Iran, in Naipaul's view, is that its past is now "irrecoverable." In Pakistan, on the other hand, he observes "[v]ital fragments of the past . . . in dress, customs, ceremonies, festivals, and, importantly, ideas of caste." Such traditions, however, do not mitigate the effects of past history, particularly what Naipaul calls the "Muslim insecurity" resulting from the breach between Indian Hindus and Muslims during the years of the British conquest, which led to the creation of Pakistan. "The Hindus, especially in Bengal, welcomed the New Learning of Europe and the institutions the British brought. The Muslims, wounded by their loss of power, and out of old religious scruples, stood aside." The demand for the new state was accompanied by "an idea of old glory," of invasion and conquest, a "fantasy [that] still lives; and for the Muslim converts of the subcontinent, it is the start of their neurosis, because in this fantasy the convert forgets who or what he is and becomes the violator." This shaky national identity had no core apart from "the triumph of the faith" in the division of "Hindustan." No realistic concept of nationhood unifies Pakistan. Without democratic institutions or a "modern economy," it came to depend on the backing of the United States and the export of its population, becoming "in part a remittance economy." Islamic identity relied on faith; Islamic law on intimidation and suppression.

Several of the stories Naipaul has collected recount the dilemmas of people who accept Islam yet are victimized by the injustices of the political and social structures that control their lives. Thus, they waver between commitment and doubt, ever warding off psychic chaos. In Lahore Naipaul meets a poor woman in a shelter run by a human rights group. Abused by her husband who mutilated her nose, deprived of her children, rejected by her family, her only defense is a state described by the lawyer of the group as "callous," a term that the woman herself explicates when she says, "I am not supposed to feel pleasure or happiness." Her parents had not permitted her to attend school and had chosen her husband because it "was against Islam for a girl not to be married." Having obeyed all the rules of her society and the demands of her husband, she is now without resources, left to punish herself for the suffering she has endured. Only at the end of her interview with Naipaul does she break through the callousness she has accepted as her due. When "suddenly she began to laugh," Naipaul felt she was laughing at his "strange questions," his "clothes," his need for an interpreter. It "had been building up inside of her." This laughter, which she could not control, seems more than a response to the immediate occasion. It is surely a reaction against her suppression of her own feelings, a kind of hysterical release from her acceptance of total passivity.

Not only the poor and the uneducated are powerless when they cannot rely on humane laws for protection. Although the courts, like other institutions established by the British, still exist, they have been corrupted by "too much political interference, too much litigation . . . too many false witnesses." Naipaul tells the story of Rana who, as an adolescent, out of a desire to protect himself and his family, wanted to obtain a position of power. Having decided at first to become a policeman and later on a lawyer, he was to become disillusioned in both aspirations. Observing that "the police were trained to treat ordinary people like criminals," he realized that power could lead to harshness, even cruelty, and, at his father's insistence, he studied law. Having obtained the position of junior attorney, he again witnessed the abuse of power by the police who brought false charges and by the judges who heard petitions. Sohail, a friend of Rana's, who accompanied him and Naipaul to the courts, sums up their predicament: "There are two kinds of people who are living well in Pakistan. People with names, and people with money. Everybody else are like insects, worms. They have no power. No approach. Powers are in limited hands, and money is also in limited hands." Disheartened about his profession, his future, Rana tries to emigrate to England only to be refused a visa by the British consulate. He remains in Pakistan, "living now on his nerves." Rana's goals, both of which derived from a need for power as protection, are a telling commentary on life in Pakistan, ruled by Islamic law.

Yet painful as it is, his is not the most disastrous of the tales Naipaul hears. For some of the mohajirs, Muslims who had emigrated from India, the partition, "once a cause for joy, had become like a wound." Unwelcome in Karachi, they faced "political barriers, some overt, some hidden." "Nearly half a century later," their descendants, still regarded as "strangers . . . unrepresented, cheated, without power, had taken up arms against the state in a merciless guerrilla war."

The accounts of individual mohajirs whom Naipaul quotes depict the disenchantment of young people who had been devout Muslims and the crushing of the spirit of the great city of Karachi. Salman's is among the most moving of these stories, perhaps because he has internalized events that occurred at the very beginning of the partition, before his birth. Reading about his effort to reconstruct the murder of his grandmother and the anguish of his grandfather's escape to Pakistan is reading history as inherited psychic torment. When he was fifteen he heard about the massacre of Muslims that took place in August 1947, in which his grandmother and other members of her family were killed in their home in Jalandhar. When his grandfather, who had been hiding, returned to the house, he found no bodies, only "blood spattered on the walls." Seeking to escape, he caught a train to Pakistan. "The train was attacked on the way. He arrived in Lahore buried under dead bodies. He was one of the few survivors." The details of this massacre, on which Salman ruminated obsessively, became the historical and emotional core of his development as a Pakistani.

As a young man he accepted the jihad and other forms of coercion as necessary defenses of Islam. But even as he participated in a "schoolboy demonstration," against a book, *The Warrior Prophet*, he doubted its justification. Clinging to his faith even as he began to doubt, he was finally able to admit that he was no longer a believer when his brother, whose judgment he valued, told him that both he and their sister had given up the faith. What had bound Salman to Islam was his loyalty to those who were murdered in Jalandhar in 1947; now he no longer feared that he was deserting their memory. Actually he had not entirely given up this preoccupation but had redirected it into a need for revenge. When he was twenty he joined the army and "was very vocal," he says, "about going back to war with India." Fortunately, he soon outgrew his involvement with the army and his desire for vengeance.

Having moved to Karachi and married, he eventually started his own business, but owing to bad investments he and his wife lost all their money. Even worse, they had arrived in Karachi at the very time that "the Sindhi-Punjabi-mohajir tensions were about to turn nasty." Salman tells of the years 1987–1989 when a "solitary pedestrian" in Karachi "at night would be approached from behind by a motorcyclist and stabbed in the back." When, one night, he ran out of petrol while driving and had to walk home, he was frightened. "I have never felt such a raging fear," he says, "it was surging inside me." When he heard the sound of a motorcycle behind him, he was "utterly and completely terrified." As it turned out, the cyclist was friendly, spoke of the danger of the streets, and took him home. But the episode was enough to convince Salman that he and his wife must leave Karachi and return to Lahore. Once again he incorporates the trauma of an era when he says: "It wasn't really fear. Fear for my own life. It was the sorrow of living in an unjust, cruel society. Everything was collapsing." Reverting to the events of 1947, he demands, even after all the years that have passed, that they have some meaning, that his forbears' catastrophe have a place in the nation's consciousness: "It's as though those poor people who died in Jalandhar died in vain. Why should my aunts and grandparents have to pay with their lives—for nothing? There was no bitterness. Just a sense of the unfairness in it all."

While he was still in Karachi, Salman joined other people "who had lost hope" in a "peace rally" that, from his description, seems to have been a ritual of mourning for the city that had once been "kindhearted . . . especially good to its poorer inhabitants." Soon after, "there was a massacre of some three hundred people in the city of Hyderabad, the second city of Sindh. . . . It was part of the mohajir war. Sometimes the mohajirs did the killing, sometimes the army." On the day of this slaughter Salman and his wife decided the time had come to leave Karachi.

Naipaul's summary of the mohajirs' war in Karachi, which lasted ten years, is his most striking depiction of the internal division and strife

Pakistan has endured since its establishment as a nation. It was, Naipaul says, "not a clear-cut war, mohajirs against the state." There was the influence of "governments [which] sought to use the passions of various groups." There also was division even among the mohajirs: "two militant and mutually hostile . . . factions." The reactions of people to life in Karachi in 1995 differ at times, but Naipaul's subjects all describe a divided city terrorized by violence. An editor of an Urdu-language newspaper tells of "three thousand young men" detained by the police, some of whom will be "tortured." He himself "had changed houses four times . . . to protect himself not only against the police but also against the militant mohajir movement," which "had become as brutal as its enemies." Another man, Abdul, asked "What are things like now in Karachi?" replies, "Very good," because it is the government that is committing the murders. "It's the Urdu-speaking people basically who are dying, and this is the sacrifice." He points out that two million "died for the creation of Pakistan. . . . We have to make sacrifices for our rights." Nusrat, Naipaul's friend, explains, "He is talking of a mohajir nation. They are talking of separatism now." The mohajirs who, Naipaul says, "became the fifth nationality of Pakistan," seem to illustrate a movement noted by a member of a fundamentalist commune, the Assembly of Islam at Mansura: "The modern state was giving way to 'separate fiefdoms' as in the past." Decades of internal strife, not only in Karachi, but elsewhere in Pakistan, for example, in 1997 between contending Muslim sects in Lahore, as well as assassinations, political and financial corruption, widespread poverty and illiteracy do not necessarily predict separatism, but they certainly indicate that Pakistan has not yet achieved a unified national goal or an idea of nationhood. Given these conditions, as well as continuous violence, an unstable economy, incompetent leaders, a populace fearful of denunciation, and a history of military rule, the coup by the army in October 1999 seems almost inevitable.

Naipaul's "Malaysian Postscript," the brief final section of *Beyond Belief,* begins with a comparison between his visit to Kuala Lumpur in 1979 and his subsequent one sixteen years later. As in Indonesia, he has come at a time of rapid industrialization and prosperity that preceded the sudden economic collapse with its political repercussions of 1998. He now finds the Holiday Inn where he had stayed in 1979 "surrounded by towers of concrete and steel," and throughout the city excavations of large areas in preparation for further construction. What remained untouched was a view of the Kuala Lumpur hills that he remembers and now perceives as "half mythical, like the Roman hills before the building of Rome." The view evokes associations to his past visit as well as to the deep past of the ancient world on which Malaysia, even with its changing prospect, also has a claim.

The past preoccupies him as he tries to renew his acquaintance with Shafi, a Malay he came to know and whose confidence he won by revealing his own values and aims even as he tried to apprehend the young man's dedication to the new Islam.[59] Now, searching for Shafi, he recalls that before his full-time commitment to the Muslim youth movement, he had worked for a construction company and even started one himself. Both companies had failed, but Naipaul wonders whether now, as a mature man of forty-eight, Shafi might have taken advantage of government support and returned to a business career. These reflections, it seems, are actually hopes that are to remain unfulfilled. He never finds Shafi and what he does learn only saddens him. It becomes apparent to Naipaul that "no one among his former associates particularly wanted me to meet him." When Naipaul first met Shafi, "he had been at the center of the Muslim youth movement in Malaysia. . . . Now, though he had remained true to those early beliefs, he was on the outside."

Fundamental changes in Malay culture since Naipaul's last visit are implicit in reactions to Shafi: "It embarrassed people to be reminded of him; he was a man who had taken the idea of the religious life to extremes." Shafi's conception of Malays "as a pastoral, tropical people . . . not commercially minded," was now out of fashion. As a young lawyer explains: "That's been laid aside. Destroyed almost. It has been replaced by the idea of the Malays as a trading and manufacturing and innovative people. These are all words you would not have associated with Malays in the past." Clearly the new prosperity created by business supported by the government has conditioned people's image of themselves as individuals conforming to national economic goals.

Naipaul's depiction of Shafi as an idealistic young man in *Among the Believers* is so appealing that one grieves for his lonely adherence to a way of life that has passed, even as one cannot help admiring his fidelity to his convictions as he endures rejection by former friends. In contrast, Nasar, his former colleague in the Muslim youth movement, has successfully adapted to the new Malaysian ethos. Having acquired a diploma in international relations as well as a law degree, now at forty-one, he is "running a holding company that managed the diverse affairs of eight companies." The young man from the village has been transformed into an executive. Yet he retains the "openness" to which Naipaul had responded in the past, and speaks freely "of the internal demons—the phobias, the lack of confidence—that as a small-town Malay he had had to quieten before he could be what I now saw."

Nasar attributes Shafi's nostalgia for village life, which was incorporated into his "religious view," to his failure in business, a rather superficial explanation influenced, it seems likely, by the fact that his own conception of Islam has been altered by his involvement in business and government. Speaking of the past, he says, "We talked about religion theoretically. Now we are talking about Islam as a way of life in practice. Now I confront the real world." He speaks of his values and his choices, the extent to which he is guided by his religion when dealing with government contracts and other business. Naipaul infers that he may be thinking of Shafi when he contrasts his own need to consider many elements in making ethical decisions in his work with those who "are always right" because they are not "confronted with reality." Yet he is grateful for the education he received in the Muslim youth movement; he has responded to the opportunities that Malaysian material and social progress have offered him, "but it had also to be said that religion had given him the important first push."

The different roads taken by these two men, Shafi and Nasar, cannot be explained merely by the failure in business of the one and the success of the other. Inevitably in a society changing as rapidly as that of Malaysia, some will adapt and others will cling to their old ways. To understand their choices one would have to know more about their inner lives than Naipaul's brief account provides. What does emerge is that both are men of integrity, acting on the basis of values learned in their youth, which elicit respect. They are sufficiently defined as characters so that, even after a brief acquaintance with them, questions about their future come to mind, especially what effects the economic collapse and the demonstrations against the government of 1998 have had on their very different ways of life.

It is clear that both Nasar's achievements and Shafi's ostracism by his former colleagues are outgrowths of the changes in Malaysian society produced by the new wealth. No doubt the direction of many other lives was determined, at least to some extent, by the expanding economy. However, one of the most moving figures Naipaul portrays, the playwright Syed Alwi, seems to be unaffected materially or in any other important way by the Malaysian boom. Although he never earned a great deal, when he was in his early sixties, he was able to buy a plot of land in a village "far out of Kuala Lumpur," where he arranged to have a house built by one of his relatives. "It was a calamity," Naipaul says. "The money was consumed and the house was unfinished and the builder had gone away." Alwi's father, who had become schizophrenic when he was twenty-two, had a similar disaster. During a lucid period, he had also planned to build a house in the Kampung, but had run out of money before the second story was constructed. He tried a second time and again lacked sufficient money. The father suffering a mental illness, the son who is a writer, the hopes for houses that remain unfinished—all recall Mr. Biswas, his son, his many efforts to build his house, and in the end, the dignity of his endurance.

Syed Alwi grew up in his father's unfinished house, and his father, after his breakdown, lived there, cared for by his family for twenty-three years until his death. They were difficult years as the father moved between two worlds, the world of everyday reality and "his private world," in which, his son believed, he "was searching for the meaning of life." He had different personalities in each of these phases; for example, he preferred to speak English only in his private world.

The family lived through the anguish of the Japanese invasion for three years and eight months. Syed Alwi tells of seeing "staked heads," said to be those of Chinese victims "near the market in Taiping." Food became scarce; "disease became rampant. . . . We couldn't cope with the breakdown of society." Yet Syed Alwi's family managed to survive and to protect the old father in both of the worlds he inhabited. He had a brief lucid period before he died. "It was as if, at the very end, he hadn't wanted to die alone in the other world." In the last paragraph of *Beyond Belief* Naipaul quotes Syed Alwi's tribute to his mother, whom he describes as "the community. From her Malay upbringing, her Islamic upbringing, she provided [her husband] the support that enabled him to have his two worlds." In this family traditional Malay customs and values, loyalty to and respect for a human being—whatever inner world he might inhabit—transcended the boom and undoubtedly the later financial collapse and social upheaval. These values are also basic to Syed Alwi's writings, another manifestation of continuity and transcendence.

NOTES

1. Quoted from a letter from William James to Dickenson S. Miller by Hilary and Ruth Anna Putnam in "What the Spilled Beans Can Spell: The Difficult and Deep Realism of William James," *Times Literary Supplement* (June 17, 1996): 14.

2. Wole Soyinka, *The Open Sore of a Continent: A Personal Narrative of the Nigerian Crisis* (New York: Oxford University Press, 1996), 117–118.

3. Berlin, 252.

4. V. S. Naipaul, *The Loss of El Dorado: A History* (1969; reprint, New York: Vintage, 1984), 12.

5. V. S. Naipaul, "Michael X and the Black Power Killings in Trinidad," 43–44.

6. V. S. Naipaul, "A Handful of Dust; Return to Guiana," *The New York Review of Books* (April 11, 1991), 15–20.

7. "A Handful of Dust," 16.

8. Mukherjee and Boyers, 13.

9. Gordon Rohlehr, "The Ironic Approach to the Novels of V. S. Naipaul," *The Islands in Between: Essays in West Indian Literature*, ed. Louis James (New York: Oxford University Press, 1968), 130–31.

10. Cudjoe, 77–85.

11. Nixon, 45.

12. Peggy Nightingale, *Journey Through Darkness: The Writing of V. S. Naipaul* (St. Lucia: University of Queensland Press, 1987), 59.

13. Nixon, 45–48.

14. "Prologue to an Autobiography," *Finding the Center*, 12.

15. In chapter 2, 43.

16. Nixon, 11–12.

17. Nixon, 6.

18. V. S. Naipaul, "St Kitts: Papa and the Power Set," *The Overcrowded Barracoon* (New York: Knopf, 1973), 221–24. First published in *The New York Review of Books*, May 8, 1969.

19. V. S. Naipaul, "The Overcrowded Barracoon," *The Overcrowded Barracoon*, 256–86. First published in the *Sunday Times Magazine*, July 16, 1972.

20. V. S. Naipaul, "Columbus and Crusoe," *The Overcrowded Barracoon*, 203–207. First published in *The Listener*, December 28, 1967.

21. *The Enigma of Arrival*, 155–56.

22. Hussein, 4.

23. Stephen Schiff, "The Ultimate Exile," *The New Yorker* (May 23, 1994), 70.

24. Hussein, 3–4.

25. V. S. Naipaul, "The End of Peronism?" *The New York Review of Books* (February 13, 1992): 53.

26. *The Return of Eva Perón*, 109.

27. V. S. Naipaul, "Argentina: Living With Cruelty," *The New York Review of Books* (January 30, 1992): 13–18.

28. "The End of Peronism," 47–50.

29. *A Congo Diary*, 35–36.

30. V. S. Naipaul, "A New King for the Congo," *The Return of Eva Perón*, 186–88. First published in *The New York Review of Books* (June 26, 1975).

31. Nixon, 100.

32. "The Crocodiles of Yamoussoukro," *Finding the Center*, 81.

33. *India: A Wounded Civilization*, viii.

34. *India: A Wounded Civilization*, 184–85.

35. Anantha Murthy, 150.

36. Narayan, *Gods, Demons, and Others*, 201.

37. *India: A Wounded Civilization*, 185–186.

38. Sunil Khilnani, *The Idea of India* (New York: Farrar, Straus, Giroux, 1998), 141–44.

39. *India: A Wounded Civilization*, 72.

40. *India: A Million Mutinies Now*, 217–26.

41. V. S. Naipaul, "A Million Mutinies," *India Today* (August 18, 1997), 21.

42. *India: A Million Mutinies Now*, 274.

43. Khilnani, 58.

44. Pankaj Mishra, "A New, Nuclear, India?" *The New York Review of Books* (June 25, 1998): 63–64.

45. "A Million Mutinies," 22.

46. "A Million Mutinies," 22.

47. "A Million Mutinies," 22.

48. V. S. Naipaul, *Among the Believers*, 141–42.

49. V. S. Naipaul, "Our Universal Civilization," 23.

50. *Among the Believers*, 194.

51. See chapter 2, 64–65.

52. V. S. Naipaul, *Beyond Belief: Islamic Excursions Among the Converted Peoples* (New York: Random House, 1998), 3.

53. Fouad Ajami, "The Traveler's Luck," *The New Republic* (July 13, 1998): 27–33.

54. *Among the Believers*, 178.

55. Margaret Scott, "Epilogue," *The New York Review of Books* (May 14, 1988). Her entire interview appears on page 45.

56. Ajami, 30.

57. Margaret Scott, "Indonesia Reborn?" *The New York Review of Books*, (August 13, 1998): 43.

58. Sandra Mackey, *The Iranians: Persia, Islam, and the Soul of A Nation* (New York: Dutton, 1996), 368.

59. See chapter 2, 63–64.

4

FICTION

In his stories and novels Naipaul transforms actual societies he has known, their rulers and subjects, into fictional communities that generate narrators and characters more vivid than their models. Emerging from different social classes, with various talents, goals, levels of education, and accomplishment, a number of these protagonists are linked to each other and to their progenitor by an impulse to pursue truths about themselves and their world, however circuitous the course. Many contemporary novelists have described their fiction as an access to truth, but no two are alike in either their conception of truth or the means they use to express it. Still there are certain ways in which they resemble each other, among them a recognition of the ambiguity inherent in the very processes of discovery and articulation. Speaking "publicly . . . from a personal point of view" in a lecture delivered in October 1982, Nadine Gordimer insists, "nothing I say here will be as true as my fiction."[1] Elsewhere she refers to "the double process" involved in writing:

> excessive preoccupation and identification with the lives of others, and at the same moment a monstrous detachment. For identification brings the superficial loyalties (that is, to the self) of concealment and privacy, while detachment brings the harsher fidelities (to the truth about the self) of revealment and exposure. The tension between standing apart and being fully involved; that is what makes a writer.[2]

The ambiguities of truth, a major theme of Philip Roth in *The Ghost Writer, Deception,* and other novels, reach a seriocomic climax in *The Facts: A Novelist's Autobiography,* in which Roth and Nathan Zuckerman, his fictive alter ego, exchange letters on the question of Roth's truthfulness. It would be hard to refute Zuckerman's claim that Roth reveals more of himself in his fiction than in his facts. Zuckerman expects the "personal historian" to resist the common inclination to "tell in order not to tell . . . the ordinary impulse to falsify, distort, and deny."[3]

Naipaul's conception of truth in fiction evolved out of a long period of uncertainty about his subject matter. With few exceptions the fiction he read as a boy in Trinidad seemed to have little connection to the reality of his own experience: "A novel was something made up; that was almost its definition. At the same time it was expected to be true, to be drawn from life; so that part of the point of a novel came from half rejecting the fiction, or looking through it to a reality." The problem solved itself, as we have seen, in his realization that it was in his own beginnings, in "the country life" and later "the city street" of Trinidad that his truth lay. Only after he had found "the language, the tone, the voice" to recreate remembrances of his observations and feelings did he "understand Evelyn Waugh's definition of fiction as 'experience totally transformed.'" Writing fiction led to the discovery that the "two spheres of darkness" which had "separated" him from the books he was exposed to as a boy, "the childhood world of our remembered India and the more colonial world of our city . . . had become [his] subject."[4]

Naipaul delivers his versions of truth in fiction via characters simultaneously identified with and detached from their author. Uniting the "personal historian," remembering, traveling, observing, with the reporter and the storyteller, he has forged his own method of exposing what is withheld in the very act of telling as his narrators and characters reveal more of their truth than they can bear to acknowledge. Although in recent years he has disparaged "invented stories," he nonetheless links fictional characters and events with historical ones to depict the lives of people contending with the impermanence of institutions and values, of government itself, people who embody the wounds of the past as they enact contemporary history.

COMIC AND TRAGIC REALISM

Writing about his first book, *Miguel Street*, in "Prologue to an Autobiography," Naipaul says of its initial two sentences: "Though they had left out everything—the setting, the historical time, the racial and social complexities of the people concerned—they had suggested it all; they had created the world of the street." The interlaced stories of *Miguel*

Street[5] depict the way of life of a group of East Indians and blacks in Port of Spain, Trinidad, as they are viewed through the eyes of a first-person narrator looking back on his boyhood and youth in the 1940s. His empathy with and distance from his friends—youths and adults alike—are implicit in the contrast between the standard English of his narration and the local dialect he spoke as a boy: the language of most of the people with whom he is involved, which vividly communicates the comedy and sadness of their marginal existence.

They adopt or are given names to suit their style, choose and discard mates, work or remain idle according to a code of the street that calls for bravado in response to opposition or failure. Originally named Patience because he played that card game all day long, when the film Casablanca came to Port of Spain, Bogart was one of the "hundreds of young men [who] began adopting the hard-boiled Bogartian attitude." Yet Bogart is by no means a consistent figure. The name Patience seems to fit the passive man who "never liked cards" and who plays as if waiting for a new role to appear. Only after he returns from the first of several disappearances from Miguel Street does he take on the tough-guy stance of Bogart while his friend Hat assumes the manner and accent of Rex Harrison. The wit and charm of their performances do not alter the reality of Bogart's recent history of smuggling and managing a brothel in Georgetown, for which he was arrested by police who had accepted his bribes. Nor does his pride in these exploits, as his Bogartian persona recounts them, lessen one's awareness that movie actor imitations are the only versions of heroic manhood to which he and Hat can aspire. At times there is desperation in his imitations: he "became the most feared man in the street." He "drank and swore and gambled with the best. He shouted rude remarks at girls walking by themselves in the street." Soon Bogart leaves Miguel Street once more, only to return with an American accent and the manner of a benevolent American—probably modeled on a soldier from the nearby army base—handing out money and advice to children. After his third departure and return, the now fatherly Bogart is hauled off to jail charged with bigamy.

In 1977 Naipaul sought out Bogart who had left Trinidad shortly after he had and was now living on the island of Margarita. Bogart, he discovers, had never been the bigamist he "had cruelly made him."[6] On his several trips away from Trinidad he had visited a woman in Venezuela with whom he had become involved and who had borne his child. Seeking freedom, he could not, then or now as an old man, commit himself to this family. In his youth, freedom consisted of the alternating passivity and playacting of his days in Miguel Street; in old age, having lost his job with an oil company, he owns a small shop where he sells "[s]hoddy goods." The man who had seemed an "adventurer" to the boy on Miguel Street now lives with an adolescent girl and seeks comfort in the little he knows of Hindu ritual, invoking the god Rama every morning. Yet these facts that Naipaul uncovers many years after he and Bogart have left Trinidad do not reveal Bogart's motives as satisfactorily as does Hat's explanation in *Miguel Street* for Bogart's so-called "bigamy." When Eddoes asks him why Bogart left his wife and baby, Hat replies, "To be a man, among we men." Neither judgmental nor sanctimonious, converting their friends' and their own weaknesses into aspirations, the people of *Miguel Street* have invented their own means of negotiating with adversity.

No one has tried harder than Elias to overcome the disadvantages of his heritage. His father, George, who is not a member of the Miguel Street "gang," is known chiefly for beating his wife, whom he finally kills, his daughter, and Elias who, despite the brutality he witnesses and endures, never cries or speaks "a hard word" to him. Unlike the other boys in *Miguel Street* who want to become "cart-drivers," men who collect "the rubbish the sweepers had gathered into heaps," Elias has lofty aspirations. At fourteen his ambition is to become a doctor.

He is so determined, so conscientious in his studies that the narrator and the other boys are convinced he will succeed. However, when he sits for the Cambridge Senior School Certificate, he fails the first time, manages to get only a third the next time and, in an attempt to improve his grade, fails again the third time. His friends do not question his ability or his preparation. After his first failure, their belief in his "brains" is unwavering, and they rally to his defense, convinced that it is his status as a colonial that has defeated him. As one of the boys says, "What else you expect? Who correct the papers? English man, not so? You expect them to give Elias a pass?" Implicit in his shift from "English man" to "them" is the general skepticism regarding colonial justice.

His teacher, Titus Hoyt, encourages Elias to try a second time as a challenge to English prejudice: "We go show those Englishmen and them." To Hat, Elias's third failure is again evidence of the dishonesty of the English: "You see how we catch these Englishmen and them. Nobody here can tell me that the boy didn't pass the exam, but you think they go want to give him a better grade? Ha!"

Though all agree, "Is a real shame," it is also clear that none believe they can alter the outcome. Elias is ready to compromise: he will become a sanitary inspector, a position that also requires passing an examination, but at least not one that is sent to England. By now, however, he fears any exam, and sure enough, he fails three times. Convinced that in Trinidad, "You got to bribe everybody if you want your toenail cut," he takes the exam in British Guiana and in Barbados and fails both. The studious, trusting young man has become as skeptical as the others on Miguel Street with a comic resilience that can defy but cannot compensate for the deprivations of a colonial culture. When the narrator gets a second grade in the Cambridge Senior School Certificate Examination and a job in Customs, Elias asks, "What your mother do to get you that?" His envy belies his assurance to others that he likes his own job as a cart-driver, his final concession to the limited possibilities his society offers, which he had hoped to surpass.

The people of *Miguel Street*, and especially the narrator, are aware of the disparities between ambition and realization, between appearance and reality:

> A stranger could drive through Miguel Street and just say, "Slum!" because he could see no more. But we, who lived there, saw our street as a world, where everybody was quite different from everybody else. Man-man was mad; George was stupid; Big Foot was a bully; Hat was an adventurer; Popo was a philosopher; and Morgan was our comedian.

Looking back "after so many years," the narrator thinks that Morgan did not get the respect he deserved because he adopted the role of clown and enjoyed making people laugh at him. Hat perceives the pain beneath the pose: "Is a damn nuisance, having that man trying to be funny all the time, when all of we well know that he is not so happy after all." Morgan is an "artist," who loves fireworks, but is frustrated and angry because few Trinidadians use the ones he produces. The narrator believes that, even when he is "playing the fool," he is "thinking about beauty." As it turns out, Morgan's final comic appearance is involuntary; he is displayed by his wife as a near-naked adulterer, and only when a fire in his house sets off his fireworks do people witness the "splendour" of his invention.

The narrator's interest in and empathy with the people he meets attract adults who treat him as an equal as he comes to know their secrets. B. Wordsworth, the would-be poet, finally confesses that he has lied about "the greatest poem in the world," which he had claimed to be composing. Yet the narrator does not resent the deception. Nor does he entirely abandon the fantasy world to which Wordsworth has introduced him as he identifies with his friend in his sadness at losing him: "I left the house, and ran home crying, like a poet, for everything I saw." When he discovers that Big Foot, the most "dangerous" man on Miguel Street, feared by everyone, is himself terrified by a little dog, he keeps his secret, more out of fear of retribution than out of loyalty. Yet after Big Foot's weakness is disclosed as he weeps over losing a fight to an English boxer, the narrator does not join in the general ridicule. All the people who had bet on Big Foot laugh at him. "All except me," he says. "For I knew how he felt although he was a big man and I was a boy." Still he regrets having lost the six cents he bet on Big Foot.

The narrator's disillusionment with his friends begins with changes in Hat's behavior. The imitator of Rex Harrison, the man seemingly content with reading the newspaper, with sports and talk and getting drunk on Christmas Eve and New Year's Eve, suddenly acts out of character, by bringing home a woman, Dolly, for whom he buys "a lot of joolry," chains his dog, and cages his birds. When she leaves him for another man, he beats her severely and, concluding that he has killed her, gives himself up to the police. She is not dead, but Hat receives a sentence of four years. The realization that Hat who before had always managed to get away with no more than a fine for minor infractions is now being treated as a criminal challenges the assumptions of Miguel Street that wit and resourcefulness can evade the rules of the sanctimonious and even the law. "When Hat went to jail," says the narrator, "part of me had died."

During the three years that Hat was imprisoned the narrator has grown up and has become increasingly critical of Trinidad and the people of Miguel Street. He is the first of Naipaul's protagonists impelled by the limited opportunities of their homelands to seek a life elsewhere. "I just want to go away," he says, refusing to remain a victim of a long history of exploitation and deprivation he cannot even define. In the last story, "How I Left Miguel Street," he is aided by Ganesh Pundit, the author of a booklet, *What God Told Me,* who appears several times in Naipaul's early fiction. In "My Aunt Gold Teeth,"[7] written in 1954, he already shows signs of the self-serving latitude that is to distinguish him as the dubious hero of Naipaul's first novel, *The Mystic Masseur* where, highly valued as a mystic, he abandons that career for politics. His reputation follows him into *The Suffrage of Elvira,* in which the Muslim political leader Baksh regrets that Ganesh is no longer available to "drive away a spirit."[8]

As in *Miguel Street*, the comedy of *The Mystic Masseur* and *The Suffrage of Elvira* is undercut by the reality that the characters are trapped by the poverty of their education, the lack of opportunities for intellectual and cultural development in their surroundings and, no doubt as a result, the shallowness of their emotional lives. Yet some aspire to improve their lot by any means they can devise. Ganesh, more complex if less sympathetic than the people of Miguel Street, prefigures the drive of Naipaul's later protagonists to compensate for the deprivations of their heritage. His struggle is both pathetic and comic, beginning with his name, which serves as the satiric norm of his story. Lest the reader miss the irony that he is named for the elephant god Ganesha, Naipaul has Leela, his wife, commission "two stone elephants" to be built on the roof of his mansion "representing the Hindu elephant god Ganesh. Ganesh thoroughly approved of Leela's decorations and designed the elephants himself."[9] The comic effect of the two names side by side is multifaceted.

The god Ganesha, whose father, Shiva, cut off his head, received its replacement, his elephant's head, from Nandin, "an attendant of Shiva." Among his other gifts was "a writing pen with coloured inks" given him by the goddess Sarasvati,[10] with which he wrote down the *Mahabharata*, as dictated by Vyasa. He is the god who overcomes obstacles for those undertaking a journey, trade, or other business, and is worshipped for his wisdom and support of scholarship and literature.

The Ganesh of *The Mystic Masseur*, continually recreating himself as schoolmaster, masseur, author, mystic, and statesman, enacts a bathetic reduction of the god's noble functions. Hired to teach boys who have learned nothing for years, "the mentally maimed," he soon gives up trying and simply marks "improvement in his Record Book." When he is criticized, he quits this job. Lacking a realistic direction for his life, he turns minor coincidences into a "providential pattern." Having convinced himself that he is destined to be a writer, he tricks his father-in-law into financing a "Cultural Institute" with an exalted scholarly agenda: "The aim of the proposed Institute, which has yet to be named, will be the furthering of Hindu Cultural and Science of Thought in Trinidad." This so-called Institute is located in Fuente Grove, an isolated town, where the only event that takes place is an annual "harvest festival," which Naipaul says is "like the gaiety of a starving child," a simile that exceeds its immediate context, suggesting the quality of much of the humor of this novel. Here, having failed as a masseur, Ganesh, turns to reading and, like many of Naipaul's protagonists, to writing.

His belief that these are his destined occupations is amusing but also a touching vestige of the traditional Hindu veneration of learning in an environment that does little to sustain it. With no direction, purely by chance, he begins to build a library. When his friend, Beharry, receives a list of Everyman books from "these people in England," Ganesh assumes their contents have value; he is impressed by the quantity— 930—and determines the price for the lot—$460, convinced that if one read them all, nobody could equal him "in the line of education. Not even the Governor." In fact, says Beharry, if the "Governor and them" were "really educated they wouldn't want to leave England where they printing books night and day and come to a place like Trinidad." British books and British speech accentuate the inferiority of Trinidadians that Ganesh and Beharry take for granted. When Ganesh orders 300 Everyman volumes, and in his own way becomes an autodidact, he is hardly conscious of his desire to associate himself with this assumed superior culture.

After six months of reading in Everymans, he buys more books, "big ones, on philosophy and history" and begins to transcribe passages in notebooks. He becomes knowledgeable about typefaces but, enchanted as he is with the idea of becoming a writer, he has difficulty finding a subject for his first book. Urged on by his friend Beharry, he finally pays for the printing of a thirty-page pamphlet, *A Hundred and One Questions and Answers on the Hindu Religion*, by Ganesh Ramsumair, B. A., justifying the degree he has awarded himself by criticizing the "modern method of education" which creates the impression that it "is the little piece of paper that matter." The pamphlet's elementary questions and answers, for example, "What is Hinduism? Answer: The religion of the Hindus" indicate that as yet Ganesh has nothing to say but, as he struggles on, in the very act of writing he is to find subjects he cares about and in so doing to form self-images that reflect his current interest.

Ganesh's development as a writer begins with his work as a professional mystic. In both these careers a mixture of naiveté, honest effort, and guile combine to ensure his success. After his first spectacular achievement as a mystic, when his wife asks him if he used "a trick on them," the narrator remarks, "Ganesh didn't say." That he did use trickery is, of course, obvious, but it is also clear that he is genuinely concerned for those seeking his help. As he reads books on psychology and Hindu philosophy, his increasing knowledge gives him the confidence to believe he can rid people of the "evil spirits" that rob them of their psychic and physical health. Although even he is surprised by "the extent of his own powers," it is evident that they derive from his role as "a good listener. People poured out their souls to him and he didn't make them feel uncomfortable."

As his reputation grows, his poor little primer, *A Hundred and One Questions and Answers on the Hindu Religion*, neglected at first, becomes a best seller, "the first . . . in the history of Trinidad publishing," and he goes on to write a number of books on psychological and philosophical subjects, such as *The Road to Happiness, The Soul as I See It*, his autobiography, *The Years of Guilt*, and *What God Told Me*. To illustrate the standing of *What God Told Me* as "a classic," the narrator informs us that the "book set a fashion. Many people in many parts of Trinidad began seeing God. The most celebrated was Man-man of Miguel Street in Port of Spain. Man-man saw God, tried to crucify himself, and had to be put away." The contrast between the impressive title *What God Told Me* and the book's effect on large sections of the population mocks Ganesh's claim. Most telling is the injury to Man-man, whose psyche was fragile to begin with but, before he was tempted by the promise that the book held out to him, had managed to survive unrestrained.[11] To add to the confusion, two months after *What God Told Me* was published, Ganesh's *Profitable Evacuations* appeared, seemingly relevant to the Second World War. It was soon discovered, however, that the book was actually "concerned more or less with constipation," which Ganesh sought to alleviate, assuring his readers that "evacuation could be made not only pleasurable but profitable, a means of strengthening the abdominal muscles." Moving from God to evacuation, Ganesh apparently believes in his power to help people, to remove obstacles to their tranquility, in his ability to write down his thoughts on what he considers important issues. But implicit in the subjects of these last two books, amusing as they are, is the question of how self-deception operates in certain forms of self-expression. This process is even more evident as Ganesh goes on to greater success.

His career as a statesman originates not in ambition or in a sense of civic responsibility but in response to the enmity of the editor of a cheap little magazine, *The Hindu*. Narayan, who aspires to equal Ganesh as a mystic, names him "the business Man of God," and continually attacks him in a column entitled *A Little Bird Tells Us*. When Ganesh's friends urge him to run against Narayan in the island elections of 1946, he replies, "I ain't burning to be one of those damn crooks who does go up for elections," a declaration he believes is sincere at the time. Yet, after being elected president of the Hindu Association of Trinidad and Tobago, he learns that his disdainful old classmate, Indarsingh, now thoroughly anglicized, has "decided to go up in [his] ward" for member of the Legislative Council. That is enough to make Ganesh run in the election, which he wins. Gradually he gives up his work as a mystic, moves to Port of Spain, gets involved in politics, and becomes "a public figure of great importance," known for the "walkout" as a means of protest. Even before a calypso appears containing clear allusions to *Profitable Evacuation*, he has found that his former "mystic career" has become "an embarrassment." He withdraws his books and closes Ganesh Publishing Company Limited.

Whatever idealism, or self-deception, drives Ganesh to stage his walkouts and expose corruption soon gives way to opportunism. When a strike breaks out in sugar estates in south Trinidad, ignorant of the circumstances, he arrives "to bring about an amicable settlement." Introduced as "a man of good and God," instead of expressing his allegiance with the strikers, as was expected, he lectures them on politics and economics, "constitutions and tariffs," and is soon the butt of heckling and anger. From then on he takes the low road that will eventually lead to further success. He denounces the labor movement in Trinidad as "dominated by communists," and he represents the British government at the United Nations, defending "British colonial rule." His reward comes in 1953 when he is made an M.B.E. Not only has he changed his profession and his convictions, he has changed his name to suit his new self-image: Pundit Ganesh Ramsumair has become G. Ramsay Muir.

It is easy to laugh at Ganesh while scorning his adoption of various roles and professions only to discard them when a new opportunity arises. But Ganesh is more a representative than an individual figure. His "history," says the narrator, "is, in a way, the history of our time." The familiar phrase "in a way" is not mere surplusage. It suggests the limited resources he can exploit, given the particular time and place in which he was born, his flawed education, and the received opinions he both cherishes and challenges. Yet his intuitive responses and concessions to the changing conditions of his world result not only in his prosperity but in that of Fuente Grove. Comical as both idealist and opportunist, he nevertheless converts the very obstacles facing a poor East Indian in Trinidad into his own means of surmounting them. That is his way, sometimes devious, often bizarre, of functioning in the historical process.

In Naipaul's fiction there are many other ways. Even the farcical connivances of the candidates for Member of the Legislative Council, which comprise the plot of *The Suffrage of Elvira*, are microversions of corrupt electoral practices all too familiar in "the history of our times."

The time of the novel, Naipaul tells us, is 1950, only four years after universal adult suffrage has come to Trinidad. As an ambitious seventeen-year-old boy, known by his nickname Foam, puts it, "In Trinidad this democracy is a brand-new thing. We is still creeping. We is a creeping nation." The characters, with few exceptions, are not individualized; they act as products of their different ethnic groups, all of whose customs and religious values have been debased by the intellectual and moral poverty of colonial exile. The election exposes the lack of an ethical structure, individual or social, among all of them—the Hindu, Muslim, Black, and Spanish communities. The opportunism of the first three groups surpasses their fear of evil spirits sent by opponents. The Spanish, however, withdraw from the election because they have been convinced by Jehovah's Witnesses that politics is not "a divine thing."

Peggy Nightingale's discussion of the political background of *The Suffrage of Elvira*, refers to the complaint of Naipaul's uncle "that many elements of Harbans's [the Hindu candidate's] story are based on his own election campaign." She also mentions a possible "echo from further back in Naipaul's family history," the involvement of "two senior sons-in-law in his mother's family . . . with establishing the Local Road Board and with the politics of the island Legislative Council." In addition, she refers to sociological and historical studies that deal with the relation between "the structures of the Indian community," and East Indian politics in Trinidad, which help to explain "the belief that everybody in the society is pursuing the interest of his own family" as well as his own interest, to the exclusion of the "outsider."[12]

Such attitudes are abetted by a general ignorance and even distrust of democracy, described by one member of the electorate as "a damn funny thing," by another as made for "people [Muslims and Negroes] who never like to make anything for theyself." The skepticism of colonials is expressed by the teacher who refuses to vote and regards the "new constitution" as "[j]ust another British trick to demoralize the people."

The unsavory practices that create the brilliant comedy of *The Suffrage of Elvira* are not restricted to the Indian or any of the other communities that make up the population of Elvira. Both candidates and voters assume that support is sought by offers of money and goods and promises of future favors. Candidates affect a humility and a commitment they do not feel. Voters take pride in the unwritten rules governing bribery: "The people of Elvira," says Pundit Dhaniram, "have their little funny ways, but I could say one thing for them: you don't have to bribe them twice."

Surujpat Harbans, the Hindu candidate, is introduced deriving satisfaction from every pothole he encounters in the roads of Elvira, since his transport service delivers supplies for the minor repairs he has arranged to be made. He has persuaded the chief engineer of the county to "keep his hands off the Elvira roads" so "[b]ig repairs were never attempted," and his own business continues to thrive. Harbans fears omens and weeps often, especially when he hears that some Hindus are supporting the Negro candidate, known as Preacher. Still, he chooses Foam, a Muslim, as his campaign manager, no doubt as a means of winning the backing of his father, Baksh, the head of the Muslim community. Harbans's moods range from subdued optimism to anger and despair. At one moment he displays his assets, his "coo" and the "flash" of his false teeth, to woo potential supporters; at another, he rages at the expense of his campaign. He tearfully accuses his backers of greed: "I ain't got no friends or helpers or nothing. Everybody only want money money," one of his rare valid complaints. When his associates object and remind him that he has recently said that "money ain't everything," he quickly changes his tune: "Is true," repeating the lie for emphasis, "Is true. . . . You is all faithful." Money remains one of his chief preoccupations. Finally persuaded to pay the "entrance fees," he vents his anger on the town he is so eager to represent: he "shook his small fist at the dark countryside behind him. 'Elvira,' he shouted. 'You is a bitch! A bitch! A bitch!'"

Harbans's craving for victory in the election leads him to offer up his eighteen-year-old son as a potential husband for Nelly, the daughter of Chittaranjan, a wealthy goldsmith whose support he seeks. In a reversal of the usual roles, owing to the election, it is the boy's father who is obliged to please the girl's father, despite the prestige that Harbans's son has gained merely by planning "to take up doctoring." Pundit Dhaniram and Baksh both see through Harbans's scheme, predicting that he will nullify the engagement, and so he does once he wins the election.

This is by no means his only defection. On the evening of his victory he leaves Elvira for Port of Spain, "intending never to return." He does appear, however, at what was to be a presentation of a case of whiskey donated by Ramlogan, the owner of a rum shop, to the "committee of the winning candidate." Harbans arrives in a new Jaguar, all dressed up for the occasion. When Chittaranjan suggests that the whiskey be refused and instead a *kattha* be said for Harbans, he immediately proposes that the people who elected him first make "a little collection" of money to which he will add an equal amount to pay for this reading from the Hindu scriptures. Foam's approval of the plan only incites the crowd, already angry at Harbans's ingratitude and hypocrisy. As a farewell gesture they burn his Jaguar, which, Naipaul wryly adds, is replaced by his insurance company.

If this is Naipaul's tour de force of comic dialogue, for which he has been widely praised, the humor of extravagant response and gesture, of ingenuity in deception and distorted logic transmits a sadness at wasted vitality. Still, there are some hopeful signs that young people are reacting against the constrictive practices of their elders, finding forms of pleasure and self-fulfillment in the world outside Elvira. Nelly, Chittaranjan's daughter, does not want to marry Harbans's son, whom she finds physically unattractive and vulgar. She dreams of going to the Regent Polytechnic in London. Nelly is honest; she admits she is not a good student. To her the "Poly" offers the chance to attend dances, to enjoy the freedom and opportunities for fun that Elvira cannot give her. She is twice victorious: she is no longer obliged to marry a man chosen by her father, and she gets her father to grant her wish.

Even more fortunate is Lorkhoor, the young Hindu who managed Preacher's campaign. The favorite pupil of Teacher Francis, Lorkhoor has gradually created the self-image of "the village intellectual." His "stringent determination to speak correct English at all times" as well as his obvious intelligence and ambition have made him unpopular. Unlike his fellow Elvirians, he does not accept suffrage as merely a gift or an imposition of the British: "We had to fight for it," he says, asserting a sense of his own dignity and sense of responsibility that his elders seem to lack. His greatest asset, in Naipaul's eyes, is his desire to be a writer. Having moved to Port of Spain and applied unsuccessfully for jobs as a journalist, he writes an account of the burning of Harbans's Jaguar, entitled "A Case of Whiskey, the New Jaguar and the Suffrage of Elvira," which wins him a job on the *Trinidad Sentinel*. In the reckoning of losses and gains at the end of the novel, his is the greatest prize.

In Naipaul's first three novels truth emerges in the comic action, in the disparity between the characters' inflated self-representations and the poverty of their inner lives unsustained by any firm ethos or personal vocation. Chief among the many differences between these characters and the protagonist of *A House for Mr. Biswas* is his struggle to define himself by his tripartite vocation: to build his house, to succeed as a journalist, and to prepare his son to leave home for study and a new life abroad. These three aims are linked in the action of this comic/tragic figure as he contends with the limits of his society, his background, and his own character and, even when he is forced to compromise, does not deny the truth he perceives. My discussion of *A House for Mr. Biswas* in the chapter on autobiography is centered on the relationship between Mr. Biswas and his son, Anand, which Naipaul has suggested is a fictional evocation of his bond with his own father, who initiated him into the vocation of writer. Clearly what Naipaul calls this novel's "truth" is inherent not only in this relationship but in his portrayal of Mr. Biswas's contest with the fate assigned to him by the lore of his people and the meager opportunities open to a poor, ill-educated Trinidadian Indian.

Mr. Biswas, as he is called from infancy to death, is introduced as a legendary figure. Like the infant in Seepersad Naipaul's story, "They Named Him Mohun,"[13] his birth is inauspicious: "Six-fingered, and born in the wrong way," says the midwife, who prophesies that he "will eat up his own mother and father." The pundit warns the family to keep him away from water and to guard against his "unlucky sneeze." The one cheerful note regarding his birth is the first name chosen for him, Mohun, which the pundit explains means "the beloved, and was the name given by the milkmaids to Lord Krishna." As the pundit's "eyes softened at the thought of the legend," he seems momentarily to forget about both Mr. Biswas and the grandmother who had suggested the name, and we soon learn that the legend Mr. Biswas is to enact is far different from that of the happy Lord Krishna. Disobeying the pundit's admonitions, he goes to a "forbidden stream" to watch the fish, loses a calf he was caring for, hides, fearing punishment, and inadvertently causes the death of his father, an expert diver who drowns searching for him. Afterward, food tastes like "raw white flesh" to Mr. Biswas.

The connections and disparities between the legendary, the historical, and the comic elements of the novel merge in Mr. Biswas's determination, despite failures and retreats, even a descent into madness, to encounter "[r]eal life, and its special sweetness," the feeling that "he was still beginning." The very use of the title Mr. throughout the novel acknowledges the dignity of his aspirations, even as many of his endeavors end in comic disarray. If, as Naipaul's heading for the first chapter of the novel indicates, the early setting is "pastoral," it is also an impoverished locale of marginal existence where, but for his transgression, Mr. Biswas could at most have lived out his life as an illiterate worker in the cane fields. His father's death results in the breakup of the family; the hut that had been home is sold, and "for the next thirty-five years [Mr. Biswas] was to be a wanderer with no place he could call his own," a legendary role that is enacted in realistic detail. Ironically, his initial and continual unwillingness to conform as well as the consequent losses recurring throughout his life, are also his gains.

Supported by an aunt in Pagotes, his mother, Bipti, and he live not with her family but with other "dependent relations in a back trace far from the Main Road." He is sent to a primitive school where he learns to read and write, then studies to be a pundit but offends his master and is dismissed. Working at various jobs, living in temporary quarters, often in a room in the home of his hated in-laws, the Tulsis, Mr. Biswas never gives up his "claim" to his "portion of the earth." His impractical, often comic, efforts to build his own home in the face of poverty, his ignorance and the skepticism of his family enact his struggle for autonomy. The house, into which he and his family move near the end of the novel and where he dies not long after, reflects the naiveté of its owner and the petty corruption of his society, but it remains standing.

Equally important and intimately related to this visible sign of self-respect is his devotion to reading and writing. With fewer than six years of elementary schooling, without guidance or encouragement, Mr. Biswas turns to reading for self-improvement and later to writing as a means of self-expression. In his youth, he is drawn to the inspirational works of Samuel Smiles, an English writer of the second half of the nineteenth century. Identifying himself with Smiles's portraits of humble, self-taught young men struggling to succeed, he realizes that these heroes, unlike him, "lived in countries where ambitions could be pursued and had a meaning." Later in life, when discouraged, he "wondered what Smiles would have thought of him." Other self-help books he owns are as varied in subject matter as Bell's *Standard Elocutionist* and "the seven volumes of *Hawkins' Electrical Guide*." For consolation he turns to the works of the Stoic philosophers Marcus Aurelius and Epictetus, who teach acceptance and endurance, and to Dickens in whose ridicule of his "grotesques" he is able to displace his own fear and anger.

Driven by his partly articulated unwillingness to accommodate himself to the routine jobs to which his class and his role in society have assigned him, displaying his talent for imaginative, even bizarre, interpretations of events, Mr. Biswas manages to get a job as a journalist on the *Sentinel*. At first his assignments allow him to express his "fantasy," his "facetiousness," "something of his own." But his job offers no more security than do any of the other economic or social conditions of his life. When his sympathetic editor, Mr. Burnett, is fired and a "new regime" takes over the newspaper, rules he regards as ridiculous are enforced, and he is assigned to cover funerals, courts, and cricket matches. In retaliation, he asserts himself in the only way he can: "He had in fact mentally composed many sonorous letters of resignation, varying from the abusive to the dignified to the humorous and even to the charitable (these ended with his best wishes for the continued success of the *Sentinel.*)"

Now instead of writing an article entitled "I Am Trinidad's Maddest Man," he is obliged to write "about the splendid work of the Lunatic Asylum." More troubling even than the loss of his freedom to improvise, the prohibition on the playfulness and wit so natural to him, is the demand that he suppress the truth he perceives. "It was his duty to praise, to look always beyond the facts to the official figures. . . . He had not so much to distort as to ignore: to forget the bare, toughened feet of the children in an orphanage, the sullen look of dread, the shameful uniforms." However, he does not forget: "writing words he did not feel, he was cramped, and the time came when he was not sure what he did feel." The need to compromise results in headaches and depression. He no longer takes pleasure in seeing his work in print.

Other ways of channeling his feelings in writing end in frustration. Among the most revealing and at the same time among the funniest is a story he begins again and again, but can never finish. Entitled "Escape," it generally consists of only the following: "At the age of thirty-three, when he was already the father of four children. . ." There were times, however, when he continued the tale: "Sometimes the hero had a Hindi name; then he was short and unattractive and poor, surrounded by ugliness, which was anatomized in bitter detail," clearly a portrait of the writer at his most self-deprecatory. At other times "his hero had a Western name; he was then faceless, but tall and broad-shouldered; he was a reporter and moved in a world derived from the novels Mr. Biswas had read and the films he had seen." Whether Hindu or Western, his hero, like Mr. Biswas, feels trapped by his obligations to his wife and children. Seemingly to the rescue comes a slender "young girl . . . dressed in white. She is fresh, tender, unkissed," and most important, "unable to bear children." At this point he can write no more. The details of his story are too close to his actual experience of attempting to live out the fantasy with young women who work in advertising at the *Sentinel*. Having invited a few of them to lunch, he found that when his invitation was accepted, "his passion at once died," and "he withdrew the invitation." His desire to escape, if only imaginatively, from the tensions of life with the Tulsis is obviously in conflict with his loyalty to his family and perhaps even more with his moral fastidiousness, his feeling that there is something "unclean" about his very fantasies. Paradoxically, his obvious unsuitability for a romantic fling is part of his charm.

Adding to his predicament, his wife, Shama, comes upon these stories, calls him by the name he has given one of his heroes, suggests that he take Sibyl, one of his "untouched, barren heroines," to the movies, and even recognizes an unflattering version of herself. Still, neither failure nor embarrassment can entirely squelch Mr. Biswas's expression of his discontent. After a while, in order "to test" his typewriter, he returns to the same sad beginning of his unfinished story. It does come near to meeting its end when he observes the outcome of enacting such a fantasy. He is summoned by his uncle Bhandat who had been unfaithful to his wife and, when she died, had abandoned his sons for his Chinese mistress. Mr. Biswas finds the couple in Port of Spain, impoverished and living in squalor. Even the humor of Bhandat's request for his help in "the Lux slogan competition" and Mr. Biswas's suggestion, "I use Lux Toilet Soap because it is antiseptic, refreshing, fragrant, and inexpensive," only intensifies the ugliness of their surroundings. When he returns home, Mr. Biswas gathers "his unfinished Escape stories" and flushes them down the toilet in the yard. Bhandat had treated him cruelly when he was a boy, but he takes no pleasure in his degradation. He views it as an enactment of the truth his aborted stories never lived to tell. Nonetheless, when he is invited to join a literary group and required to read "something of his own," he thinks of resurrecting the story, but again gets no further than his first fragment of a sentence.

Other facets of Mr. Biswas's need and hesitancy to reveal himself in writing appear in a letter that bares the tragic core of his comic responses to the "trap" he feels his life has become. Responding to a brief letter from his former editor, Mr. Burnett, which Naipaul describes as "a joke," Mr. Biswas pours out his anger and pain: he "went on for pages, writing detailed denigrations of the new members of the staff." On rereading the letter and realizing "how bitter he appeared, how much he had revealed of himself," he tears it up. The self his words have portrayed is too uncompromising to survive in the narrow domain to which he must somehow adapt, yet even as he destroys this evidence of its existence, he is aware that he has created it.

Finally, after the death of his mother, Mr. Biswas writes, and this time posts, a letter that releases his vulnerability to the crass and the unfeeling and declares his capacity to withstand the pain they inflict. He had not been close to his mother. After her husband's death, living with her son in one room of a mud hut, dependent on her sister, Bipti gave way to anger and depression, feelings she transmitted to Mr. Biswas. When, disgraced, he was sent back to her by the pundit with whom he had been studying, he felt that she did not welcome him. Still, years later, when he builds one of his ill-fated houses on the way to his final one—this one in Shorthills—he invites Bipti for a visit, fulfilling a promise he had made many times since boyhood. Observing her with his family, friendly to Shama, who treats her with great respect, and helpful "with the housework and on the land," he senses a renewal of the fundamental connection of parent and offspring. For Mr. Biswas this brief visit leaves memories earlier even than those of his childhood in Pagotes. After Bipti's death, he recalls returning home from work to find that the "ground in front of the house . . . which he had left that morning cumbered and unbroken, had been cleared and levelled and forked. . . . In the setting sun, the sad dusk, with Bipti working in a garden that looked, for a moment, like a garden he had known a dark time ages ago, the intervening years fell away."

It is this primal tie with his mother, all the more precious because he has had so little contact with her in later years, that causes his outrage when he hears about the "disrespect" the doctor displayed when he had examined and certified Bipti's body. Beginning to write a letter to this Dr. Rameshwar, he is surprised by the unexpected support of Shama and his children, which leads him to enlarge the scope of his protest against the doctor's conduct. His original drafts were "hysterical and libellous," but with his new sense of security, "after many re-writings, the letter turned into a broad philosophical essay on the nature of man." Anand and he agree that the letter is "humorous, charitable and in parts correctly condescending." They imagine the doctor's surprise at reading this letter from "the relation of someone he had thought to be only a peasant." Their rage at the insult to Bipti has turned into a demand that she be associated with their own self-assertion, that their own dignity be acknowledged. Even Mr. Biswas's denunciations of the doctor are a way of revealing authentic feelings about himself and his family. Comparing the doctor "to an angry hero of a Hindu epic," he may be showing off, but he is also claiming the respect due to standards that derive from learning. When he asks forgiveness "for mentioning the Hindu epics to an Indian who has abandoned his religion for a recent superstition"—Christianity—he refers to common unprincipled conversions for "political reasons or social reasons, or simply to escape from his caste." Then he crowns this accusation with a statement that is as much a threat as a truism: "no one could escape from what he was," and ends his letter with the warning that "no one could deny his humanity and keep his self-respect." With quotations from Shakespeare, the New Testament, and the *Gita,* the letter has strayed far from its subject, but it has converted grief and humiliation into a protest against mistreatment of the weak and the humble.

Yet Bipti seems to have gotten lost among the extravagant rebukes and allusions. The letter, typed and posted, has not fulfilled Mr. Biswas's need to assuage "the wound . . . too deep for anger or thoughts of retribution." He feels he must set the record straight: though "[w]hat had happened was locked away in time . . . it was an error, not a part of the truth," and it is this error that he wants to correct. Wishing to honor the mother "whom he had never loved," he can do so only by resurrecting the truth of their actual relationship. He is moved to write a poem addressed to his mother in simple language, using "no cheating abstract words." He begins with seeing signs of her work on his ground, the "marks of the spade, the indentations of the fork prongs," which revived his earliest memories. Then he turns to his journey home from the pundit, and her kindness to him, unappreciated at the time, "the circumstances improved to allegory: the journey, the welcome, the food, the shelter." So true to his long-repressed feelings is this poem that when he reads it to his literary group, after beginning "boldly, and even with a touch of self-mockery," he is overwhelmed by emotion. His "hands began to shake," and at the part about the journey, "his voice fail[s]" him, and he is near tears. He remains silent for the rest of the evening and, "in his shame and confusion," drinks so much whiskey that on returning home, "he shamed Shama by being noisily sick in the outdoor lavatory." Once again, exposing his self without the defenses of irony or learned references is so painful that he retreats to his familiar self abnegation.

Still, he never gives up his struggle against his own internalization of the historical forces that threaten his autonomy; he is part of the Trinidadian Indian community, yet he constantly questions its customs and values. As a young man, painting signs for a living, even as he dreams of success, he is realistic enough to ask himself what he could accomplish in "this hot land, apart from opening a shop or buying a motor bus." Later, living among the Tulsis, working at a variety of menial jobs, he defies their authority, exposes their pretensions, their arrogance, sometimes with "vile abuse," and at others, with piercing sarcasm. Unlike the other sons-in-law, he makes it clear that he will never surrender to the Tulsis. Among his most effective defenses against them is his tacit evidence of his inner life, his retreat to his bed with his cigarettes, his Epictetus, and his Marcus Aurelius.

As a reporter and later as a welfare officer, he adapts to the "widening world" into which he has ventured. But it is his own house where he finally lives with Shama and his children that remains as his monument. Defying traditional legend, Mr. Biswas creates his own. One of Naipaul's achievements in this novel, and later in *A Bend in the River*, is not to depict heroes but to rescue from history's leavings its seemingly least endowed, its poor uneducated victims. It is their unwillingness to accept the limits of their *moira* that constitutes the tragic realism of his fiction.

The protagonist of Naipaul's next novel, *Mr. Stone and the Knights Companion,* is a sixty-two-year-old bachelor living in South London, reserved, timid, apparently dull. Yet different as he seems from the mercurial Mr. Biswas, the two men are not unlike in their imaginative defenses against the constraints with which they live and in their fundamental integrity. Until he marries, Mr. Stone is known only by his title and surname, and afterward only his wife calls him Richard. As in *A House for Mr. Biswas*, the narrator uses this formality to create the ironic distance of comedy even as it signifies an inherent dignity in this unheroic protagonist's aspirations. Although their settings and backgrounds are worlds apart, Mr. Biswas and Mr. Stone are alike in their need to create "something of [their] own" out of the means available to them.

When we meet Mr. Stone, apart from his fear of his neighbors' cat, he seems to live a tranquil if boring life, working as librarian of a firm called Excal and gardening in his spare time. Yet this seemingly conventional gentleman when alone in his house "found himself prey to fancies which he knew to be grotesque but which he ceaselessly indulged."[14] His imagination produces what Mr. Biswas would call "amazing scenes," in one of which Mr. Stone, standing on his "private moving strip," glides along the pavement while "walkers on either side [look] on in amazement." In another fantasy, like an ancient god, he can fly over the city, "indifferent to" the "stupefaction" of the people who observe him. "Seated in his armchair," as he flies "up and down the corridors of his office," he distorts the appearances and movements of his fellow employees while remaining calm in his flight. Clearly Mr. Stone is not as impassive as he seems. Another fantasy—which he reveals "with gruesome elaboration" at a dinner party—is "of boiling" his neighbors' cat "in oil or water." His visions of superhuman power, of being above it all—the daily grind of unrewarding work—his testiness, his compulsive tidiness, his preoccupation with the numbers of years that marked the events of his life are ways of escaping the actual world in which he lives, the present, which he finds "flavourless" and which holds out the prospect of death. They are unconscious means of controlling—at least in his thoughts—threats of the unknown, of nothingness.

For years, observing the life cycle of a tree outside his window, he had seen only regeneration, signifying his own "lengthening past." Now, he has begun to feel an inexplicable "unease," which he attributes to the aging of his maid, Miss Millington, who, he feels, is "soon to die," a fear, as yet inarticulate, that her decline is a foreboding of his own death, the actual cause of his disturbance. So intense and persistent is this half-conscious awareness that Mr. Stone uncharacteristically departs from his familiar routine at home and at work: he marries and soon after embarks on a project that, he hopes, will revitalize his later years and remain after his death as his memorial.

His marriage to Margaret Springer, a middle-aged widow, produces a sudden confrontation with a reality he had hitherto avoided. On their first night in his house the sight of her false teeth in the bathroom shocks him, leaving him feeling "cheated and annoyed." When he places his own teeth beside hers, the comic sadness of the scene is a prelude to his increasing awareness of the transience of his life: "every racing week drew him nearer to retirement, inactivity, corruption." During their honeymoon in Cornwall, when he and Margaret lose their way, encounter a fire, and are surrounded by smoke, Mr. Stone feels "panic," a "hallucinatory moment, when earth and life and senses had been suspended. . . . It was like an experience of nothingness, an experience of death." During that same holiday, a bizarre encounter in a teashop with a recently retired man along with his "keepers," the difficulty of adjusting to the "new and disturbing experience" of being with Margaret constantly, added to the "white void" he had endured, all lead to his formulation of the idea that was to be named the Knights Companion. The impulse toward creation to counter intimations of the final nothingness.

Before Naipaul explains what this project entails, he portrays Mr. Stone at work, putting his ideas on paper, actually a depiction of the physical process by which the hand writing embodies the act of creation. Reading the typescript, he is "struck anew by the perfection and inevitability of what he had written." Mr. Stone has enjoyed a satisfaction, a delight in his own powers that nothing else in his life has afforded him. The plan is ingenious in its simplicity and in its potential benefits. Pensioners of Excal are to be invited to become "Visitors or Companions." Those who accept, the "active" ones, will visit the "inactive," bringing friendship and a small gift. The head of the firm, Sir Harry, is impressed. Mr. Stone is elevated to the Welfare Department; he is moved to a new office in a new building, and his salary is raised. Now it is success that gives him "the delicious sensation of flying in his chair," soaring beyond his fears of old age and death.

For Mr. Stone the validity of the project lies in "the concern and fear out of which the plan had arisen" and the integrity of the emotions that entered into its "elaboration." These origins he cannot transmit to Whymper, the young public relations officer assigned to assist him. From the beginning the two men are at cross-purposes—Mr. Stone concerned only for the altruistic aims of his undertaking; Whymper for its "benefits to Excal." Still, Mr. Stone tries to cut through Whymper's "perversity" with an explanation eloquent in its directness: "He had solved some of the problems of old age. He rescued men from inactivity; he protected them from cruelty. He preserved for men the comradeship of the office, which released them from the confinement of family relationships. He kept alive loyalty to the company." The basic incompatibility of these two men can be inferred from Whymper's reply to this moving statement of purpose: "A society . . . for the protection of the impotent male." Yet it is Whymper who gives the project its exalted name and who exploits its Arthurian associations for the sake of publicity.

Despite his initial disapproval of Whymper, for a while Mr. Stone allows himself to be taken in by the man's cleverness and enthusiasm. Before long, however, he realizes that "Whymper was 'riding to success on his back.'" His "single creation" has been taken over by a public relations man "whose boast was that he made nothing." Nevertheless, he does not deny that Whymper's work has contributed to the success of the Knights Companion, especially in devising ways of publicizing the "Unit," as he calls it. It is Whymper who arranges for a competition for "Knights Companion of the Year," who is awarded the sword *Excal*ibur at the "Christmas Round Table Dinner." Even Mr. Stone is impressed when a photograph of Sir Harry presenting this prize appears in the newspapers the next day. On this occasion, when Mr. Stone and Whymper are congratulated by Sir Harry, and at a dinner party at his friends, the Tomlinsons', the next evening, Mr. Stone puts aside his reservations and enjoys the rewards of achievement.

Even more satisfying than the public acknowledgment is the evening at the Tomlinsons', where Margaret and he had met two years before, which fills his need for recognition by his friends as someone of consequence. He revels in Margaret's and his "position of command," which allows him to state openly what he had felt obliged to suppress in dealing with Whymper: "This is not to help Excal. This is to help all those poor old people without friends, without relations, without—without anything." He is to recall this evening and "see that it marked the climax of his life."

It also marks the beginning of his disillusionment, his realization that "[o]ther people had made his idea their property." He was no longer needed. If he should die, "the Whympers and Sir Harrys would continue to present *Excali*burs." Gradually he acknowledges the deeper cause of his discontent: the awareness that he cannot recover the drive out of which the Knights Companion was born. He looks back on his brief period of creativity, "the only pure moments, the only true moments were those he had spent in his study, writing out of a feeling whose depth he realized only as he wrote." But even this expression in words "was a faint and artificial rendering of that emotion, and the scheme as the Unit had practiced it was but a shadow of that shadow." Caught up in "administration and success," he had turned away from that truth, which he had known all along. Now, this most honest of men forces himself to face the inevitable compromises that make society possible and concludes that "All that he had done and even the anguish he was feeling now, was a betrayal of that good emotion. All action, all creation was a betrayal of feeling and truth."

Ironically, his disparagement of the expression and application of his idea leads to his articulation of his uncompromising conception of truth. In fact, the project itself has uncovered aspects of reality he had hitherto avoided: "the distress and need, . . . the neglect and cruelty," endured by many old people with whom he now empathizes. His work for The Knights Companion has given his marriage a focus and inspired feelings of affection long repressed as he shared at least some of his concerns with Margaret. Now he takes no pleasure in these gains as he judges his own accommodations to the world of commerce and public relations as a violation of the creative process: "It was not by creation that man demonstrated his power . . . but by destruction." Even "Nature's attempt to reassert herself became a mockery." Yet he will take no part in this process. Concluding that he is "no destroyer," he finds comfort in remembering that he survived before when "the world had collapsed about him" and "in time calm would come to him again." Like many of Naipaul's protagonists, he arrives at a conception of truth by acknowledging the inevitable nothingness by which human life is bound. Still, despite, or perhaps because of, such knowledge, looking at signs of spring outside his window, the tree, the dahlia bush, he asks, "I mean, don't you think it's just the same with us? That we too will have our spring?" Neither Margaret nor Miss Millington understands that this is his sole response to the coming darkness.

OUTSIDERS EVERYWHERE

In a London suburb, where self-deprecation mingles with pretentiousness to block genuine human communication, Mr. Stone finds himself obsessed with the issue of truth and its inevitable betrayal. Yet for him this narrow locale, with its petty feuds and showy respectability, is home, where he has enjoyed the brief triumph of creation and can find a measure of comfort, of hope, in his despair. Ralph Singh, the narrator of *The Mimic Men*, has known different aspects of London—the boarding houses and university of his student days, the "intervening visits"[15] to hotels and government buildings as a political leader from the colony of Isabella (Trinidad), and finally a suburban hotel, the site of his exile, where he lives and writes his memoir to atone for his betrayal of truth. Mr. Stone discovers to his dismay that his version of truth, born out of the needs of his time, is debased in the realms of business and public relations, the very background of its conception. His only defense is to define truth as ahistorical, inoperable in society. The truth Ralph Singh seeks, after years of evasion, resides in his own personal, social, and political history.

In his memoir Singh tells of his unfulfilled wish to write history, his desire to fix the uncontrollable, to record the ephemeral: "It is the vision that is with me now. This man, this room, this city; this story, this language, this form." How like and how different from Naipaul's own description of himself as a writer quoted in the Introduction: "I begin with myself: this man, this language, this island, this background, this school, this time. I begin from all that and I try to investigate it, I try to understand it. I try to arrive at some degree of self-knowledge, and it is the kind of self-knowledge that cannot deny any aspect of the truth."

Actually the resemblance of the narrator's vision to the author's commitment points up the differences in their approach to such knowledge. For Naipaul it is a vantage point for exploration and discovery beyond his limited experience. For Singh it is "a moment that dies," a fragment of an "ideal narrative" that he will never write, in which he might identify "a disorder . . . beyond any one man to control." Unlike Naipaul, Singh, having evaded self-knowledge for much of his life in compromise and betrayal, faces his deceptions only in writing his memoir. He approaches the truth regarding his personal and professional life warily, sometimes contradicting himself, changing his position, and in the end he has earned the perception he shares with his creator that "writing, for all its initial distortions, clarifies and even becomes a process of life."

Writing from the point of view of a man of forty looking back on his unfulfilled aspirations, Singh recalls his early years in London when he hopes for a future of accomplishment and honor. After the death of his landlord, Mr. Shylock, he discovers in the attic of the boarding house only "a mattress, a writing table," and a photograph of a young girl, undoubtedly Mr. Shylock's mistress. He responds to the sordidness of the scene with a kind of secular prayer: "Let it not happen to me." He accepts the reality of death, which "comes to all," but he asks to "leave more behind. Let my relics be honoured. Let me not be mocked." Even as he writes, as he tries "to put words to what I felt," he is all too aware that "my own journey scarcely begun, had ended in the shipwreck which all my life I had sought to avoid."

Peggy Nightingale proposes that the image of shipwreck, which recurs throughout *The Mimic Men*, "conjures up all Singh's fears of the 'haphazard, disordered and mixed society of his island'. . . . Further, shipwreck suggests the experience of being stranded without the necessities of life," which she relates to Naipaul's "own contention . . . that Caribbean communities are culturally starved."[16] Singh does refer to Isabella as the "shipwrecked island," but the phrase seems more a projection of his own feelings about himself than a reasoned judgment. Writing about his early days in London, he remarks on his use of the word: "Shipwreck: I have used this word before. With my island background, it was the word that always came to me. And this was what I felt I had encountered again in the great city: this feeling of being adrift, a cell of perception, little more, that might be altered, if only fleetingly by any encounter." He had hoped for order in London, for a secure sense of his own identity. Yet, as early as his initial journey to England, he had interpreted a cryptic message from a friend, "ending in dots," as telling him "that all my notions of shipwreck were false, telling me this against my will, telling me I had created my past, that patterns of happiness or unhappiness had already been more or less decided." Unwilling to come to terms with such knowledge, he avoids it, choosing the character of the "dandy," an artifice to cover the "panic of ceasing to feel myself as a whole person." He sees himself as one of those who came to the "great city" only to lose "some of our solidity," who, in a "growing dissociation between ourselves and the city . . . became nothing more than perceivers." It is not only in writing about London that the image of ship-wreck continues to occur to him. The threat of failure, or actual fail-ure—his father's, his own—in Isabella all take on its chaotic, perilous character. Despite Singh's dismissal of his "notions of shipwreck" as false, his obsessive return to the image indicates how accurately it conveys his feelings about himself, how ambiguous are his versions of truth.

In contrast with this image are his various associations with the Latin language and with ancient Rome, which signify order, stability, and a lasting cultural tradition. As Umberto Eco points out, the very syntax of Latin expresses boundaries. "Time is irreversible. This principle was to govern Latin syntax." His explication of the ablative absolute explains, at least in part, why Naipaul and his narrator at times turn to Latin for assurance: "That masterpiece of factual realism which is the ablative ab-solute establishes that, once something has been done, or presupposed, then it may never again be called into question."[17]

It is noteworthy that Singh's first reference to Latin is the word Vir-tus, as he speculates on a young Swiss girl's reaction to him. Had she seen "the absence of virtue"? Implicit in the contrast between the capitalized Latin and the lower case English is Singh's ideal image of himself and his inability to live up to it in his relations with the people he comes to know. A more critical event evokes a passage from the *Aeneid*. After his marriage to Sandra at a registry office, "appalled" at what he has com-mitted himself to, he flees to a pub in Holborn. In his memoir, he asks the reader to "[t]hink of" him, pretending to read the evening paper, and "being really frightened."

Trying to achieve some distance from "his recent terrible adven-ture," he twice invokes Vergil's "Quantum mutatus ab illo," from Ae-neas's dream of the fallen Hector, "How changed from that Hector" (*Aeneid* II, 274) who for a time was triumphant over the Greeks. The words reiterated in his head "became the emotion of loss and sadness and sweetness and apprehension," and gradually he is able to regard himself with a kind of melancholy humor as the victim of "nemesis" exacting retribution from "the dandy, the creation of London," the debased sur-rogate of his idea of selfhood.

In this novel Naipaul moves back and forth, portraying the processes of Singh's memory as he recalls various stages of his past, evaluating their relation to each other and their meaning in the present. Immediately after his mock-heroic description of his postnuptial flight, he tells of his return with his wife to Isabella, a trip he had never expected to make. His feeling that this return was "a failure and a humiliation" he "buried" along with his "unease," his alienation. Now, looking back, he believes that this self-deception, this fundamental flaw, was the incipience of his failure as a political leader.

It is not his belief in justice, but rather in "a moral balance" that makes him conclude: "If only we look down deeply enough, we can spot the beginning of the misfortunes that eventually overtake us in just such a small suppression of the truth, in just such a tiny corruption." He now admits that he should never have returned to Isabella, never have disembarked as a would-be celebrant, knowing as he did that the "tainted island is not for me." He finds excuses in the very "mood of celebration," with which he left London and which seemed to compensate for his aimless, troubled time there, and also in the possibility that after his marriage to Sandra he had "begun to surrender the direction of [his] life, not simply to her, but to events." Yet he is aware that these are only further self-deceptions: "dishonesty linked to dishonesty, unease to unease." Having admitted his evasions of his true feelings, he now explains that they were a defense against psychic disintegration: "to have examined my reactions more closely would have meant making myself open again to that feeling of drift and helplessness, the nightmare I had combated on so many evenings by the thought of the Luger at my head." This is by no means Singh's final conception of truth or his only explanation of his difficulty in accepting what he judges to be his authentic reactions. He returns to this issue repeatedly, interpreting the changing circumstances of his personal life in relation to the cultural and political realms in which he is involved.

In Isabella, Singh and Sandra immediately find a place among a group of rich young people, professional men and their expatriate wives, "mainly Indian, with a couple of local whites and coloured." The word "dazzled" that Singh uses to describe Sandra's and his responses to being accepted in this circle contains the contradiction inherent in this phase of their life: their attraction to the seemingly sophisticated mores of their new acquaintances and the constriction of their vision, their blindness to the superficial values, the petty concerns of these people whom they mimic as they seek their friendship. Their example encourages Singh to claim his place among the wealthy; and soon, using money and land he has inherited from the Bela Bela Bottling Works owned by his grandfather, he makes a fortune by developing this land and dividing it into small plots, which he sells at a fair price. For a time Singh enjoys a new "placidity," the inner core of his "new life of activity." In this placidity, he believes, lies his strength, his true character. He feels that he "would never allow [himself] to be damaged again."

What he does not reckon with is his increasing sense of separation from his continuing financial success and, at the same time, his and Sandra's separation from their group of friends. Singh attributes their friends' alienation not to "jealousy or envy" but rather to a feeling that they do not really belong, that their real commitment is to "making a fortune." Actually, what Singh's account discloses is that half-consciously he and Sandra have created their own estrangement from the group and from each other. Sandra's famous "gift of the phrase," which has become her means of belittling her former friends, and his own ironic comments on the rituals of Isabella society are ways of striking out less at their ostensible victims than at the fraudulence of the roles they themselves have been playing.

As their marriage fails Singh decides to build a "Roman house." What attracts him to examples of such a house, which he finds in a book, are its "simplicity, . . . its outward austerity, its inner private magnificence," all qualities connoting an authenticity and a permanence that he longs for and patently lacks. Once again the contrast between the outward manifestation, in this case, the house, a "sacred symbol" awaiting only "the installing of the household gods," and the apathy of Singh and Sandra, emphasizes the emotional damage of self-deception. Finally, at the housewarming, the household gods are violated as the guests repay their hosts for their wit, their irony, their apartness. In a kind of frenzy they play a destructive game, throwing a ball from the pool to the house and back again, breaking objects in its path, a window, plates, and glasses. At first Singh feels "a deep, blind, damaging anger" at the chaos around him. Then, driving away, he is overcome by "a nameless pain," not for the injury to his house, which can be repaired, but a "despair" that is "absolute." He identifies himself with Alexander who, he now believes, wept for "a deeper cause" than having no more worlds to conquer. In Alexander's history he sees his own "sense of futility, an awareness of the lack of sympathy between man and the earth he walks on." To understand and thus control his pain, Singh views it through the lens of ancient history, for him a guide and a solace even in its tragic course.

The opening section of *The Mimic Men* ends with Singh's remembrance of his "first instinct," to write history, which surprised him during "moments of stillness and withdrawal . . . in the days of power" as a politician. Before he turns to the events of those days, however, he abruptly shifts to memories of his boyhood and youth, the background of his achievements and inevitable failures. In the second and longest section Naipaul uses and transforms autobiographical material, including his reactions to Trinidad as reported in *The Middle Passage*. There are, however, critical differences in his and Singh's responses to their milieu and in the psychic processes involved in their frustrating, painful, often tragic perception of the self that emerged from its confines. For example, Naipaul, in the chapter on Trinidad in *The Middle Passage*, and Singh are both distressed on returning to their homeland after living in London, and it is only through the process of writing that both examine this reaction. But there are dissimilarities beyond their roles—the reporter as opposed to the wealthy real estate developer-turned-politician—in the consequences of their earlier refusal to scrutinize their fears of becoming victims of "the land of failures"[18] they have fled. The details they perceive and remember, the contrasting reported and invented associations with people, their narrative styles toned to self-observation and self-expression, all generate versions of experience that complement each other in their very divergences. Their explorations of the historical processes that produced "mimic men" may be contiguous, but they disclose different temperaments and values. Asked by an interviewer whether Singh echoes his own views when he says: in trying "to put myself in the place of those I thought were distressed, . . . I failed to see much. I minimized the quality of personality. But so it is when we seek to forget ourselves by taking on the burden of others," Naipaul replied, "No, no, no, that isn't me."[19]

Singh's recollections of his childhood have been "edited," he says, by a "complying memory," which "has obliterated many" of his "burdensome secrets," yet even the "brief cinematic blur" remaining is painful. The secrets are both those characteristic of many intelligent, sensitive adolescents and those peculiar to Singh's character and circumstances. Chief among these last are his alteration of his name, his feelings about his father, and his consciousness that "a celestial camera recorded my every movement, impartially, without judgment or pity." Like Naipaul, as a young boy, Singh is aware that his family is anomalous, materially and culturally: his maternal grandparents, owners of Bela Bela Bottling Works and the "local bottlers of Coca-Cola," are wealthy, while his father, a poor schoolteacher, resents and despises them. Singh, envying his rich cousin, Cecil, and Deschampsneufs, another boy from a wealthy and distinguished family, compensates for his feelings of inadequacy by changing his name from Ranjit Kripalsingh to Ralph Singh. This abnegation of his patronymic and his Indian given name is viewed by his father as disrespectful of him and favoring his mother's family. Actually Singh is merely competing with Deschampsneufs, whose many names herald his exalted status. Throughout his changing reactions to his father, Singh never entirely rejects him. In fact, he comes to realize that his own destiny "was to be linked to his." As a boy, reading in *The Missionary Martyr* of Isabella about his father's oratorical skills when he was a young missionary, Singh conceives an ideal image of "a man who had been cut off from his real country," a glorious place, from which he had been "shipwrecked" on the island. This heroic figure is a far cry from the "embittered schoolteacher" who, in his rage at his in-laws' influence on his son, breaks ninety-six bottles of Coca-Cola at a soda fountain. Yet he is admired for this act by local people, who interpret it as an assertion of the poor against the rich. It is the inception of his role as Gurudeva, a name he adopts when he leaves his home and his job to lead striking dockworkers and other followers in a quasi-religious revolt against the injustices of their society.

The name Gurudeva, which evokes the dubious hero of Seepersad Naipaul's "The Adventures of Gurudeva" who starts out as a hoodlum and ends as a lonely aspiring brahmin, creates an ambiguous connection between Singh's father and both Seepersad Naipaul and his creation. Like Seepersad Naipaul, Singh's father endures emotional distress before his radical departure from his customary life, but there are many differences in their backgrounds and conduct. Seepersad Naipaul's psychotic episode was brought on, at least in part, by the ostracism of his clan and his torment at ceding to their threats. He suffered his breakdown, fled from home, and recovered, alone. Singh's father is a theatrical figure, "in the hills, a preacher, a leader, with a growing frenzied following." His son, contemplating the role of "the widow of the transport contractor," says that he "always saw method in my father's madness." It was she who "saw him entering the stage of meditation before the final renunciation. It was an idea he received from her and exploited." Different as is the course of his life from Seepersad Naipaul's, in this last stage, he approaches his namesake Gurudeva, who has come to resemble his creator in his devotion to brahmin values.[20]

Through these associations, Naipaul indicates that, whatever Singh's reservations regarding his father's movement, he is a figure who elicits sympathy. Even after Singh's "horror" at Gurudeva's involvement in *Asvamedha,* the "horse-sacrifice," he acknowledges the necessity for the violent act: "without it a mood is useless and burns itself out. . . . The killing of a racehorse, favourite for the Malay Cup, was outrageous and obscene to everyone on that sport-crazed island. Yet it became an acceptable rallying point of righteous, underground emotion." Asked to pay Gurudeva's debt of thirty dollars to the son of the woman he lives with, Singh weeps for his father's "pain" mingled with his own "humiliation." Later, remembering the scene, he is struck by his own "surprise" at his "sudden and intense sympathy for [his] father. Poor Gurudeva! There on the beach I had felt linked to his power, madness and humiliation." On Singh's final visit to his father, he is told, "It is his day of silence. He has given up the world. He has become a true sanyasi," a holy man. Although he does not speak, he embraces his son, who is left with "sympathy . . . for the idea of him: Gurudeva *asvamedha*," a leader committed to the horse sacrifice in order to challenge authority.

Having renounced his plan to record history because he is himself "too much a victim of the restlessness" with which he would have dealt, Singh nonetheless portrays his personal history, like that of all of Naipaul's major characters, as a yield of colonialism. But not entirely. In the third section of *The Mimic Men*, Singh's shifting loci of truth confront and revise his earlier conclusions. "As I write," he says, my own vision of my actions alters." An investigative narrator, he questions the very notion of entirely dishonest action, and finds within the affectation and disorder of his life a "pattern" of personality and conduct that leads him to a harsh but authentic assessment of his role and his failure as a political leader. In the act of writing he has come to understand the falsity of his former declaration that "nothing in [his] life had prepared" him for a political career, his vanity in acting as though this career was merely "another aspect of [his] dandyism." The intensity of his feelings regarding such misrepresentations to himself as well as to others emerges in his comment, "Criminal error!" which suggests that such conduct harmed not only him but people who put their trust in his leadership. He goes on to say that he has in fact "been describing the youth and early manhood of a leader of some sort, a politician, or at least a disturber." What's more, a "name of peculiar power had been prepared for me." The name, of course, is Gurudeva.

Singh's political career begins with an invitation to "proclaim" that name. When his former classmate, Browne, now a journalist and editor, asks him to write the "main article" on his father for an issue of his paper, *The Socialist*, commemorating "the anniversary of the dockworkers' exodus from the city," Singh enthusiastically accepts. His preparations for Browne's visit to the Roman house, with the Loeb edition of Martial displayed, exemplifies Singh's way of revealing himself in what may seem to be mere posturing. He says that he meant "to create the picture of a man who," despite the disorder of his personal life, "had achieved a certain poise." The elegance of the Roman house and the Martial, his "therapy," serve that purpose. He does not mention any pleasure in reading the *Epigrams*, but he does tell of the benefits of returning to Latin: "the acquisition in easy stages of a dead language, through an easy author" he finds soothing, a routine that lends order to his days.[21] The book adds to the impression of the stability of the house, a defense against his "special relationship" with Browne, with whom he shares comradeship, understanding, and misunderstanding of the Indian and black backgrounds of their childhood.

Having accepted Browne's invitation, Singh found that the essay about his father "wrote itself." At the time he believed that his writing was effortless "because I was making a confession, proclaiming the name, making an act of expiation." Actually, he goes on to say,

> the article was, deeply, dishonest. It was the work of a convert, a man just created, just presented with a picture of himself. It was the first of many such pieces: balanced, fair with the final truth evaded, until at last this truth was lost. The writing of this book has been more than a release from those articles; it has been an attempt to rediscover that truth.

As Singh delves for hidden self-deceptions, he continually addresses his readers, inviting them to share his quest, for example: "Consider"; "See then"; "Understand"; "See how" repeated three times—guiding us in following his approach to truth from his success as a public figure, a nationalist leader, to his downfall, ousted from politics in disgrace. With Browne elected Chief Minister and Singh editing *The Socialist* and leading the "party organization," the two built a movement whose followers, "unproductive, uncreative" men, responded to their program out of "bitterness." Now he admits, "in this response we saw the success of our appeal and its truth." He makes it clear that Browne and he saw truth where they wished it to exist. From the distance of his present writing, Singh views his movement in Isabella as one that occurred "in twenty places, twenty countries, islands, colonies, territories," where truth is evaded in "borrowed phrases," where people are led to believe that the choice of a "particular" word "alters the truth," where a leader like Singh appears "to have been suddenly given a glimpse of the truth."

It is only in retrospect that he admits his failure to address the "negative frenzy of a deep violation" rooted in colonial rule, which could lead to violence if no action were taken to prevent it. Nor had he realized that his restlessness was an unacknowledged internalization of this violation. His recognition of the "bigger truth . . . that in a society like ours, fragmented, inorganic . . .there was no internal source of power, and that no power was real that did not come from the outside" does not free him of responsibility for the "open racial conflict," the "organized violence" that broke out. He realizes that he could have availed himself of both outside and internal interests from the "banks," the "bauxite companies," and "the Stockwells" (Lord Stockwell, he is to learn, greatly admired his father) to the "middle class" and the "rural workers, picturesque Asiatics like myself." Mingling external controls with internal resources, he "might have rescued [himself] from the falseness of the position of the simple sharer of distress," the colonial victim, incapable of action.

Browne and he, longing "for freedom and the truth of our personalities," escape from the challenges of their positions through a correspondence that obliquely explains their "action or inaction." Part of this correspondence, Singh's essay on the "puzzle" of Pompey's conduct during the Civil War in Rome, is clearly a way of avoiding his own motivations. He first attributes his inaction to his "vision of a disorder which it was beyond any one man to put right," but then reaches further into his own responsibility, baring the "romance" which he "distrusted" but to whose satisfactions he nonetheless "yielded": his initial distress at returning to Isabella, "the slave island," where he did not belong, he, "the picturesque Asiatic born for other landscapes." He has learned that neither a single deceit nor historical inevitability alone has determined the course of his life, that the links between personal and social history are complex and ever changing.

When he realizes that he must leave Isabella, Singh looks forward to his final departure, expecting to find "fulfillment and truth." In exile, as remembrance leads to contradictory remembrance, rationalization to exposure, denial to the acceptance of responsibility, he gradually frees himself from his past. The Latin word *Dixi*, with which he ends his memoir, denotes completed action; his preoccupation with his self-delusion, his fantasies and failures, is over. His exile, he says, has been "fruitful," and now, having "fulfilled the fourfold division of life prescribed by our Aryan ancestors," he is prepared for, if somewhat fearful of, "fresh action." His quest for truth is the story of one man's relation to the history of his homeland. Sometimes he has written, as he says, "from both sides," from that of the "old order" with its so-called "benevolence and service . . . imposed" even on his grandfather who could be "an object of easy satire" and at others from that of the naive, ill-prepared leader who hoped to overthrow a corrupt political establishment. Although some of his background and some of his experience resemble Naipaul's, this is not Naipaul's memoir. Singh is a highly individualized figure, at times a dandy and a snob; he is egotistical, and he can be unfeeling, even cruel, all qualities that respond to and affect the political events in which he is involved. It is his effort to get at the truth of his history, his shortcomings and his gifts, his refusal of the consolations of victimhood, a fundamental integrity, that redeem him. In this last respect he comes closest to his creator.

In societies seeking independence and in those having recently attained it, the narrators and characters of Naipaul's novels contend with political and social upheaval in a variety of ways. They enter into the fray; they retreat in helpless despair; they use any available resources to escape the chaos threatening them. Mundane experiences reflect an amorphous state without and within. An automobile, or some other moving vehicle, becomes more than a means of transport. As the protagonists of *The Mimic Men, In a Free State, Guerrillas*, and *A Bend in the River* drive through city and bush, they internalize the landscape, heading for the locus of themselves. Ralph Singh, driving through the city and past it, away from the eruption of violence at the Roman house, regains his sense of proportion: "over the wheel of my motor car, I returned to myself," and finally finds release from his anger in tears. The "Prologue" and "Epilogue" from journal entries, the two stories and the title novella that comprise *In a Free State*,[22] deal with travelers going to or having arrived at places even more inhospitable than those they have left. As the anonymous TLS reviewer puts it: "In this . . . book the placelessness is global."[23]

The journal entry with which *In a Free State* begins tells of Naipaul's crossing from Piraeus to Alexandria, a trip dominated by the presence of a tramp, an old man whose claim to thirty-eight years of travel and whose view of himself as "a citizen of the world" only confirm the sense that he belongs nowhere. His apparent disorientation and his physical frailty evoke Naipaul's pity, but he avoids involvement with him even when he is the victim of a cruel game that his cabin mates engage in. This contrasts with Naipaul's description in the "Epilogue" of his intervention in Luxor where he stops the cruel "Egyptian game" in which children are whipped as they run to collect food thrown on the sand by tourists.[24] The tramp is the most bizarre example of the dispossessed, but there are others on this ship, ordinary people who seem to have no permanent home: Egyptian Greeks, "deck-passengers" expelled from Egypt, now "refugees," returning as "tourists"; a Lebanese furniture-maker whose business in Cairo has diminished, he says, "since the Europeans have left" and who vows that he will leave Egypt rather than "go modern." His inordinate rage at the tramp, the extremity of homelessness, seems motivated by his own insecurity.

The two short stories that follow deal with the particularities of the "free state" as Naipaul explores the psychic cost of being an outsider in both one's native and adopted lands. Santosh, an Indian who has come to Washington D.C. as a cook for a diplomat, sums up his position at the beginning of "One Out of Many": "Many people, both here and in India, will feel that I have done well. But." The single-word sentence "But" introduces and later elaborates Santosh's dilemma: caught between the portion that was dealt him and his decision "to be free," he ends by renouncing the very freedom he gained: "All that my freedom has brought me is the knowledge that I have a face and have a body, that I must feed this body and clothe this body for a certain number of years. Then it will be over." This, the end of his narration, is not his whole story.

He claims to have been happy in Bombay, living in the street among other servants, "respected" because he worked for "an important man." Then his identity was based on what he experienced as contentment in being "part of" his "employer's presence," considering himself only "dirt" in relation to him. As he gradually ventures forth on his own into Washington, he begins to form a self-image separate from that imposed on him by his history, particularly his caste. Now, reconsidering his description of himself as dirt, he says, "I *used to*[25] tell him [his employer] then that beside him I was as dirt." First he tries to justify this self-deprecation by explaining that "it was only a way of talking, one of the courtesies of our language," but he does not deny that "it had something of truth." Acknowledging that as dirt, he had "experienced the world through" his employer, he realizes that he is now ceasing to regard himself "as part of [his] employer's presence" and is forming a realistic image of this man who, in some respects, is not unlike himself. Having given up the dubious satisfaction of merging with his opinions, he is free to feel disappointment in his employer's reaction to a crass American who brags of having gotten a guide in India to "hack off" a head from "an ancient temple." It is the insult to himself that upsets his employer, whereas Santosh regrets the violation of the temple.

Soon after this revelation he has an "adventure," amusing in itself but also important in determining his future. He has met a black woman (hubshi, he calls her), a neighbor's maid who attempts to "frolick" with him. Even as he fears her, her size, her odor, he fears his own desire: "in our country," he says, "we frankly do not care for the hubshi. It is written in our books, both holy and not so holy, that it is indecent and wrong for a man of our blood to embrace the hubshi woman. Nonetheless, he is "falling"; being "found attractive," he examines his face in the mirror and discovers that he is handsome. Ashamed of the ragged servant's clothes he used to wear, he becomes "obsessed" with his appearance. He has become so attractive to the black woman that she forces him down on the couch in his employer's apartment, and as he delicately puts it, "the act took over and completed itself." He associates the woman with Kali, "goddess of death and destruction, coal-black, with a red tongue and white eyeballs and many powerful arms" and seems disappointed when she turns out to be "playful," laughing all the while she embraces him. Still, to undo the "dishonour," after she leaves, he bathes, pays penance, and meditates.

Santosh has considered himself a "prisoner" (a word he uses repeatedly) all the time he has been in Washington, but now he is inspired by riots, as the blacks burn houses and shops, exhilarated by their power to destroy. Unaware that they are burning the signs and structures of discrimination against them, Santosh welcomes the fires and hopes for destruction so profound as to prevent any means of escape from his present situation, an idea he has not before acknowledged. Yet, walking in the streets, observing the "smiling" black people, he "shared their exhilaration." Now he admits that he "couldn't easily become part of someone else's presence again," that he no longer wants to return to his old life in Bombay.

His "escape," as he calls it, brings him a good job in a restaurant, a large increase in salary, a friend in his employer, Priya, and marriage, which provides citizenship, to the black woman he had feared. But a free state for Santosh means that he accepts the role of "stranger." He has lost his curiosity, and does not want to experience more of the society in which he now lives, its language or its people. Having "decided to act and see for himself," he has escaped imprisonment in a static and servile role by empathizing with rioters and marrying a woman he viewed as Kali. It seems that for this timid, gentle man, only association with violence could remove the hold of his past. Still, he has not found a satisfactory alternative, a center, to replace the rigid Hindu hierarchy which had determined his place. It is, he says, "as though I have had several lives." Though he does not "wish to add to these," at least he has lived for a time as his own person, merging with no one else's assumptions or values. In his renunciation, he has accepted the loneliness inevitable in this choice, one of the few that "freedom" has offered him.

For the narrator of "Tell Me Who to Kill," freedom seems an escape from the shame engendered by the poverty and ignorance of his colonial heritage. We first meet him when he is a passenger on a train, looking out the window at the rain falling on towns with "little bits of country between" them, the whole scene finally resembling "a big wet rubbish dump." His view of the landscape reflects his despair as he heads for London to attend his brother's wedding, an event that concludes a lifetime of devotion to visions of love and freedom that inevitably betray him.

Like Santosh, the narrator is an exile in a world so inhospitable that he envies a boy with his mother on the train who, he assumes, knows "where they are going when the train stop[s]." The narrator has not even the security of nostalgia for the place he has left. In his humble position as a "domestic," Santosh can take pride in being a member of an ancient culture, its arts, its beliefs and customs. The narrator of "Tell Me Who to Kill," a West Indian, has no memories and little knowledge of his Indian origins. His past, as he sees it, was barren. He does not expect his friend Frank, who accompanies him, "to understand how ordinary the world was for [him], with nothing good in it, nothing to see except sugarcane and the pitch road, and how from small I know I had no life." The poverty of his experience is evident in his chief associations, American films, his heroes the actors whose names he cannot spell correctly but who are paradigms or warnings in his vision of the future he will create for his brother Dayo.

He recalls the day he first dedicated himself to his brother's well-being: the donkey's pen beneath their house "wet and dirty with mud and manure and fresh grass mixed up with old grass," the smoke and odors from his mother's cooking, the heat and the mosquitoes and in "a bare room," his little brother Dayo, "trembling with the ague, lying on the floor on a floursack spread on a sugarsack, with another floursack for counterpane." The beauty of the child, "like Errol Flim or Fairley Granger" seems "like a wonder," which he must rescue from the sordidness of the island. Yet early on he is conscious of danger. Once again a film (*Rebecca*) is his frame of reference, in this case the setting for a dreamlike fantasy in which his brother has accidentally killed a friend he has made while "pursuing his studies" in England. Even worse, the narrator says, his brother and he hide the body "in a chest, like in *Rope* with Fairley Granger," and eat dinner with the dead boy's parents. The hatred that consumes the narrator throughout this story is here contained in his description of the parents: "They could be like any of the white people on this train. Like that woman with the boy writing on the wet window." In his fantasy he acts out his obsessive need to hurt those who make his "life spoil," who have prevented him from developing into his own ideal of an educated, successful man and who now threaten to ruin his brother's chances. They are not individuals, just "any of the white people," representatives of imperial power as it filters down to the quotidian life of its colonial subjects.

As "the fourth child" of his family, the narrator has seen the "world around [him] change," people going abroad "to further their studies." Regretting all that he and his family have been deprived of, his father's illiteracy, his older siblings' and his own few years of schooling, he takes on "the ambition and the shame for all of them." He is their scapegoat, "always hurting," determined at any cost to himself to rescue his younger brother. But his ignorance of the nature of education conveyed in the vague phrases he uses to describe it, the language of received ideas—"pursuing his studies," "to further his studies"—leaves him open to Dayo's deception, his insistence that he leave for England with his friends without any evidence of acceptance in a college in which he claims that by simply paying his fees he can enroll in a course in aeronautical engineering. Although the narrator yields to Dayo's insistence that he must leave at once, he is wary. He has encountered too many obstacles to change, to freedom, to be entirely taken in by his brother's story: "I feel the whole thing was too easy, that something so easy cannot end well." Of course, it does not.

Like Santosh, the narrator, Dayo and the rest of his family are products and victims of past and present history. In the changing world, the narrator observes, he is an unwelcome stranger. When the narrator goes to England to care for Dayo, he hates everything he sees: "houses, shops, traffic, all those settled people, those children playing games in fields," all those who seem to belong to their country, their time in history. Yet, for a few years, working at two jobs, saving money, living with Dayo in a squalid basement apartment, the narrator is happy. The two thousand pounds he saves gives him a new sense of security, but it does not last. Once again his ignorance of the world in which he has tried to realize his ambition, to rid himself of the shame of his background, defeats him. He buys a roti and curry shop, and is almost instantly conscious that he has made a foolish move, and is now the victim of the "prejudice" of inspectors and the cruelty of the "young English louts" who torment him. The only time he feels "like a free man" is when he acknowledges his delusions, admitting that the brother he tried so hard to help, professing to love him, rejects him for the world of his white bride; that he is now left with nothing. Only hate, which he cannot focus on any particular object, remains, turned inward in self-execration. In him Naipaul has created a figure whose increasing rage and alienation from a society that has scorned him are his only defenses against a total descent into madness.

The action of the title novella, *In a Free State*, takes place chiefly during a drive from the capital of a newly-independent African country to an area four hundred miles to the south "still known by its colonial name of the Southern Collectorate." The third-person narrator's introductory paragraph sets the scene for the two major characters' confrontation with the Africa they have avoided in their chosen exile there, the political struggle involving not only the recent internal combatants but a history of conflict and exploitation that has led to the present crisis:

> In this country in Africa there was a president and there was also a king. They belonged to different tribes. The enmity of the tribes was old, and with independence their anxieties about one another became acute. The king and the president intrigued with the local representatives of **white** governments. The white men who were appealed to liked the king personally. But the president was stronger; the new army was wholly his, of his tribe; and the white men decided that the president was to be supported. So that at last, this weekend, the president was able to send his army against the king's people.

Bobby, an English homosexual, who works as an "administrative officer" in the Collectorate, unaware of this crisis, has spent a week attending a seminar with "more English participants than African" in the capital, "still a colonial city" where everyone "was far from home." An episode that takes place on the evening before his drive back to the Collectorate foreshadows his discovery of how precarious is the freedom he has sought and believes he has found in Africa. In the bar of the New Shropshire Hotel, known as an "interracial pick-up spot," Bobby, wearing a so-called "native shirt," makes a pass at a Zulu he has identified as a "whore," only to have the man spit in his face. Having broken one of his own "rules" by pursuing "a boy dealing only in money," thus, in his eyes, a "whore," he doesn't blame the Zulu. Still, that night anxieties that he has suppressed emerge in his dream of lying on his back "in a place like the New Shropshire" where "the liveried boy [is] standing above him" and he is unable to see the boy's "face," to know if "the face" is laughing, the anonymity both tantalizing and frightening. Later, on the road, frustrated and angry when an African, supposedly cleaning his windscreen, actually damages it, he makes himself "think of the bar of the New Shropshire" and the Zulu, himself an exile, who led him on only to insult him. This time he wills himself to recall a warning that he refuses to heed.

Looking forward to his drive, unprepared for any difficulties, Bobby's anticipation is diminished only when he is asked to take on a passenger, Linda, "one of the 'compound wives' from the Collectorate." Linda has also come to Africa "for the freedom," as Bobby is to remind her. In both cases this consists of opportunities for social status and sexual adventures, hers with her compatriots, his with African boys "built like men." Their conversations on the road, tense, hostile, but also, in spite of themselves, confessional and even at times compassionate, expose the desperation of colonials facing history's interference with the compromises of their personal history. Like earlier colonists, they came to Africa because they could not quite "make it" financially, socially, or psychically at "home," as they still refer to England.

In a letter to Paul Theroux (dated September 18, 1972), Naipaul remarks on "how tightly constructed 'Free State' is, how every line of dialogue has a job of work to do."[26] Even before Linda's appearance, Bobby's internal monologue is a concise self-characterization. With extraordinary economy Naipaul discloses the nature of Bobby's need for the boys he seeks. Ruminating on past flirtations during long "drives on open roads," Bobby recalls himself making the first move: "You want lift? You big boy, you no go school? No, no, you no frighten. Look, I give you shilling." And so on. His use of pidgin, his empty promises: "I give you shilling buy schoolbooks. Buy books, learn read, get big job," divulge his pathetic, but ultimately cruel, attempt to get the boys to join him in enacting a fantasy in which he can clothe contempt for himself and for them in fellowship. The narrator's comment, equally compressed, "Sweet infantilism, almost without language: in language lay mockery and self-disgust," exposes the psychic drive for a measure of self-acceptance, of affection, that Bobby has persuaded himself can be bought with shillings and lies.

After Linda and he have set out on their drive and have begun to feel fairly comfortable with one another, Bobby casually mentions having seen a psychiatrist in the past, then "too calmly" explains, "I had a breakdown at Oxford." It is clear that this ordeal—"like watching yourself become a ghost"—the loss of his fragile hold on selfhood, has determined his choice of exile. "Africa," he says, "saved my life." The comment that follows, two clauses introduced by "as though," expresses Bobby's intent while it discloses the narrator's skepticism: "As though it was a complete statement, explaining everything; as though he was at once punishing and forgiving all who misunderstood him." After his overreaction to the scratches on his windscreen, to which Linda responds sympathetically, Bobby returns to the subject of his breakdown. Obviously, his original confession was hardly "complete." He finds it "strange" that although he hadn't learned to drive before he came to Africa, during his breakdown, he "consoled" himself with "the fantasy of driving through a cold and rainy night, driving endless miles, until [he] came to a cottage right at the top of a hill" with the warmth of a fire and the assurance of safety. He also imagined himself in a room in which everything was white, with a view of "green hills" and "a very blue sea." Bobby assents to Linda's suggestion that this sounds "like a hospital on a Greek island," admitting to her and to himself that this was a fantasy of total self-abnegation, a "wish to give up, to be nothing, to do nothing." It is from this state that Africa has freed him, and it is through this dependence that he views Africa. Soon he perceives the "mountains, the rain, the forest" of their present drive as "the sort of drive I used to dream of," finally merging his fantasy with the road they are actually on, until Linda calls out, "Bobby," summoning him back to the reality that their car is skidding in the rain and mud.

Linda, despite her "reputation as a man-eater," is a conventional bored colonial wife, who derives satisfaction out of her supposed superiority to the Africans and her occasional sexual adventures. Although she is attached to the beauty of Africa and the freedom she has found there, she is also obsessive about so called African customs, which Bobby believes are mere gossip she has picked up in the capital: the eating of excrement and dirt and "oaths of hate." She and her husband, "an old radio man," came to Africa because at the BBC he was reduced to "putting out rubbish," and he hoped to do better as a colonist. Now, more realistic than Bobby about the impending crisis, she knows that she and her husband must leave soon, even as Bobby insists, "My life is here."

He is soon to discover what actually is here, despite his efforts to escape into the "free state" of his fantasies. Bobby is consistently defensive about Africa. He is there, he says, "to serve." He has no wish "to tell them how to run their country." Even after Linda and he pass a crowd of Africans whose blank stares unnerve him, he says, "Speaking personally, I haven't found any . . . 'prejudice.'" But he does not admit his own, although Naipaul's three periods before the word "prejudice" indicate not an ellipsis of words spoken but surely of thoughts and words suppressed. One has only to recall Bobby's contempt for the African who damaged his windscreen, his threat to call the police, his outburst when the man began to walk away: "I'm a government officer! How dare you turn your back on me while I'm addressing you?" his arm lifted as if to strike the man.

After this episode, for a while the drive seems familiar and peaceful. However, when they encounter a roadblock and are obliged to take the road to the mountains, they come upon an older Africa than the urban one they have become accustomed to, "bush on both sides of the road," and, as they climb higher into the mountains, "it seemed they were on the roof of the world, at the heart of the continent," the last phrase no doubt an allusion to Joseph Conrad's *Heart of Darkness*. A line of Africans, the "bright colours" of their clothing and the "leaves over their heads" creating a kind of "camouflage," makes Linda "feel that sort of forest life has been going on forever." To which Bobby responds, "You've been reading too much Conrad. I hate that book, don't you?" Linda, who has learned that "the only lies for which we are truly punished are those we tell ourselves," counters his evasion, "You mean they're probably just going to a wedding or an annual general meeting." Bobby's hatred of *Heart of Darkness* springs from his evasion of Africa's past and present history. He says that he knew nothing about the country when he arrived, and he has learned little since. His need of Africa as a personal haven prohibits his acceptance of Conrad's depiction of the "horror" of colonial rule, which repudiated any so-called "idea"[27] of service, the very claim by which Bobby justifies his own presence there.

His fantasy drive, which he had compared with the present one, is suddenly obliterated as he finds his car "skidding, slithering," and finally stuck in mud. As Linda and he try to release it, they become muddy, "soaking and frenzied in separate parts of the bush," looking for sticks "to clear the exhaust." This is only the beginning of their descent into the heart of the newly independent African state. The town they enter is an image of total neglect: the "drives of villas," "the park," "the sidewalks" are all overgrown. Everywhere things are broken, rusty, decayed, corrupted, as is the hotel where they stop for the night. The owner, known as the colonel, is a prototype of the arrogant, patronizing settler, manipulating and often brutal to the African staff in his decrepit hotel, originally a resort for colonists, "who thought they had come to Africa to stay," now a mockery of that intention. When Bobby goes out for a walk he sees houses converted by Africans "to re-create the shelter of the round forest hut." He observes an Israeli trying to train soldiers for the new regime, only to find that they have "fallen into the trance-like dance of the forest."

The ways in which the police state of the president has already begun to supersede the encroachment of the colonists and the remnants of tribal customs are enacted in a dialogue between the colonel and Peter, his servant, or "boy," as he calls him. The two are bound by years of sizing up one another's attitudes, years of mistrust, mutual dependence, envy, and hatred. Peter has been with the colonel since boyhood when he was brought to the hotel from the bush, in the colonel's view, an elevation for which he is expected to be grateful. He is handsome and clever; at times his accent has "echoes of the colonel's accent," but he reverts to pidgin when he is challenged.

Peter appears in the dining room claiming that he is going to the "cinema," but cannot remember the film he plans to see, an obvious lie. Aware that Peter intends to join a meeting of Africans supporting the president and wishes to arrive there in his Volkswagen, the colonel demands the keys to the car. Peter's denial that he has taken them becomes an occasion for the colonel to taunt and humiliate him: "You like going in to some black hole to eat filth and dance naked. You will steal and lie to do that, won't you?" Then he threatens him: "If I die you will starve, Peter. You will go back to bush." Peter's response, "That is true, sir," is one in a series in which he professes agreement, affection, gratitude, none of which, it is obvious, he means. Finally, the colonel is so exasperated by these vestiges of formulas which once served as defenses that he reminds Peter of the torments he and other servants endured in the past: talk of "extermination," "a boy who was locked in the refrigerator," "whippings," and finally "the crops you weren't allowed to grow." This time, when he asks, "You say you like me?" Peter again gives him the answer that he wants, only this time it is the truth: "I hate you, sir," and a little later, "I will always hate you, sir." The colonel has wrung this admission out of Peter to support his suspicion, which he now voices, that Peter plans one day to kill him, and to justify his own threat: "You won't come past that door. I'll kill you. I'll shoot you dead," a warning that animates Peter, who returns the car keys and leaves. It is clear that he thinks he will ultimately win this contest; as Linda says, "They're waiting to kill" the colonel.

The rest of Linda and Bobby's journey is filled with tension, fear of the unknown, and danger in what they discover. Driving along, they see two naked men covered with white chalk running on the road. Later, Linda is to complain that Bobby did not react to this "apparition," did not even mention it. But all his efforts to evade or deny what he cannot understand or control are in vain. When they come upon what seems to be a wrecked Volkswagon on the road, Linda realizes that this is a staged accident; "they've killed the king," she says. Again, Bobby resists what he cannot face, until finally he responds bitterly, "The wogs got him." Linda, crude and prejudiced, nonetheless continues to confront him with the collusion of exploiter and exploited: "Everybody just lies and lies and lies."

Near the end of their drive they are stopped by the president's soldiers. Their prisoners, men of the king's tribe, mostly naked, sit on the ground, some of them "roped up in the traditional forest way, neck to neck, in groups of three or four, as though for delivery to the slave-merchant," another association with Conrad's Congo, only this time it is Africans violating Africans. Even after seeing this horror, Bobby does not realize the danger he himself faces. When he refuses to turn over his watch to a soldier, he is beaten, and his wrist is fractured. Still, finally safe in the compound at the end of the novel, he vacillates between the necessity of leaving the country and the temporary measure of firing his houseboy, who belongs to the king's tribe and has laughed at his distress. Like the protagonists of the other stories of *In a Free State*, Bobby is essentially homeless. When he keeps insisting that he is a government officer, one is left asking, which government? He has no family in Africa, no loyal friends, no memories or associations, no sense of continuity, all of which render a place loved or at least familiar.

At the beginning of his "Epilogue, from a Journal," with which *In a Free State* concludes, Naipaul, now in Luxor, sees two Chinese men leaving the dining room of his hotel. His first reaction, "Fellow Asiatics, the three of us, . . . wanderers in industrial Europe," soon turns out to be mere wishful thinking of some kind of fellowship as he realizes that they have no interest in him. They are immediately joined by many of their compatriots, members of a circus visiting from Communist China. A "wanderer," Naipaul characteristically looks for signs of continuity amid the changes brought about by the Egyptian revolution. When he visits the tombs, he is moved by the work of the "ancient artist, recording the life of a lesser personage" than the kings. He depicted the ordinary "pleasures of that life, . . . of the river, full of fish and birds, the pleasures of food and drink. . . . It was the special vision of men who knew no other land and saw what they had as rich and complete." After his effort to rescue the young boys from the camel-whip used in "an Egyptian game," after observing the lack of concern for them of the German, Italian, and English tourists, and the smugness of the Chinese,[28] traveling to Cairo, he recalls that vision, but he can no longer believe in the "pure time" he had imagined. Seeing with his "stranger's eye" the mundane life of people working in the fields, "agitated" peasants at railway stations, he suggests that perhaps it was the "yearning" for this vision, always a "fabrication," that actually inspired the ancient artist. The prologue and epilogue, the personal frame for the stories and the novella, like them, are rooted in history. The epilogue ends with a description of "soldiers from Sinai, peasants in bulky woollen uniforms going back on leave to their villages. Seventeen months later these men, or men like them," defeated in the Six-Day War with Israel, were to be photographed "from helicopters flying down low" revealing them "lost, trying to walk back home, casting long shadows on the sand," pictures, unlike those on the tombs, of the continuity of strife and suffering in human history.

VIOLENCE, SELFHOOD, AND THE AMBIGUITIES OF TRUTH

Guerrillas, Naipaul's fictional version of the Black Power murders in Trinidad, depicts this continuity of cruelty and strife in a setting far different from the Egyptian desert but even more emotionally charged. A mood of loss permeates *Guerrillas,* in which everybody, staying or leaving, is a wanderer in one way or another.

James Ahmed, who has a major role, is a fictional version of Michael X, a.k.a. Michael Abdul Malik, a Black Power leader in London and Trinidad during the late 1960s and early 1970s. Once a controversial figure, admired by some, scorned by others, Malik, though now generally forgotten, retains a historical and literary interest as an example of the charismatic con man and as the model who hardly seems to warrant the sympathy his fictive counterpart can evoke.

Malik's brief career can be gleaned from a number of sources, among them newspaper articles that appeared in London and Trinidad, his own ghosted autobiography, *From Michael de Freitas to Michael X,*[29] Derek Humphry and David Tindall's *False Messiah: The Story of Michael X*[30] and Naipaul's essay, "Michael X and the Black Power Killings in Trinidad."[31] Together they cover his years in England and Trinidad, where his activities ranged from dealing in drugs and women, to leading a Black Power movement, and finally to murder, for which he was sentenced to death. These sources provide the background of the referential action of *Guerrillas*, which depicts individual internalizations of the racial conflict of the 1960s and 1970s. Referential, obviously not as objective accounts or as bases of legal or moral judgments but as material for the introspective narratives that Michael X and his followers enacted in fact and in fiction. The very divergences of these accounts contribute to our understanding of the violent yet somehow pathetic figure who in Naipaul's fictive characterization finally confronts truths about himself he has long evaded, even while driven to betray them as fiction.

How does Naipaul educe this measure of dignity from his model, a self-described "hustler," a pimp, drug-pusher, questionable Black activist, would-be writer, and finally murderer? What truths about himself, his society, and the people with whom his life intersects does Jimmy Ahmed, Malik's fictive counterpart, reveal and discover? How are his efforts both to define himself and to retreat from self-knowledge central to the action and theme of *Guerrillas*? The answers to these questions, I believe, lead to an understanding of the complexity of this novel, as well as an apprehension of the magnitude of its vision.

As an activist in London, Malik was able to attract prominent and wealthy white supporters who donated large sums of money to his various projects. But the Racial Adjustment Action Society (RAAS), the Black House, and other institutions he founded received little of these contributions, most of which Malik appropriated. By the end of 1970, facing a criminal indictment for extortion by physical abuse from the manager of an employment agency, he withdrew from leadership of the Black House and, early in February 1971, fled to Trinidad. There, on the strength of his reputation as a leader in London, he was able to raise money for a so-called commune in Arima, where he was joined by former associates, among them his old friends Stanley Abbott and Steve Yeates, and visited by others who had not known him personally but were drawn by his putative accomplishments. Hakim Jamal, a Black American, and Gale Benson, a white Englishwoman, whom Naipaul describes as "an itinerant hustling team,"[32] came seeking refuge. The couple, who had met in England and traveled together to France, Morocco, the United States, and Guyana, performed their own Muslim marriage ceremony. Both psychologically fragile, they provided, however bizarre the means, some measure of stability for one another. Gale announced her symbiotic attachment to Hakim by calling herself Hale Kimga, an anagram of their names. She accepted his designation of himself as God and worshipped him accordingly. He basked in her adoration, encouraged in his projects, comforted in his failures.

Disheartened by the rejection of his various proposals to the government of Guyana and his expulsion from the country, Hakim accepted a passive role in the commune in Trinidad, even surrendering his divinity to Malik. But Gale soon became suspicious of Malik, who concluded that she was a spy. Facing discord among members of his commune, finding it increasingly difficult to raise money, he decided to assert his authority and to reunite his followers through a ritual sacrifice:[33] the scapegoat was Gale Benson. Although Malik instigated the murder and others knew about or were involved in it, it was actually Steve Yeates who on January 2, 1972, struck the final blow. A month later, when Malik's cousin, Joseph Skerritt, became suspicious about Gale Benson's disappearance, Malik himself murdered Skerritt.[34] When the bodies were discovered, Malik was in Guyana, where the police found him hiding in the woods. In August 1972 he was pronounced guilty and sentenced to death for the murder of Skerritt. His appeal was supported by many prominent people, among them William Kunstler, Kate Millett, Dick Gregory, William Burroughs, and John Lennon and Yoko Ono,"[35] but to no avail. He was hanged on May 16, 1975.

From Michael de Freitas to Michael X and Naipaul's essay on the Black Power killings provide some insight into the temperament of the man whose life was so bleak and violent, and his metamorphosis into Jimmy Ahmed. The "I" of *From Michael de Freitas to Michael X* is most engaging in its contradictions, resulting mainly, but not entirely, from his representation of himself as a black man struggling for survival in a white society. Explaining his choice of a white ghost writer, whom he names John X, Malik writes of his surprise and delight in their capacity to traverse what has seemed to him impassable avenues of "thought and expression" between the races. But even if the Sunday *Times* (September 24, 1967) had not reported that John X was an officer of the Central Office of Information, obvious disparities between voice and subject would suggest the very barriers that Malik denies. Malik left school at fourteen and for many years was either a seaman or a pimp, yet the language of large parts of the autobiography, especially the sections on social and racial issues, is, with some concessions, that of an educated man. The tone, while sympathetic toward oppressed blacks, is often impersonal. After a passage of reporting and brief analysis of racial conflict, the first-person narrator returns as a surprise. Occasionally, when John X tries to capture the idiom of the shebeen or the marijuana- and alcohol-inspired revels, only a ghostly approximation emerges.

Malik's decisions and projects consistently reveal contradictions between his ambitions and his meager emotional and moral investment in any undertaking. Inspired by one of his lovers, a white Jewish woman, he decided to study "sociology, which was a subject I found increasingly interesting." But, as he explains, he needed money and thus returned to hustling. Finding little or no time left for college, he dropped out after "twenty lessons in all." Yet in the autobiography his ghost presents him as a man of sociological insight, an articulate teacher and lecturer. His personal relations disclose similar separations of act and affect. Having settled down with Desirée, a woman he claims to love, he soon becomes sexually involved with a prostitute, a relationship he or his ghost calls "a commercial proposition." His use of women for sex and money or both persists throughout the portion of his life recorded in *From Michael de Freitas to Michael X.*

The autobiography repeatedly asserts that communication and trust are impossible between blacks and whites, yet among Malik's friends and supporters were middle- and upper-class whites. The only woman who emerges as a person in her own right is Nancy, a white Jew. "Talking with Nancy," he says, "a slow transformation began in me." He tells of beginning to read seriously and to recognize "how limited my vocabulary and general knowledge were." He admits to the superficiality of his ideas and the inadequacy of his arguments. But, at least from the evidence of his autobiography, his transformation was merely into a temporary new guise. Examining himself after he had become a Black Power leader, he feels obliged to admit his hypocrisy: all the while he was lecturing others on the evils of whites and on the degradation of black men in their relations with white women, he had been involved in an affair with a wealthy white woman whom he used as a "source of income" for RAAS. Characteristically, he blames not himself but the inevitable "effects of the ghetto."

Malik's autobiography ends with an assertion and a prophecy. "I have no fear of losing my own identity," he insists, as he declares his objections to interracial marriage and predicts that increasing hostility between blacks and whites in England will end in an "explosion." About himself he was, as usual, deluded. Yet this autobiography tells more about Malik than he was aware of or perhaps wished to reveal. It portrays a man continually adopting pseudo-identities—lover, husband, black leader, painter, writer, humanitarian—all unearned, authentic only as failed efforts to achieve psychic integration. According to one account, even the name Michael X, which the title of his book suggests is a form of self-definition, was acquired through a misunderstanding during his brief association with Malcolm X, who referred to him as his "brother."[36] As to the "explosion," racial clashes did continue to occur, but certainly not on the scale that Malik predicted.

From Michael de Freitas to Michael X is more interesting for what it suggests than for what it tells, for the clues to what is omitted, which Naipaul followed in his essay and in his novel. In both works he deals with events following the period covered in the autobiography, but he weaves facts about Malik's earlier life and, especially in *Guerrillas*, feelings unexpressed but intimated into the violent outcome of Malik's return to Trinidad. Throughout "Michael X and the Black Power Killings in Trinidad" he views Malik as "shallow and unoriginal, . . . an entertainer." Of the autobiography he says: "It is not the story of a life or the development of a personality." Malik "is without a personality; he is only a haphazard succession of roles." Still, when he briefly explores the etiology of Malik's instability, his shifting "personalities," it is with compassion for a figure whose conduct hardly elicits it.

Naipaul's leading clue is Malik's relationship with his mother who, as portrayed in *From Michael de Freitas to Michael X*, "is as puzzling as Malik." His summary of this puzzle includes Malik's mixed parentage— his mother was black, his father a Portuguese shopkeeper, de Freitas, who deserted her and their son—and the contradictory behavior of the mother, as Malik describes her, a racist snob, "forever preaching the beauty of whiteness," which she equated with propriety, but herself a drunkard, a "hustler," and a "brothel keeper." "Certain facts about his mother are too important to the narrator for him to leave out," says Naipaul. "But the facts have been scattered about the picaresque narrative: a pain greater than the one stated is being concealed." What Naipaul surmises is that the mother, who came from Barbados and was a stranger in Trinidad, now married to a black man, "was disgraced" by her "red bastard" son, as he was disgraced by her bizarre conduct. "She was uneducated, drunken, vicious."

Naipaul considers a letter that Malik sent to his mother from London, defining himself as a "negro" and recalling how she had repeatedly humiliated him, "the truest thing Malik ever wrote, and the most moving. It explains . . . the change of names from de Freitas to X, the assumption of so many personalities, the anxiety to please. A real torment was buried in the clowning of the racial entertainer. Black power gave order and logic to the life; it provided Malik with a complete system." As the autobiography and Naipaul's further comments on his exploits demonstrate, the Black Power movement was but one of several avenues in Malik's quest for self-definition. In fact, each time Naipaul touches on this central unfulfilled need, the harshness of his portrayal of Malik is mitigated by his apprehension of Malik's "torment."

The autobiography confirms Naipaul's view that Malik regarded the educated, professional black as "not quite a Negro," that the "real Negro" who "lived in a place called the 'ghetto' . . . was a ponce or a drug peddler; he begged and stole; he was that attractive Negro thing, 'a hustler.'" But Naipaul's conclusion that to Malik the "real Negro" was "someone like" himself speaks for only one of the self-images Malik enacted. The other, the would-be writer, teacher, lecturer who had white friends and lovers, comes all too close to being "not quite a Negro."

If the first image was, as Naipaul says, "a construct for a commercial market," it was fundamentally, I believe, a retaliation against the mother who denied his blackness and thus his elemental connection with herself. The second image, which conformed, however meretriciously, to his mother's demands, was yet to be used in the service of the first. Hence, while defying the mother he rejected, he never quite relinquished his desire to be the son she would accept. This conflict, at the heart of Malik's anguish, remained unresolved; he enacted it throughout his life.

"Michael X and the Black Power Killings in Trinidad" contains examples of Malik's writings, even with their errors in spelling and grammar and their "borrowed words," straining for an ideal of himself that would integrate these two roles. As author, narrator, or character he is famous and handsome, "his beautiful golden brown skin" uniting his African and Portuguese heritage. In notes he took while still in England for a planned but unwritten sequel to his autobiography, he refers to his "Hero Image," which is "greater overseas." As Naipaul's quotations from the novel Malik was writing in Trinidad suggest, this exalted image was only part of his psychic and fictive narrative. In fragments of this novel Naipaul sees evidence of a "resentment, soon settling into hatred . . . of the English middle class [Malik] had got to know." Malik, who appears in the novel under his own name, is at first a figure who inspires admiration and even awe among the powerful English characters, but they soon grow to fear him. In Guyana, where the novel is set, he is regarded as a "hero," and in Naipaul's paraphrase, "there are people in the streets who shout for him to be king." The narrators shift from Lena-Boyd Richardson, a young Englishwoman, to third person, to Sir Harold, a friend of Lena's father. As narrator, Lena is contemptuous of the "natives," but clearly has mixed feelings about Mike (Malik), whom she de-

scribes as "like some statue on a Pedestal, some god," worshipped by his
followers. Since he appears to be well read, she is astonished when he
addresses her alternately in pidgin and in Cockney, and she is troubled
by evidence of his "weird double Life." She then admits to being "scared
. . . mortally afraid of this man of this Mike the grinning ape," whom she
can't help liking. An episode Lena recounts suggests that she has good
reason to fear his apparently motiveless rage with its threat of violence.
These fragments, says Naipaul, "survived the events they seem so curi-
ously to foreshadow."

If Malik, writing this novel in his commune in Trinidad, was arriving, as Naipaul says, "at some new definition of himself," it consisted of
more grandiose versions of his earlier conflicting images: of the canny
black hustler who could best the white middle class and the cultured
black leader apotheosized. But nothing that Malik could achieve in
Trinidad—neither his agricultural commune nor his comfortable house
in Arima nor the aid of supporters in England and the United States—
could match his own fictive imaginings. No Sir Richard would ever
shout: "We go crown him king." Finally, he enacted the alienation and
rage that motivated these fantasies of omnipotence in murder.

Converting his interpretation of Malik's inner narrative into fiction,
Naipaul condensed the multifarious enactments of his "personalities"
into a few episodes which allude to the events they transform. The plot
of *Guerrillas* lends Jimmy Ahmed—and indirectly Malik—a coherence
that "Michael X" only hints at and that Malik could not achieve for
himself in his ghosted autobiography, his articles, letters, or fiction. In
Guerrillas Jimmy Ahmed emerges as a more vivid figure than his model;
he elucidates Malik's aspirations, his struggle for autonomy, his pain, and
his violence. Jimmy's fiction, like Malik's, is part of this revelation, as are
his relations with other characters in the novel.

Guerrillas[37] portrays the elaborate political and psychic stratagems
devised to avoid the truth of experience during a period of racial conflict on an unidentified Caribbean island that bears a strong resemblance
to Trinidad. Jimmy is but one of three leading characters. His mother,
like Malik's, was black, but his father was Chinese, a heritage even more
problematic than Malik's, producing not even conflict but only a void in
cultural identity. Like Malik, he has fled from the law in London, but unlike Malik, who was accompanied by his wife and children, Jimmy arrives alone. His deepest erotic attraction is to one of the members of his
commune, Bryant, a poor uneducated young man who can only "grieve
for what was denied him": the opportunity to become "what he truly

was," a man as loved and as happy as Sidney Poitier in the film *For Love of Ivy*.

The two major characters involved with Jimmy are Peter Roche, a white South African, who seems culturally and psychologically related to Malik's British supporters, and Jane (she is given no surname), his English lover, who bears some resemblance to Naipaul's depiction of Gale Benson in his essay. Roche, who was tortured in his homeland for engaging in protests against apartheid, now works in public relations for Sablich's, a firm eager to atone for its unsavory history as slave traders by sponsoring Jimmy's so-called agricultural commune. His dubious role on the island exacts his admission that "every decision he had made had been made after he had disregarded some element of the truth." Jane has come from England to join Roche, hoping to identify herself with a man and a cause. Chief among the other characters who enact the narrator's multifaceted conception of truth are Meredith Herbert, a black journalist, solicitor, and politician whose wish "just to be oneself" articulates a goal he cannot achieve or abandon; and Harry de Tunja, a Jew in perpetual exile, whom Meredith describes as "never blind. . . . The one man in the country."

The novel opens soon after Jane's arrival as she and Roche are on their way to visit Jimmy at his commune, Thrushcross Grange. As they drive the windows of these outsiders' car frame politics, commerce, and nature reacting on each other: political slogans, a sea smelling of "swamp" and "bauxite dust," a dump, a new housing development already decaying, hills, suburbs, and factories. The approach to the commune is indicated by signs announcing For the Land and the Revolution, donated by American and local firms protecting their investments by cynical accommodation to Jimmy's demands. Roche's and Jane's disillusion with each other is intensified by the atmosphere of waste, rot, exploitation. Soon after Jane is introduced to Jimmy, the three are bound together in their despair of finding satisfaction in who they are or what they do, as each recognizes the others' efforts to buttress a fragile sense of self by embracing the struggle against racial discrimination.

After their first meeting Jimmy uses Jane as a fictive projection of his fantasies of omnipotence—a blend of hate and longing for esteem. Disturbed by his reaction to Jane and Roche's visit, he seeks relief from feelings of depersonalization, from "a vision of darkness," in a narrative written from her first-person point of view, harsh toward the island with its "good-for-nothing natives" and adoring toward him. Having perceived the beginnings of Jane's disillusionment with Roche, he attributes to her surrogate his own contempt for Peter's motives as Sablich's representative at the commune: he is merely using the "natives," including Jimmy himself, to enhance his own reputation as a leader who endured torture for the black people of South Africa.

Jimmy, on the other hand, who "was like a celebrity" in London, is "like a savior" who "understands and loves the common man" and inspires fear in "the rich white firms." She responds to his color, "not black, but a lovely golden color, like some bronze god." Physically and ideologically this man she longs for is Jimmy's film-star version of himself. Roche, she says, is becoming "jealous" of him and has become "repugnant" to her. Only at the end of this outpouring of self-adulation does Jimmy, writing with mounting excitement, grant his smitten narrator the insight he has gained in the act of writing as he fuses a memory of his brief triumph in London with his present fantasy, which is a clue to his future. After his fictional Jane acknowledges that Jimmy "must hate people like me," since she is "middle-class born and bred," she echoes a description of him by a woman quoted in an English newspaper: "I only have to look in his eyes to understand the meaning of hate." The reader learns that it is a quotation only later in the novel when Meredith mockingly asks Jane, "Did you look into his eyes and understand the meaning of hate?" and then goes on to reveal its source. Through Meredith's prescience Naipaul unites fact and several levels of fiction: Malik's calculating approach to the women he lured in London and his reputation as a dangerous ladies' man become part of Jimmy's past—the background of his present conduct and of his fiction, which, like Malik's, "never lies." Meredith's question also presages the danger that Jane is to court in her flirtation with Jimmy.

The distortions of Jimmy's narrative, like those of a dream, disclose the processes of their creation: his self-hatred projected on the "natives" and transformed into its opposite in his grandiose image of benevolence and power. The world he has fashioned Jane to represent, which he envies and wishes to possess and to destroy, is condensed in her adoration, her desire to take him in and to be possessed. But recognition of the generation of his desire in hatred leaves Jimmy spent. Only the source of his narrative remains: "Melancholy . . . like fatigue, like rage, like a sense of doom." When he tries to resume writing, the words are "false." A short time later, he begins a letter to an English friend named Roy to whom he is more direct in expressing his despair, which comprises pity and rage at the condition to which those for whom "the world is made" have reduced the underprivileged, particularly the boys at his commune, deprived even of hope. His only recourse, he says, is to "destroy the world" that has betrayed him and them. But his "destructive urge" passes, replaced by an admission that all he can actually do is exploit "liberals" like Roche, whom he despises: "I play along, what can you do——." Like Bryant, Jimmy sees himself as "lost" and, turning to him, seeks comfort in embracing this most forlorn image of himself.

This episode foreshadows the two "sexual scenes" on which Naipaul has said the novel "hangs."[38] These, which involve Jimmy and Jane, with Roche and Bryant as accessories, have nothing to do with affection or even physical attraction. Parodies of lovemaking, they are desperate forays into a fantasy domain of selfhood by people who lack the psychological and moral integrity to withstand or counter the political cynicism and cultural instability of their society. These scenes are focal because they enact the most extreme effects of alienation on society's most vulnerable individuals, whatever their race or class.

Jane was drawn to Peter Roche in London after reading his recently published book on his imprisonment and torture in South Africa. Aimless, emotionally empty, regarding herself as a victim, she had chosen him as her guide to "real events and real action," her rescuer from the decay she perceived in the middle-class environment into which she was born and which she blamed for the blight on her early marriage, on her love affairs, on her very hopes for personal fulfillment. Imagining Roche as the "doer" who had chosen to leave London for "some new and as yet unsuspected center of world disturbance," she had joined him on the island, only to discover that once again her homemade hero was no longer of use to her and, like all her earlier products, disposable. It is an old story in life and in art, but Naipaul invests it with a new psychological complexity that reveals how intimately individual conduct is linked to the political and social consequences of colonialism.

Having realized that Roche, the seeming enemy of imperialism, is actually its offspring and has become its appeaser, a "half colonial" himself, Jane plans to return to London. She has given up not only on Roche but on life on the Ridge, a suburb inhabited by transient bureaucrats and expatriates intimidated by newspaper reports of guerrillas threatening what little stability the island has offered them. But she puts off her departure. Four months after her arrival, she is ripe for another victimization, this time by Jimmy.

The prelude to the first "sexual scene" repeats the pattern of Jimmy's reaction to Jane and Roche's visit with which the novel begins: Jimmy writing, his uneasiness at his own disclosures, his reaching out to

Bryant for physical and emotional comfort. This time, however, he will attempt to enact his written narrative with Jane, who remains the narrator of his novel, now named Clarissa. Jimmy has been writing about a meeting with Clarissa, who once again expresses her conviction that only "a woman of [her] class" can appreciate his intrinsic nobility, and foresees the day when the "shiftless" blacks will present him with a crown. Longing for Jimmy, Clarissa confesses that she phoned him but was so overcome by her feelings that she was unable to speak when he answered. "I put the phone down," says the narrator. Soon after writing this passage Jimmy phones Jane twice to arrange for a meeting. The first time, hearing her maid's voice, he "put the telephone down." Jimmy then returns to Clarissa who, seeking knowledge of her hero in the newspaper, discovers that he is to address the Lions at the Prince Albert Hotel, where she encounters him after his speech.

Again Jimmy's narrative method becomes that of a dream, merging past with present as Jane/Clarissa is abruptly metamorphosed into a figure out of Jimmy's boyhood. He knew only her story, told by his classmates, "but it had become like a memory." A white girl who had been raped by a gang on a beach had screamed, then fainted, and one of the rapists had brought her water from a creek nearby. This story of an abused, bleeding girl responding with "grateful eyes, remembering terror" to the "cupped hands offering water" had become Jimmy's prototype of romance. Identifying himself with both victim and aggressor, he has fantasized himself involved in a conquest in which he asserts power through sexual cruelty and humiliation, thus incorporating what he hates and envies. In his adaptation of this fantasy to fiction Jane/Clarissa becomes the raped girl, assuming her "terror" and anticipating the moment when her hero "will bring water in his own cupped hands and I will drink water from his tender hands and I will not be afraid of him anymore."

Writing this passage, Jimmy has become sexually aroused but, as the fantasy fades, he grows uneasy, aware of the "emptiness" of the present. He cannot continue writing. Having long since internalized the raped girl, he conceives of himself as a victim: "he could have screamed like the girl on the Ford fender." After turning to Bryant for comfort, he abruptly leaves him to again phone Jane, asking her to meet him at the Prince Albert the next day, pretending that he has an appointment there with some business executives.

Naipaul, it will be recalled, described Malik in "Michael X and the Black Power Killings in Trinidad" as "only a succession of roles." In

Guerrillas, depicting Jimmy, like Malik, merging with various figures he knows or invents—Bryant, the raped girl, and now Jane—he portrays this process manifested in Jimmy's fiction and then in the devious turns of the narrative enacted with a partner whose responses are, to a large extent, beyond his control.

When Jane and Jimmy meet at the Prince Albert it is clear that he is hardly motivated by sexual attraction. As Jane approaches the lobby Jimmy notices her "clumsy" walk, her "characterless" face, her mouth intimating weakness and "cruelty." Jane asks about his "meeting," but Jimmy has momentarily forgotten his pretense: "As in a dream he saw confused swift events: a drive to his house, her reading of his writings, exposure." On some level Jimmy perceives the connection between the sadomasochistic fantasies of his novel and his interest in Jane. When she refers to his speech to the businessmen, he asks, "The Lions?" an allusion to his fiction, now fused with the telephone invitation in which he had mentioned only executives. Jane's immediate association is Roche. "Peter is a Lion," she says. "Was he there?" Jimmy's response is a bitter attack on Sablich's, founded by slave traders, hated for its past corruption and present efforts at respectability. "Massa's firm," he calls it. To Jane's insistence, "But not mine," Jimmy replies ambiguously, "Look. I don't want us to be friends." Suppressing her initial uneasiness, Jane interprets the comment as an avowal of sexual interest, evading the implications of his refusal to accept her dissociation from Roche's guilt.

On the way to Jimmy's house a moving car is once more a literal and figurative vehicle of perception as Jane, looking out the window, observes details of the city she had hitherto ignored. Focusing on an old female vendor, beggars, dying dogs, slums infesting natural beauty, she projects on the city her own emotional slumming, fearing yet seeking psychic dissolution. Yet, when they arrive, the excitement she has induced is gone. His home, Jimmy himself, have become all too mundane, and she turns to the business of the afternoon, sex, with aggressive detachment.

From the beginning their efforts at lovemaking are frustrating, Jane's demands and Jimmy's fantasies unfulfilled. Soon they are interrupted by a phone call from Roche, followed by Bryant's footsteps "somewhere in the house," both foreshadowing political turmoil and personal disaster. The fruitless exertions to which they return—her contrivances, his rage emerging in an attempt at sodomy, and finally her effort to evoke some feeling with the ritualistic formula "Love love"—end in impotence and hatred. Three times Naipaul refers to Jimmy's disappointment in "losing the moment" he had wished to "witness," the moment of his conquest of the rich white adversary reduced to his adoring slave. But Jane has refused the role of Clarissa or the raped girl. As she leaves him, Jimmy associates her with a "prostitute," emerging "triumphant" after "defeat and degradation." In pain and despair, he longs for "Bryant's warm, firm flesh and his relieving mouth and tongue."

Typically, Jimmy's image of Jane as "triumphant" is a reaction to his spoiled narrative. It has nothing to do with the actual woman whom he has no desire to understand. On the way home in a hired car, Jane feels only the "distress" of repeated frustration as an inner voice reviews her own past and present conduct: "I've looked everywhere. I've looked and looked." Shifting from his character's narrative to his own, Naipaul uses the word "looked" three times, as she does, conveying empathy in the repetition: "She looked at the driver's mirror," feeling judged as she met his stare. Trying to escape him, she "looked" out the window, but she was drawn back to the mirror, "and whenever she looked . . . she saw his red assessing eyes." There is empathy also in the contrast between the two ways of looking: Jane's looking "everywhere" has been an evasion of herself, a search for a projected savior, which has led her to the present reality that she feels compelled to confront in the driver's eyes. Now the warning, "I've been playing with fire," comes to her "like an intimation of the truth." For readers acquainted with Naipaul's essay "Michael X and the Black Power Killings in Trinidad," it is as if the narrator, who has modeled her neediness and vulnerability on Gale Benson's, would save both of them from themselves. But, given his truth to the events that compel him and the character of Jane, he cannot.

That night Jane turns to Roche for comfort, asking him to share her bed. Meanwhile Jimmy, impatiently awaiting Bryant's return, continues writing his letter to Roy, in which he depicts himself as the despairing leader who can no longer "control the revolution." He mentions Stephens, a young gang leader who has left the Grange and whom he now considers a rival and a threat. Here he enlarges on his earlier contemptuous assessment of Stephens, "Everybody wants to be a leader," with the statement that Naipaul uses as his epigraph: "When everybody wants to fight, there's nothing to fight for. Everybody wants to fight his own little war, everybody is a guerrilla."

Bryant appears, obviously enraged by Jane's visit, but nonetheless the representative of lost, subservient youth dependent on the master, a presence comforting enough to lift Jimmy's despair and restore his sense of control. When he continues writing, he takes up his novel and the voice of Clarissa, who is obviously being punished for Jane's rejection of her assigned role. This section of Jimmy's novel begins where the last one left off, repeating the same motifs; only here his hatred and fear are intensified by his failure to subjugate his oppressors represented by Jane. When Clarissa warns the hero that "they" (the oppressors) intend to "destroy the leaders," he accuses her of belonging to "the establishment." Hatred of the vestiges of colonialism in his society and in himself are expressed in sexual terms throughout this passage. Jimmy tells Clarissa that she is "rotten meat," and she senses his judgment in the eyes of waiters and taxi drivers, in "every face I see." The seemingly innocuous phrase "Of course" takes on sinister implications as it introduces her confession (and through hers, Jimmy's own) of hatred for the "shiftless" people and the acknowledgment that "this hate and scorn . . . is bringing retribution." Finally she is chased by boys who look like Bryant and she becomes the raped girl. At this point Bryant, who has been sitting in the room, screams, "Jimmy, I see the white rat today!" Jimmy's response is a promise to "give her to" him.

By the end of the first third of *Guerrillas* Jimmy has plotted his narrative for the next sexual scene, which is to take place a few pages before the book's conclusion. Between these two episodes rebellion against the government intensifies, indicating that however megalomaniacal Jimmy's fictive self-image and however melodramatic his view of the inevitable "revolution," he is a shrewd observer of the political scene and of the individuals involved as participants or victims. More acute than Malik, he is as incapable as his model of action immune from his self-destructive impulses.

At a gathering at the beach house of Harry de Tunja, whose surname is one of several his family has come by as people identified them by "the last place" they had fled, he tells his guests of an old black man he encountered on the street recently who pointed at him and said, "You! You is a Jew!" For Harry the episode is but one of many signs that he does not belong on the island, that it is again time to flee. To the consternation of Jane, Roche, and other middle-class Caucasians, the de Tunjas have been planning to move to Canada. Equally unsettling is the news that Harry's wife has left him. The couple, whom they had chosen to represent harmonious family life, has become another example of the instability threatening them all.

With the arrival of Meredith Herbert at the beach house, the tension increases as precarious political and social affiliations merge to arouse suspicion in relations that had once seemed secure. Roche had admired Meredith's integrity, his pleasure in his work as solicitor and radio interviewer as well as in his family; but gradually, influenced by Jane, he had begun to mistrust "the personality that had attracted him and seemed so restful," regarding it as a mere "creation." Harry, the most open and direct of men, suspects Meredith of "getting a little closer to the powers that be." Both assessments have some validity, but both fall short of apprehending the complex figure Naipaul has portrayed as simultaneously bound to and reacting against historical forces. For Naipaul, self-creation is not the disguise that Roche assumes it is. The "hysteria, . . . rages, deprivations, and unappeased ambition" that Roche senses behind Meredith's domesticity are no more definitive than is his image of personal wholeness in a fragmented society. Implicit in Meredith's expression of the wish "to express myself fully" is a lifetime's struggle against the oppression his race and class have endured. The very intelligence and talent that have made it possible for him to achieve a leading role in his society have rendered whatever compromises he made on the way violations of the self-image he retains against all odds.

Meredith seems compelled to speak of Jimmy whom he had known as a child and had encountered later in London where he had become "this great Negro leader." Jimmy's "English glamour" he says, is "dangerous," a cover for his inner emptiness: "he's nothing at all" and thus can be used to "create chaos." Jimmy, he says, cannot be satisfied with his present project, "Land, the revolution based on land. That was the London programing . . . Jimmy has to go on and on. There's a kind of—what's the word? Not dynamism." It is clear that for Meredith Herbert, educated, articulate, this is not a deficiency of vocabulary. He is resisting the modish word, which Jane then supplies. "Dynamic," she says, and Meredith takes it up, investing it with his insight and anger to remind the others that Jimmy's career in England "ended with rape and indecent assault. The same dynamic," he predicts, "will take him to the end here." Ironically, Jane, who has supplied the key word, avoids its meaning even when Meredith reiterates, "the white-woman rape," an unwitting prophecy of her own fate.

This conversation takes place as riots break out in reaction to the killing of Stephens by the police that very morning. In the state of emergency declared by the government amid fires and explosions, the rebellion seems to have no center, no program or established leaders. Harry de Tunja, on hearing that the police are abandoning their posts, confirms Jimmy's earlier observations: "I don't see how you can blame the police. They don't know who they fighting or who they fighting for. Everybody down there is a leader now."

Isolated on the Ridge, Jane and Roche rely on Harry for whatever information he can obtain. His levelheadedness in this crisis contrasts with their confusion, his kindness to them with their open hatred for one another. Feeling themselves trapped on the island, their customary defenses useless, each faces the situation alone. Down in the city, Jimmy, leading the rioters bearing Stephens's body through the streets, and Meredith, representing a government he mistrusts, are alike in denying what they know. Both pay for their compromises. Jimmy is soon dropped by the rioters, replaced by others who declare themselves leaders. Meredith is stripped and assailed by the mob. As Harry says, "A child could have told Meredith that they were calling him back to the government just to throw him to the crowd."

With the arrival of the American helicopters the rebellion comes to an end. "The Americans are not going to let anybody here stop them lifting bauxite," says Harry, yet he has scoffed at the radio news report that "the disturbances were sparked off by radical youth groups protesting against unemployment and what they see as continued foreign domination of the economy." It is true that the young gang leaders' slogans reveal no consciousness of the bases of their dissatisfactions, only messianic visions of undefined black power. In "Michael X and the Black Power Killings in Trinidad," Naipaul regards race as an "irrelevance" in Trinidad, "but the situation" as "well suited to the hysteria and evasions of racial politics." The situation he describes is one in which "agriculture . . . declines," and "industry, where it exists, is rudimentary, protected, and inflationary." Poverty and unemployment are widespread. There is "the sense of a land being pillaged rather than built up." Still, in his portraits of Malik in that essay and, in *Guerrillas,* of Jimmy, and of Meredith (so different from both except in this one respect), race is not irrelevant. The past of colonialism and slavery continues to exert its hold on the present in the economic, cultural, and psychic deprivations recurrent in Jimmy and Meredith's memories and are the heritage of the black gang leaders. The outcome of the contest between the gangs and the American helicopters was never in question. Acceding, however ambivalently, to Sablich's paternalism, to foreign exploitation of the island's natural resources, Roche thinks it odd that people on the island should talk about their childhood as a time they have only begun to comprehend. Ever an outsider, he does not realize that a measure of political independence so recently acquired exposes the infirmities of the self formed in servitude. Disorganized and ultimately ineffectual, the rioters nonetheless communicate a desire for self-determination. Malik and

Jimmy's final cruelty and violence enact the most disastrous effects of what Naipaul considers the essential "problems" of their society: "dignity and identity."[39]

As the city returns to normal, Meredith uses a radio interview with Roche to strengthen his restored position as minister in the surviving government. In a dusty, stifling room, the air conditioning intentionally turned off, Roche is again a victim, this time submitting to intellectual bullying reinforced by physical discomfort, a milder version of his treatment in South Africa. Too passive to protest, he is gradually manipulated into mentioning Jimmy, opening the way for Meredith's denunciation of him as a dangerous fraud. Questions about Roche's book and thus about his admittedly fruitless guerrilla activities in South Africa lead to the issue of Thrushcross Grange as a "cover for the guerrillas." Naipaul's portrayal of Roche's submission to Meredith's prodding suggests that the author, along with Jane and the reader, gradually comes to know Roche through his relations with other people.

Discussing the interview with Jane, Roche can only assent to her judgment: "You've left Jimmy out there for Meredith and those other people to kill." For Roche the interview had been a public confession of the failure of his work with Jimmy and the so-called commune, of the shallowness of his commitment to the cause of racial equality, of a life without focus, personal or political. Now, prolonging his humiliation, he confesses to Jane that he left England not out of conviction but out of fear of a neo-Nazi who threatened to kill him, which she interprets as a personal affront, an exposure of the last traces of her spoiled fantasy. She retaliates by announcing that Jimmy has been her lover, their one frustrated attempt at loveless coupling her only defense against nothingness. To this she returns.

Once again before Jane's visit, Jimmy is writing, this time a letter to Marjorie, a woman with whom he had an affair in London, telling her that her prophecy is "coming true. I am dying alone and unloved and I will die in anger." Part self-analysis, part apologia, the letter conveys the convergence of impulses to be enacted in the rape and murder of Jane. To Marjorie, the woman who first revealed his "manhood" to him and who, like everyone else, has betrayed him, Jimmy writes in his own person of the hate that his fictional persona Clarissa had seen in his eyes. His portrayal of Marjorie, his "maker and destroyer," is an indictment of all women. With her he could "know the joy" of being himself, but the consequences of such knowledge were renunciations of the disguises he had first assumed in childhood and the admission that he was indeed "that child in the back room" of his Chinese father's shop. Inveighing against women who "have no shame and thought for the children who come after them who have to endure all they did," he is no doubt thinking of his mother, described by Meredith as one of "our women [who] went to live with Chinese shopkeepers" for the economic security they offered. Like Malik, Jimmy is bitter about his anomalous heritage, especially the mother who deprived him of his black identity, his source of an authentic self. Like Malik, too, he is finally unable to displace his personal alienation in social programs and revolutionary schemes, however spurious. Only his earliest rage and shame remain. Rejected by his former adherents in London, he was sent back to the island "to be nothing," the very word Meredith had used to describe him. Rejected there as a leader by the people he claimed to represent, he is, he admits, "a lost man," lost since childhood.

In the past, writing had aroused him sexually as he concocted sadistic fantasies embellished by his role as savior. Now, having identified himself ironically in the last words of his letter with "dead men [who] come once," he exerts the only control left him in the anal rape and murder of Jane, his vengeance on those he perceives to have used him and finally abandoned him to his enemies. Helpless against the government, Meredith, and Roche, he passes sentence on Jane, the last object of his skewed fantasy of power and romance. Calling her "rotten meat," as he had addressed Clarissa, he demands recognition, "You know what you are now," a revised version of Naipaul's interpretation of Gale Benson's struggle against her murderers. Voiced by Jimmy, its falsity only emphasizes the pathos of Jane who knows so little about herself emotionally and sexually. To the end she does not understand what is happening to her. After the rape she says she will phone for a taxi, but she allows Jimmy to dissuade her. Nor does she struggle when she is cut by Bryant and strangled by Jimmy. Having defined herself as a victim for most of her life, she goes to her final victimization passively, as if she could experience herself in no other way.

In "The Black Power Killings in Trinidad," Naipaul could only speculate on the motives for the murder of Gale Benson. He suggests that Benson's middle-class background, her "African-style clothes," her cultic adoration of Jamal aroused suspicion among the members of Malik's commune. This outsider could even be a British agent. He quotes Mrs. Malik's assessment of her as a "fake," and seems to accept this view, remarking on the danger of being "a fake among fakes." Describing her murder ("She was held by the neck and stabbed and stabbed") and her attempts to defend herself, Naipaul concludes: "At that moment all the lunacy and play fell from her; she knew who she was then, and wanted to live. Perhaps the motives for the killing lay only in that: the surprise, a secure life ending in an extended moment of terror."

The characterization of Benson as a fake seems too facile. Malik's wife was hardly an objective source. Nor is worshipful attachment necessarily a sign of the fraudulent. It may in fact be a defense against psychic deprivation so painful as to motivate elaborate displacement. We simply cannot know what drew Benson to Jamal and what her feelings were as she met her death. Nor from the available evidence are the motives for her murder clear. It is apparent that Naipaul was unsatisfied with his own speculation as later in the essay he twice returned to this question, repeating the perception of Benson as an "outsider" and adding another possible cause: Malik held Benson responsible for the stress Jamal was suffering and demanded "blood." Paradoxically, more credible motives for the actual murder are conveyed through the changes Naipaul made in the fictional one, in which Jimmy has but one ineffectual accomplice. Murder in *Guerrillas* is the inevitable outcome of the complex of individual, political, and social determinants—of inner emptiness finally enacted in the rage of impotence. In Jimmy the investigative narrator bares the sources of Malik's psychic narrative.

After he murders Jane, Jimmy feels "nothing except desolation." His bizarre fantasies, which in the past had provided relief from frustration and anger, now confront him with the violence that was their ultimate aim. Jane's dead eyes, on which he can project "nothing," dismiss the girl raped on the beach who had offered him love. He is lost in "a void."

At the end of the novel, Jimmy, aware that Roche knows he has murdered Jane, nonetheless phones him asking for help. Roche's subterfuge, which he assumes Jimmy will comprehend, is that Jane and he are returning to England. Only indirectly does he threaten Jimmy: "I'm leaving you alone," he says. "That's the way it's going to be." Abandoned to be killed, Jimmy replies in the last word of the novel, "Massa." All that is left him is this double-edged epithet, his final self-mockery hurled at the oppressor who came in the name of benefactor.

Roche cannot know that by now Jimmy has accepted the defeat of his long struggle to avoid extinction. Bizarre as his writings are, they constitute his defense against the threat of depersonalization, failed attempts literally to make something of himself. His fiction and letters are a record of pain and rage against injustice distorted into megalomania, cruelty, and even—as in Clarissa in the role of the raped girl—a warped compassion. They are revelations of the inner emptiness he has tried to fill with visions of leadership and power. His final admissions to Marjorie that he " knew I was fooling myself" and to himself, after Jane's murder, that he "didn't know who or what he was" obviously do not justify or even explain his terrible deeds, but they are a testament to a lifetime's conflict between a need to evade and a compulsion to face truths about himself so damaging as to finally destroy him.

Like *Guerrillas*, *A Bend in the River* is a fictional version of events Naipaul dealt with as a journalist. The titles of both articles he wrote refer to a leading figure, Michael X in the first instance, and Mobutu as "A New King for the Congo" in the second. There is a major difference, however, in the connections between these articles and their fictional analogues: whereas Michael X is transformed into a leading character in *Guerrillas*, the new King, though his influence, like his photograph, is everywhere in the town where the novel is mainly set, does not appear as a character in *A Bend in the River*.

The protagonist of that novel, Salim, who is also its narrator, embodies a period of history of which he and Mobutu are a part. He identifies his family as Muslim, but as "a special group . . . distinct from the Arabs and other Muslims of the coast; in our customs and attitudes we were closer to the Hindus of northwestern India, from which we had originally come."[40] The east coast of Africa, where his family had lived "for centuries," he says, "was not truly African. It was an Arab-Indian-Persian-Portuguese place." Thus, Salim introduces himself as the very product of Naipaul's conception of history as "an interplay of various peoples, and it's gone on forever."[41] Through Salim's voice Naipaul converts first-person narration into the mental and psychological activity that creates individuality in contemporary history.

His story begins with his drive from his family home to an unnamed town, no doubt Kisangani, formerly Stanleyville, in an unnamed country, obviously, Zaire, in the interior. The first sentence of the novel, "The world is what it is; men who are nothing, who allow themselves to become nothing, have no place in it," immediately conveys the narrator's adaptation to the historical, political, social, and cultural forces that shape his individual existence. These are his limits and his challenge. The opening clause, which Naipaul repeats later in the novel, "The world is what it is," is developed in the destructiveness, the lies, the self-serving ambitions, the resourcefulness, the cunning, the continual struggle to survive, to rebuild and renew out of rubble, of which life in the town at the bend in the river consists. The three negatives of the second clause, "men who are nothing, who allow themselves to become nothing, have no place in it," make clear that whatever small capacity for self-assertion exists must contend with a society where negation is internalized.

Salim is no hero; he is a man whose background and temperament have provided him with no stability and few choices. Born into a family of merchants, he identifies himself with neither the religion and customs of his relatives nor with those of the Africans of the interior in their recent independence. His education is limited; though he is bright, his intellectual and emotional capacities are not extraordinary. Yet, as a young man, recognizing that the way of life his family had established and maintained for centuries is doomed ("another tide of history was coming to wash us away," he says), he takes what seems to be his one opportunity to survive as an individual: "I could be master of my fate only if I stood alone." Staying with his family would be giving way to disaster: "We couldn't protect ourselves; we could only in various ways hide from the truth." More than the loss of his home, as he foresees "the political system we had known . . . coming to an end," he fears "the lies—black men assuming the lies of white men." In fact, Salim's most appealing quality is his uncompromising quest for the truth of whatever situation, problem, or danger he encounters. The nature of truth itself interests him, even the "special kind of truth" used by "newspapers in small colonial places." Now, admitting the dangers of inaction, he has arranged to move on. But it is not only the truth that history has taught him that impels Salim. As always in Naipaul's novels, choice is contingent on individual reactions to historical forces. Salim had been expected to remain in the family business and to marry the daughter of Nazruddin, a family friend, a "stifling" prospect to him. Instead he buys a shop owned by Nazruddin in the town at the bend in the river, nearly destroyed by internal conflict after independence, in the expectation that the inevitable time of renewal is imminent.

As narrator, Salim is participant, observer, creator, and creation. At times he is unaware of his drives and motivations operating unconsciously in diverse combinations with external circumstances; at others he is a perceptive, conscious interpreter of his own thoughts and actions. Naipaul depicts both types of mental acts with extraordinary precision. At the beginning of the novel, as Salim drives from the coast to the interior in his Peugeot, the man at the wheel is himself driven "through bush and more bush," feeling the "madness" of his aim, telling himself that he is "going in the wrong direction" as he persists in his need to create a "new life" in the ruins left by violence and anarchy.

Yet he drives on: "Each day's drive was like an achievement." A compassionate as well as a "life-loving man," he thinks of the psychic compromises of slaves who in an earlier time had been forced to make a similar journey. Yet, if the external circumstances are similar, he has grasped at the measure of freedom open to him. He reminds himself that he, after all, is going in the "opposite direction"; driving to the heart of the bush, he is reacting with his own instinctual impulses to the pressures of history. "The greater the discouragements of the journey, the keener I was to press on and embrace my new life."

A little later he moderates these aims, diverting them into rational thoughts as he evaluates what he has done. Realizing that he is "breaking faith with Nazruddin" in "breaking away from [his] unspoken commitment" to marry his daughter, Salim also recognizes the ambiguity of the situation: in "breaking away" (a term that recurs in his thoughts), he is keeping faith with his image of Nazruddin. An alien presence among his people, an "exotic," European in his manner, Nazruddin was successful, fortunate. For Nazruddin, things seemingly "worked out beautifully" but he always "lived with a vision of things turning out badly." Salim has identified himself with Nazruddin in this view of life: "I thought: This is how a man should behave; and I felt close to him after that, closer than I did to members of my own family." Now, if in leaving his intended bride, there is a breach of faith in regard to her father, there is also loyalty to him: "Yet he—a relisher of life, a seeker after experience—had been my exemplar; and it was to his town that I drove." Loyalty to Nazruddin is, of course, a means of defining and defending his own needs, but Salim at this point can only act them out; he cannot foresee the consequences of such action. As he approaches the town he recalls Nazruddin's stories of what the place was like. Memories of the merchant's allusions to wine evoke fantasies of "pure bliss." Knowing that the town is in ruins, he nonetheless allows himself to imagine its old life "re-created" for him. The town he actually finds "had returned to the bush." Wine, with its associations of pleasure, is obviously out of the question. The simplest food is hard to find, and daily life is primitive. Yet the self that functions there is created by the daydreamer as well as the driver, for these are both expressions of the same impulses and memories and the same historical processes.

Critics have questioned Salim's credibility because at times he seems to change his mind about issues without sufficient reason and, at others, his convictions seem to bear the authority of the trained, sophisticated intelligence of his creator.[42] This seems to me too facile a judgment of the most complex of Naipaul's fictional investigative narrators, contending with the world as it is by various and sometimes contradictory means. To be sure, Naipaul has endowed Salim with something of his own curiosity and skepticism, his commitment to seek out the truth within himself and to apprehend the corruption that political machinations and cultural pretensions would obscure. But he has deprived him of his own advantages. Naipaul's autobiographical allusions throughout his writings reveal that, for all his complaints about the narrowness of his background, he had the opportunity to transform his "limitations into virtues."[43] His education was keyed to escape from the restrictions of his early environment, first to Oxford, then to London and the world beyond, which he continues to explore. Most important, of course, was the inexplicable, the great inborn gift that determined his dedication to writing under the most trying circumstances. The journalist exploring Salim's terrain conveys these marks of privilege.

Salim's vantage point as a shopkeeper casting about for a way of life is utterly different from Naipaul's in *A Congo Diary*, "A New King for the Congo," and "Conrad's Darkness," which yet provide vital clues to the narrator, plot, and setting of *A Bend in the River*. Salim could be Naipaul's image of one of "the people, le petit peuple of Mobutu" extending to the outsider he would expel, whose "value" Naipaul suggested in *A Congo Diary*, was the "most important" of Mobutu's ideas. This concept, he says, "points to the future." However, as I indicated in chapter 3, even then he was dubious, "clutching at straws." His doubts confirmed, his portrayal of Salim embodies a fragile hope for a measure of individual assertion accommodating a history of obstruction and yet enduring.

As the town begins to rise again and Salim rebuilds his store, he becomes involved with other people, and it is in relation to them that he struggles to define himself. These include Ali, a half-African family servant a few years younger than Salim, who had asked to be sent to him; Zabeth, a trader, one of his first customers; her son Ferdinand, a boy from the bush, now enrolled in the town's lycée; Father Huismans, the head of the lycée; Indar, a wealthy friend from the coast; Shoba and Mahesh, an Indian couple; Yvette, a Belgian with whom Salim falls in love; and her husband Raymond. Salim's connections with them are intertwined with political and economic developments in the town. Political ambition and power, a recurrence of "the semi-tribal war that had broken out at independence," the instability of daily life, exert their influence on the very psychic processes and intimate acts of the characters.

Determined to establish a new way of life, Salim is aware that he has gone from one stifling environment to another. Observing Metty developing "a new idea of his worth" and Ferdinand trying out various images of himself, Salim feels compelled to demonstrate his separation from "Ferdinand and the life of the bush about me." Having "no means in my day-to-day life of asserting this difference, of exhibiting my true self," he shows Ferdinand his binoculars, his camera, and the "popular science" magazines that he reads, reflecting that he should have devoted himself to studying "the particular science or field I was reading about . . . adding knowledge to knowledge, making discoveries, making something of myself, using all my faculties." Yet he knows that these aspirations will never be fulfilled, his potentialities never realized.

Such regrets are not fruitless as Salim applies his desire to explore and learn to the limited realm available to him—the town and its people. During the new uprising, soon to be aborted by the intervention of foreigners, "white men" called in by the president, he is torn between compassion for the hotel workers who are "abject" in the presence of these strangers, and relief at the security they offer. "This was how the place worked on you: you never knew what to think or feel. Fear or shame—there seemed to be nothing in between." His ambivalence seems similar to Naipaul's in "A New King for the Congo" in response to Mobutu's Domain at Nsele. But Salim is personally involved, in this case, with the fate of the workers. Naipaul, however empathic, is the reporter as "visitor," evaluating Mobutu's claims. Their language reflects the differences in their points of view. Salim admits that he is unable to come up with an appropriate response, both fear and shame being demeaning; the journalist, describing what he assumes is an inevitable reaction to inherent contradictions, writes of "moods" rather than of intense emotions. Yet both are self-examinations in the interest of truth.

One of the people who introduce Salim to the range of Africa's hold on the outsider is Father Huismans, a Catholic priest who is enthralled by all things African—the food, the religious beliefs, the art—yet also reveres the remnants of European colonization. Salim is drawn to Huismans in part because of their differences. Father Huismans's "interests," which Salim tries to comprehend, seem to him an avenue to knowledge of the country, of himself. Using the motto of the lycée, "Semper aliquid novi," Father Huismans explains that in the masks and carvings he collects there is "always something new," a unique "religious purpose" absent in copies. Salim is surprised by Father Huismans's involvement in an art he himself does not admire and in beliefs ignored in his upbringing on the coast. Unlike him, Father Huismans is indifferent to "the state of the country," a man, says Salim, whose "Africa, of bush and river, was different from mine. His Africa was a wonderful place full of new things."

Naipaul soon uses a second Latin quotation to cast doubt on this idyllic picture of Africa and on Father Huismans's knowledge of the history of the land in which he feels so much at home. He tells Salim that "the second motto of the town" is a line from the *Aeneid* "carved on the ruined monument near the dock gate: Miscerique probat populos et foedera jungi," which he translates as: "He approves of the mingling of the peoples and their bonds of union." Actually, in *Aeneid* IV (110-12), Venus tells Juno that she is uncertain as to whether Jupiter would approve of the blending of the peoples (Tyrians and Trojans) and their being joined in a union. When Father Huismans explains that in the line on the ruined monument "three words were altered to reverse the meaning," Salim is "staggered" by the audacity of the act, the identification of the town with Rome. He reflects, but not wishing to offend Father Huismans, does not say, "Twisting two-thousand-year old words to celebrate sixty years of the steamer service from the capital! Rome was Rome. What was this place? To carve the words on a monument beside this African river was surely to invite the destruction of the town." He wonders at the lack of the "anxiety" that was present in the original line of the Latin poem, and observes that soon after it was erected, "the monument had been destroyed, leaving only bits of bronze and the mocking words, gibberish to the people who now used the open space in front as a market and bivouac."

Father Huismans reacts differently. The paired Latin quotations define his conception of his role in Africa. He takes delight in each new revelation of the spiritual life of the country and uses the altered quotation from the *Aeneid* to place himself within "an immense flow of history," as a European to whom the Latin words apply. In this flow the town at the bend in the river has always existed and will continue to exist, its history as a colony, "the opening up of the river," to be revered as much as the life of the bush, to which he returns periodically. His equanimity, it turns out, is not enough to protect him from the reality of contemporary Africa, in which he takes little interest. Soon after peace is restored after the second rebellion, during a visit to the bush, he is killed, his body sent down the "main river" in a dugout, his head "cut off and spiked." Although in the "flow of history," the ruling powers and their subjects are now reversed, Huismans's spiked head evokes and is linked with the horror of the shrunken heads on stakes surrounding Kurtz's house in *Heart of Darkness*.

In Edward Said's view, "it is precisely the fervent innocence of [Graham] Greene's Pyle or Naipaul's Father Huismans, men for whom the native can be educated into 'our' civilization, that turns out to produce the murder, subversion, and endless instability of 'primitive' societies."[44] In Salim's eyes and, no doubt, in Naipaul's, Father Huismans is not simply a representative of colonial condescension. Salim mourns the loss of his "knowledge . . . and what to me was more than knowledge—his attitudes, his relish for Africa, his feelings for the beliefs of the forest." These qualities, Salim believes, derived from his "idea of his civilization," which fostered a spirit of inquiry: "it had made him find human richness where the rest of us saw bush or had stopped seeing anything at all." Still, Salim, who has spent his life in Africa, realizes that Father Huismans's "idea" was "also like his vanity," which made him rely too much on "that mingling of peoples by our river, and he had paid for it." Father Huismans's "innocence" may have been instrumental in bringing about his death, but it hardly had the power to subvert the whole society, to which he actually paid too little attention.

There is no lack of affection in Salim's judgment. In fact, it grows out of much that he has learned from Father Huismans, from his view of himself "as part of a great historical process," which Salim and other "outsiders" share, "but from a different angle." Like Father Huismans, who "would have seen his own death as unimportant," they see themselves as "expendable," like "ants," whose labor might be destroyed at any time, but who "kept on."

In the "boom" that follows the end of the rebellion, "order and money" are the framework provided by the ruling powers; the "confidence" these bring and the "energy" they release promote Salim's deeper concerns, the sense that he must somehow define his own role within the processes of history. His observations of the president's new development, the Domain of the State at Nsele, and his relations with the people he meets there help him to formulate the possibilities open to him and the hazards he must somehow meet. His early reactions to the creation of the Domain, like Naipaul's in "A New King for the Congo," are ambivalent. It seems to be a town in itself that conveys instability even as it projects an image of power. It transmits the president's message that "Africans had become modern men who built in concrete and glass and sat in cushioned chairs covered in imitation velvet." For a while no one knows how the Domain, with its huge buildings, its farm, swimming pool, and conference hall, is to be used. Eventually, it becomes "a university city and a research centre" to train the future administrators of the nation. In "A New King for the Congo" Naipaul, attempting to explain the "extravagance" of the Domain, and the "nationalizations" as an effort to heal the wound Africa has endured, finally admits that the domain is "shoddy" and the nationalizations "bogus." The response he gives Salim both echoes and departs significantly from this judgment. Salim sees the Domain "with its shoddy grandeur" as a "hoax," built out of foreign greed and African opportunism. Yet, remembering Father Huismans's belief in the altered lines out of Vergil, the motto that was an "earlier hoax" and yet "had helped to make men of the country in a certain way," he believes that "men will also be made by this new hoax." In his own case, ironically, its very deceptions seem to stimulate his interest in the African society into which he was born and the Africa he now inhabits as well as a more authentic conception of his own capacities and limits.

He is introduced to the Domain by Indar, an old friend from the coast, who describes himself as "a guest of the government," in Salim's eyes, one of the "new-style foreigners" who live in this creation of the president. Indar, who had left home to study at an English university, returned to find that his formerly wealthy family had lost their property and now was "scattered," like Salim's own family. Nonetheless, his impressive appearance, his superior manner and his appointment at the polytechnic for a term at first recreate the old distance between him and Salim. Eager for Indar's friendship, for the knowledge of the world outside that he has to offer, Salim is willing to show him the admiration he does feel and that Indar so obviously needs. Soon Indar becomes his guide to "the strange world of the Domain," to which Salim becomes strongly attracted: "To travel those few miles between the town and the Domain was always to make some adjustment, to assume a new attitude, and each time almost to see another country." The image of Africa among the people he knows in the town is of a place "where we had to survive," a place barren of intellectual or aesthetic stimulation. In the Domain, by contrast, "another Africa had been created," and with it a new African man. As Salim responds to the "educated talk" with its references to "famous cities," the Domain becomes a substitute for the education he missed, seeming to offer fulfillment of his desire to explore and learn.

Still, always on the lookout for the fraudulent, seeking the truth beneath the evident, Salim continues to question. Even after he is impressed by the discussion at one of Indar's seminars, he wonders whether

Indar and he "weren't fooling ourselves and whether we weren't allowing the Africa we talked about to become too different from the Africa
we knew." To return to the town he has come to know—the squalor, the
poverty, with "the presence of the river and the forest all around"—is

> to grasp reality again. Did Indar believe in the Africa of words? Did
> anyone on the Domain believe? Wasn't the truth what we in the
> town lived with—the salesmen's chat in the van der Weyden and the
> bars, the photographs of the President in government offices and in
> our shops, the army barracks in the converted palace of the man of
> our community?

Indar's cynical response, "Does one believe in anything? Does it
matter?" is unacceptable to Salim. He probes into the "dishonesty" that
he feels exists between them as a clue to their present evasion of the
truth: their avoidance of their common past—the "smashed life of our
community," the past history that foreshadows the future. The questions
he raises lead to even more fundamental ones: Can the Domain be a
hoax and yet "real" because of the "serious men (and a few women)"
who function there? and even more challenging: "Was there a truth outside men? Didn't men make the truth for themselves?" For Salim these
are not merely interesting philosophical inquiries; they are issues of psychic and physical survival, which become increasingly pressing as conditions in the country grow more precarious.

Further discussion of the nature of truth takes place at a party in the
Domain, to which Salim has been taken by Indar, at the home of Raymond, a middle-aged European historian who works for the president,
and his young wife Yvette. Raymond, who has been "the Big Man's
white man," praises the president as the most gifted of leaders, all the
while aware that he himself is no longer needed. As Indar later tells
Salim, "Everybody knows that, but Raymond thinks they don't." This
denial seems to motivate Raymond's "wonder . . . whether the truth ever
gets known," his feeling "that everything one does is just going to
waste." From this general disillusion he moves on to question whether
"the history of the Roman Empire" can be known, and finally to his particular concern: "Do you think we will ever get to know the truth about
what has happened in Africa in the last hundred or even fifty years?" A
little later his reference to the great historian of Rome, Theodor
Mommsen, as "the giant of modern historical writing," suggests that this
man who has been made and is soon to be unmade by the president has
chosen Mommsen as his fantasized model. Lest he not live up to this

image, he is careful to point out that Mommsen had the advantage of a great subject. The Western tradition—Rome with its German interpreter—is the standard, against which Africa is the unknown: "We have no idea," he says, "where the continent is going. We can only carry on." In some respects Raymond is a touching figure in his generosity and loyalty, and especially in his effort to objectify his own situation but, as Salim is to learn, he has no real understanding of Africa; his knowledge of the country is chiefly of "letters" and "missionary reports."

In the beginning Salim's love affair with Yvette is based on his exalted image of Raymond's position and her apparent "glamour," fantasies soon to be dispelled. Even when he realizes that had he "understood more about Raymond" earlier, he might have seen "her more clearly— her ambition, her bad judgment, her failure," and would not have become "involved with people as trapped as myself," he also admits that he is now "possessed by" her. With Yvette he experiences a joy and satisfaction he had never before known in an erotic relationship. His past sexual experience, chiefly with women in brothels, had produced only contempt for himself and his partners. Now all his "energy and mind . . . devoted to that new end of winning the person," he enacts in his aggressive sexuality "a great need for tenderness," and in his desire to "see," to comprehend the woman he embraces, he feels the emergence of a "new self." As Yvette becomes the focus of his days, he exults in the feeling that he is "revitalized," in the "newness" of his very "skin," but he is also frightened by a vision of "the decay of the man I had known myself to be," for he neglects his shop, caring only for his meetings with her. Yet the qualities of self that develop as this love affair progresses, and eventually ends, are far more complicated than either of these attitudes imply. His love for Yvette transforms the "broken-down town, in which [he] had felt neutered," into "the place where it had all come to me." Investing the town with his own sense of discovery, he develops "a new kind of political concern, almost a political anxiety." Feeling "bound to Raymond" through Yvette, Salim experiences the president's power "as a personal thing, to which we were all attached as with strings, which he might pull or let dangle."

As Salim recognizes the dangers implicit in the president's silent dismissal of Raymond, with its threat to Europeans and other foreigners, the growing visibility of his managers and soldiers, the "arbitrariness" of life in the town, these become determinants of the self he enacts and observes: "We stood for ourselves. We all had to survive." Personal need and desire are intensified and qualified by political tensions, riots, and rebellion. Yvette and Salim must leave the country and each other; psychic and physical survival demands the break.

Salim resists this knowledge. Yet it is inherent in the deeper ambivalence of the self manifested in his love for Yvette, which produces both "self-esteem" and "shame, to have reduced my manhood just to that." But this ambivalence leads to a more fundamental self-awareness. In this period of tense expectation, Salim records the very processes of thinking verbally as his anxiety about his self-regard leads him to a concept of selfhood, which comes to him as a question conveying its tentative nature: "She gave me the idea of my manliness I had grown to need. Wasn't my attachment to her an attachment to that idea?" His psychic growth demands a recognition that the self he has tried to define and to fix in relation to Yvette is itself a historical development, the continual adaptation of cognitive and psychic processes to social and political necessity:

> And oddly involved with this idea of myself, and myself and Yvette, was the town itself—the flat, the house in the Domain, the way both our lives were arranged, the absence of a community, the isolation in which we both lived. In no other place would it be just like this; and perhaps in no other place would our relationship be possible.

Implicit in this understanding is that in his "certainty of the end" of his life in the town, of his affair with Yvette, lies his "security." As Salim and Yvette face this end, their talk takes on a quality of indirection, "lying and not lying, making those signals at the truth which people in certain situations find it necessary to make." At their last meeting Yvette's posturing goes beyond indirection to what Salim considers betrayal. His brutality—striking and spitting at her—are violent reactions to what he sees as her dishonesty, but also to his loss of love for a woman with whom he discovered sexual pleasure and grew in self-knowledge.

It is this recognition that makes him write to Nazruddin, now in London, to tell him that he plans to come for a visit. Once there, he chooses to stand alone no longer, and becomes engaged to Nazruddin's daughter, Kareisha, a pharmacist, intelligent, serene, a guide to the city and the new life for which this visit is a preparation. Before he can commit himself to a new beginning, however, he must return to Africa, ostensibly to wind up his affairs, actually to renounce what he clings to, a phase of his past, "the idea of the other place," which he has internalized and transformed into aspects of his own being. He also knows that "There could be no going back; there was nothing to go back to. We had become what the world outside had made us; we had to live in the world as it existed."

His visit to the town confirms this perception. Under a policy of "radicalization," his shop has been "nationalized." The town is "in a state of insurrection," and he is placed in "preventive detention." Once released he knows he must leave as quickly as possible and, with Ferdinand's help, he escapes just in time. Paradoxically, Salim's acknowledgment that he must live in the world as it is expresses his conception of individuality. If he is, as he says, what the world outside has made him, he is no passive victim. Circumscribed geographically, economically, socially, he develops what seems to him a remarkable capacity to look outward from himself, to apprehend the nature of a woman who herself internalizes a nation in flux. He comes to realize that his sophisticated friend Indar is in need of his guidance, that the European "experts" are as vulnerable as he, and he feels closer than ever to African fellow prisoners who "had prepared themselves for death . . . crazed with the idea of who they were," and yet "far away" from them in his determination to survive.

This is not, as it has often been judged, a pessimistic novel. There is a tragic optimism in this individual struggle to create a self pitted against continents whose past and present history seems calculated to negate it. Salim's continuous and ever-changing inner transformations of his environment, his questioning and revision of his memories, his defenses against his erotic drives even as he submits to their aims, his efforts to discover truths about himself and his place in the ever-changing world, even his renunciations engage the reader in the risks and satisfactions of individual "energy and mind" conceiving and narrating their presence.

THE AUTHOR IN HISTORY

The Enigma of Arrival and *A Way in the World* both deal with changes in the writer as he interacts with the history of his changing backgrounds. In *The Enigma of Arrival*, it is Wiltshire, site of England's ancient past, the more recent past, and Naipaul's present home; in *A Way in the World*, it is Trinidad, his first home, to which he returns repeatedly in his writings in order to establish its way in the world, as well as his own.

Naipaul has "split" himself into a variety of characters who share certain of his traits and qualities of his background. This is especially true of those who write. The affinity between Ralph Singh or Salim and their author, for example, is readily apparent. But even Jimmy Ahmed, whom Naipaul has afflicted with a narrative style that is laughable or frightening, or both at once, resembles him in finding relief from anxiety or panic in writing. In *The Enigma of Arrival*, however, he distinguishes the author writing in his "own person" from fictional characters who interact with him to illuminate the writing process. Naipaul has used autobiographical material earlier in *A House for Mr. Biswas*, as reminiscence or association in his travel narratives, and has written a more organized survey of important events of his early life in "Prologue to an Autobiography." In *The Enigma of Arrival* he reviews his personal history from a new vantage point, recreating it within the context of the history of Wiltshire, where he lives in a rented cottage on a decaying estate.

A major subject of the novel, one of Naipaul's continuous explorations of the manifold ways of knowing, is the great emotional effort involved in acknowledging what one somehow apprehends. Both autobiography and fiction are centered on the activities of observing and learning to perceive what at first is hardly noticed or is actually misinterpreted. For the writer such exploration began with "an acknowledgment of myself," actually of "the worlds I contained within myself," and has become an ongoing process encompassing new experiences, new worlds and their peoples, self-questionings and self-corrections, nightmares, losses, and confrontations with mortality.

The first section, "Jack's Garden," consists of a series of gradual discoveries regarding the land and its people, and especially of Jack who, whether based on an actual acquaintance, as seems likely, or entirely concocted, is central to the plot. The narrator's approach to Wiltshire and its history develops from his early fantasies about this farm worker whom he first observes as an adjunct to his garden. His initial image of Jack "rooted to the earth" as opposed to his own rootlessness has something of the quality of an imaginary childhood friend functioning in an adult realm of anxiety and emotional need. Early on he realizes that his notion of the "unchanging world" of Wiltshire was wrong.

> Change was constant. People died; people grew old; people changed houses; houses came up for sale. That was one kind of change. My own presence in the valley, in the cottage of the manor, was an aspect of another kind of change. The barbed-wire fence down the straight stretch of the driveway—that was also change. Everyone was aging; everything was being renewed or discarded.

Still, he holds on to his belief that Jack is "a remnant of the past." This too, and only after Jack has died, he finally rejects as "wrong." It takes him many years to understand that this man "with a high ideal of himself" had "created his own life, his own world, almost his own continent." Jack had come to terms with the decay of the once flourishing farms, with abandoned homes, with change in renewal by creating "a garden on the edge of a swamp and a ruined farmyard." Knowing that he was dying, he had embraced the last pleasure his life afforded him, celebrating Christmas Eve at a pub with his friends. For the narrator, Jack's grace in asserting himself within the cyclic patterns of external and human nature conveys the "primacy" of life in the face of inevitable annihilation. It establishes his deepest bond with a fictional character in this novel.

After recovering from a debilitating illness owing in part to the dampness of the area and the cold of his cottage, Naipaul plans to leave it for a new home a few miles away. This is a difficult decision; he admits that the "beauty of the place, the great love [he] had grown to feel for it, . . . the second, happier childhood" he had known there have held him "too long." For years he has been willing to trade the discomforts of his cottage for these virtues and for his satisfaction in the work he has done there. It is this security that leads him in the second section, "The Journey," to explore "the idea of death," which has oppressed him since childhood.

He begins by explaining the meaning of his title. In his first days in the cottage, he comes upon a booklet on the early surrealist paintings of Giorgio de Chirico, left by a previous tenant. He is unimpressed by most of the reproductions, whose contents seem superficial "with an occasional applied touch of easy mystery," but one, "perhaps because of the title," he says twice, which was given it by Apollinaire, "referred to something in my own experience." The painting, *The Enigma of Arrival*, as he interprets it, is a "classical scene, Mediterranean, ancient-Roman," with two figures on a wharf, in the background, "the top of the mast of an antique vessel. . . . The scene is of desolation and mystery: it speaks of the mystery of arrival."

The painting suggests to him quite a different story from the one on which he is now working. Although Naipaul does not identify it, this is clearly *In a Free State*, which, set in contemporary Africa during a period of tribal conflict, is "a violent book—not violent in its incidents, but in its emotions." It is "a book about fear." The story inspired by the de Chirico painting is set in the classical period, a fantasy about a voyager who arrives with "a sense of mission" but, after various experiences in the city he enters, comes to feel that he is lost. In panic he attempts to return to the ship, only to find that it is gone and that he "has lived out his life." Naipaul never wrote this story, and only later did he realize that it was "no more than a version of the story [he] was already writing" as well as a means of giving "coherence" to a recurrent nightmare that ended in the feeling that an "explosion" had taken place in his head, throwing him to the floor or the ground. The dreamer was also the observer, aware that he was experiencing his own death.

The dream narrative is related to past and present distress, what Naipaul calls "intellectual fatigue and something like grief." He recalls the long years of study and preparation for his writing career and his present feeling of having been "undermined" by his publisher's misunderstanding and rejection of *The Loss of El Dorado*, his history of the world that had first formed him. But more fundamental than these anxieties and disappointments is his fear of extinction, which seems to him inherent in the vocation of writer.

As if for affirmation, he turns from his recurring dream of death to the first journey "that had seeded all the others," which took him briefly to New York, then on to England and Oxford, and traces major events of his life as they relate to his work, up to and including his life in Wiltshire. I have referred to much of this material in "Becoming a Writer," in chapter 2; as part of this novel the factual details are most engaging in the way Naipaul remembers them. Various layers of the past are present in the consciousness of the man writing as he records the accretion of feelings and fantasies his imagination has produced. On his return to New York nineteen years after his initial journey, for example, passing the Wellington, where he stayed overnight on his way to England, he is astounded to find an ordinary hotel rather than the "archaeological site" it should have been "to match its mythical nature in [his] mind." He experiences "sensations" that are like "dreams rather than memories," which he feels are "suited to the occasion" because on his first day away from Trinidad "space and time had become one."

Another merging—this time, of fictional and actual landscape and persons—is also related to the convergence of time and space. In childhood Naipaul had projected the English novels he read "onto the Trinidad landscape, the Trinidad countryside, the Port of Spain streets." Although aware that Dickens "was all English," he imaginatively transformed Dickens characters into a "multiracial" cast. Now, writing *In a*

Free State, he continues to use this technique of his childhood, reversing the process as he projects the violent Africa of that novel onto the safe atmosphere of Wiltshire so that the world of his African novel becomes one with the world he inhabits in *The Enigma of Arrival*, to which he returns in the next section, "Ivy."

This section begins with a description of a walk Naipaul took during one of his early years in Wiltshire and his discovery of the "ragged, half-rotted-away carcass of a hare," which reminds him of a skeleton of a pelican that he saw years later in the channel between Trinidad and Venezuela. These are the first of many images of decay and death that pervade this section: the beech trees that are "now like a natural—wasting—monument" of his landlord's "father's grandeur"; "the overgrown orchard": the vegetation that "was partly strangled and decayed"; photographs that are "a kind of memento mori"; in parts of the estate "only bush and forest debris" and bridges rotted; a boathouse that is "a spectacular ruin." The most dramatic example of decay is the ivy which Naipaul's landlord has ordered not to be cut and which has already killed many trees. As he speculates about the landlord's inner life, Naipaul wonders about the man's reaction to this decay—did he "cherish" it as "a comforting reflection" of his persistent depression?

Naipaul himself has come to accept decline and death as inherent in external and human nature: "I lived not with the idea of decay—that idea I quickly shed—so much as with the idea of change, of flux, and learned, profoundly, not to grieve for it." As his nightmares of his exploding head disclose, this acceptance has come only after his confrontations with his fears of death. Now he says, "Decay implied an ideal, a perfection in the past." Imagining that past for himself, he prefers the present.

Flux is also a theme in the lives of the people who work on the estate. At first Naipaul projects on them traditional qualities characteristic of their roles. Later, when he learns that these suppositions were wrong, he is interested in the ambiguity of their lives. Having learned that Phillips, the chauffeur, and his wife are not typical "staff servants" but people who had come to the manor only a year before he had rented his cottage and were "in fact rootless," he then, as a novelist, uses the details of their lives that he does know to weave a story about them, their personalities, their motivations, their pleasures. In the gardener, Pitton's, choice of clothing appropriate to the changing seasons Naipaul sees a kind of ritual "to match" his wife's beauty. Pitton, as Naipaul describes him, seems also to use his clothes to provide a front of security that he actually lacks, subject as he is to the landlord's whim or financial straits, and sure enough, he is fired.

As he creates the particularities of these characters, Naipaul identifies himself with them as "a camper in the ruins, living with what he found, delighted by the evidence of the life of the past—like a barbarian coming upon an ancient Roman villa in Gloucestershire, momentarily delighted by the wonder and ruin of a heating system he no longer understood or needed." To extend and reinforce the image, he then compares himself and the workers on the estate—so unlike him yet similar as part of the general flux—to "a barbarian in North Africa, brushing away new desert sand from a mosaic floor with gods as mysterious and unnecessary as the craft of the mosaic floor itself." The contrast between the beauty of the floor (and the prose that recreates it) and the emphasis on its dispensability conveys the loss inevitable in the acceptance of change.

This acceptance has nothing to do with the "certainty" that Derek Walcott believes Naipaul "found . . . on the imperial soil of England."[45] In fact, it is the post-imperial, the changing, decaying world of the estate in which Naipaul comes to terms with his own uncertainties and fears. Writing of his incorporation of the idea of change, he imagines the estate at its imperial perfection. "But would I have cared to be in my cottage while the sixteen gardeners worked? When every growing plant aroused anxiety, every failure pain or criticism? Wasn't the place now, for me, at its peak?" And it is Pitton, the one remaining gardener, "like Jack, marking out and maintaining areas of cultivation in the midst of wasteland" whom Naipaul befriends after he is fired. His way of reaching Pitton is to imagine himself in the place of the man who "had lost touch with the idea of work," from the writer's point of view one of the profoundest of the losses that change may effect.

In "Rooks," the section named for the "birds of death" that have settled in the beeches of the deteriorating estate, Naipaul writes about further changes in his life and the lives of people he has invented or known. As the book draws to a close, he returns to the subject of death, which his account of Jack's garden had introduced. He tells of the suicide of Alan, the would-be writer who could not face but only act out the "psychological damage he had suffered" as a boy. He then writes of the death of Mr. Phillips, who had cared for his landlord and had supervised whatever work was still done on the estate.

To Naipaul, Mr. Phillips's death and the incompetent people who are hired to replace him and Pitton, both of whom he admired, mean the loss of security he had enjoyed in this setting for many years. More personal and more moving is his account of the death of his sister Sati and his journey to Trinidad for "the ceremony of farewell." His response to these deaths is linked with his vision of the "abyss" with which he had lived since childhood. Jack's death, the other fictional or semi-fictional deaths, and the actual ones: his brother Shiva's death recorded in the dedication, his sister's, mourned at the end, all have a role in his "new awareness of death," out of which, he says, he "began at last to write." The conflict between the two gifts his father had bestowed on him, the "vocation" and the "subsidiary" fear of extinction, seems to be resolved. In Wiltshire, in the healing "landscape of down and barrow," through painful memories, nightmares, and illness, the "subsidiary" (literally, supporting) gift has been his golden bough leading him into his own and others' psychic inferno, his "vocation," a summoning back to the self's narration, which became this book. "Death," Naipaul says, "was the motif." Coming to terms with this central reality, like Jack, he has created his own world.

Like *The Enigma of Arrival*, *A Way in the World* deals with continuous change. In developing this motif Naipaul again blends history with autobiography and fiction, introducing Sir Walter Raleigh's last voyage on the Destiny as "perhaps a play or a screen play, or a mixture of both" and treating the careers of fictional Foster Morris and Lebrun as part of literary and political history, in which the narrator is involved. As in *The Enigma of Arrival*, he shares his writing processes with his readers, telling them, in the third chapter, his idea for a story he is "partly working. . . out for the first time." In *The Enigma of Arrival* his outline for a novel based on the de Chirico painting refers to a possible "hero" as "a man on the run, a man passionate to get away to a cleaner air." He never wrote that novel, although he came to feel that it was related to *In a Free State*. But he obviously remained attached to the figure of "a man on the run" who is first considered as narrator of his new projected story set in "an unnamed South American country" but is rejected in favor of a "revolutionary of the 1970s . . . seeking the help of up-country Amerindians to overthrow the African government on the coast. Such a situation wouldn't only echo the truth of more than one country in the region. It would also hold certain historical ironies."

This narrator, a revolutionary "infiltrator," after a long march through the forest with two guides, arrives at a village where he is expected. On the way he has been told by his guides of the "kanaima, the spirit of death of the forests," and he believes he has had "a brush" with such a spirit, which, in his case, manifests itself as feelings of uncertainty, of insecurity that will remain with him. While bathing in a pool, he experiences a sense of nothingness; Naipaul uses the word "nothing" four times to describe the change in him from determination to help the people of the forest to doubt regarding his own intentions and premonitions of his project's failure. He feels trapped in the forest even as he foresees that he will be remembered by the people he professed to love as "the man who stayed long and wasn't straight with them, who promised many things and then went away."

This elliptical summary of an unwritten story is actually a preview of major themes of the nine linked narratives that comprise *A Way in the World*: the instability of seemingly firm positions, the revolutionary, the practical doer who turns out to be "the man on the run," the continuity of betrayal, all of them rooted in colonial conquest and related to changes in the narrator and the societies he explores. His acquaintance with Foster Morris, a composite of English literary figures of the 1930s, enacts the first of these motifs. As a young man setting out to become a writer, the narrator is impressed by the very fact that Morris has written a book about the oilfield strike that took place in Trinidad in 1937 and the men who led it, especially their leader, Tubal Uriah Buzz Butler. He finds this apparently sympathetic account, *The Shadowed Livery*, "well-intentioned but wrong," lacking "the sense of the absurd, the idea of comedy" that Morris did not recognize as inherent in Trinidadian attitudes, even in so critical a situation. Still, he admires Morris's knowledge and is grateful to him for his frank dismissal of a manuscript with which he himself was dissatisfied and now felt free to give up and turn to more authentic material—the street life of Port of Spain, which proved to be so fruitful.

Only after knowing Morris better does the narrator realize how questionable are his views as a reporter, how hypocritical his praise. Morris admits that he had regarded Butler and his followers as "a bunch of racial fanatics" and Butler himself as "a crazy black preacher," but one simply couldn't write such things, and gradually reveals himself as a bit of a hack who, out of his own failure and envy of others, has come to disapprove of all his successful contemporaries. Among these is the narrator, who is both disillusioned and enlightened by the realization that beneath the "courtesy" that Morris extends to him at a luncheon is "a constant indirect criticism" of his recent writings. When he sends Morris a copy of *A House for Mr. Biswas* and receives a response, the opening of which is so nasty that he feels compelled to stop reading, he is finally ready to give up "this disciple-guru relationship." The break with Morris signifies the narrator's confidence in the way he has chosen to live and work as a writer. Years later, more objective about *The Shadowed Livery*, he concludes that, with all its limitations, the book nonetheless has a place in "the great chain of changing outside vision" of the world into which he was born. It is part of the recorded history of Trinidad from the Renaissance to the present.

He has come a long way from the naive seventeen-year-old boy who was soon to go abroad to study at Oxford. Yet in a fundamental respect even then his character had already been formed. Taken by a classmate to meet his father, he is shocked when this "famous" lawyer mistakenly claims that his name, Evander, can be found in Homer rather than in Vergil. Before he can assimilate this "flaw" in the famous man's "character," he is even more surprised when the lawyer extends "his forearm across the table in a gesture of strength and . . . with a smile, and as a kind of pledge," says, "The race! The race, man!" The narrator, writing from a distance of many years and much experience as a traveler and writer, remarks on how unexpected in the late 1940s was this idea of "a way ahead," an association of black people. In fact, the general view of Evander was of a "self-made black man who wanted only to be white," and "was fighting only for himself." Realizing that he is being let into what was "like a family secret," the narrator is "moved." Yet, though he "understood their feelings, shared them to some extent," he could not join a "group." At seventeen he already knows that to become the writer he envisions, he must "belong to" himself. This brief episode foreshadows a more complex but similar experience of the mature narrator in his relations with Lebrun.

In Lebrun, obviously based on C. L. R. James, Naipaul finally creates his man on the run, a semi-fictional character who is central to the narrator's view of his own history. He had heard of Lebrun, "the Trinidadian-Panamanian communist of the 1930s" from Foster Morris, who described him as "one of the most dangerous men around Butler, the oil strike leader." As Naipaul portrays him, Lebrun is less dangerous than provocative, "an impressario of revolution" rather than a participant. "He had always been on the run, a revolutionary without a base . . . never having to live with the consequences of his action, always being free to move on." Moving from place to place, he is not merely fleeing authority or former associates; he grows and changes in the countries he visits and moves on to different political positions. At heart, Lebrun, like C. L. R. James, is a humanist, subtle in thought, learned and eloquent in speech. Beginning as a Marxist, he changes with the world he travels. In his later years he relinquishes the role of revolutionary and becomes "the man of true African or black redemption."

An article Lebrun had written about the narrator's early books, which was published in a Russian magazine, becomes "a lasting part of [the narrator's] way of looking" at the world. Typically, Lebrun's approach is original, delving beneath the writer's comic episodes and manner to "the material itself," to the characters whose "colonial setting mocked" their "delusions, . . . their ambitions, their belief in perfectibility, their jealousies." In short, his books "were subversive." In his description of the narrator's response to Lebrun's article, Naipaul seems to be summarizing the themes and contents of *The Loss of El Dorado* and his chapters on the history of Trinidad in the present book. The narrator, he says, appeared to have

> been granted a vision of history speeded up, had seen, as I might have seen the opening and dying of a flower, the destruction and shifting about of peoples, had seen all the strands that had gone into the creation of the agricultural colony, and had understood what simple purposes—after such activity—that colony served.

Ironically, the narrator's gratitude toward Lebrun, his recognition of "something of myself in his struggle" create barriers between them. A resentful remark about Lebrun made by a "chief minister" of a small West Indian island, "The man want to take you over," comes to the narrator's mind as he realizes that Lebrun's friends and allies would welcome him as a follower, would "make room for" him. As a boy of seventeen he had known himself well enough to refuse a similar invitation, risking aloneness before he had achieved very much. Now, with a body of work behind him, with a commitment to his vocation, he can articulate his reasons for declining to join a group. He can identify the "yearnings" that in his mature years he has assuaged and will continue to gratify: "my own earned security, a wish for my writing gift to last and grow, a dream of working at yet unknown books, accumulations of fruitful days, achievement. These yearnings could be assuaged only in the self I knew." Secure in this knowledge, he yet admits that he would never again receive "an invitation so wholehearted or so seductive," his very refusal a tribute to all that Lebrun represents.

Still, he has not entirely turned down this invitation; he has converted it to his own "yearnings," joining Lebrun in recreating the little-known history of Trinidad. As a boy he had come across Lebrun's first book in the "sixth-form library" of Queens Royal College, but did not read it until many years later. The book, which Naipaul does not name, deals with "some of the Spanish-American or Venezuelan revolutionaries before Bolívar, and he had concentrated on those with Trinidad connections." Impressed by Lebrun's effort to reunite the Caribbean islands with "the great historical processes of the continent," the narrator remarks, "What a spirit was locked in its pages! Always there, waiting to speak to me." He has made Lebrun's book the inspiration for the next three chapters of *A Way in the World*, which interrupt the autobiographical narrative to tell Naipaul's own version of Sir Walter Raleigh as invader and of the Venezuelan revolutionary Francisco Miranda, whose lust for power and wealth and whose exploitation of the indigenous people are intrinsic to the history of Trinidad. This suggestion that Lebrun is Naipaul's muse of history is no doubt part of the fiction, but his admiration for the model for this character, C. L. R. James, transcends the fictional portrait. Referring to the "profile writers and the television interviewers" who sought to use his accomplishments and his fame for their own purposes, Naipaul says:

> They risked nothing at all. They had no means of understanding or assessing a man who had been born early in the century into a very hard world, whose intellectual growth had at every stage been accompanied by a growing rawness of sensibility, and whose political resolutions, expressing the wish not to go mad, had been in the nature of spiritual struggles, occurring in the depth of his being.

Lebrun, the man on the run, is a portrait of essential integrity, a norm measured against which betrayals of the past and present are heightened. At the end of chapter 3 of *A Way in the World*, "New Clothes: An Unwritten Story," one of the guides tells the narrator the story of his grandfather who believed the English people's promises that they would come and build houses, but they never came. The young guide continues to believe that an English friend of his grandfather will send for him. To prove his point he brings out some clothing that was sent to his grandfather, "modern clothes, for the houses they were going to build," but what he uncovers is actually "a doublet of Tudor times, new clothes of three hundred and fifty years before, relic of an old betrayal." This episode is linked to the section on Raleigh, who allowed Don José, his servant, to choose for himself from some of his own fine clothing, a token of approval for the Indian whose people Raleigh had said he would rule, only to desert them, leaving them to be punished and "resettled" by the Spanish invaders. Don José is himself betrayed by Raleigh's patronage; absorbed in Raleigh's needs in his last days, lamenting his execution, he struggles to retain his own identity. He exemplifies one of "the themes of that story," Naipaul says, "that the enemy becomes the man you love." Yet Don José's integrity, like Lebrun's, saves him from total immersion in this madness that threatens him in his own "very hard world."

A Way in the World ends with a return to the story of Blair, whom Naipaul had introduced early in the book, in the second chapter, where the narrator summarizes his story. He had met Blair when he was seventeen, copying documents in the Registrar General's Department in Trinidad, a temporary job he held before leaving for Oxford. Blair, a tall, impressive black man, then a senior clerk, seemed to the narrator a person "of ambition and strength." He was to enter local politics and later "to have an international career." But his success, his pleasure in an appointment in an independent East African country, could not save him from betrayal and murder "by agents of some wild men in the government who felt threatened by him." In this first narration Naipaul says he does not "know whether the ironies of his death made a mockery of that career or undid the virtue of it," but promises to raise this question later on. Now, addressing his readers he twice asks them to "Remember" Blair as he was in his youth, like the writer, "at the most hopeful time of his life." It is an image of him deeply connected with Trinidad and the narrator's own youth.

When the narrator and Blair meet again twenty years later in the East African country where Blair has a government position, remembrances of this early affiliation suggest to the narrator that Blair, the "self-made man," perhaps, like him, might have decided "to remake himself." He is never to know. After this one meeting, Blair is murdered because he was doing his job too well; he had become aware of "the smuggling out of ivory and gold." The narrator, in his shock and sorrow, is left with the question he mentioned earlier, which he approaches by inventing still another narrative. Instead of Blair's dead body found in a model banana field, he imagines Blair alive there, but during "a moment in that great silence," conscious "that he was being destroyed." He now is convinced that if "while the brain still sparked, a question could have been lodged in that brain—'Does this betrayal mock your life?'—the answer immediately after death would have been 'No! No! No!'" The vehemence of that repeated negative is an affirmation of Blair's life, the intensity of his commitment to change, his assertion that "the world [he] will be leaving is better than the one" he was born into, his satisfaction in knowing that "the revolution he had taken part in had succeeded." Naipaul's response insists that even the continuity of betrayal cannot invalidate the lives of those who struggle to exceed the limits of their times.

NOTES

1. Nadine Gordimer, "Living in the Interregnum, *The Essential Gesture: Writing, Politics and Places*, ed. Stephen Clingman (1988; reprint, New York: Penguin, 1989), 263–64.

2. Gordimer, "Selecting my Stories," *The Essential Gesture*, 114.

3. Philip Roth, *The Facts: A Novelist's Autobiography* (1988; reprint, New York: Penguin, 1989), 164.

4. V. S. Naipaul, "Reading and Writing," *The New York Review of Books* (February 18, 1999): 16–18.

5. V. S. Naipaul, *Miguel Street* (1959, reprint, New York: Penguin, 1979).

6. "Prologue to an Autobiography," *Finding the Center*, 34.

7. V. S. Naipaul, *A Flag on the Island* (New York: Macmillan, 1967), 15–17.

8. V. S. Naipaul, *The Suffrage of Elvira* (1958; reprint, New York: Penguin, 1981), 65, 80.

9. V. S. Naipaul, *The Mystic Masseur* (1957; reprint, New York: Vintage, 1984), 156.

10. *Hindu Myths: A Sourcebook Translated From the Sanskrit*, with an Introduction by Wendy Doniger O'Flaherty (New York: Penguin, 1975), 348, 268.

11. *Miguel Street*, 38–44.

12. Nightingale, 34–35.

13. See chapter 2, 32–33.

14. V. S. Naipaul, *Mr. Stone and the Knights Companion* (1963; reprint, New York: Penguin, 1973), 8.

15. V. S. Naipaul, *The Mimic Men* (1967; reprint, New York: Penguin, 1978), 10.

16. Nightingale, 103.

17. Eco, 28.

18. *The Middle Passage*, 54.

19. Mukherjee and Boyers, 21.

20. See chapter 2, 33–34.

21. These comments suggest another—in this case, amusing—difference between Naipaul and Singh. In a letter to Paul Theroux (dated February 21, 1967), Naipaul, who obviously has been urging Theroux to read Martial, says, "I'm glad you have got on to Martial at last; he is a delicious writer and brings Rome back more vividly than others." However, he objects to Theroux's com-

ments on Latin: "But he [Martial] is hardly someone from whom one could generalise about the word Latin, as you swiftly did. The issue is somewhat more complex." *The New Yorker* (June 26 and July 3, 1995): 146. Naipaul's is clearly the exact opposite of Singh's approach to Martial.

22. V. S. Naipaul, *In a Free State* (1971; reprint, New York: Penguin, 1980).

23. "Nowhere to Go," *Times Literary Supplement* (October 8, 1971): 1199.

24. See chapter 1, 10–11.

25. Italics mine.

26. *The New Yorker* (June 26 and July 3, 1995): 148.

27. See *Heart of Darkness, The Portable Conrad,* ed. Morton Dauwen Zabel (New York: Viking, 1957), 495–96.

28. See chapter 1, 10.

29. Michael Abdul Malik, *From Michael de Freitas to Michael X* (London: Andre Deutsch, 1968).

30. Derek Humphry and David Tindall, *False Messiah: The Story of Michael X* (London: Hart-Davis, Mac Gibbon, 1997).

31. "Michael X and the Black Power Killings in Trinidad," *The Return of Eva Perón,* 3–97.

32. "Michael X and the Black Power Killings in Trinidad," 59. A more sympathetic view of the pair, especially of Jamal, can be found in Diana Athill, *Make Believe* (London: Sinclair-Stevenson, 1993).

33. "Michael X and the Black Power Killings," 93.

34. Humphry and Tindall, 160–63. Naipaul suggests that "Skerritt had become uneasy with Malik; he began to hide from him," in "Michael X and the Black Power Killings," 20.

35. Humphry and Tindall, 206–208.

36. Humphry and Tindall, 48.

37. V. S. Naipaul, *Guerrillas* (1975; reprint, New York: Vintage, 1980).

38. Mukherjee and Boyers, 16.

39. "Power," *The Overcrowded Barracoon*, 250.

40. *A Bend in the River*, 11.

41. "Delivering the Truth," 4.

42. See, for example, Robert Boyers, *Atrocity and Amnesia: The Political Novel Since 1945* (New York: Oxford, 1985), 36.

43. Mukherjee and Boyers, 8.

44. Said, xix.

45. Derek Walcott, "The Garden Path: *The Enigma of Arrival* by V. S. Naipaul," *The New Republic* April 13, 1987): 27.

5

AFTERWORD

In two interviews, thirteen years apart, Naipaul explained his differences from other modern and contemporary writers on the basis of
their internalization of imperial values from which they derived a certain security. "Graham Greene and others," he says, are "travelers in a
world made safe for them by empire." Whereas these writers "travel for
the picturesque, I'm *desperately* [italics his] concerned about the countries
I'm in."[1] Speaking to another interviewer more recently, he returns to
this subject: Asked about James Joyce, Virginia Woolf, and D. H.
Lawrence, he refers to them as writers "from the imperial period . . .
without knowing it, without considering themselves imperial writers.
They inhabit a world where you don't see the other half or three-quarters."[2] It is that other three-quarters, their various cultures, and their individual lives that have been his primary subjects.

During the many years in which he has explored postcolonial societies and recreated them in fiction and nonfiction, he has taught himself
to see the world through the eyes of the people whose culture he has
absorbed. He ends his first book on India with the sad confession that
this was "a journey that ought not to have been made." After many returns over the years, he has not only come to feel at home in India; his
conception of how to write about India has changed. "The idea came
to me," he says, "that the truth about India wasn't what I thought about
India; it's what they are living through."[3] In *A Million Mutinies Now,* he
depicts the protests and achievements that represent the changes that the
people of India are undergoing. Still, both books disclose how genuine
is Naipaul's concern with his subject, a concern that is inextricably
linked with the autobiographical revelations of their author, particularly
his emotional and intellectual investment in his Indian heritage.

As a writer, Naipaul has said, he begins with himself, a center that comprises his background, his education, and his vocation. Yet the self that emerges in the body of his work also changes as he internalizes his growing knowledge of the societies he explores and the people he meets, who appear in his nonfiction as friends or antagonists, in his fiction, transformed by the merging of some of their models' characteristics with some of the author's. Determined to express the truth of his experience, in his early autobiographical references, he exposes the intensity of his pain and anger and his occasional churlishness, but also his willingness to reconsider his judgments, to correct his vision.

Since few writers—and indeed few other human beings—have escaped psychic trauma and conflict, one must ask why Naipaul's frank revelations of episodes of panic and intimations of mortality have been used repeatedly in critical attacks on his work. The very opponents who have not taken up his challenge to produce evidence refuting his observations have been most dogmatic in this respect. Others besides Cudjoe and Nixon, whom I have cited, have converted his autobiographical allusions into instruments for assigning him a political stance that they find unacceptable. Amon Saba Saakana, for example, describes him as

> a man whose violent psychological turmoil in not being born into a
> metropolitan society articulates itself in vitriolics, whose assumptions
> of the world are dictated by the primacy of psychic trauma, of deep
> inferiority, which results in stasis, rather than political comprehension,
> analysis, or studied reaction in terms of rational political thought.[4]

The crudeness of this statement is obvious, primarily because it ignores the complexity of autobiography as a literary vehicle. Autobiography is neither a case history nor, unless intended as such, a political one. It is a reminiscence, an evocation of past experience, by a present consciousness, selective, organized for a particular purpose. If fiction is often autobiographical, autobiography has its own fictional qualities. The person writing it has created the subject, has chosen details of setting, atmosphere, social, and familial influences to produce a plot and a theme that serve a present end. Such qualifiers do not detract from its reliability as personal revelation, nor do they define it as fiction. They do suggest that autobiography mined to detect ideology will inevitably yield distortion.

Naipaul's stories and novels illuminate differences between fictional truth and the veracity of reporting and autobiography. The struggles of many of his characters to define truth for themselves seem to me central to his fiction. Characters as different from each other as Mr. Stone and Jimmy Ahmed resemble their author as they seek the multiform nuclei of truth, sometimes evading its consequences even as they cannot relinquish the quest. But their methods and findings differ from those of the reporter or autobiographer. Comparisons between Naipaul's fiction and nonfiction, however similar their subjects and locales, reveal important differences in detail and technique. An example is his use of comedy, which, he says, is "a covering up" in *The Middle Passage*, but in the novels is clearly a means of exposing the suppressed feelings of characters like Bogart, Morgan, or Mohun Biswas. The wild fantasies of their inner monologues and bizarre stories express desires their conduct hides or enacts obliquely. Individual as these feelings are, they are never merely personal, for they simultaneously incorporate and challenge cherished assumptions of their society and class. Naipaul's protagonists are funniest and at the same time most touching when their rebellion conveys the blend of truth and guile that comprises their uneasy accommodation to conditions they cannot bear or alter.

One standard that Naipaul has set for himself and for other writers is:

How much of the modern world does his work contain? You should be able to see the lineaments of today's society in the work of a good writer. . . . I just feel that we're living in such an interesting world. One must capture all the interest of this period. I don't believe that the world has all been written about. The world is so new.[5]

Naipaul himself has covered much of the twentieth century. In the overlapping concerns and settings of his fiction and nonfiction, he has moved on from the world of his childhood in Trinidad of the 1930s and 1940s through the years up to the present, to many of the other postcolonial societies of the West Indies, South America, the Middle East, Africa, and Asia. In all his portrayals of these various nations and their peoples—whether in fiction or nonfiction, or the union of the two, as in his most recent books—personal and social history converge as narrators, informants, among them historical figures, past and present, and his characters reveal their vantage points.

The author's diverse affiliations with these narrators, subjects of interviews, historical and fictional characters, and their relationships with each other, create the various situations in which truth can be approached. In the doctor's interview with Raleigh, in the dialogues of Roche and Jimmy, Naipaul shows how even the barriers that past and present history and individual human beings have erected to distort or conceal reality are part of the search and, paradoxically, the discovery, of long suppressed truths.

In his reconstructions of the history of Trinidad in *The Loss of El Dorado* and more recently in *A Way in the World*, Naipaul produces what Brent Staples calls "an archeology of the colonial impulse."[6] This study of origins is characteristic of Naipaul's method as a reporter and novelist; the ancient world of Rome, the colonial history of the countries he explores, are bases for uncovering the hidden "lineaments of today's" societies. They are also avenues to the self-knowledge intrinsic to his search for truth. His concern for the "three-fourths" who are generally neglected informs all his writings, as does his personal involvement in their history. Commenting on his interpretation of that history in *A Way in the World*, his ambivalence regarding Trinidad by now resolved, he speaks of having recovered the "parent," the "slave society,"[7] that had left its traces in his homeland.

NOTES

1. Charles Michener, "The Dark Visions of V. S. Naipaul," *Newsweek* (November 16, 1981): 109.

2. "Delivering the Truth," 3.

3. "Delivering the Truth," 3.

4. Amon Saba Saakana, *The Colonial Legacy in Caribbean Literature* (Trenton, New Jersey: Africa World Press, 1987), 90.

5. V. S. Naipaul, quoted in Mel Gussow, "Writer without Roots," *The New York Times Magazine* (December 26, 1976): 19–22.

6. Staples, 43.

7. "Delivering the Truth," 3.

CHRONOLOGY OF
WORKS BY V. S. NAIPAUL

1957   *The Mystic Masseur*
1958   *The Suffrage of Elvira*
1959   *Miguel Street*
1961   *A House for Mr. Biswas*
1962   *The Middle Passage*
1963   *Mr. Stone and the Knights Companion*
1964   *An Area of Darkness*
1967   *A Flag on the Island*
1967   *The Mimic Men*
1969   *The Loss of El Dorado*
1971   *In a Free State*
1972   *The Overcrowded Barracoon*
1975   *Guerrillas*
1977   *India: A Wounded Civilization*
1979   *A Bend in the River*
1980   *The Return of Eva Perón with the Killings in Trinidad*
1981   *Among the Believers*
1984   *Finding the Centre*
1987   *The Enigma of Arrival*
1989   *A Turn in the South*
1990   *India: A Million Mutinies Now*
1994   *A Way in the World*
1998   *Beyond Belief: Islamic Excursions among the Converted Peoples*
1999   *Letters between a Father and Son*

INDEX

Abbott, Stanley, 206
Abdul (Pakistani), 155
Abidjan, Ivory Coast, 122
Abu Bakr, 83
Acharya (in *Samskara*), 56–58, 91
The Adventures of Gurudeva and Other Stories (S. Naipaul), 27, 30–31, 33–34, 190
Aeneid (Vergil), 9–11, 186, 229, 231
African authenticity, 115, 117
African customs and beliefs, 121
Against Sainte-Beuve (Proust), 76
Agricola (Tacitus), 80–81
Ahmadis of Pakistan, 59
Ahmed, James (in *Guerrillas*), 19, 205–6, 211–24, 236
Ajami, Fouad, 139–40, 143
Alan (in *The Enigma of Arrival*), 240
Ali (Iranian), 149–50
Ali (in *A Bend in the River*), 227
alienation from society, 199, 214, 222
Alwi, Syed, 157–58
Amaranth, Cave of, 10, 48, 75
Among the Believers (V. S. Naipaul), 18, 59, 70, 139–40, 143, 156
Anand (in *A House for Mr. Biswas*), 35–40
Anantha Murthy, U. R., 18; *Samskara*, 56–58, 74, 91

ancestor worship, 109
The Ancient City (Coulange), 10, 31
Andrée (West Indian expatriate), 121
anger, 10–11, 43; as self-assertion, 41
anti-government marches, 82–83
Anwar, Dewi Fortuna, 145–46
Appalachians, 68
Applewhite, James, 68
Arash (wealthy Iranian), 148–49
archetypes, 104–5
An Area of Darkness (V. S. Naipaul), 10, 13, 44–46, 69, 90–91
Argentina, 107–11; future of, 114; guerillas, 111–13
"Argentina: Living with Cruelty" (V. S. Naipaul), 112
"Argentine Terror: A Memoir" (V. S. Naipaul), 111–12
Arlette (black woman from Martinique), 121–22
Aryans, 130
Assembly of Islam, 155
Association of Muslim Intellectuals, 141–43
At Last: A Christmas in the West Indies (Kingsley), 89
attraction/rejection, 59
Austen, Jane, 90

255

autobiography, 188–89, 250;
combined with history and
fiction, 18–20, 100, 252; as dreams
rather than memories, 238–39; as
fiction, 6, 11, 26, 36–41, 194, 227,
236
automatic writing, 54
automobiles, as vehicles of
perception, 194, 212, 216, 224–26
Aziz (a Sunní Muslim), 47–50, 75

Babri Masjid, destruction of, 126
Baksh (in *The Suffrage of Elvira*), 166,
172
Baptist service, 62
Basijis, 148
Bayley, John, 1
beggars, 10–11
Beharry (in *The Mystic Masseur*),
168
Behzad (communist Iranian guide),
60–61, 136
Bela Bela Bottling Works, 187, 189
Belgian Congo, 110–11
Belize, 68
A Bend in the River (V. S. Naipaul),
11, 19, 112, 118, 224–35
Benson, Gale, 206–7, 212, 222–23
Berlin, Isaiah, 16–17, 79
Berrio, Antonio de, 95–96
Best, Lloyd, 83
betrayal, 242, 246
*Beyond Belief: Islamic Excursions among
the Converted People* (V. S.
Naipaul), 139–40, 155, 158
Bhandat (in *A House for Mr. Biswas*),
177
Bharatiya Janata Party, 133
Bhindranwale (Sikh fundamentalist
leader), 132
Big Foot (in *Miguel Street*), 166
Bipti (in *A House for Mr. Biswas*), 175,
177–79

Biswas, Mohun (in *A House for Mr.
Biswas*), 12, 174–80; relationship
with his son, 174
Black Dalits, 127–28
Black House, 206
Black Muslims, 83
Blair (in *A Way in the World*), 246–47
boarding schools, religious, 144
Bobby (in *In a Free State*), 199–205
Bogart (in *Miguel Street*), 163–64
Bombay, India, 124–26
Bombay Municipal Corporation,
125–26
Borges, Jorge Luis, 110; *Fervour of
Buenos Aires*, 109
Bowen, North Carolina, 62
Bradshaw, Robert, 94
brahmins, 71–74; discrimination by,
130–31
bribery, 171
bridge crossing dream, 66
British Guiana, 44, 84–87
Browne (in *The Mimic Men*), 191–93
Bryant (in *Guerrillas*), 211, 214,
216–18
Budi (Muslim partner in a software
company), 146
Bunty (in *An Area of Darkness*), 47
Burnett (in *A House for Mr. Biswas*),
175, 177
Burnham, Forbes, 44, 84–86
Buruma, Ian, 1
Butler, Tubal Uriah Buzz (in *A Way
in the World*), 242–43

Calderon, Luisa, 96–96, 99
Caro (Miranda's agent), 97
caste system, 123–24; brahmins,
71–74, 130–31; rebellion against,
129–30; untouchables, 127–28
Catholicism, 113
Cecil (in *The Mimic Men*), 189
Chandri (in *Samskara*), 56–57

change, 72, 204; adaptation to, 45–46, 151, 156–57; analogous in countries and individuals, 75–76, 236, 239–40; in conflict with traditions, 55, 65–66, 70

characters, 20, 161, 163; allegorical, 57; as composite creations, 12, 18, 47; identified with and detached from their author, 162, 235–36; multiracial, 238; in Seepersad Naipaul's stories, 31–34. *See also* protagonists; *specific characters*

Charleston, South Carolina, 11

childhood, 6, 71; comprehension of, 220, 221; recollections of, 189; transformed into fiction, 26, 36–41, 236

Chirico, Giorgio de, 237, 241

Chittaranjan (in *The Suffrage of Elvira*), 172–73

Christianity, 140

civilization as enslavement, 80

clans: ambivalent feelings about, 3, 36, 73; surrender to the will of, 28, 35

Clausell, Bernyce, Reverend, 67

cloth for a jacket dream, 51

Cohen, Roger, 114

the colonel (in *In a Free State*), 202–3

colonialism, 13; condescension of, 230; cultural and psychological effects of, 71, 80, 164, 214, 218; distorting the identity of the subject people, 43, 191–92; heritage of, 87, 220, 252; indictment of, 90; intellectual and moral poverty of, 79, 171, 197; of Islam, 135; justified by universal civilization, 15–16; Naipaul's presumed bias toward, 3

colonizers, 89, 200–203; mimicry of, 47

Columbus (Landstrom), 95

Columbus, Christopher, 95

comedy, 165, 171; revealing truth, 173, 251

compassion, 93, 103–4

Congo, Democratic Republic of the (formerly Zaire), 115–19, 224

A Congo Diary (V. S. Naipaul), 115–16, 227

Conrad, Joseph, 4–5, 21n13, 29, 118; *Heart of Darkness*, 4, 110–11, 202, 204, 230; *Lord Jim*, 5; *Nostromo*, 5; *The Secret Agent*, 5; *Under Western Eyes*, 5

conversions, religious, 139–40, 178

cooperative socialism, 86

Coulange, Fustel de, *The Ancient City*, 10, 31

crocodiles, 119

cruelty, 113, 152, 154, 221; of an Egyptian game, 194, 205; gratuitous acts of, 51

Cudjoe, Selwyn, 2–3, 89

cult of the leader, 115; as substitute for national cohesion, 122. *See also* despots

culture: degeneration of, 110; effects of colonialism on, 71, 80, 164, 214, 218; identification with, 79. *See also* traditions

Dalits, 127–28

Dalit Panthers, 127–28

The Dark Room (Narayan), 54–55

Darma-sastro, 64

Dayo (in "Tell Me Who to Kill"), 197

death, 181, 237–41, 246; fear of, 39, 181, 238, 241; rites for, 10; spirit of (kanaima), 241

de Freitas, Michael. *See* Michael X

democracy, 15, 133; ignorance of, 171

demotic Marathi language, 127

Deschampsneufs (in *The Mimic Men*), 189

Desirée (in *From Michael de Freitas to Michael X*), 208

despots, 79, 107–8, 115–16; atrocities of, 136. *See also* cult of the leader

Destiny (ship), 100, 241

de Tunja, Harry (in *Guerrillas*), 212, 218–20

Dhaniram (in *The Suffrage of Elvira*), 171–72

dharma, 123, 134

Dhasal, Mallika, *I Want to Destroy Myself*, 127–28

Dhasal, Namdeo, 128; "The Road to the Shrine," 127

dialogues, imaginary, 100

diaries, 25–26

Dickens's characters as multiracial, 238

dictatorships, 108, 115

di Giovanni, Norman Thomas, 86–87, 109

The Discovery of the Large, Rich, and Beautiful Empire of Guiana (Raleigh), 101

discrimination, 137; by brahmins, 130–31

dishonesty, 192, 232, 234, 242

disillusionment, 112–13, 148–50, 152, 183

DMK (Dravidian Progressive Movement), 128–31

Dolly (in *Miguel Street*), 166

Domain of the State, 230–32

"Dookhani and Mungal" (Seepersad Naipaul), 32

doom, sense of, 104

Dravidian Progressive Movement (DMK), 128–31

dreams: cloth for a jacket, 51; crossing a bridge, 66; explosion nightmares, 238–39; snakes, 38

drowning, fear of, 39

drummologie, 121

Dutch language, 93

Eco, Umberto, 6, 186

Egyptian game, cruelty of, 194, 205

El Dorado, 95–96, 101

elections, African elder's responses to, 120

Elias (in *Miguel Street*), 164

Emerald Publishers, 130

emotional intimacy, 50

The English in the West Indies (Froude), 88–90

English language, 130

The Enigma of Arrival (V. S. Naipaul), 9, 11, 25–26, 43, 71, 235–41; as autobiography, 18–20

epics, 34, 64, 101; heroic codes, 110

epigraphs, 80–81, 88–90

"Epilogue, from a Journal" (V. S. Naipaul), 204

escape, 176–77, 179, 196; from the actual world, 180

espiritismo, 109

Evander (in *A Way in the World*), 243

exploitation, 68, 95

"eye" of V. S. Naipaul, 7, 13, 100; revision of, 46, 79

The Facts: A Novelist's Autobiography (Roth), 161–62

False Messiah: The Story of Michael X (Humphry and Tindall), 205

Fanon, Frantz, 16

fantasies: of conquest, 95–96, 107; romantic career as a writer, 4; sadomasochistic, 216, 222–23; of self-abnegation, 201; of slaves, 99–100; of superhuman power, 180, 182; of violence, 198, 211

father/son relationships, 36–38, 40; Seepersad and V. S. Naipaul, 26–35, 174 fear, 150–51, 154, 237; escape from, 182; of extinction, 39, 181, 238, 241; of extinction allayed by writing, 30, 36, 38–41, 236

feelings, moderation of, 46

Ferdinand (in *A Bend in the River*), 227–28, 235

Fervour of Buenos Aires (Borges), 109

feticheurs, 122

fiction: autobiography in, 6, 11, 26, 36–41, 194, 227, 236; combined with history and autobiography, 18–20, 100, 252; compared to nonfiction, 250–51; and history, 96 searching for truth, 94, 162

Finding the Centre (V. S. Naipaul), 25–27

flying fantasies, 180, 182

Foam (in *The Suffrage of Elvira*), 171–73

Foreigner (Rachlin), 18

Forster, E. M., 90

Foundation for the Development and Management of Human Resources, 141

freedom, 132, 163, 197

From Michael de Freitas to Michael X (John X), 205, 207–11

Froude, James Anthony, *The English in the West Indies*, 88–90

Fullarton, William, 96, 98

Gandhi, Indira, 132

Gandhi, Mohandas K., 18, 53, 123–25, 129; *The Story of My Experiments with Truth*, 55

Ganesh (a.k.a. G. Ramsay Muir or Ganesh Ramsumair) (in *Miguel Street, The Mystic Masseur,* and *The Suffrage of Elvira*), 166–70

Ganesha (elephant god), 167

Geertz, Clifford, 144–45

Genovese, Eugene, 67, 78

genre fusion, 8

George (in *Miguel Street*), 164

Georgetown, British Guiana, 93

Ghate (Shiv Sena leader), 126

The Ghost Writer, Deception (Roth), 161

ghost writers, 207

Glynn, Patrick, 15

goat, sacrifice of, 28

Golden Temple of Amritsar, 132

Gopalakrishnan (rebel against brahmin discrimination), 130–31

Gordimer, Nadine, 1, 161

greed, 111

Greene, Graham, 249

guerrillas: Argentine, 111–13; mohajir, 153–55

Guerrillas (V. S. Naipaul), 3, 9, 82, 205–6, 211–24; incorporating facts about Malik, 209–11

Gulmarg, Kashmir, 48

Gurudeva (in "The Adventures of Gurudeva"), 33–34

Gurudeva (in *The Mimic Men*), 190–91

Guyana, 206–7, 210

Habibie, 141–45

Hadrian, Emperor, 10

Hannibal, 11

happiness, pursuit of, 17

Harbans, Surujpat (in *The Suffrage of Elvira*), 171–72

Hat (in *Miguel Street*), 163–66

hate, 221; turned inward, 199, 213

Hazlitt, William, 145

Heart of Darkness (Conrad), 4, 110–11, 202, 204, 230

Herbert, Meredith (in *Guerrillas*), 212–13, 218–22

heritage: of colonialism, 87, 220, 252; ethnic and paternal, 51; of slavery, 81–82, 220, 252

heroic codes of epics, 110
Himalayas, 13, 48–49
Hindi language, 130
Hindu philosophy and religion,
51–56, 123–24, 130, 134; rituals,
46, 73; in Trinidad, 31, 36, 41;
veneration of learning, 168
Hislop, General (governor of
Trinidad), 100
historical perspective, 45, 47, 80, 205,
219; absence of, 116, 135; and
individual identity, 67–68, 72, 127,
170, 225–27, 251; integration of
past and present, 100, 193
history, 13, 93, 188, 224; as the basis
for novels, 19; foreshadowing the
future, 232; Islamic revisions of,
135; Roman, 80, 145, 155–56,
186, 233; Roman, Naipaul's study
of, 9–11, 31
homelessness, 204
horse-sacrifices, 190–91
Houphouët-Boigny, Felix, 119,
122–23
A House for Mr. Biswas (V. S. Naipaul),
18, 27, 31, 33–41, 173–80, 236;
Morris's critique of, 242
houses: as a reflection of family and
society, 175; as a reflection of self,
188
Howe, Irving, 1–2
Hoyt, Titus (in *Miguel Street*),
164
hubshi woman (in "One Out of
Many"), 195–96
Huismans, Father (in *A Bend in the
River*), 227–31
humane laws, 152
human possibility, 52, 134–35
humiliation, 47, 127
Humphry, Derek, 205
*A Hundred and One Questions and
Answers on the Hindu Religion*

(Ganesh or Ramsumair) (in *The
Mystic Masseur*), 168–69
Huntington, Samuel, 15
Hutus, 119
hypocrisy, 208

idealists, tainted, 105
ideals, 29
identification with the aggressor,
82
identity, 52, 69, 146; cultural, 79;
distorted by colonialism, 43,
191–92; within a historical
perspective, 67–68, 72, 127, 170,
225–27, 251; loss of, 29, 64–65,
138; national, 81, 123–34, 152,
155; pseudo-identities, 208–9,
215–16, 221
ideology, tyranny of, 65
Imaduddin, 65–66, 139–44
imperialism, 2, 21n13, 249; Arabian,
135
In a Free State (V. S. Naipaul), 194,
199–205, 237–38
Indar (in *A Bend in the River*), 227,
231
Indarsingh (in *The Mystic Masseur*),
169–70
India, 13, 44–51, 58–59, 69, 249;
changes after British conquest, 72;
Independence, 1947, 82; national
identity, 123–34
India: A Million Mutinies Now (V. S.
Naipaul), 13, 58–59, 69, 125–26,
249
India: A Wounded Civilization (V. S.
Naipaul), 13, 52, 58, 69, 124–26
Indian attitudes, 52–55; negation, 51,
53; underdeveloped egos, 55–56
Indian politicians, 133–34
individuals: changes analogous with
countries, 75–76, 224; reaction to
social mores, 52; survival, 224–25

Indonesia, 137–38; and airplane design, 141, 143; as an Islamic state, 140
inferiority taken for granted, 168
injustice, 10–11, 91, 97, 154, 223
interracial marriage, 208
investigative narrators, 9, 191
Iran, 134–35, 146; as an Islamic state, 140; eight-year war, 147–51
irony, 91, 108
Islam, 137–38, 142–44, 153–58; colonialism of, 135; conversion to, 139–40, 151–52; fundamentalist, 136; Shia Islam, 14, 59–61; union with science, 141, 146. *See also* Muslims
Israelites, ancient dilemma of, 80
Ivory Coast, 119–23
I Want to Destroy Myself (M. Dhasal), 127–28

Jabavu, Noni, 87–88
Jack (in *The Enigma of Arrival*), 20, 236–37
Jacquet (sugar estate head-man), 99
Jagan (in *The Vendor of Sweets*), 53–54, 58
Jagan, Cheddi, 44, 84–87
Jagan, Janet, 84–87
Jamaica, 87–88
Jamal, Hakim, 206–7
James, C. L. R., 243, 245
James, William, 79
Jane (in *Guerrillas*), 212–23; as Jane/Clarissa, 215, 217–18, 223
Janet (Guyanese woman), 120
Java, 64
jihad, 153
Jimmy (in *Guerrillas*), 19, 205–6, 211–24, 236; based on Malik, 209–211
Johansson, Bertram B., 87

John X, *From Michael de Freitas to Michael X*, 205, 207–11
José, Don (in *A Way in the World*), 102–6, 245–46
Journey through Darkness: The Writing of V. S. Naipaul (Nightingale), 90, 171, 185
Joyce, James, 249
justice, 6, 164

Kabila, Laurent Desire, 115, 118–19
Kakar, Dr. Sudhir, 55
Kakusthan (brahmin), 73–74, 131
Kala (Indian woman), 73
Kali (goddess of death and destruction), 196
kanaima (the spirit of death), 241
Karachi, Pakistan, 62, 153–55
Kareisha (in *A Bend in the River*), 234
karma, 53, 69
Kashmir, 47–48, 75
Kazin, Alfred, 1
Keymis, Laurence, 96, 102
Khalkhalli, Ayatollah, 60–61, 149–50
Khilnani, Sunil, 126–27, 133
Khomeini, Ayatollah, 135–36, 150
Kimga, Hale (name assumed by Gale Benson), 206
kings as descendants of ancient priest-kings, 122
Kingsley, Charles, *At Last: A Christmas in the West Indies*, 89
Kripalsingh, Ranjit (in *The Mimic Men*), 189
Kuala Lumpur, Malaysia, 155

lacrimae rerum, 41
lamentation, 93
landlords, society-approved nastiness of, 43–44
Landstrom, Bjorn, *Columbus*, 95
language, concern with, 5

languages: demotic Marathi, 127;
  Dutch, 93; English, 130; Hindi,
  130; Latin, 12, 186, 192, 228–29,
  231; Tamil, 129–30
Latin language, 12, 186, 192; mottos,
  228, 229, 231
Lawrence, D. H., 249
learning, veneration of, 168
Lebrun (in *A Way in the World*), 241,
  243–45
Leela (in *The Mystic Masseur*), 167
Leopold II (Belgium), 116
Level de Goda, Luis, 106
Linda (in *In a Free State*), 199–204
lingam of Shiva, 10, 48–49
Liward (later corrected to Leeward)
  Hotel, 47–48, 75
*London Calling: V. S. Naipaul,
  Postcolonial Mandarin* (Nixon), 2–3
looking: imagery of, 217; without
  seeing, 104
Lord Jim (Conrad), 5
Lorkhoor (in *The Suffrage of Elvira*),
  173
The Loss of El Dorado (V. S. Naipaul),
  81, 94–100, 238, 244, 252
love, parodies of, 214
Luxor, Egypt, 10–11

MacGowan, Gault, 28
Mackey, Sandra, 147
Madras, India, 128–31
magic, 66, 121; as an apparatus for
  survival, 123; as a form of religion,
  122
Mahabharata, 64, 138
Malaysia, 62–63, 137, 155–58; as an
  Islamic state, 140
Malcolm X, 209
Mali (in *The Vendor of Sweets*), 53–54
Malik, Michael Abdul (a.k.a. Michael
  X), 19, 82, 205–11, 220
Man-man (in *The Mystic Masseur*), 169

Mann, Thomas, *Tables of the Law*, 80
Marathas, 124
marriage, interracial, 208
Martinique Island, 68
Martyrs' Cemetery, 148
Masood (disillusioned Pakistani), 135
Mauritius, 94
Mehrdad (Iranian guide), 147–48, 150
Memoir (Narayan), 55
memory, process of, 186
Menem, Carlos, 114
Menon, Sadanand, 129, 131
mental training, 64–65, 138
Metty (in *A Bend in the River*), 228
Michael X (a.k.a. Michael Abdul
  Malik), 19, 82, 205–11, 220
"Michael X and the Black Power
  Killings in Trinidad," 19, 205–11,
  215–16, 220, 222
The Middle Passage (V. S. Naipaul), 3,
  42–44, 71, 81, 84, 251; epigraphs,
  80, 88–90; reviews of, 86–87;
  tones in, 92–93
Miguel Street (V. S. Naipaul), 26–27,
  44, 91, 99, 162–66
Miss Millington (in *Mr. Stone and the
  Knights Companion*), 181
The Mimic Men (V. S. Naipaul), 11,
  184–87, 190–94; as autobiography,
  188–89
Miranda, Francisco, 96–96, 99,
  104–7, 245
Mishra, Pankaj, 133
missionaries, 137
Mobutu Sese Seko, 115–17, 224
mohajir guerrilla war, 153–55
Mohenjo-Daro, Pakistan, 135
moira, 9
Mommsen, Theodor, 232–33
monkey simile, 90–92
Montazeri, Ayatollah, 150
morality, 176; lack of, 171; moral
  ideas, 114

Morgan (in *Miguel Street*), 165
Morris, Foster (in *A Way in the
World*), 241; *The Shadowed Livery*,
242–43
mothers, relationships with, 35, 175,
177–79, 209–10, 222
movie actors as models, 163, 197, 212
Mr. Sampath (Narayan), 52–53
Mr. Stone and the Knights Companion
(V. S. Naipaul), 180–84
Muir, G. Ramsay (a.k.a. Ganesh), 170
mullahs, 65
Muslim countries, 14
Muslims: Black, 83; riots against, 126;
Sunni, 47.
See also Islam
Mustafa, Fawzia, 4–5
The Mystic Masseur (V. S. Naipaul),
35, 166–70
mythmaking, 107, 110, 122
myths: of Africanness, 117; of sacred
places, 145
"My Uncle Dalloo" (S. Naipaul),
31–32

Nahdlatul Ulama (NU), 144
Naipaul, Seepersad, 12, 26–35,
40–41; *The Adventures of Gurudeva
and Other Stories*, 27, 30–31,
33 34, 190; "Dookhani and
Mungal," 32; gifts to V. S. Naipaul,
29, 241; "My Uncle Dalloo,"
31–32; "Panchayat," 32; "They
Named Him Mohun," 32–33,
174; in V. S. Naipaul's writings, 27,
31; writing for the *Trinidad
Guardian*, 28–29, 39
Naipaul, V. S., 17; childhood of, 6, 71;
chronology of works, 253; early
life transformed into fiction, 11,
26, 36–41, 236; education, 9–11,
25, 31; friendships, 51; as a man
without religion, 60, 62; not

joining groups, 243–44;
psychopolitical biography of, 2–3;
relationship with his father, 26–35,
174; relationship with his mother
and extended family, 35; suspected
of being a guerrilla, 111–12
Naipaul, V. S., works: *Among the
Believers*, 18, 59, 70, 139–40, 143,
156; *An Area of Darkness*, 10, 13,
44–46, 69, 90–91; "Argentina:
Living with Cruelty," 112;
"Argentine Terror: A Memoir,"
111–12; *A Bend in the River*, 11,
19, 112, 118, 224–35; *Beyond
Belief: Islamic Excursions among the
Converted Peoples*, 139–40, 155,
158; *A Congo Diary*, 115–16, 227;
"Conrad's Darkness," 4–5, 21, 29,
77 "The Crocodiles of
Yamoussoukro," 66; *The Enigma of
Arrival*, 9, 11, 18–20, 25–26, 43,
71, 235–41; "Epilogue, from a
Journal," 204; *Finding the Centre*,
25–27; *In a Free State*, 194,
199–205, 237–38; *Guerrillas*, 3, 9,
82, 205–6, 209–24; *A House for
Mr. Biswas*, 18, 27, 31, 33–41,
173–80, 236, 242; *India: A Million
Mutinies Now*, 13, 58–59, 69,
125 26, 249; *India: A Wounded
Civilization*, 13, 52, 58, 69,
124–26; *The Loss of El Dorado*, 81,
94–100, 238, 244, 252; *The Middle
Passage*, 3, 42–44, 71, 80–81, 84,
86–90, 92–93, 251; *Miguel Street*,
26–27, 44, 91, 99, 162–66; *The
Mimic Men*, 11, 184–94; *Mr. Stone
and the Knights Companion*,
180–84; *The Mystic Masseur*, 35,
166–70; "A New King for the
Congo: Mobutu and the Nihilism
of Africa," 19, 115–17, 224, 227,
230–31; "One Out of Many,"

195–97; "Our Universal
Civilization," 14, 17; "Prologue to
an Autobiography," 11, 40, 66,
236; *The Return of Eva Perón with
the Killings in Trinidad,* 108–9, 111,
114; *The Suffrage of Elvira,* 35,
166–67, 170–73; "Tell Me Who
to Kill," 197–99; *A Turn in the
South,* 62, 66–67, 71; *A Way in the
World,* 18–20, 81, 83, 99–100,
102–4, 235, 241–47, 252
Nancy (in *From Michael de Freitas to
Michael X*), 208
Nandy, Ashis, 15–16
Naranappa (in *Samskara*), 56–57
Narayan (in *The Mystic Masseur*),
169
Narayan, R. K., 18, 123; *The Dark
Room,* 54–55; *Memoir,* 55; *The
Painter of Signs,* 55; *Mr. Sampath,*
52–53; *The Vendor of Sweets,*
52–53; *The World of Nagaraj,* 55
narratives, 46, 139; dramatic, 100;
inner, 8
narrators, 12, 18, 162, 241; addressing
readers, 192; first-person, 9, 11,
224–25; identified with and
detached from their author, 26;
investigative, 9, 191; more vivid
than their models, 161; shifting
within a work, 210; third-person,
9, 199, 210
Nasar (Malaysian executive), 156–57
Nath, Vishwa, 73
national identity: India, 123–34;
Pakistan, 152, 155
nationalism, 79, 85
nationalization, 115
nationhood: deterred, 122; no
concept of, 111, 119, 124; as the
source of law and civility, 133;
striving toward, 93
Nazir (son of Aziz), 75

Nazruddin (in *A Bend in the River*),
225–26, 234
Nelly (in *The Suffrage of Elvira*),
172–73
neocolonialism, 2
"A New King for the Congo:
Mobutu and the Nihilism of
Africa" (V. S. Naipaul), 19,
115–17, 224, 227, 230–31
Niangoran-Bouah, Georges, 121
Nightingale, Peggy (*Journey through
Darkness: The Writing of V. S.
Naipaul*), 90, 171, 185
nightmares of explosions,
238–39
Nixon, Rob, 89–92, 118; *London
Calling: V. S. Naipaul, Postcolonial
Mandarin,* 2–3
nonviolence, 53
Nostromo (Conrad), 5
novels, 18–19, 162; based on history,
19; defined, 58; outlined but not
written, 241–42
Nsele, Zaire, 117
NU (Nahdlatul Ulama), 144
Nusrat (Pakistani), 155

O'Brien, Conor Cruise, 1–2
observation, 12, 45, 55, 63, 87
"One Out of Many" (V. S. Naipaul),
195–97
The Open Sore of a Continent
(Soyinka), 79
"Our Universal Civilization" (V. S.
Naipaul), 14, 17
outsiders, 171, 184–205, 222

pacifism, contempt for, 125
Pakistan, 134–37, 151–55; as an
Islamic state, 140
Palani (rebel against brahmin
discrimination), 130–31

Palomeque, Don (in *A Way in the World*), 102–4
"Panchayat" (Seepersad Naipaul), 32
Panday, Basdeo, 84
parentage, mixed, 209
Pariyangan, West Sumatra, 145
Patagonian estates, 114
Patience (in *Miguel Street*), 163
Patil (Shiv Sena leader), 125
Periyar (Self-Respect Movement founder), 129–30
Perón, Eva, 108–9
Perón, Juan Domingo, 107–8
Peter (in *In a Free State*), 203
pharaohs, 122
Philip (English expatriate), 120
Phillips (in *The Enigma of Arrival*), 239–40
Picton, Thomas, 96–98
Pitton (in *The Enigma of Arrival*), 239–40
politics, 141; as an extension of human relationships, 14, 233; and change, 3
Polybius, 10
Port of Spain, Trinidad, 94, 99, 163
possibilities, human, 52, 134–35
postcolonial societies, 249, 251
poverty, 61, 69–70, 79, 124; of colonialism, 79, 171, 197
power, abuse of, 152
powerlessness, 152
Praneshacharya, an Acharya (in *Samskara*), 56–58, 91
Prasojo (guide), 64
Pravas (engineer), 72
Preacher (in *The Suffrage of Elvira*), 172
prejudice, 201
pride, 104
prison imagery, 98, 196
privatization, 114
Profitable Evacuations (Ganesh) (in *The Mystic Masseur*), 169

"Prologue to an Autobiography" (V. S. Naipaul), 11, 40, 66, 236
protagonists: compensating for the deprivations of their heritage, 167; struggling to define themselves, 173; tragic, 107. *See also* characters
Proust, Marcel, *Against Sainte-Beuve*, 76
pseudo-identities, 208–9, 215–16, 221
psychopolitical biographies of V. S. Naipaul, 2–3
puppet shows, 64–65, 138
Putta (in *Samskara*), 57

Rachlin, Nahid, *Foreigner*, 18
Racial Adjustment Action Society (RAAS), 206
racial conflict, 90, 193, 206–8
racial division, 84–85
racialism, 2, 50, 82–83
rage, 131–32, 199
Raleigh, Sir Walter, 96, 100–104, 241, 245–46; *The Discovery of the Large, Rich, and Beautiful Empire of Guiana*, 101
Ramanujan, A. K., 57, 74, 123
Ramayana, 64, 138
Rameshwar (in *A House for Mr. Biswas*), 178–79
Ramsumair, Ganesh (a.k.a. Ganesh) (in *The Mystic Masseur*), 166–70
Rana (disillusioned Pakistani), 152–53
Raote (Shiv Sena leader), 126
Ras Tafarians, 87
Raymond (in *A Bend in the River*), 227, 232–33
reading for self-improvement, 175
reality: desolation of, 98; of the world as it is, 227, 232, 235
Rega, José López, 108

religions: composite of Islam, Hinduism, and Buddhism, 64, 137–38; conversion to, 139–40, 178; rebellion against, 129; revealed, 140; substitutes for, 61; union with science, 141

reporting, 12–13, 17, 42, 76

rerum natura of natural law, 7

The Return of Eva Perón with the Killings in Trinidad (V. S. Naipaul), 108–9, 111, 114

revenge, 151, 154

revolution: and slavery, 94; as a substitute for religion, 61

Richardson, Lena-Boyd (in "Michael X and the Black Power Killings in Trinidad"), 210–11

rituals, 46, 73

Robinson, Arthur N. R., 83

Roca, President (of Argentina), 110

Roche, Peter (in *Guerrillas*), 212–14, 216–17, 220–23

Rohlehr, Gordon, 88

Roman history, 80, 145, 155–56, 186, 233; Naipaul's study of, 9–11, 31

Roth, Philip: *The Facts: A Novelist's Autobiography*, 161–62; *The Ghost Writer, Deception*, 161

Rushdie, Salman, 19

Saakana, Amon Saba, 250

sacredness, 145

Said, Edward, 15, 21n13, 230

Saint Kitts Island, 93–94

Salim (in *A Bend in the River*), 227–28, 235; driving to the interior, 224–26; relationship with Father Huismans, 228–31; relationship with Yvette, 232–34

Salman (disillusioned Muslim in Pakistan), 153–54

Samskara (Anantha Murthy), 56–58, 74, 91

Sandra (in *The Mimic Men*), 186–87

Santosh (in "One Out of Many"), 195–96

Schiff, Stephen, 101

schizophrenia, 158

Scott, Margaret, 140, 142, 144

The Secret Agent (Conrad), 5

Seghir (Iranian woman), 151

self-abnegation, 179, 195–96, 201

self-assertion of anger, 41

self-contempt, 17, 44–45, 82

self-definition, 210, 233–34

self-delusion, 97, 169, 187–88, 192–93, 232

self-examination in the interest of truth, 228

self-expression, 28, 175

selfhood, 9, 25, 70, 186; annihilation of, 30, 200; formed through constructive work, 58–59, 63; fragile sense of, 212; and social roles, 49, 220; as a vehicle for truth, 8, 20, 53

self-images, heroic, 106

self-interest, 79, 171

self-knowledge, 184

self-made men, 105–6

self-representations: false, 191; multiple, 208–9

Self-Respect Movement, 129

self-revelation, 12; in writing, 177, 179

servants, 48

Shafi (Malaysian guide), 63–64, 70, 137–38, 156–57

Shama (in *A House for Mr. Biswas*), 36–37, 177

Shia Islam, 14, 59–61, 61

Shiites of Iran, 59

shipwreck imagery, 185–86, 190

Shirazi, Ayatollah, 60

Shiva, lingam of, 10, 48–49

Shivaji (seventeenth-century Maratha guerrilla leader), 124

Shiv Sena movement, 124–27

Shylock (in *The Mimic Men*), 185

a Sikh (unnamed), 47, 50, 91

Sikhs, 132

Simon (educated Zairian manager), 118

Simón, Fray (in *A Way in the World*), 102–4

Singh, Ralph (in *The Mimic Men*), 184–94, 235

Sir Harold (in "Michael X and the Black Power Killings in Trinidad"), 210

Skerritt, Joseph, 207

slavery, 13, 87, 93; heritage of, 81–82, 220, 252; and revolution, 94

slaves' mimicry and mockery of oppressors, 99

Smiles, Samuel, 175

snake dreams, 38

socialism, cooperative, 86

social mores, 52

Sohail (disillusioned Pakistani), 153

sorcerers, 122

Soyinka, Wole, 93; *The Open Sore of a Continent*, 79

Spanish conquest, 107, 113

Springer, Margaret (in *Mr. Stone and the Knights Companion*), 181

Srinivas (in *Mr. Sampath*), 53

Staples, Brent, 1–2, 15

Stephens (in *Guerrillas*), 217, 219–20

Stone, Richard (in *Mr. Stone and the Knights Companion*), 180–84

The Story of My Experiments with Truth (Gandhi), 55

story-writing machine, 54

Subandrio (physician and political prisoner in Indonesia), 141, 143

Subramaniam (brahmin scientist), 71–72

The Suffrage of Elvira (V. S. Naipaul), 35, 166–67, 170–73

Sugar (self-made holy man), 128

Suharto, 140, 143

suicide, 240

Sunnis, 59

surgeon to Sir Walter Raleigh, 100–104

Surinam, 93

survival as an individual, 224–25

sweeping of yards, 68

Tables of the Law (Mann), 80

Tacitus, 10, 145; *Agricola*, 80–81

Tamil language, 129–30

Tamil Nadu, Madras, 128–31

technology, 62–63

Tehran, Iran, 135, 147–48

"Tell Me Who to Kill" (V. S. Naipaul), 197–99

"The Crocodiles of Yamoussoukro" (V. S. Naipaul), 66

themis, 123

"The Road to the Shrine" (N. Dhasal), 127

Theroux, Paul, 12, 200, 247–48n21

"The Unfortunate Traveller" (Walcott), 92

"They Named Him Mohun" (S. Naipaul), 32–33, 174

Thrushcross Grange, 212, 221

Tindall, David, 205

tones in Naipaul's work, 92–93

traditions, 32, 45–46, 57, 158; adapting to change, 74, 156–57; blending of, 64; in conflict with change, 55, 65–66, 70; nostalgia for, 137–38

tragic optimism, 235

tragic protagonists, 107

tramp (in *In a Free State*), 194–95

travel as a means to discover other states of mind, 66, 194, 212

travel books, 11–13, 18

Trinidad, 20, 35, 41–44, 71, 166;
    elections, 83–84; history of,
    80–82, 94–95, 99–100, 244–45;
    rebellions, 82–83
Trinidad Guardian, 28
Trollope, Anthony, *The West Indies
    and the Spanish Main*, 89
truth, 161, 183–84, 192, 225, 232;
    ambivalence toward seeking, 224;
    imaginative, 18, 58, 104; not
    relevant to legends, 109; objective,
    7; personal, 7, 206; revealed,
    60–61; shifting loci of, 191;
    suppression of, 176, 187, 212
truth, methods of searching for, 5–8,
    139; comedy, 173, 251; fiction, 94,
    162; fiction, history, and
    autobiography, 18–20, 100, 252;
    fiction and history, 96;
    observation, 12, 45, 55, 63, 87
truth of experience, 7, 17, 19, 26,
    226, 250–51; avoided, 211; fidelity
    to sensations, 4, 30; perceptions, 1,
    44
Tulsis, 175, 179
A Turn in the South (V. S. Naipaul),
    62, 66–67, 71
Tutsis, 119

Under Western Eyes (Conrad), 5
universal civilization, 14, 17, 62;
    justifying colonialism, 15–16
universal values, 15–16, 62

values: universal, 15–16, 62; Western,
    15
The Vendor of Sweets (Narayan),
    52–53
Venezuelan revolutions, 96–97
Venus, 145
Vera, Domingo de, 95
victims, 180, 193, 198, 214–15;
    passive, 222

violence, 40–41, 50, 126, 213, 221;
    depersonalization of, 138;
    removing the hold of the past, 196
vocations, 63, 241

Wahid (Nahdlatul Ulama leader), 144
Walcott, Derek, 240; "The
    Unfortunate Traveller," 92
Warner, Thomas, 94
The Warrior Prophet, 153
water, caste prejudices about, 127, 130
Waugh, Evelyn, 162
A Way in the World (V. S. Naipaul), 81,
    83, 99, 102–4, 235, 241–47;
    uniting autobiography, history, and
    fiction, 18–20, 100, 252
Western values, 15
West Indians, 88
The West Indies and the Spanish Main
    (Trollope), 89
West Sumatra, 145
What God Told Me (Ganesh) (in *The
    Mystic Masseur*), 166, 169
Whymper (in *Mr. Stone and the
    Knights Companion*), 182
Wiltshire, England, 235–41
withdrawal from a changing society, 53
women: mistreatment of, 32–33, 55;
    unmarried, 147; used by men, 208
Women's Era, 73
Woolf, Virginia, 249
Wordsworth, B. (in *Miguel Street*), 165
writers: aesthetic models for, 1; ghost,
    207; psychic and intellectual risks,
    42
writing, 34, 167–68, 184–85; allaying
    the fear of extinction, 30, 36,
    38–41, 236; to report responses to
    the world, 6, 189; revealing falsity,
    191; as a romantic career, 4; as
    self-expression, 28, 175; self-
    revelation in, 177, 179; without a
    spiritual core, 54

writing process, 25–27, 66, 76, 161, 235–36; automatic, 54; methods, 139; shared with readers, 241; unfinished works, 176–77; works not written, 238, 241–42

xenophobia, 125–26

Yamoussoukro, Ivory Coast, 119
Yeates, Steve, 206

Yeats, William Butler, 26, 98
Yvette (in *A Bend in the River*), 227, 232–34

Zabeth (in *A Bend in the River*), 227
Zaire (renamed The Democratic Republic of the Congo), 115–19, 224
Zuckerman, Nathan (in *The Facts: A Novelist's Autobiography*), 161–62

ABOUT THE AUTHOR

Lillian Feder is Distinguished Professor Emerita of English, Classics, and Comparative Literature, Graduate School, City University of New York. She is the author of *The Handbook of Classical Literature*, *Ancient Myth in Modern Poetry*, and *Madness in Literature*.